Microsoft® Access 2010

COMPLETE

by Pasewark and Pasewark*, Cable, Evans

Microsoft® Access 2010

COMPLETE

by Pasewark and Pasewark*, Cable, Evans

William R. Pasewark, Sr., Ph.D.
Professor Emeritus, Business Education, Texas Tech
University

Scott G. Pasewark, B.S.
Occupational Education, Computer Technologist

William R. Pasewark, Jr., Ph.D., CPA
Professor, Accounting, Texas Tech University

Carolyn Denny Pasewark, M.Ed.
National Computer Consultant, Reading and Math
Certified Elementary Teacher, K-12 Certified Counselor

Jan Pasewark Stogner, MBA
Financial Planner

Beth Pasewark Wadsworth, B.A.
Graphic Designer

Sandra Cable, Ed. D.
Texas A&M University

Jessica Evans
Contributing Author

*Pasewark and Pasewark is a trademark of the Pasewark LTD.

COURSE TECHNOLOGY
CENGAGE Learning™

Australia • Brazil • Japan • Korea • Mexico • Singapore • Spain • United Kingdom • United States

COURSE TECHNOLOGY
CENGAGE Learning™

Microsoft Access 2010 Complete
Pasewark and Pasewark, Cable, Evans

Author: Sandra Cable

Contributing Author: Jessica Evans

Executive Editor: Donna Gridley

Product Manager: Allison O'Meara McDonald

Development Editors: Rachel Biheller Bunin, Ann Fisher

Associate Product Manager: Amanda Lyons

Editorial Assistant: Kim Klasner

Senior Content Project Manager: Catherine DiMassa

Associate Marketing Manager: Julie Schuster

Director of Manufacturing: Denise Powers

Text Designer: Shawn Girsberger

Photo Researcher: Abigail Reip

Manuscript Quality Assurance Lead: Jeff Schwartz

Manuscript Quality Assurance Reviewers: Green Pen QA, Serge Palladino, Susan Pedicini, Jeff Schwartz, Danielle Shaw, Marianne Snow, Susan Whalen

Copy Editor: Michael Beckett

Proofreader: Kim Kosmatka

Indexer: Sharon Hilgenberg

Art Director: Faith Brosnan

Cover Designer: Hannah Wellman

Cover Image: © Neil Brennan / Canopy Illustration / Veer

Compositor: GEX Publishing Services

For product information and technology assistance, contact us at
Cengage Learning Customer & Sales Support, 1-800-354-9706
For permission to use material from this text or product, submit all requests online at **www.cengage.com/permissions**.
Further permissions questions can be e-mailed to
permissionrequest@cengage.com.

Library of Congress Control Number: 2010943254

Hardcover
ISBN-13: 978-1-111-52990-1
ISBN-10: 1-111-52990-6

Course Technology
20 Channel Center Street
Boston, Massachusetts 02210
USA

Cengage Learning is a leading provider of customized learning solutions with office locations around the globe, including Singapore, the United Kingdom, Australia, Mexico, Brazil, and Japan. Locate your local office at:
international.cengage.com/region

Cengage Learning products are represented in Canada by Nelson Education, Ltd.

To learn more about Course Technology, visit **www.cengage.com/coursetechnology**

To learn more about Cengage Learning, visit **www.cengage.com**

Any fictional data related to persons or companies or URLs used throughout this book is intended for instructional purposes only. At the time this book was printed, any such data was fictional and not belonging to any real persons or companies.

Printed in the United States of America
1 2 3 4 5 6 7 15 14 13 12 11

ABOUT THIS BOOK

Microsoft Access 2010 Complete is designed for beginning users of Microsoft Access 2010. Students will learn to use the application through a variety of activities, simulations, and case projects. Microsoft Access 2010 Complete demonstrates the tools and features for this program in an easy-to-follow hands-on approach.

This self-paced step-by-step book with corresponding screen shots makes learning easy and enjoyable. End-of-lesson exercises reinforce the content covered in each lesson and provide students the opportunity to apply the skills that they have learned. It is important to work through each lesson within a unit in the order presented, as each lesson builds on what was learned in previous lessons.

Illustrations provide visual reinforcement of features and concepts, and sidebars provide notes, tips, and concepts related to the lesson topics. Step-by-Step exercises provide guidance for using the features. End-of-lesson projects concentrate on the main concepts covered in the lesson and provide valuable opportunities to apply or extend the skills learned in the lesson, and instructors can assign as many or as few of the projects at the end of the lesson as they like.

The lessons in the **Introductory Access** unit teach students how to develop, design, and create tables with primary keys and field properties set for fields; to create queries based on one or more tables and set criteria; to develop and create forms to display the data in one or more tables and use the form to find, enter, and view data; to create reports to present data in an efficient, organized way; and finally, to use Access to merge records stored in a database with a Word document.

The lessons in the **Advanced Access** unit teach students enhanced table design that helps with data entry accuracy; how to create professional queries using different search data each time the query is opened; how to develop advanced forms with command buttons and themes; how to add sub-reports and charts to reports; how to create embedded macros; how to develop navigation forms to be used as menus for the database; and how to write functions and procedures for programming in Access. Please note that some concepts introduced in the Introductory unit will be expanded upon in the Advanced unit.

To complete all lessons and End-of-Lesson material, this book will require approximately 24 hours.

Start-Up Checklist
Hardware

- Computer and processor 500-megahertz (MHz) processor or higher
- Memory: 256 megabytes (MB) of RAM or higher
- Hard disk: 3.5 gigabyte (GB) available disk space
- Display 1024 × 768 or higher-resolution monitor

Software:

- Operating system: Windows XP with Service Pack 3, Windows Vista with SP1, or Windows 7

INSIDE THIS BOOK

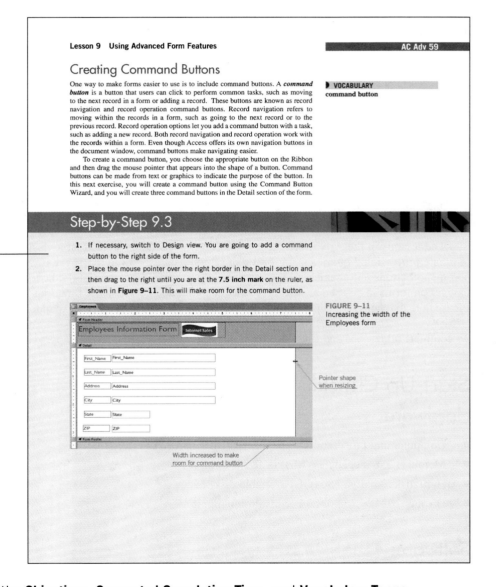

Step-by-Step Exercises offer "hands-on practice" of the material just learned. Each exercise uses a data file or requires you to create a file from scratch.

Within the figure:

Creating Command Buttons

One way to make forms easier to use is to include command buttons. A *command button* is a button that users can click to perform common tasks, such as moving to the next record in a form or adding a record. These buttons are known as record navigation and record operation command buttons. Record navigation refers to moving within the records in a form, such as going to the next record or to the previous record. Record operation options let you add a command button with a task, such as adding a new record. Both record navigation and record operation work with the records within a form. Even though Access offers its own navigation buttons in the document window, command buttons make navigating easier.

To create a command button, you choose the appropriate button on the Ribbon and then drag the mouse pointer that appears into the shape of a button. Command buttons can be made from text or graphics to indicate the purpose of the button. In this next exercise, you will create a command button using the Command Button Wizard, and you will create three command buttons in the Detail section of the form.

▶ VOCABULARY
command button

Step-by-Step 9.3

1. If necessary, switch to Design view. You are going to add a command button to the right side of the form.

2. Place the mouse pointer over the right border in the Detail section and then drag to the right until you are at the **7.5 inch mark** on the ruler, as shown in **Figure 9–11**. This will make room for the command button.

FIGURE 9–11
Increasing the width of the Employees form

Pointer shape when resizing

Width increased to make room for command button

Lesson opener elements include the **Objectives, Suggested Completion Time**, and **Vocabulary Terms**.

End of Lesson elements include the **Summary, Vocabulary Review, Review Questions, Lesson Projects**, and **Critical Thinking Activities**.

Instructor Resources Disk

ISBN-13: 978-0-538-47523-5
ISBN-10: 0-538-47523-4

The Instructor Resources CD or DVD contains the following teaching resources:

The Data and Solution files for this course.

ExamView® tests for each lesson.

Instructor's Manual that includes lecture notes for each lesson and references to the end-of-lesson activities and Unit Review projects.

Answer Keys that include solutions to the end-of- lesson and unit review questions.

Critical thinking solution files that provide possible solutions for critical thinking activities.

Copies of the figures that appear in the student text.

Suggested Syllabus with block, two quarter, and 18-week schedule.

Annotated Solutions and Grading Rubrics.

PowerPoint presentations for each lesson.

Spanish glossary and Spanish test bank.

Appendices that include models for formatted documents, an e-mail writing guide, and a letter writing guide.

Proofreader's Marks.

ExamView®

This textbook is accompanied by ExamView, a powerful testing software package that allows instructors to create and administer printed, computer (LAN-based), and Internet exams. ExamView includes hundreds of questions that correspond to the topics covered in this text, enabling students to generate detailed study guides that include page references for further review. The computer-based and Internet testing components allow students to take exams at their computers, and save the instructor time by grading each exam automatically.

Online Companion

This book uses an Online Companion Web site that contains valuable resources to help enhance your learning.

- Student data files to complete text projects and activities
- Key terms and definitions for each lesson
- PowerPoint presentations for each lesson
- Additional Internet boxes with links to important Web sites
- Link to CourseCasts

CourseCasts

CourseCasts—Learning on the Go. Always Available…Always Relevant.

Want to keep up with the latest technology trends relevant to you? Visit our site to find a library of podcasts, CourseCasts, featuring a "CourseCast of the Week," and download them to your mp3 player at http://coursecasts.course.com.

Our fast-paced world is driven by technology. You know because you're an active participant—always on the go, always keeping up with technological trends, and always learning new ways to embrace technology to power your life.

Ken Baldauf, a faculty member of the Florida State University Computer Science Department, is responsible for teaching technology classes to thousands of FSU students each year. He knows what you want to know; he knows what you want to learn. He's also an expert in the latest technology and will sort through and aggregate the most pertinent news and information so you can spend your time enjoying technology, rather than trying to figure it out.

Visit us at http://coursecasts.course.com to learn on the go!

SAM 2010 SAM

SAM 2010 Assessment, Projects, and Training version 1.0 offers a real-world approach to applying Microsoft Office 2010 skills. The Assessment portion of this powerful and easy to use software simulates Office 2010 applications, allowing users to demonstrate their computer knowledge in a hands-on environment. The Projects portion allows students to work live-in-the-application on project-based assignments. The Training portion helps students learn in the way that works best for them by reading, watching, or receiving guided help.

- SAM 2010 captures the key features of the actual Office 2010 software, allowing students to work in high-fidelity, multi-pathway simulation exercises for a real-world experience.
- SAM 2010 includes realistic and explorable simulations of Office 2010, Windows 7 coverage, and a new user interface.
- Easy, web-based deployment means SAM is more accessible than ever to both you and your students.
- Direct correlation to the skills covered on a chapter-by-chapter basis in your Course Technology textbooks allows you to create a detailed lesson plan.
- SAM Projects offers live-in-the-application project-based assignments. Student work is automatically graded, providing instant feedback. A unique cheating detection feature identifies students who may have shared files.
- Because SAM Training is tied to textbook exams and study guides, instructors can spend more time teaching and let SAM Training help those who need additional time to grasp concepts

Note: This textbook may or may not be available in SAM Projects at this time. Please check with your sales representative for the most recent information on when this title will be live in SAM Projects.

About the Pasewark Author Team

Pasewark LTD is a family-owned business with more than 90 years of combined experience authoring award-winning textbooks. They have written over 100 books about computers, accounting, and office technology. During that time, they developed their mission statement: To help our students live better lives.

Pasewark LTD authors are members of several professional associations that help authors write better books. The authors have been recognized with numerous awards for classroom teaching and believe that effective classroom teaching is a major ingredient for writing effective textbooks.

Sandra Cable, Texas A&M University – Commerce

Sandra Cable received her doctorate in Education from Texas A&M University —Commerce in 2003. In addition to working as an adjunct professor, she teaches computer classes at corporations that want to enhance the computer skills of their employees. Sandra also volunteers at schools and not-for-profit organizations, giving seminars that demonstrate simple approaches to using computer applications.

I would like to thank the great team at Course Technology: Donna Gridley, Executive Editor; Allison O'Meara McDonald, Product Manager; Cathie DiMassa, Senior Content Project Manager. This team is truly the best group of individuals with whom I have worked! I would also like to give special thanks to Ann Fisher, the Developmental Editor. Thank you so much for all of your great work, coordination efforts, and incredible sense of humor. You are truly wonderful to work with. To the thousands of students and clients that I have taught over the years, many thanks for your encouragement and for all you have taught me. Finally, I am very grateful to my family, Keith and Meridith Albright, for their enduring support.— **Sandra Cable**

From the Contributing Author

It has been a privilege to be a part of this project and the talented group of people who have worked on it. Thank you Donna Gridley, Allison O'Meara McDonald, Amanda Lyons, and Cathie DiMassa of Course Technology for managing the many details of this project; thank you to my co-authors Kitty, Robin, and Rachel, for their support and friendship while we were all busy writing; and special thanks to Rachel for her thoughtful edits of my lessons. Finally, thank you Richard and Hannah for your patience, understanding, humor, and support during this book's development. When I count my blessings, you share the top spot on my list. — **Jessica Evans**

Microsoft Office 2010 Advanced
Casebound
ISBN-13: 978-0-538-48129-8
Hard Spiral
ISBN-13: 978-0-538-48142-7
Soft Perfect
ISBN-13: 978-0-538-48143-4

Microsoft Excel 2010 Complete
Hardcover
ISBN-13: 978-1-111-52952-9

Microsoft Word 2010 Complete
Hardcover
ISBN-13: 978-1-111-52951-2

Microsoft PowerPoint 2010 Complete
Hardcover
ISBN-13: 978-1-111-52953-6

CONTENTS

ADVANCED MICROSOFT ACCESS 2010 UNIT

CONTENTS

ACCESS 2010 COMPLETE DATA FILES GRID

APPLICATION	LESSON	DATA FILE	SOLUTION FILE
INTRODUCTION	1	Class Descriptions.docx	Blackfoot Resort.pptx
		Clients.accdb	Final Spectrum Follow-up.docx
		Historic Preservation.pptx	First Qtr Sales.xlsx
		January Sales.xlsx	Historic Housing.pptx
		JC's Data.mdb	JC's Updated Data.accdb
		Sales Report.xlsx	Revised Sales Report.xlsx
		Spectrum Follow-up.docx	Updated Class Descriptions.docx
			Updated Clients.accdb

ACCESS *(continued)*

APPLICATION	LESSON	DATA FILE	SOLUTION FILE
ACCESS	1	Employees.accdb	Employees Solution.accdb
		Members.accdb	Members Solution.accdb
		Restaurants.accdb	Restaurants Solution.accdb
		Stores.accdb	Stores Solution.accdb
	2	Company.accdb	Company Solution.accdb
			Interviews Solution.accdb
			Music Solution.accdb
			RetailStores Solution.accdb
			Database.accdb (student supplies filename)

ACCESS *(continued)*

APPLICATION	LESSON	DATA FILE	SOLUTION FILE
	3	Agents.accdb	Agents Solution.accdb
		Listings.accdb	Listings Solution.accdb
		Product.accdb	Product Solution.accdb
		Properties.accdb	Properties Solution.accdb
		Realtors.accdb	Realtors Solution.accdb
	4	Broker.accdb	Broker Solution.accdb
		Class.accdb	Class Solution.accdb
		Recreation.accdb	Recreation Solution.accdb
		Teacher.accdb	Teacher Solution.accdb
	5	Agencies.accdb	Agencies Solution.accdb
		Office.gif	Sales Solution.accdb
		Supplies.accdb	Staff Solution.accdb
		Teacher.gif	Supplies Solution.accdb
		Staff.accdb	
		Sales.accdb	

DATA FILES

ACCESS *(continued)*

APPLICATION	LESSON	DATA FILE	SOLUTION FILE
	6	Abbott.docx	Abbott Solution.docx
		Clubs.txt	Club Officials Solution.xlsx
		InfoTech.accdb	InfoTech Solution.accdb
		Inventory.accdb	Inventory Solution accdb
		Items.accdb	Items Solution.accdb
		Lakewood.docx	Lakewood Solution.docx
		Officials.xlsx	Products Solution.txt
		Products.xlsx	Sales Solution.docx
		Sales.docx	School Solution.accdb
		School.accdb	Student Solution.rtf
		Student.txt	Student Word Solution.xlsx
		Student Excel.xlsx	Swimming Solution.accdb

ACCESS *(continued)*

APPLICATION	LESSON	DATA FILE	SOLUTION FILE
Unit Review		Dining.accdb	Dining Solution.accdb
		Favorites.accdb	Favorites Solution.accdb
		Java.accdb	Java Solution.accdb
		Meals.accdb	Meals Solution.accdb
		Personnel.accdb	Personnel Solution.accdb
		Price.accdb	Price Solution.accdb
		Reminder.docx	Reminder Solution.docx
	7	Division Sales.accdb	Division Sales Database.accdb
		Internet Sales.accdb	Internet Sales Database.accdb
		P & K Industry.accdb	P & K Industry Database.accdb
		Pacific Sales.accdb	Pacific Sales Database.accdb
		Pet Sales.accdb	Pet Sales Database.accdb
		Sales.accdb	Sales Database.accdb
		Student Teams.accdb	Student Teams Database.accdb

ACCESS *(continued)*

APPLICATION	LESSON	DATA FILE	SOLUTION FILE
	8	Atlantic Sales.accdb	Atlantic Sales Database.accdb
		Book Sales.accdb	Book Sales Database.accdb
		Healthcare Training.accdb	Healthcare Training Database.accdb
		Pet Supplies.accdb	Pet Supplies Database.accdb
		Regional Sales.accdb	Regional Sales Database.accdb
		Teams.accdb	Teams Database.accdb
	9	Animal Supply Industry.accdb	Animal Supply Industry Database.accdb
		Book Sales.accdb	Book Sales Database.accdb
		Coastal Sales.accdb	Coastal Sales Database.accdb
		Healthcare Training.accdb	Healthcare Training Database.accdb
		Internet Sales Logo.tif	Internet Sales Database.accdb
		Internet Sales.accdb	My Form.accdb
		Pets Unlimited.accdb	Pets Unlimited Database.accdb

ACCESS *(continued)*

APPLICATION	LESSON	DATA FILE	SOLUTION FILE
	10	Book Sales.accdb	Book Sales Databsae.accdb
		Computer Sales.accdb	Computer Sales Database.accdb
		Pacific Sales.accdb	Pacific Sales Database.accdb
		Pet Supplies.accdb	Pet Supplies Database.accdb
		Regional Sales.accdb	Regional Sales Database.accdb
	11	Book Sales.accdb	Book Sales Database.accdb
		Computer Sales.accdb	Computer Sales Database.accdb
		Internet Sales.accdb	Internet Sales Database.accdb
		Regional Sales.accdb	Regional Sales Database.accdb
		Supplies for Happy Pets.accdb	Supplies for Happy Pets Database.accdb

ACCESS *(continued)*

APPLICATION	LESSON	DATA FILE	SOLUTION FILE
	12	Book Sales Logo.tif	Book Sales Database.accdb
		Book Sales.accdb	
		Coastal Sales.accdb	Coastal Sales Database.accdb
		Online Sales Logo.tif	Online Sales Dtabase.accdb
		Online Sales.accdb	
		Pets.accdb	Pets Database.accdb
		Region Sales.accdb	Region Sales Database.accdb
	13	End of Year Sales.accdb	End of Year Sales Database.accdb
		Epic Internet Sales.accdb	Epic Internet Sales Database.accdb
		National Events.accdb	National Events Database.accdb
		New Sales.accdb	New Sales Database.accdb
		Wholesale International Sales.accdb	Wholesale International Sales Database.accdb

ACCESS *(continued)*

APPLICATION	LESSON	DATA FILE	SOLUTION FILE
	14	Book Sales.accdb	Book Sales Database.accdb
			Book Sales Database_2014-09-20.accdb
		Coach Files.accdb	Coach Files Database.accdb
		Coastal Sales.accdb	Coastal Sales Database.accdb
			doc_rptObjects - Student Teams.pdf
			doc_rptObjects.pdf
		Employee Sales.accdb	Employee Sales Database 2.accdb
			Employee Sales Database 2_2014-09-18.accdb
			Employee Sales Database.accdb
		Happy Pets.accdb	Happy Pets Database.accdb
		Student Teams.accdb	Student Teams Database.accdb
Unit Review		New Book Sales.accdb	New Book Sales Database.accdb
		New Generation.accdb	New Generation Database.accdb
		Pet Supplies.accdb	Pet Supplies Database.accdb
		Revelation Sales.accdb	Revelation Sales Database.accdb
		West Coast Sales.accdb	West Coast Sales Database.accdb
		Winter Sales.accdb	Winter Sales Database.accdb
			doc_rptObjects - West Coast Sales.pdf

ADVANCED

INTRODUCTION

LESSON 1   2 HRS.

Microsoft Office 2010 and the Internet

LESSON 1

Microsoft Office 2010 and the Internet

■ OBJECTIVES

Upon completion of this lesson, you should be able to:

- Apply basic Microsoft Word, Excel, Access, PowerPoint, and Outlook features.
- Search for information on the World Wide Web.
- Evaluate Web sites.
- Bookmark favorite Web sites.
- Manage the history of the Web sites visited.

■ VOCABULARY

bookmark

browser

hits

keywords

search engine

wildcard

ADVANCED Introduction Unit

Microsoft Office 2010 is a complete set of computer applications that equips you with the tools you need to produce a variety of documents and files, and to help streamline your everyday computing activities. This course focuses on the more complex and advanced capabilities of the Word, Excel, Access, PowerPoint, and Outlook applications.

This lesson provides a review of basic application features and will help you refresh your application skills. In this lesson, you will also learn more about how to access resources on the World Wide Web.

Applying Word Features

As you know, Microsoft Word is a powerful, full-featured word processor with comprehensive writing tools. You've already learned many of the basic features that enable you to complete common word-processing documents. The Word lessons in this course will introduce you to features that will enable you to further enhance the appearance of your documents and save time preparing and editing documents. Developing a document often involves multiple team members, and Word offers several tools to help you share documents and effectively collaborate on projects.

However, before you begin to explore these and other advanced features in Word, complete the following Step-by-Step, which provides a review of many basic Word skills.

Step-by-Step 1.1

1. Launch Word and then open the **Class Descriptions.docx** file from the drive and folder where your Data Files are stored. Save the document as **Updated Class Descriptions**, followed by your initials.

2. Edit the document as shown in **Figure 1–1**.

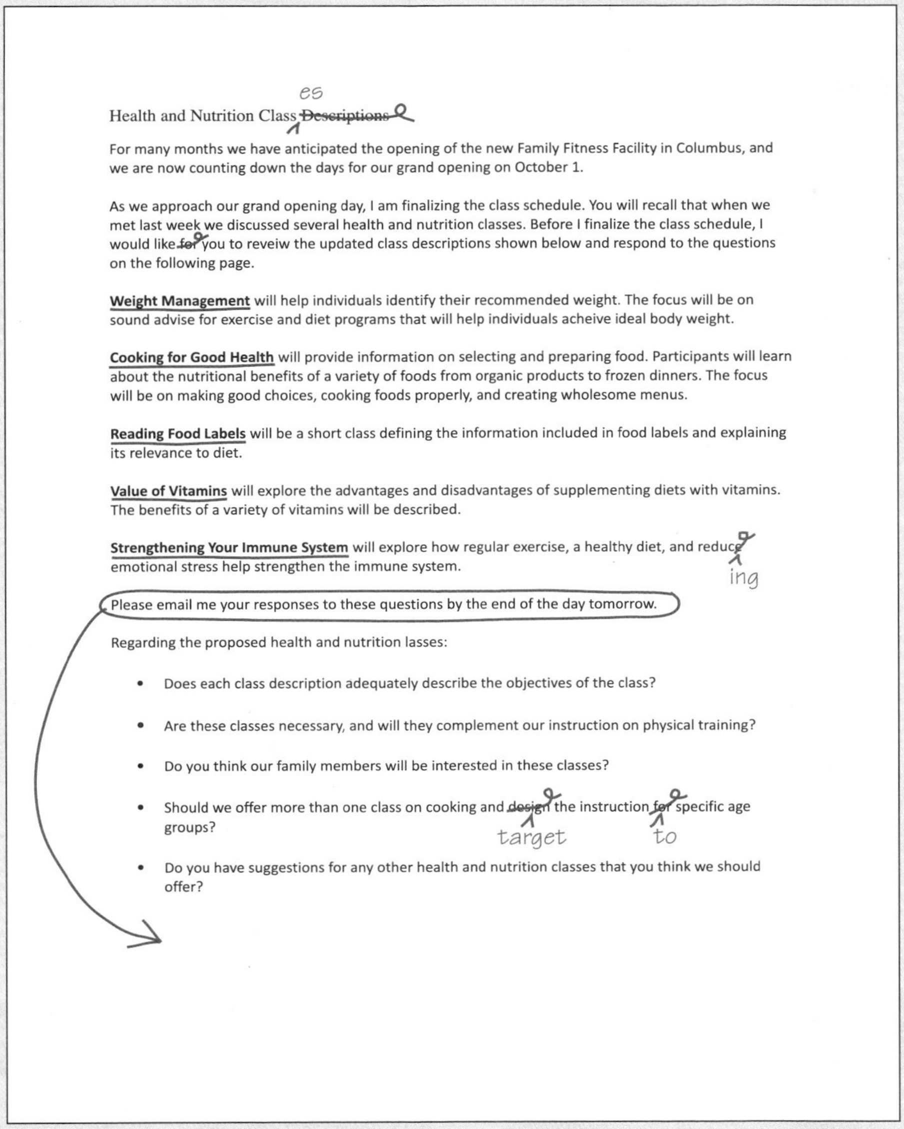

FIGURE 1–1
Edits for document in
Step-by-Step 1.1

Health and Nutrition Class Descriptions   *es*

For many months we have anticipated the opening of the new Family Fitness Facility in Columbus, and we are now counting down the days for our grand opening on October 1.

As we approach our grand opening day, I am finalizing the class schedule. You will recall that when we met last week we discussed several health and nutrition classes. Before I finalize the class schedule, I would like for you to reveiw the updated class descriptions shown below and respond to the questions on the following page.

Weight Management will help individuals identify their recommended weight. The focus will be on sound advise for exercise and diet programs that will help individuals acheive ideal body weight.

Cooking for Good Health will provide information on selecting and preparing food. Participants will learn about the nutritional benefits of a variety of foods from organic products to frozen dinners. The focus will be on making good choices, cooking foods properly, and creating wholesome menus.

Reading Food Labels will be a short class defining the information included in food labels and explaining its relevance to diet.

Value of Vitamins will explore the advantages and disadvantages of supplementing diets with vitamins. The benefits of a variety of vitamins will be described.

Strengthening Your Immune System will explore how regular exercise, a healthy diet, and reduc ~~e~~   *ing*
emotional stress help strengthen the immune system.

Please email me your responses to these questions by the end of the day tomorrow.

Regarding the proposed health and nutrition lasses:

- Does each class description adequately describe the objectives of the class?

- Are these classes necessary, and will they complement our instruction on physical training?

- Do you think our family members will be interested in these classes?

- Should we offer more than one class on cooking and ~~design~~ the instruction ~~for~~ specific age groups?   *target*   *to*

- Do you have suggestions for any other health and nutrition classes that you think we should offer?

3. Center and bold the title, and then change the font to Arial 18 point. Change the title text to all uppercase.

4. Select the paragraphs that describe the five classes and format all the paragraphs with a left indent of 0.5" and a right indent of 5.5" (0.5" from the right margin).

5. Select the list of bulleted questions at the end of the document and apply the number format (1., 2., 3.) to create an enumerated list.

6. Position the insertion point anywhere in the first numbered paragraph and add space after the paragraph. Then use the Format Painter feature to copy the new paragraph format to the other paragraphs in the numbered list.

7. Search for the word *email* and replace it with **e-mail**.

8. Change the document margins to **Office 2003 Default** setting (1" top and bottom and 1.25" left and right).

9. Position the insertion point in front of the paragraph that begins *Regarding the proposed...* and insert a page break.

10. Create a header for only the second page of the document. Use the Blank (Three Columns) format for the header, and then type the title **Health and Nutrition Classes** in the center of the header.

11. Check the document for spelling and grammar and make any necessary corrections. The spelling checker doesn't catch mistypes if they are the same as correctly spelled words.

12. Save the changes. Close the document, and then exit Word.

Applying Excel Features

Excel is the spreadsheet application in the Office suite. As you've discovered, spreadsheets are used for entering, calculating, and analyzing data. You should now be familiar with the basic features for creating, editing, and formatting worksheet information. Excel's advanced features enable you to perform complex calculations and in-depth analysis that you'd normally leave up to an economist or mathematician! With Excel's data analysis tools, you can generate reports, charts, and tables that are every bit as professional looking and accurate as those created by the experts. In this course, you'll also learn how to share workbooks with colleagues.

Before you venture into the advanced features of Excel, complete the following Step-by-Step, which provides a review of the Excel basic skills.

Step-by-Step 1.2

1. Launch Excel and then open the **Sales Report.xlsx** file from the drive and folder where your Data Files are stored. Save the workbook as **Revised Sales Report**, followed by your initials.

2. Go to cell M5 and type the column heading **TOTAL**.

3. Go to cell M6 and enter a formula to calculate the sum of the numbers in cells B6:L6. Fill the formula down through cell M12.

4. Go to cell A14 and type the row heading **TOTAL**.

5. Go to cell B14 and enter a formula to calculate the sum of the numbers in cells B6:B13. Fill the formula across through cell M14.

6. Insert a new column to the left of the *TOTAL* column. In the new column, type the heading **Dec**, and then enter the following data in the new column:

   61258

   50211

   61858

   50212

   61855

   50215

   61852

7. Copy the formula in cell L14 and paste it in cell M14.

8. Merge and center the title *Division Sales Report* over cells A1:N1. Format the title text bold and italic, and change the font size to 14 point.

9. Delete rows 2 and 3.

10. Format the column and row headings bold, and then center the column headings.

11. Apply a currency format to all the numeric data, with no decimal points. If necessary, automatically adjust the column widths.

12. Create a 3-D pie chart on a new sheet, using only the data in the cell ranges A4:A10 and N4:N10. Add the title **Total Sales by Division** to the chart and apply a chart style of your choice.

13. Format the worksheet to fit on one page in landscape orientation.

14. Save the changes. Close the file, and then exit Excel.

Applying Access Features

Access is the database application in the Office suite that is used for storing and organizing information. Databases are made up of objects, including tables, queries, forms, and reports. You now should be familiar with the basic techniques for creating these objects. In the advanced lessons, you will learn about features that give you even more control over how database records are viewed, edited, and professionally analyzed. You'll learn how to streamline data entry and editing and to present the data in an attractive, reader-friendly manner.

Before you begin exploring advanced features in Access, walk through the following Step-by-Step to review the application's basic features.

Step-by-Step 1.3

1. Launch Access and open the **JC's Data.accdb** file from the drive and folder where your Data Files are stored. Save the database as **JC's Updated Data**, followed by your initials.

2. Open the EMPLOYEE table in Design View. Between the *Employee ID* and *Last Name* fields, insert a new field titled **Department**. Define the field data type as **Text**.

3. Save the changes to the table and then switch to Datasheet View.

4. Sort the table alphabetically by last name and then update the records to include the department name in which each employee works:

Dominquez:	**Marketing**
Gonzalez:	**Administrative**
Keplinger:	**Sales**
Mann:	**Accounting**
Pullis:	**Accounting**
Thomsen:	**Sales**
Ti:	**Marketing**
Wong:	**Sales**

5. Sort the table by Employee ID, and then add a new record to the table and enter the following information:

Employee ID:	**9**
Department:	**Sales**
Last Name:	**Barkin**
First Name:	**Dave**
Salary:	**$145,000**
Home Phone:	**608-555-5121**
Date Hired:	**3/24/13**

6. Adjust the column widths to show all the data, and then show the table in Print Preview.

7. Change the page layout to **Landscape** and close Print Preview. Save the changes and close the table.

8. Open the PRODUCTS table and filter the data to show only those products with a price greater than $10. The filter should produce eleven records. Remove the filter and close the table. When prompted, save the changes.

9. Use the Form Wizard to create a form based on the EMPLOYEE table.

   a. Include all the fields in the form.

   b. Select the **Columnar** layout.

   c. Name the form **EMPLOYEE FORM**.

10. Use the Report Wizard to create a report based on the EMPLOYEE table.

   a. Include all the fields except *Salary* and *Date Hired*.

   b. Group the records by **Department**.

   c. Sort the records in ascending order by **Last Name**.

   d. Apply the **Stepped** layout and **Portrait** orientation.

   e. Name the report **EMPLOYEE TELEPHONE REPORT**.

11. Close the report and the form, and then exit Access.

Applying PowerPoint Features

PowerPoint is a presentation graphics program that enables you to create presentation materials for a variety of audiences, including slide shows using a projector and online presentations that everyone on a network can view. In the PowerPoint unit, you will explore some of its more advanced features. To make your presentations more interesting and effective, PowerPoint provides tools to add multimedia effects to your slides. The many customizing features PowerPoint offers enable you to create your own color schemes, backgrounds, and design templates. When preparing for your final presentation, PowerPoint has many options for distributing your slide show, including sharing via e-mail or presenting it remotely over a Web page or network.

Before you explore these advanced PowerPoint features, complete the following Step-by-Step to review your PowerPoint skills.

Step-by-Step 1.4

1. Launch PowerPoint, and then open the **Historic Preservation.pptx** file from the drive and folder where your Data Files are stored. Save the presentation as **Historic Housing**, followed by your initials.

2. On the title slide, replace *Your Name* with your own first and last names.

3. Add a new slide after the title slide, using the **Two Content** layout for the new slide.

4. In the title placeholder, type **Stabilization**. In the text placeholder on the left, type the following two lines of text. The text should automatically be formatted with bullets.

   Reestablish structural stability.

   Maintain essential form.

5. Move slide #5 (with the title *Resources)* so it is the last slide in the presentation.

6. Add graphics to slides 2–9. If possible, search Office.com for the graphics. *Hint*: Try search terms such as *house, fix, historic, tools,* and *blueprints.*

7. Apply a built-in design, and, if desired, change the color theme and/or fonts.

8. Apply a transition to all slides in the presentation. Adjust the timing of the transitions as needed.

9. Apply custom animations to the text and graphics on slides 2–10 to control when and how the objects appear.

10. Run the slide show and observe your transitions and animations, and make any necessary changes.

11. Save your changes. Close the presentation, and then exit PowerPoint.

Applying Outlook Features

Outlook is a desktop information management application. As you already know, using Outlook helps you keep track of e-mail messages, appointments, meetings, contact information, and tasks you need to complete. In this course, you will explore some of Outlook's more advanced features. You will learn about features that make it even easier to manage contact information, manage e-mails, and communicate with others. You will also learn about many features and tools that make it easier for you to schedule events and track progress on tasks.

Before you explore Outlook's advanced features, complete the following Step-by-Step to review the basic skills and features for Outlook.

Step-by-Step 1.5

1. Launch Outlook. Open a new journal entry and enter the information below. Then start the timer and leave the journal entry open.

   Subject: **Step-by-Step 1.5**

   Entry type: **Task**

2. Open the Contacts folder. Create a new contact group and name the group **Fitness Trainers**.

3. Add the following contacts to the new group and save the group.

Name:	**Sharon McKee**
E-mail:	**smckee@familyfit.xyz**
Name:	**Ronald DeVilliers**
E-mail:	**rdevillers@familyfit.xyz**
Name:	**Alisa Mandez**
E-mail:	**amandez@familyfit.xyz**

4. Create a new e-mail message. Send the message to the Fitness Trainers group, and type **Health and Nutrition Classes** in the Subject box. Then type the following in the message area:

   Please review the attached document and give me your feedback by the end of the day tomorrow.

5. Attach your solution file **Updated Class Descriptions.docx** to the e-mail message, and save the e-mail message as a draft. Do not attempt to send the e-mail.

6. Create the following two notes:

   Upload the health and nutrition class descriptions to the Web site.

   Confirm yoga class schedule with Bonnie.

7. Open the Calendar and show the calendar for a week from the current date. Create an appointment with your dentist for 10 a.m. and set a reminder. The appointment should last 45 minutes.

8. Open the Tasks folder and create the following new task. Give the task high priority and specify that it be completed within a week.

   Gather information for dental bills to submit for insurance.

9. Delete the dentist appointment.

10. Delete the contact group and contacts you created, and then delete the e-mail draft.

11. Delete the insurance task.

12. Delete the two notes.

13. Return to the journal entry and pause the timer. Make note of how much time you spent on this activity, and then delete the journal entry.

14. Exit Outlook.

Accessing Internet Resources

Microsoft Office 2010 is designed to give you quick and easy access to the World Wide Web, regardless of which Office application you are currently using. A *browser* is a program that connects you to remote computers and gives you the capability to access, view, and download data from the Web. Microsoft's browser program is Microsoft Internet Explorer.

▶ **VOCABULARY**
browser

Searching for Information and Evaluating Web Sites

Each day, millions of people use the World Wide Web to find information. To get the information they're looking for, they must navigate through an enormous amount of data. As a result, even with high-speed connections and powerful search engines, searching for specific information can be very time consuming.

ADVANCED   Introduction Unit

▶ **VOCABULARY**
search engine
keywords
hits
wildcard

A *search engine*, such as Microsoft's Bing, is a tool designed to find information on the Web. When you enter *keywords*, words that describe the information you are seeking, the search engine generates a list of Web sites that potentially match the search criteria. These search results (the best matching Web sites) are often referred to as *hits*. Searches often produce a long list of hits; if you wish to narrow the search results, you need to be more specific in the keywords that you provide. **Table 1–1** describes several options for refining a search so you can find information quickly and effectively.

TABLE 1–1   Options for refining searches

SEARCH OPTIONS	DESCRIPTION
Capitalization	If you want the results to include occurrences of both upper and lowercase letters, enter the keywords using all lowercase letters. However, if you want to narrow your results to words that begin with capital letters (such as Central Intelligence Agency) or all capital letters (such as CIA), enter the keywords with the same capitalization.
Plurals	Most search engines consider singular keywords as both singular and plural. For example, results for the keyword *agent* will include hits with the word *agents*. If you want the results to include only hits with a plural word, be sure the keyword is plural.
Phrases	Search for a group of words by including quotation marks before and after the sequence of words. With the quotation marks, only hits with all of the words in the exact same sequence will appear in the results. Without the quotation marks, the results will include hits that contain all or most of the words anywhere within a Web site.
Operators	Narrow or broaden the search using operators including *+*, *&*, *and*, *-*, *not*, and *or*. For example, if you are searching for information about international exchange students, use the following keywords in the search engine to exclude hits for currency exchange rates: **+international +exchange +students -currency** or **international and exchange and students not currency**
Related pages	Many search engines provide options to include hits for Web pages with similar information. Look for links such as *Similar pages, Also try,* or *Related searches*.
Truncation	Some search engines support the use of a symbol, sometimes referred to as a ***wildcard***, that allows for variations in the spelling of words. When an asterisk (*) symbol is used in a word, the search results include hits with alternate spellings for the word at the point that the asterisk appears. For example, *extra** generates hits for Web pages with *extra, extras, extract,* and *extraordinary*.
Domains	You can limit search results to a specific domain, such as an educational institution or a government Web site. For example, to find information about environmental research at an educational institution, in the search engine, enter the following keywords: **+domain:edu +environmental +research** or **domain:edu and environmental and research**

When the search results appear, read the information carefully before clicking any of the links. You can determine the validity of some of the hits by looking at the URLs. For example, if you're looking for information about deadlines for filing forms for personal income taxes, you want to click a link that includes IRS in the URL. Also, domain name extensions help to identify the type of entity. **Table 1–2** shows common domain extensions and the type of entity related to them.

TABLE 1–2   Common domain extensions

DOMAIN EXTENSIONS	DESCRIPTIONS
.com	Commercial business
.edu	Educational institution
.gov	Governmental institution
.org	Nonprofit organization
.mil	Military site
.net	Network site
.us	Abbreviation that indicates a country; for example: .us (United States), .ja (Japan), .uk (United Kingdom), .ca (Canada), and .hk (Hong Kong)

 EXTRA FOR EXPERTS

Most search engines include links that provide information about advanced search features. Be sure to access these links to learn how to make your searches more effective.

Just about anyone can publish information on the Web—often for free, and usually unmonitored. So how do you know if you can trust the information that you find? When you depend on the Web for sources of information, it is your responsibility to determine the integrity and validity of the information and its source. **Table 1–3** provides questions that will guide you through an evaluation process.

TABLE 1–3   A guide for evaluating information on the Web

QUESTIONS TO ASK	WHAT TO CONSIDER
Is the information relevant to my query?	The information should help you to accomplish your goals and objectives. Make sure you analyze the information and determine if it meets your needs.
Is the information current?	Check for a date on the Web page that indicates when the information was last updated.
Is the Web site published by a company or an entity, or is it a personal Web site?	The URL often includes a company name. If you are familiar with the company or entity, consider whether you trust information from this source. If you are not familiar with the company, or the individual, look for links such as *About Us*, *Background*, or *Biography*.
What is the purpose of the Web site?	Use the domain name to identify the type of Web site. For example: a domain name ending with .com is a business, and the intent of the Web site is to sell or promote a product or service.
Who is the author?	Look for information that explains who the author is and how the author is connected to the subject. Verify that the author is qualified to address the subject. Individuals sometimes falsify their credentials, so research the author's background and confirm that the author is credible. For example, if information at the Web site indicates that the author is a professor at a university, go to the university Web site and check the faculty roster.
Is the author biased in his/her opinion?	When looking for facts, be sure the author provides objective viewpoints and cites information with credible sources.
Is the Web site presented professionally?	Information should be well organized and presented accurately, free from spelling and grammar errors.
Are the links legitimate and credible?	Confirm that links are up to date. Links to a credible Web site, such as a business or an organization, do not mean that the business or organization approves of or supports the content on the linked Web page.

Step-by-Step 1.6

1. If necessary, log onto the Internet and open your browser.

2. In the address bar, type **www.bing.com** and then press **Enter** to open the Bing search engine.

3. In the Bing search box, type **lake tahoe ski** and then click the **Search** button, or press **Enter**.

4. Note that the number of hits is indicated at the top of the search results. Scroll down and review the first set of results. Each link provides a brief preview of the Web page content, and the keywords are highlighted in the preview. Occurrences of the word *skiing* may also appear highlighted in the previews.

5. Edit the text in the search box to read **+lake +tahoe +ski -water**. Click the **Search** button, or press **Enter**. Scroll down through the first set of results. Note that the number of hits is greatly reduced, and the word *water* is not found in any of the previews.

6. Edit the text in the search box to read **"lake tahoe water ski"** and then click the **Search** button, or press **Enter**. Note that the number of hits is considerably less because adding more keywords often narrows the search.

7. Delete the text in the search box and then type **domain:org and tahoe and ski**. Click the **Search** button, or press **Enter**. Scroll down through the first set of results. Notice every URL has a .org extension.

8. Type **www.nasa.gov** in the address bar and then press **Enter**. The NASA home page opens.

9. Navigate the Web site and find the following information:
   a. the date when the site was last updated
   b. NASA locations
   c. blogs
   d. the names of the authors of the site's articles and blogs
   e. any available information about the authors' backgrounds
   f. information for contacting NASA

10. Return to the home page for the NASA Web site.

11. Leave the NASA Web site open for the next Step-by-Step.

Revisiting Web Sites

As you rely more and more on the Web as a primary source of information on any topic, you'll find that there are sites you visit frequently or that you know you'll want to access again. You can create a bookmark for quick and easy access to a Web page. A *bookmark* is a link that navigates you to the Web page, and it is saved in a Favorites folder. You can create additional folders inside the Favorites folder to keep the list of sites organized.

▶ VOCABULARY
bookmark

Your browser keeps track of the sites you have visited, so you can also quickly revisit a site by selecting the Web site from the History list. The History list can be organized by date, site, most visited, and the order the sites were visited on the current day. You can easily delete the History list, as well as temporary Internet files, cookies, form data, and passwords.

Step-by-Step 1.7

The following steps describe bookmarking Web pages using Internet Explorer features. If you are not using Internet Explorer as your browser, you can still explore the features for creating the bookmarks, but these steps will not exactly describe your browser features.

1. If necessary, log onto the Internet, open your Internet Explorer browser, and open **www.nasa.gov**. Or navigate to the NASA home page, if necessary.

2. Click the **Favorites** button on the Command bar in the upper-left corner of the screen, as shown in **Figure 1–2**.

FIGURE 1–2
Favorites button on
the Internet Explorer browser

Favorites button

3. If necessary, click the **Favorites** tab to show a list of your favorite sites. Your favorites list will be different than the one shown in **Figure 1–3**.

FIGURE 1–3
Folders on the Favorites tab

History tab

Favorites list

4. Click the **Add to Favorites** button to open the Add a Favorite dialog box shown in **Figure 1–4**.

FIGURE 1–4
Add a Favorite dialog box

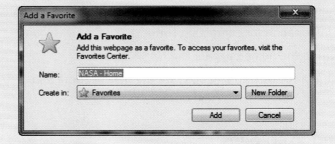

TIP

You can also quickly add Web sites to the Favorites folder using the shortcut keys Ctrl+D.

5. In the Name text box, *NASA - Home* appears. Leave the name as is and click **New Folder** on the dialog box. The Create a Folder dialog box similar to the one shown in **Figure 1–5** opens. In the Folder Name text box, type **Research** and then click **Create**. The Add a Favorite dialog box is still open. Click **Add**.

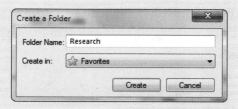

FIGURE 1–5
Create a Folder dialog box

6. Click the **Favorites** button to show your list of favorites. Click the new folder **Research** and you will see the *NASA - Home* site. You can move favorites into folders by dragging the site name to the desired folder.

7. Click the **History** tab on the Favorites pane. Click the **View By...** button at the top of the History list, and then click **View By Order Visited Today**. Notice that the NASA Web page is included in the list of documents and Web sites accessed today. Click the **View By...** button at the top of the History list again, then click **View By Most Visited**. The list is rearranged.

8. Right-click one of the Web sites in this list, click **Delete** in the shortcut menu, and then click **Yes** to confirm the deletion.

9. Click the **Favorites** button, and on the History tab, click any one of the site names on the History list. The Web page opens.

10. Click the **list arrow** at the right side of the address bar in the browser, as shown in **Figure 1–6**. A history of accessed Web sites is displayed, as well as a list of favorite sites. Click anywhere outside the History list to close it.

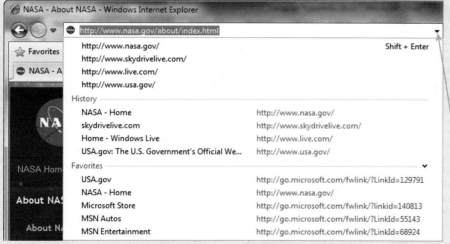

FIGURE 1–6
History and Favorites lists on the address bar

Click to display history of accessed Web sites and favorite sites

11. Click the **Safety** button on the browser toolbar, as shown in **Figure 1–7**.

Safety button

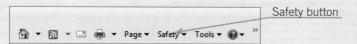

FIGURE 1–7
Safety button on browser toolbar

12. Click **Delete Browsing History** to open the dialog box in **Figure 1–8**. If necessary, change the settings so they match those shown in the figure, and then click **Delete**.

FIGURE 1–8
Delete Browsing History
dialog box

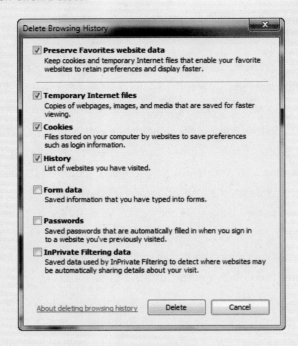

13. Click the **Favorites** button. Click the **Favorites** tab, and in the Favorites list, right-click the **Research** folder, and then click **Delete** in the short-cut menu. Click **Yes** to confirm the deletion.

14. Close Internet Explorer.

SUMMARY

In this lesson, you learned:

- Microsoft Word is a powerful, full-featured word processor. Its advanced features enable users to further enhance the appearance of documents and save time preparing and editing documents. Developing a document often involves multiple team members, and Word offers several tools to help you share documents and effectively collaborate on projects.

- Excel is the spreadsheet application in the Microsoft Office suite. Spreadsheets are used primarily for calculating and analyzing data, and Excel's advanced features enable you to perform complex calculations and in-depth analysis. Excel includes many features that enable you to generate accurate and professional-looking reports, charts, and tables.

- Access is the database application in the Office suite. Databases are used for storing and organizing information. The advanced features in Access give you more control over how database records are viewed, edited, and professionally analyzed. Effectively designed forms and reports help to streamline data entry and editing.

- Microsoft PowerPoint is a presentation graphics program that enables you to create materials for presentations of many kinds. Its advanced features include several tools for customizing slide designs and using multimedia effects to enhance your content. Remote publishing features in PowerPoint enable you to share presentations over the Internet or a network.

- Microsoft Outlook is a desktop information management program that provides several tools for scheduling appointments and meetings, managing and delegating tasks, and communicating with others. Advanced features help you customize the tools to fit your needs.

- An enormous amount of information is available on the World Wide Web. Effective search strategies not only save you time, but they also lead you to more relevant sources.

- When you depend on the Web for sources of information, it is your responsibility to determine the integrity and validity of the information and its source.

- You can bookmark Web sites that you visit frequently and save the links to the Favorites folder. You can create additional folders to organize your Favorites list.

- You can also quickly revisit a site by selecting the Web site from the History list, which can be organized by date, site, most visited, and the order the sites were visited on the current day.

VOCABULARY REVIEW

Define the following terms:

bookmark	hits	search engine
browser	keywords	wildcard

REVIEW QUESTIONS

MATCHING

Match the most appropriate application in Column 2 to the application described in Column 1.

Column 1

_____ 1. A graphics application with multimedia capabilities that can be used to create materials to present and share information with others

_____ 2. An application designed for entering, calculating, and analyzing data

_____ 3. An application used for storing and organizing information

_____ 4. A desktop information management application

_____ 5. An application that provides comprehensive writing tools for sharing information with others

Column 2

A. Microsoft Outlook

B. Microsoft PowerPoint

C. Internet Explorer

D. Microsoft Word

E. Microsoft Excel

F. Microsoft Access

MULTIPLE CHOICE

Select the best response for the following statements.

1. A _____ is a program that gives you the capability to access, view, and download data from the Web.

   A. search engine   C. browser

   B. Web page   D. tracking device

2. _____ are used to broaden or narrow an online search.

   A. Keywords   C. Operators

   B. Phrases   D. all of the above

3. Non-profit organizations commonly use the _____ extension in the domain name.

   A. .net   C. country abbreviation

   B. .org   D. .com

4. _____ are the results generated by a search engine.

   A. Hits   C. Wildcards

   B. Domains   D. Quick links

5. You can organize your Internet Explorer History list based on _____.

   A. the date sites were accessed   C. the order in which sites were visited today

   B. the names of the sites   D. all of the above

WRITTEN QUESTIONS

1. Explain how the search results are affected when you include quotation marks before and after a group of words when entering keywords in a search engine.

2. Explain how the domain name can help you identify the purpose of a Web site.

3. Give an example of when you would include operators with the keywords in a search engine.

4. How can you validate that a Web site author has credibility?

5. Name some examples of related pages options provided by some search engines.

■ PROJECTS

If you have a SAM 2010 user profile, your instructor may have assigned an autogradable version of the indicated project. If so, log into the SAM 2010 Web site at *www.cengage.com/sam2010* to download the instruction and start files.

PROJECT 1–1

1. Launch Word, then open the **Spectrum Follow-up.docx** data file from the drive and folder where your Data Files are stored. Save the document as **Final Spectrum Follow-up,** followed by your initials.

2. Make the edits indicated in **Figure 1–9.**

3. Change the left and right margins to 1.25 inches.

4. Justify the alignment of the paragraphs in the body of the letter.

5. Indent the bulleted list .5 inches from the left margin.

6. Adjust the paragraph spacing as needed to fit the entire document on one page.

7. Proofread and check for spelling and grammar errors, and make any necessary corrections.

8. Save the changes and leave the document open for the next project.

BLACKFOOT CONFERENCE RESORT
Route 2
Butler, OH 44822-0712
800-555-5436

*Arial
14 pt. bold*

Current date

Mr. Gary Ferreira
Spectrum Media Corporation
1454 West 30th Street
Minneapolis, MN 55402-1884

Gary
Dear ~~Mr. Ferreira~~:

Thank you for visiting us and considering scheduling your national conference at Blackfoot Conference Resort. As you witnessed, we offer every thing from meeting rooms to dining and recreation, and we are in the business to help you plan and execute a productive conference.

We have years of experience hosting traning conferences, and a personal coordinator will be available to assist you in planning every detail of the meeting. Your teammates will enjoy the modern, air-conditioned suites, complete with cable TV and wireless Internet connections. Each suite has a private balcony with a scenic view. But they most likely won't spend a lot of time in the guest rooms because they have all of these ~~options~~... *amenities*

- an indoor and an outdoor pool
- whirlpool spa
- a full-facility exercise room
- tennis courts
- a basketball court
- a recreational lake for boating and fishing
- two area downhill and cross-country ski resorts
- horsback riding
- 18-hole golf course
- three miles of walking trails

to ensure

We are responsive to your needs. We pay attention to details and provide quality service so your meeting is a memorable success. Choose our facility, and we will treat your conference like it is the most important event we have ever hosted!

Best,

Victoria A. Nolan
Sales Manager

FIGURE 1–9   Edits for the Word document in Project 1–1

SAM PROJECT 1–2

1. Launch PowerPoint and open a new presentation. Save the presentation as **Blackfoot Resort**, followed by your initials.

2. Create a slide show highlighting the guest amenities described in the Blackfoot Conference Resort letter in Project 1-1. This presentation will be distributed on the Internet to promote the resort.

3. Add pictures and graphics to help viewers visualize the amenities.

4. Add a creative title slide at the beginning of the presentation, and add a slide for closure at the end of the presentation.

5. Apply an appropriate design or background colors to the slides.

6. Add transitions to the slides, animations to the text, and objects on the slides to produce special effects and keep the viewer's attention.

7. Save the changes and exit PowerPoint.

PROJECT 1–3

1. If necessary, log onto the Internet and open your browser.

2. In the address bar, type **www.bing.com** and press Enter.

3. Enter the keywords **Conference Resorts Ohio** to search for Ohio-based conference resort sites that offer options for guests that are similar to the options described in the Blackfoot Conference Resort document you edited in Project 1-1.

4. When you find at least two Web sites promoting a conference center similar to the Blackfoot Conference Resort, save the sites to your Favorites list in a Conference Resort folder. *Hint*: Several hits may be sites that showcase multiple resorts, and you will need to navigate to the individual resort pages to get the required information.

5. Evaluate the Web sites and answer the following questions about each Web site.
   a. Were you able to find relevant information to compare resorts?
   b. Is the information at the site current?
   c. When was the site last updated?
   d. Is the site organized well, and is the information presented accurately and professionally?
   e. Does the site provide background information about the resort?
   f. Can you easily access information to contact the resort?
   g. Would you recommend this resort? Explain the reasons for your answer.

6. Close the browser.

PROJECT 1–4

1. Launch Excel and open the **January Sales.xlsx** file from the drive and folder where your Data Files are stored. Save the workbook as **First Qtr Sales**, followed by your initials.

2. In cell C1, type the column heading **February**. In cell D1, type the column heading **March**. In cell E1, type the column heading **Total**. In cell A7, type the row heading **Total**.

3. Enter the following data in the new columns.

	February	March
Byron Store	23112	42109
Fenton Store	38432	41002
Holly Store	31902	48111
Howell Store	27656	39202
Linden Store	29211	43007

4. Proofread the data entries to make sure you entered the numbers correctly.

5. Apply the Accounting number format to all the cells with numbers and remove the decimal places.

6. Enter a formula to calculate the sum of the cell range B2:D2 in cell E2, then fill the formula down through cell E6.

7. Enter a formula to calculate the sum of the cell range B2:B6 in cell B7, then fill the formula across through cell E7.

8. Create a 3-D column chart on the same sheet showing total sales by store. Apply a design of your choice.

9. Add a centered overlay title and type **First Qtr. Sales**. Turn off the legend options.

10. Reposition the chart on the sheet so you can see the sales data in the worksheet.

11. Save the changes and close the document.

PROJECT 1-5

1. Launch Access and open the **Clients.accdb** file from the drive and folder where your Data Files are stored. Save the database as **Updated Clients**, followed by your initials.

2. Open the CLIENTS table in Datasheet View.

3. Delete the record for Daniel Warner.

4. Update the address for Helen Sanderson. Her street address is now **709 Vienna Woods Drive, Cincinnati, OH 45211**.

5. In Design View, add a new field named **Mobile Phone**. Save the changes to the table and then switch back to Datasheet View.

6. Delete the home phone number for Paula Trobaugh and add her mobile phone number, **513-555-4465.**

7. Add two new clients:

   Penelope Rausch

   5074 Signal Hill

   Cincinnati, OH 45244

   Home Phone 513-555-0133

   Mobile Phone 513-555-0899

   Roger Williamson

   722 Red Bud Avenue

   Cincinnati, OH 45229

   Mobile Phone 513-555-1055

8. Save and close the database, then exit Access.

■ CRITICAL THINKING

ACTIVITY 1-1

Excel and Access have some similarities because both applications are used to organize data. If possible, look at two computer screens, side by side. On one computer, open an Excel worksheet. On the other computer, open an Access database table in Datasheet View. Compare the two screens, and create a list of similarities and differences between the worksheet and the database table. You should point out at least four similarities and four differences.

ACTIVITY 1-2

Open your browser and go to *www.bing.com*. Search for the keywords *Top Ten Search Engines*. Find the most current information available, and confirm that the sources are credible. Then, from the two sources, choose two search engines that you have never used and explore the features in each. Write a brief description of the features you like and why you would use them.

INTRODUCTORY UNIT

MICROSOFT ACCESS 2010

LESSON 1

Microsoft Access Basics

■ OBJECTIVES

Upon completion of this lesson, you should be able to:

- Understand databases and database terminology.
- Start Access, open a database, and open an object.
- Navigate a datasheet, edit a record, and undo a change.
- Select records and fields, and delete a record.
- Cut, copy, and paste data.
- Change the appearance of a datasheet.
- Preview and print a table.
- Close an object and exit Access.

■ VOCABULARY

best fit

compacting

database

database management system (DBMS)

datasheet

datasheet selector

Datasheet view

field

field name

field selector

field value

Navigation Pane

record

record selector

Each day, people rely on the information in databases for a variety of reasons. A database can store information about the books in a library, the medicines available at a pharmacy, or the customers at a DVD rental store. Whether you use a database to get the information you need, or a professional such as a doctor uses a database to retrieve information about you, databases are an important part of organizing your life.

Database Basics

▶ **VOCABULARY**
database management system (DBMS)

Access is a program known as a ***database management system (DBMS)***. A DBMS allows you to store, retrieve, analyze, and print information. You do not, however, need a computer to have a DBMS. A set of file folders or any system for managing data can be a DBMS. There are distinct advantages, however, to using a computerized DBMS.

A computerized DBMS is much faster, more flexible, and more accurate than using file folders. A computerized DBMS is also efficient and cost effective. A DBMS such as Access can store thousands of pieces of data that users can quickly search and sort, helping them to save time otherwise spent digging through file folders. For example, a computerized DBMS can find all the people with a certain zip code faster and more accurately than you could by searching through a large list or through folders.

Starting Access

To start Access, click the Start button on the taskbar, click All Programs, click Microsoft Office, and then click Microsoft Access 2010. After a few seconds, Access starts and opens Backstage view, as shown in **Figure 1–1**. The New tab contains options for creating a new database, opening an existing database, and getting Help while using Access.

FIGURE 1–1   New tab in Access Backstage view

Step-by-Step 1.1

1. With Windows running, click the **Start** button 🔵 on the taskbar.

2. Click **All Programs**, click **Microsoft Office**, and then click **Microsoft Access 2010**. Access opens the File tab and displays the New tab in Backstage view as shown in Figure 1–1. Leave this tab open for the next Step-by-Step.

Opening a Database

A **database** is a collection of objects. The objects work together to store, retrieve, display, and summarize data and also to automate tasks. The object types are tables, queries, forms, reports, macros, and modules. You can open an existing database by clicking Open in the navigation bar on the File tab, which displays the Open dialog box so you can browse to and open the desired database, or by clicking Recent in the navigation bar on the File tab, which displays a list of databases you have recently opened on the Recent tab. To open a database using the Recent tab, click the database name in the list.

After opening a database, the **Navigation Pane** opens on the left side of the screen, as shown in **Figure 1–2**. The Navigation Pane lists the objects in the database.

▶ **VOCABULARY**
database
Navigation Pane

FIGURE 1–2   Navigation Pane

Step-by-Step 1.2

1. On the File tab, click **Open** in the navigation bar. The Open dialog box appears.

2. Navigate to the drive and folder where your Data Files are stored, open the **Access** folder, and then open the **Access Lesson 01** folder.

3. Double-click **Members.accdb** (or **Members** if your file extensions are not displayed) in the folder. Access opens the Members database. The Navigation Pane displays the objects in the database, as shown in Figure 1–2.

4. If the Security Warning opens, as shown in Figure 1–2, click the **Enable Content** button in the Security Warning to close it. Leave the database open for the next Step-by-Step.

When you open a database, Access assumes that the database might contain something that could damage your computer. This is why you might see the Security Warning. The files in this book do not contain anything that might damage your computer. You can choose to close the Security Warning or just leave it open. In this book, when you open a database, you should click the Enable Content button in the Security Warning so your screens will match the ones shown in the book.

The Access Screen

Like other Office 2010 programs, the Access screen has a title bar, Quick Access Toolbar, and Ribbon. The status bar is located at the bottom of the screen. As you use Access, various windows and dialog boxes will open based on how you interact with the database. As in other Office programs, you can click the Microsoft Access Help button on the Ribbon to get help while you are working. You can use the Access Help window to browse for help by clicking links to topics or by typing a key term in the Search text box.

Database Objects

When you create a database, you create a file that will store all of the objects in the database. As you create objects in the database, the Navigation Pane displays them in a list. You can change the way that the Navigation Pane displays objects, so you might see them organized differently.

Each object has a different icon to identify its function. **Table 1–1** describes each type of object that you can create in a database and shows the icon used to identify the object in the Navigation Pane.

TABLE 1–1 Database objects

OBJECT	ICON	DESCRIPTION
Table		Stores all the data in the database in a format called a datasheet. A datasheet is similar in appearance to a worksheet. A database usually contains many tables.
Query		Used to search for and retrieve data from tables using conditions. A query is a question you ask the database.
Form		Displays data from one or more tables or queries in a format that might be similar in appearance to a paper form.
Report		Displays data from one or more tables or queries in a format that is usually customized for on-screen viewing or printing. A report is commonly used to summarize data and to calculate totals.
Macro		Automates database operations by allowing you to issue a single command to perform a task, such as opening a form or closing a database.
Module		Similar to a macro, but allows more complex programming of database operations. Creating a module requires the use of a programming language.

The Navigation Pane

When you open a database, the Navigation Pane displays the objects contained in the database. The database might contain any or all of the database objects described in Table 1–1 or just a single table. When you double-click a table, query, form, or report object in the Navigation Pane, the object opens in the main part of the Access window so you can view its contents. The object name appears on a tab at the top of the window to identify its name and object type, as shown in **Figure 1–3**. When many objects are open, clicking a tab displays the object. When you want to display more of the open object, you can close the Navigation Pane by clicking the Shutter Bar Open/Close Button at the top of the Navigation Pane. To open it again, click the Shutter Bar Open/Close Button on the left side of the screen.

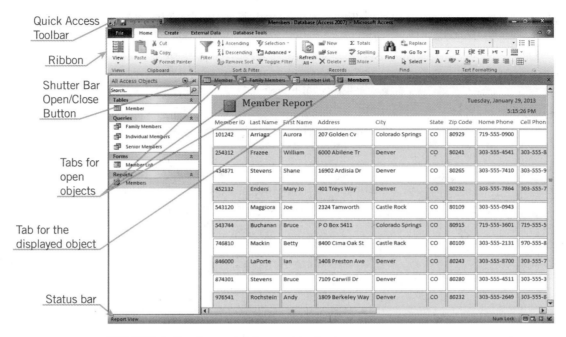

FIGURE 1–3 Open database objects

Step-by-Step 1.3

1. In the Navigation Pane, double-click **Member**. The Member table opens in Datasheet view.

2. In the Navigation Pane, double-click **Family Members**. The Family Members query opens in Query Datasheet view.

3. In the Navigation Pane, double-click **Member List**. The Member List form opens in Form view.

4. In the Navigation Pane, double-click **Members**. The Members report opens in Report view, as shown in Figure 1–3.

5. Click the **Member** tab to display the Member table datasheet.

6. Click the **Shutter Bar Open/Close Button** ≪ at the top of the Navigation Pane. The Navigation Pane closes. Leave the objects open for the next Step-by-Step.

Working with Records

Some terms are essential to know when working with databases. These terms relate to the way data is organized in a table. A *record* is a complete set of data. In the Member table, the data about each member is stored as a record. In a table, a record appears as a row, as shown in **Figure 1–4**.

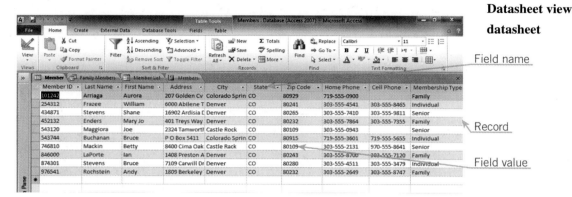

FIGURE 1–4   Records and fields in a table

Each record is made up of one or more *fields*. For example, the first name of each member is placed in a field that stores first names. In a table, fields appear as columns. To identify the fields, each field has a *field name*. The data entered into a field is called a *field value*. In the Member table, for example, the first record has *Aurora* as the field value in the First Name field.

You can enter records directly into the table using Datasheet view. In *Datasheet view*, the table displays its data in rows and columns in a *datasheet*.

The techniques used to enter records in the table should be familiar to you. Press Enter or Tab to move to the next field as you enter data. The field names describe the data that you enter in each field. For example, a Zip Code field might be designed to accept only numbers, or a State field might only accept entries consisting of two letters. When you enter an improper field value, an error message appears and tells you what to do to correct your mistake.

After entering records in a table, you do not need to save the changes as you do in other Office programs. Access automatically saves the changes you make to records.

Navigating Records in Datasheet View

You can use the pointer to move the insertion point to any field in a table by clicking in the desired field. You can also use the keys shown in **Table 1–2** to navigate a table.

TABLE 1–2   Using the keyboard to navigate in Datasheet view

KEY	DESCRIPTION
Enter, Tab, or right arrow	Moves to the next field in the current record
Left arrow or Shift+Tab	Moves to the previous field in the current record
End	Moves to the "Click to Add" column in the current record
Home	Moves to the first field in the current record
Up arrow	Moves up one record and stays in the same field
Down arrow	Moves down one record and stays in the same field
Page Up	Moves up one screen for the current field
Page Down	Moves down one screen for the current field
Ctrl+Home	Moves to the first field in the first record
Ctrl+End	Moves to the last field in the last record

Step-by-Step 1.4

1. Click the **Member ID** field for the second record, which contains the field value 254312. The insertion point appears in the field value, the Member ID field has an orange outline that identifies it as the current field, and the fields in the rest of the record appear with a blue background to indicate that the record is selected.

2. Press **Tab**. The Last Name field for the second record is selected.

3. Press the **down** key twice. The insertion point moves to the Last Name field for the fourth record, as shown in **Figure 1–5**.

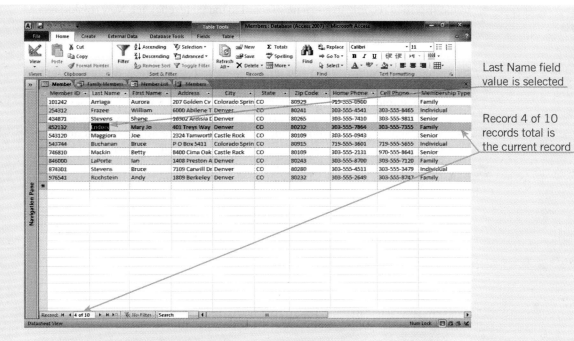

FIGURE 1–5
Navigating a table
datasheet

Last Name field value is selected

Record 4 of 10 records total is the current record

4. Press **Home**. The Member ID field for the fourth record is selected.

5. Press **Page Down**. The first field in the blank row at the bottom of the datasheet is selected.

6. Press **Ctrl+Home**. The first field value in the first record is selected. Leave the Member table open for the next Step-by-Step.

Editing Records

To make editing records easier, Access includes navigation buttons on the record navigation bar at the bottom of the datasheet. These buttons let you select records. They are very helpful when a table contains hundreds or thousands of records because they make it easy to move to the record you need. **Figure 1–6** shows the navigation buttons.

Current Record box

Previous record button

Next record button

New (blank) record button

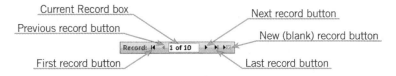

First record button

Last record button

FIGURE 1–6   Record navigation bar in Datasheet view

Clicking the First record button selects the first record in the table, and clicking the Last record button selects the last record in the table. The Next record and Previous record buttons select the next and previous record in the table. To select a specific record in a table, click in the Current Record box, select the value it contains, and then type the number of the record you want to select. Press Enter to move to the specified record. To add a new record to the table, click the New (blank) record button on the record navigation bar.

When you press Enter or Tab to move to a field, Access selects the contents of the field. When a field value is selected, you can replace the contents of the field by typing a new value. When you click a field with the pointer, the insertion point appears in the field. When the insertion point appears in a field, you can use the arrow keys to move the insertion point through the field value. Press Backspace to delete characters to the left of the insertion point, or press Delete to delete characters to the right of the insertion point. When an entire record is selected, the record selector changes color from gray to orange, and the background color of the fields in the record change from white to blue. In Figure 1–5, the fourth record is selected, as indicated by the orange record selector for that row, the blue background color of the fields in the row (except for the Last Name field, which is the active field), and the "4 of 10" that appears in the Current Record box.

Undoing Changes to a Field

If you make a mistake when typing a field value, you can click the Undo button on the Quick Access Toolbar to undo your typing and restore the field value to its original state. You can also press Esc to restore the contents of the entire field.

Step-by-Step 1.5

1. Click the **Last record** button on the record navigation bar to select the last record in the table.

2. Press **Tab** to move to the Last Name field.

3. Type **Richman**, and then press **Tab**. The First Name field is the current field.

4. Click the **First record** button on the record navigation bar to move to the First Name field in the first record. Click the **Next record** button on the record navigation bar to move to the next record.

5. Click in the **Current Record** box on the navigation bar, select the **2**, type **7**, and then press **Enter**. Record 7 is the current record.

6. Click the **Address** field value (*8400 Cima Oak*) for the seventh record. Press **Tab** to move to the City field. The field value *Castle Rack* is selected.

7. Click the insertion point to the right of the letter "R" in *Rack*. Press **Delete**, type **o**, and then press **Tab** twice.

8. Press the **down** key, type **11111**, and then press **Enter**.

9. Click the **Undo** button on the Quick Access Toolbar. The Zip Code field value *11111* returns to its original state (*80243*).

10. Press **Ctrl+Home**. Leave the Member table open for the next Step-by-Step.

Selecting Records and Fields

You can quickly select entire records and fields by clicking a record or field selector. A *field selector* appears at the top of each column in a table and contains the field name. Clicking a field selector selects the entire column. A *record selector* appears to the left of the first field for each record. Clicking a record selector selects the entire record. You can also select all of the records and fields in a table by clicking the *datasheet selector*, which is the box in the upper-left corner of a datasheet.

You can select more than one field by clicking the field selector in one column, holding down Shift, clicking the field selector in another column, and then releasing Shift. The two fields, and all the fields between them, will be selected. **Figure 1–7** shows five selected fields. You can use the same method to select multiple records. You can also select multiple fields or records by clicking and dragging across the field or record selectors.

▶ **VOCABULARY**
field selector
record selector
datasheet selector

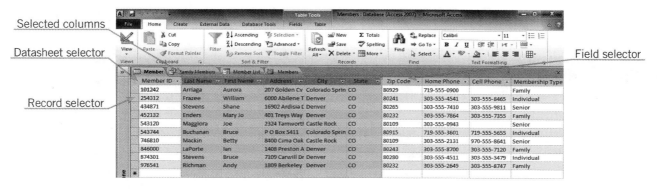

FIGURE 1–7   Selected columns in a datasheet

Step-by-Step 1.6

1. Click the **Last Name** field selector to select the entire column.

2. Press and hold down **Shift**, click the **State** field selector, and then release **Shift**. Five columns are selected, as shown in Figure 1–7.

3. Click the **Member ID** field selector. The Member ID field is selected, and the five columns are deselected.

4. Click the **Member ID** field value for the first record (*101242*) to deselect the column.

5. Click the **record selector** for the third record, with the Member ID field value *434871*. The entire record for Shane Stevens is selected.

6. Click the **datasheet selector** in the upper-left corner of the datasheet. All fields and records in the table are selected.

7. Click the **Member ID** field value for the first record (*101242*) to deselect the datasheet. Leave the table open for the next Step-by-Step.

Deleting Records

To delete a record from a table, select the record and then press Delete. A message box opens, as shown in **Figure 1–8**, warning you that you are about to delete a record. Click Yes to permanently delete the record or click No to cancel the deletion. After deleting a record, you cannot use the Undo button or press Esc to restore it. Deleting a record is permanent.

FIGURE 1–8   Message warning that you are about to delete a record

Step-by-Step 1.7

1. Click the **row selector** for the record with the Member ID *846000*.

2. Press **Delete**. A dialog box opens, as shown in Figure 1–8, warning that you are about to delete one record.

3. Click **Yes**. Leave the table open for the next Step-by-Step.

Cutting, Copying, and Pasting Data

The Cut, Copy, and Paste commands in Access work the same way as they do in other Office programs. You can use the commands to copy and move data within a table or into other tables. The Cut, Copy, and Paste commands are available as buttons on the Ribbon, as options on the shortcut menu, and as keyboard shortcuts. To cut or copy an entire record, select the record and click the Cut or Copy button in the Clipboard group on the Home tab.

Using the Cut, Copy, and Paste commands can sometimes be tricky, because data pasted in a table might overwrite the existing data. When you cut or copy an entire record and want to paste it into a table as a new record, click the arrow at the bottom of the Paste button in the Clipboard group on the Home tab, and then click Paste Append. When you select a record and click the Cut button, you will see the same warning message as when you press Delete. However, using the Cut button copies the record to the Clipboard, so you can paste it back into the table or into another table.

Step-by-Step 1.8

1. Click the **record selector** for the record for Shane Stevens (with the Member ID *434871*).

2. In the Clipboard group on the Home tab, click the **Copy** button 🗐.

3. In the Clipboard group on the Home tab, click the **Paste button arrow** 🗐. Click **Paste Append**. A copy of the record for Shane Stevens is pasted at the bottom of the datasheet.

4. In the Member ID field for the pasted record for Shane Stevens, change the Member ID field value to **457900**, and then press the **up** key.

5. Click the **record selector** for the original record for Shane Stevens (with the Member ID *434871*).

6. In the Clipboard group on the Home tab, click the **Cut** button ✂. A dialog box opens and warns that you are about to delete one record.

7. Click **Yes**. The record is deleted.

8. On the record navigation bar, click the **New (blank) record** button ▶. A new record is added to the table. The first field in the new record contains the insertion point.

9. In the Clipboard group on the Home tab, click the **Paste button arrow** 🗐, and then click **Paste Append**. The original record for Shane Stevens is pasted at the bottom of the datasheet.

10. Click the **record selector** for the record for Shane Stevens (with the Member ID *457900*), and then press **Delete**. Click **Yes**.

11. Press **Page Up**. Leave the Member table open for the next Step-by-Step.

Changing Datasheet Layout

You can make many changes to the datasheet layout, including changing row height and column width, rearranging columns, freezing columns, and changing the background color of rows in the datasheet.

Changing the Row Height

When you change the row height in a datasheet, the change affects every row in the datasheet. To change the row height, point to the bottom of any record selector. The pointer changes shape to a double arrow, as shown in **Figure 1–9**. Click and drag the row border up or down to adjust the row height.

Row resize pointer

FIGURE 1–9   Changing the row height

You can also specify an exact row height. In the Records group on the Home tab, click the More button, and then click Row Height. The Row Height dialog box opens, as shown in **Figure 1–10**. The standard (default) row height is 14.25. To change the row height to another value, select the value in the Row Height text box, type a new value, and then click OK.

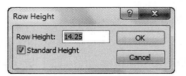

FIGURE 1–10   Row Height dialog box

Step-by-Step 1.9

1. Point to the bottom border of the record selector for the first record in the table (with the Member ID *101242*). The pointer is positioned correctly when it changes to a double-arrow shape ✛.

2. Click and drag the row border down until it appears on top of the bottom of the record selector for the second record, and then release the mouse button. The change affects every row in the table, as shown in **Figure 1–11**.

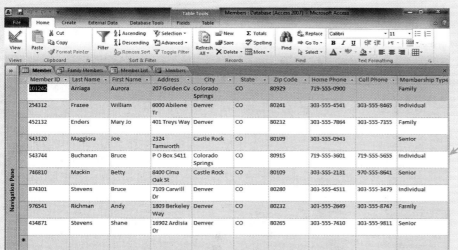

FIGURE 1–11
Datasheet after
increasing the row
height

New row height
applied to all rows

3. In the Records group on the Home tab, click the **More** button, and then click **Row Height**. The Row Height dialog box opens.

4. In the Row Height dialog box, click the **Standard Height** check box to add a check mark to it. The value in the Row Height text box changes to 14.25.

5. Click **OK**. The row height returns to the default setting. Leave the table open for the next Step-by-Step.

TIP

Another way to change the row height is to right-click any record selector, and then click Row Height on the shortcut menu.

Changing Column Width

Often, the default column widths are too wide or too narrow to display the data in the field. Adjusting the column width is similar to adjusting the row height. To change the column width, point to the right edge of the field selector for the column that you want to resize. The pointer changes to a double arrow, as shown in **Figure 1–12**. Click and drag the border to the right to make the column wider or drag the border to the left to make the column narrower. Unlike rows, which must all have the same height, each column can have a different width.

Column resize
pointer

Datasheet
selector

FIGURE 1–12   Changing the column width

▶ **VOCABULARY**
best fit

Another way of resizing a column is to change it to *best fit*, which automatically resizes the column to the best width for the data contained in the column. To resize a column to best fit, point to the right border of the field selector for the column that you want to resize, and then double-click the border.

Step-by-Step 1.10

1. Point to the right border of the **Address** field selector so the pointer changes to a double-arrow shape ✛, as shown in Figure 1–12.

2. Click and drag the right border of the **Address** field selector to the right about one-half inch (to the "t" in the word "City" in the field selector to the right of the Address field selector), and then release the mouse button. All of the data in the Address field should be visible.

3. Point to the right border of the **City** field selector so the pointer changes to a double-arrow shape ✛, and then double-click. The City field is resized to best fit the data it contains.

4. Click the **datasheet selector** to select all columns in the datasheet.

5. Point to the right border of the **Member ID** field selector so the pointer changes to a double-arrow shape ✛, and then double-click. All visible columns in the datasheet are resized to best fit.

6. Click the **Member ID** field value for the first record (*101242*) to deselect the columns. Leave the table open for the next Step-by-Step.

📼 **EXTRA FOR EXPERTS**

When a datasheet is selected and you use a field selector border to resize all columns, only the columns that are visible on the screen are resized to best fit. To resize columns that aren't visible, scroll the datasheet and resize them individually.

Rearranging Columns in a Datasheet

In Datasheet view, you can rearrange the order of the columns in a datasheet by dragging them to a new location. First, click the field selector for the column you want to move. Then, click and hold down the mouse button on the field selector and drag the column to the new location. A black vertical line follows the pointer to show where the column will be inserted. Release the mouse button to insert the column in its new location.

Step-by-Step 1.11

1. Click the **First Name** field selector.

2. Click and drag the **First Name** field selector to the left until the black vertical line appears between the Member ID and Last Name columns.

3. Release the mouse button. The First Name column appears between the Member ID and Last Name columns, as shown in **Figure 1–13**. Leave the table open for the next Step-by-Step.

FIGURE 1–13
Moving a column in a datasheet

New position of the First Name column

Freezing Columns

When a table has many columns, you might want to freeze one or more columns so you can still see them on the screen as you scroll the datasheet.

To freeze columns, select the field selectors for the columns that you want to freeze, click the More button in the Records group on the Home tab, and then click Freeze Fields. To unfreeze columns, click the More button in the Records group on the Home tab, and then click Unfreeze All Fields.

Step-by-Step 1.12

1. Click the **field selector** for the Member ID column.

2. In the Records group on the Home tab, click the **More** button, and then click **Freeze Fields**. Press **Home** to deselect the Member ID column.

3. Slowly drag the horizontal scroll bar at the bottom of the window to the right and notice that the Member ID column remains visible as you scroll the other columns. (Note: If you do not see a horizontal scroll bar, your screen is wide enough to display all of the columns. Continue to Step 4.)

4. Click the **More** button in the Records group on the Home tab, and then click **Unfreeze All Fields**. Leave the table open for the next Step-by-Step.

Changing the Background Row Color

By default, the rows in a datasheet are displayed with alternating light and dark background colors to make the data in the records easier to read. You can change the colors used by clicking the arrow on the Alternate Row Color button in the Text Formatting group on the Home tab. As shown in **Figure 1–14**, a gallery of colors opens and displays different themes and color selections. Pointing to a color in the gallery displays its name in a ScreenTip. Clicking a color in the gallery applies it to the datasheet.

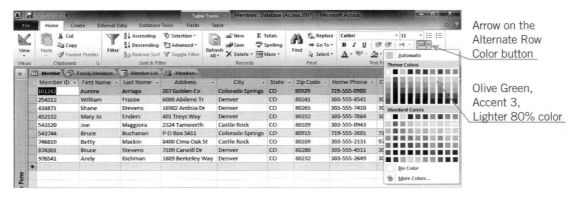

Arrow on the Alternate Row Color button

Olive Green, Accent 3, Lighter 80% color

FIGURE 1–14   Gallery with color choices for the background row color

Step-by-Step 1.13

1. In the Text Formatting group on the Home tab, click the **Alternate Row Color button arrow** .

2. In the Theme Colors section, click the **Olive Green, Accent 3, Lighter 80%** color (the seventh color in the second row). The gallery closes and the new background color appears in every other row in the datasheet. Leave the table open for the next Step-by-Step.

Previewing and Printing a Table

Before printing a datasheet or any other database object, you should view it in Print Preview so you can check the print settings. To view an object in Print Preview, click the File tab, click Print in the navigation bar, and then click Print Preview. **Figure 1–15** shows Print Preview for the Member table datasheet. You can use the options on the Ribbon to change the printer, to change the page layout (portrait or landscape and the page margins), or to change the zoom setting on the report so you can view the entire page or a close-up of its contents. You can use the page navigation bar at the bottom of Print Preview to display additional pages when the object contains them. After previewing the object and making any adjustments, click the Close Print Preview button in the Close Preview group on the Print Preview tab to return to Datasheet view.

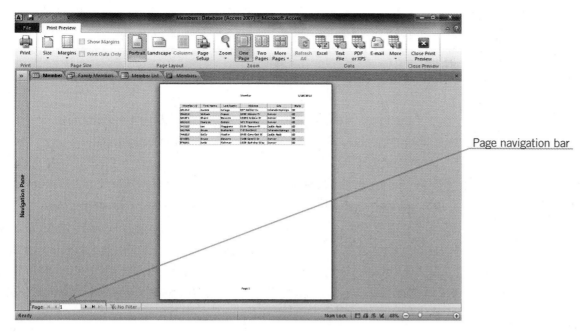

FIGURE 1–15   Print Preview for the Member table datasheet

You can print a datasheet by clicking the File tab, clicking Print in the navigation bar, and then clicking Quick Print to print the datasheet using the default printer
and the default print, or clicking Print to select a printer and adjust the print settings.
As shown in **Figure 1–16**, you can choose to print all the records, only the selected
records, or certain pages.

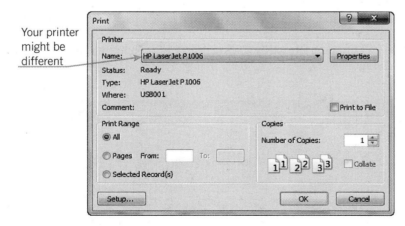

FIGURE 1–16   Print dialog box

Step-by-Step 1.14

1. Click the **File** tab, click **Print** in the navigation bar, and then click **Print
    Preview**. The Member table datasheet appears in Print Preview, as
    shown in Figure 1–15.

2. In the Page Layout group on the Print Preview tab, click the **Landscape** button.

3. On the page navigation bar, click the **Next Page** button 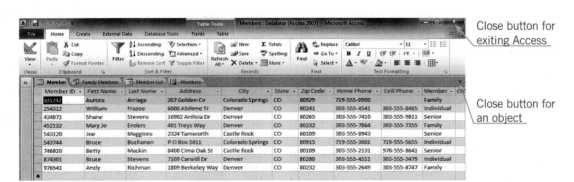 to view the second page of the datasheet.

4. In the Zoom group on the Print Preview tab, click the **Zoom** button. The zoom settings for the page change so that you can read the data in the datasheet.

5. In the Close Preview group on the Print Preview tab, click the **Close Print Preview** button. The datasheet is displayed in Datasheet view.

6. Click the **File** tab on the Ribbon, click **Print** in the navigation bar, and then click **Print**. The Print dialog box opens, as shown in Figure 1–16.

7. Make sure that your printer appears in the Name box and that the **All** option button is selected in the Print Range section. Click **OK**. Leave the table open for the next Step-by-Step.

Saving and Closing Objects

As you are entering and changing data in a table, Access saves your changes to the data automatically. When you make changes to the layout or appearance of a datasheet, such as changing row height or column widths or changing the background row colors, you must save your changes by clicking the Save button on the Quick Access Toolbar. If your table already has a name, Access saves the table when you click the Save button. If you haven't given your table a name, the Save As dialog box opens first and requests a name.

You can close an object by clicking the Close button on the object's tab, as shown in **Figure 1–17**.

> **TIP**
>
> When you make changes to the layout of a datasheet and try to close the table, Access will prompt you to save your changes.

FIGURE 1–17   Closing a database object

Step-by-Step 1.15

1. On the Quick Access Toolbar, click the **Save** button 🖫. Access saves the layout changes you made in the table.

2. Click the **Close 'Member'** button ☒ on the table window. The table closes.

3. Click the **Close 'Members'** button ☒ on the report window. The report closes.

4. Click the **Close 'Member List'** button ☒ on the form window. The form closes.

5. Click the **Close 'Family Members'** button ☒ on the query window. The query closes. Leave the database open for the next Step-by-Step.

Compacting and Repairing a Database

As you add and delete data or objects in a database, the database can become fragmented and use disk space inefficiently. *Compacting* a database rearranges how the database is stored on the disk and optimizes the performance of the database. Access combines compacting and repairing into one step. Depending on the size of the database and your computer's settings, it might take only a second or up to a minute to compact and repair a database. When the database you are compacting is small in size, like the Members database, you might not even notice that Access is compacting it because it will happen quickly.

▶ **VOCABULARY**
compacting

Step-by-Step 1.16

1. Click the **File** tab on the Ribbon. The Info tab displays information about the current database.

2. Click the **Compact & Repair Database** button. Access compacts and repairs the database, and displays the Home tab.

3. Leave the database open for the next Step-by-Step.

Closing a Database and Exiting Access

When you are finished working in a database, you can close it by clicking the File tab on the Ribbon, and then clicking Close Database in the navigation bar. After Access closes the database, the File tab opens.

As in other Office 2010 programs, you exit Access by clicking the File tab on the Ribbon, and then clicking Exit. You can also close Access by clicking the Close button on the title bar. Exiting Access takes you back to the Windows desktop.

Step-by-Step 1.17

1. Click the **File** tab on the Ribbon, and then click **Close Database** in the navigation bar. The database closes. Backstage view displays the New tab.

2. In the navigation bar, click **Exit**. Access closes.

SUMMARY

In this lesson, you learned:

- Access is a program known as a database management system (DBMS). A DBMS allows you to store, retrieve, analyze, and print information.

- A database is a collection of objects. The objects work together to store, retrieve, display, and summarize data and also to automate tasks. The object types are tables, queries, forms, reports, macros, and modules. You can open an object by double-clicking it in the Navigation Pane.

- You can open an existing database by clicking the File tab on the Ribbon, clicking Open in the navigation bar, and then browsing to and double-clicking the database you want to open. You can also click the File tab on the Ribbon, and then click Recent in the navigation bar to select the database from a list of recently opened files.

- You can use the keys on the keyboard to move through the records and fields in a datasheet. You can also use the buttons on the record navigation bar in Datasheet view to move around the datasheet. The record navigation bar buttons allow you to select the first record, the last record, the previous record, or the next record. You can also use a button to add a new record or use the Current Record box to select a specific record.

- A record is a complete set of data. Each record is made up of one or more fields. Each field is identified by a field name. The data entered into a field is called a field value. To select an entire row in a datasheet, click the record selector for the row. To select an entire field in a datasheet, click the field selector at the top of the column. To select multiple columns, click the field selector for the first column, press and hold down Shift, click a field selector in another column, and then release Shift. To select all fields and rows in a datasheet, click the datasheet selector.

- To delete a record from a table, select the record and then press Delete. Use the Cut, Copy, and Paste buttons in the Clipboard group on the Home tab to move and copy data. Clicking the arrow at the bottom of the Paste button and then clicking Paste Append appends a copied or cut record to the bottom of the datasheet.

- You can make many layout changes to a datasheet, such as changing the row height or column width, freezing columns, and changing the background row color of every other row.

- Before printing a database object, use Print Preview to check the print settings and to adjust the way the object is printed.

- You can close an object by clicking its Close button. To exit Access, click the Close button on the title bar.

■ VOCABULARY REVIEW

Define the following terms:

best fit	datasheet selector	field value
compacting	Datasheet view	Navigation Pane
database	field	record
database management system (DBMS)	field name	record selector
datasheet	field selector	

■ REVIEW QUESTIONS

TRUE / FALSE

Circle T if the statement is true or F if the statement is false.

T   F   **1.**   Microsoft Access allows you to store, retrieve, analyze, and print information.

T   F   **2.**   The object that stores data in the database is a form.

T   F   **3.**   Clicking a record selector in a datasheet selects an entire row.

T   F   **4.**   Pressing and holding down Alt allows you to select more than one column in a datasheet.

T   F   **5.**   Changing the height of one row in a datasheet changes the height of all rows.

WRITTEN QUESTIONS

Write a brief answer to each of the following questions.

1. How do you delete a record in Datasheet view?

2. What does the Paste Append command do?

3. When should you freeze columns in a datasheet?

4. Why should you preview an object before printing it?

5. Which database object allows you to search for and retrieve data?

FILL IN THE BLANK

Complete the following sentences by writing the correct word or words in the blanks provided.

1. Access is a program known as a(n) _____.

2. The _____ lists the objects in the current database.

3. To move to the first field in the current record, press _____.

4. You can select all of the records and fields in a table datasheet by clicking the _____.

5. _____ a database rearranges how the database is stored on the disk and optimizes the performance of the database.

■ PROJECTS

If you have a SAM 2010 user profile, your instructor may have assigned an autogradable version of the indicated project. If so, log into the SAM 2010 Web site at *www.cengage.com/sam2010* to download the instruction and start files.

PROJECT 1–1

1. Start Access.

2. Open the **Restaurants.accdb** database from the Access Lesson 01 folder where your Data Files are stored.

3. Open the **Favorites** table in Datasheet view.

4. Enter the records shown in **Figure 1–18**. (The first record was added for you.)

5. Resize the columns in the datasheet to best fit.

6. Preview the datasheet in Print Preview. Change the page layout to landscape.

7. Print the datasheet. Close Print Preview.

8. Save the table, and then close it.

9. Close the database, and then exit Access.

Name	Address	Phone	Specialty	Favorite Dish
Rosie's	8722 University Ave	817-555-6798	Mexican	Chicken fajitas
Health Hut	3440 Slide Rd	817-555-8971	Healthy foods	Fruit salad
Tony's BBQ	2310 S Lamar	817-555-7410	BBQ	Pulled pork sandwich
Stella's	7822 Broadway	817-555-7144	Italian	Lasagna
Westside Inn	5845 S 1st St	817-555-8200	American	Curry chicken salad
Alamo Diner	451 San Jacinto	817-555-0120	American	Chili cheese fries

FIGURE 1–18

PROJECT 1–2

1. Open the **Employees.accdb** database from the Access Lesson 01 folder where your Data Files are stored.

2. Open the **Department** table in Datasheet view.

3. Go to record 7 and change the first name to **Natalie**.

4. Go to record 11 and change the title to **Account Executive**.

5. Go to record 14 and change the department to **Marketing**.

6. Go to record 1 and change the last name to **Abraham**.

7. Undo your last change.

8. Select record 5. Delete record 5.

9. Select the datasheet (all rows and all columns). Change all columns to best fit.

10. Change the row height to **15**.

11. Move the First Name column so it appears between the Employee ID and Last Name columns.

12. Change the alternate row color in the datasheet to Dark Blue 1 (in the Standard Colors section, second row, fourth column).

13. Preview the datasheet in Print Preview. Change the page layout to landscape.

14. Print the datasheet, and then close Print Preview.

15. Save the Department table, and then close it.

16. Compact and repair the database.

17. Close the database, and then exit Access.

PROJECT 1–3

1. Open the **Stores.accdb** database from the Access Lesson 01 folder where your Data Files are stored.

2. Open the **Manager** table in Datasheet view.

3. Copy record 4 and paste it at the bottom of the datasheet.

4. In the pasted record, change the Name to **Vision Eyewear**, the Address to **7500 Hwy 15 West**, the Zip Code to **43601**, the Phone to **419-555-0122**, the Specialty to **Contemporary eyewear**, and the Manager to **Trent Rodriguez**. Press the Tab key.

5. Move the Phone column so it appears between the Name and Address columns.

6. Resize all columns to best fit.

7. Freeze the Name column.

8. Scroll to the right until the Specialty column appears to the right of the Name column.

9. Unfreeze all columns.

10. Change the alternate row color of the datasheet to Maroon 1 (in the Standard Colors section, the sixth color in the second row).

11. Preview the datasheet in Print Preview. Change the page layout to landscape.

12. Print the datasheet, and then close Print Preview.

13. Save the Manager table, and then close it.

14. Compact and repair the database.

15. Close the database, and then exit Access.

■ CRITICAL THINKING

ACTIVITY 1–1

When you are working in Access and need help completing a task, the Access Help window can help you find an answer. Start Access and click Help in the navigation bar on the File tab. Click Microsoft Office Help to open the Access Help window. In the Search text box, type **Navigation Pane**, and then click the Search button. Review the links that you find and click ones that you believe will give you more information about viewing and managing objects using the Navigation Pane. Read the information that appears. After following several links and reading their contents, write a brief summary of two new things that you learned about the Navigation Pane. When you are finished with your report, close the Access Help window and exit Access.

ACTIVITY 1–2

In this lesson, you learned how to compact and repair a database to reduce the size of a database and repair any errors. Another utility that you might use is one that creates a backup copy of the database. When you back up a database, you create a copy of everything in the database at the time of the backup. If the database ever becomes damaged or destroyed, you can restore the backup copy to minimize the amount of work you'll need to do to replace the damaged copy of the database.

Start Access, and click Help in the navigation bar on the File tab. Click Microsoft Office Help to open the Access Help window. In the Search text box, type **Back up a database**, and then click the Search button. Review the information that you find, and then answer the following questions on a sheet of paper

1. What steps do you follow to back up a database?

2. What happens when you restore a whole database?

3. What steps do you follow to restore a database?

LESSON 2

Creating a Database

■ OBJECTIVES

Upon completion of this lesson, you should be able to:

- Create a database.
- Design, create, and save a table in Datasheet view.
- Set a field's data type and name in Datasheet view.
- Add, delete, rename, and move fields in Design view.
- Change field properties in Design view.
- Set field properties in Design view.

■ VOCABULARY

alphanumeric data

AutoNumber

Blank database template

data type

Default Value property

Description property

design grid

Design view

Field Properties pane

field property

Field Size property

Format property

primary key

Required property

template

Access provides you with many options when creating databases and the tables that will store your data. In this lesson, you will learn about the different options you can use to create a database and a table. You will also create a table, add fields to a table, change a field's data type and properties, and add records to a table.

Creating a Database

The first step in creating a database is to create the file that will store the database objects. You can choose to create a database using one of the many templates that are installed with Access. These templates contain objects that you can use to organize data about events, projects, tasks, and other categories of data. When you use a ***template*** to create a database, the template creates the database and one or more table, query, form, and report objects that you use to enter and view data. Another option is to use the ***Blank database template***, which creates a database with an empty table in it.

To create a database, start Access. On the New tab in Backstage view, click the template you want to use or click the Blank database template to create a database that contains an empty table. Access asks you to specify a file name to use and a location in which to store the database, as shown in **Figure 2–1**.

▶ **VOCABULARY**
template
Blank database template

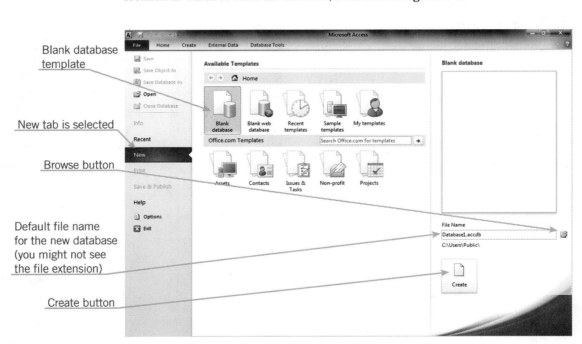

FIGURE 2–1   Creating a new, blank database

After specifying the file name and the location in which to store the database, click the Create button to create the new database and open it in Access. When you create a blank database, Access opens an empty table in Datasheet view so that you can start entering data, as shown in **Figure 2–2**.

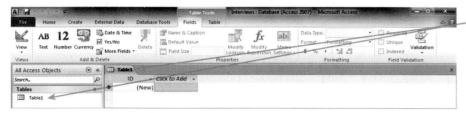

Default table name

FIGURE 2–2   New, empty table created

Step-by-Step 2.1

1. With Windows running, click the **Start** button ⊕ on the taskbar. Click **All Programs**, click **Microsoft Office**, and then click **Microsoft Access 2010**.

2. On the New tab, click the **Blank database** template, if necessary. See Figure 2–1.

3. In the Blank database pane, click the **Browse** button ⌹. The File New Database dialog box opens.

4. Navigate to the drive and folder where your Data Files are stored, and then open the **Access Lesson 02** folder. Click **OK**.

5. In the Blank database pane, click in the File Name text box to select the default database name (Database1.accdb), and then type **Interviews** followed by your initials.

6. Click the **Create** button. Access creates the Interviews database and opens it. Access also opens a new, empty table, as shown in Figure 2–2. Leave the table open for the next Step-by-Step.

TIP

Access might add the file name extension "accdb" to your file name automatically. You do not need to type it.

Creating and Saving a Table

When you create a blank database, Access creates the first table in the database for you and names it *Table1*. You can change this name when you save the table for the first time. To save a table, click the Save button on the Quick Access Toolbar. In the Save As dialog box, type the name of the table, and then click OK. The new table name appears on the tab for the table and also in the Navigation Pane, as shown in **Figure 2–3**. In many databases, data is stored in more than one table.

Save button
New table name
ID field
Applicant table in the Navigation Pane

FIGURE 2–3   Table after saving it

Step-by-Step 2.2

1. On the Quick Access Toolbar, click the **Save** button . The Save As dialog box opens. The default name *Table1* is selected.

2. In the Table Name text box, type **Applicant**.

3. Click **OK**. The tab for the table now displays the table name *Applicant*. The Applicant table appears in the Navigation Pane, as shown in Figure 2–3. Leave the table open for the next Step-by-Step.

Designing a Table

After creating a table in a database, you need to tell Access which fields to include in the table. When you create a blank database, the table that Access creates for you contains one field named *ID*. Access sets the ID field as the table's primary key. In a table, the **primary key** is the field that contains a unique field value for each record in the table. In some tables, this field is called an **AutoNumber** because it automatically adds a unique number to the primary key field for each record in the table. You can tell that Access created an AutoNumber for the ID field because of the word *(New)* in the first record's field. When you add the first record to the table, Access will change *(New)* to a unique number.

In some tables, your data might already have a field that stores unique numbers for each record. This unique field might store student identification numbers, employee numbers, or Social Security numbers. These types of values are also good candidates to use as a table's primary key field. The advantage of setting a primary key is that Access does not let you enter duplicate values for this field in different records. In other words, if you enter the student ID 1001 in the record for a student named John Hooper, Access does not let you enter the same student ID number in a record for another student. You learn more about primary key fields later in this lesson.

Understanding Data Types

Before creating all the fields for your table, you must decide which data type to assign to the field based on the field values you will enter. A field's **data type** determines the kind of data that you can enter in the field, such as numbers or text, or a combination of numbers and text (also called **alphanumeric data**). **Table 2–1** describes some common data types that you can use when you create a table.

▶ **VOCABULARY**

data type

alphanumeric data

TABLE 2–1   Common data types in Access

DATA TYPE	DESCRIPTION
Text	Accepts field values containing letters, numbers, spaces, and certain symbols such as an underscore (_). A Text field can store up to 255 characters and is used to store data such as names and addresses.
Number	Stores numbers. Number fields are usually values that will be used in calculations, such as multiplying the cost of an item by the number of items ordered to get a total. Number fields are sometimes used to restrict the entered field values to numbers.
Currency	Accepts monetary values and displays them with a dollar sign and decimal point.
Date/Time	Stores dates, times, or a combination of both.
Yes/No	Stores Yes/No, True/False, or On/Off values.
Lookup	Creates a field that lets you "look up" a value from another table or from a list of values entered by the user.
Memo	Accepts field values containing alphanumeric data, but can store field values containing up to 65,535 characters. Memo fields usually store long passages of text, such as detailed notes about a person or product.
Attachment	Stores graphics, sound, and other types of files as attachments.
Hyperlink	Stores a value that contains a hyperlink. Clicking the value activates the link and opens a Web page or other location, or addresses a message to an e-mail address.
Calculated	Opens the Expression Builder dialog box, which lets you specify fields and operators to use in calculations. The result of the calculation appears as the field's value, and determines the field's actual data type.
AutoNumber	Adds a unique numeric field value to each record in a table. AutoNumber fields are often used for primary key fields.

EXTRA FOR EXPERTS

You can also use a Quick Start selection to add commonly used fields to an existing table, such as the fields that store the street, city, state, and zip code for a person's address. In the Add & Delete group on the Fields tab, click the More Fields button, scroll down to the Quick Start section, and then click a Quick Start selection to add fields to the table.

Setting a Field's Data Type and Name in Datasheet View

When you create a table in Datasheet view, clicking the Click to Add field selector opens the list of data types show in **Figure 2–4** and described in Table 2–1. After clicking the desired data type in the list, the list closes and the default field name is selected, so you can type the field name used in your table design. The field name is added to the field selector after you press Tab or Enter. After you have added all of the fields to your table, the last column in the table contains the Click to Add field selector in case you need to add another field later.

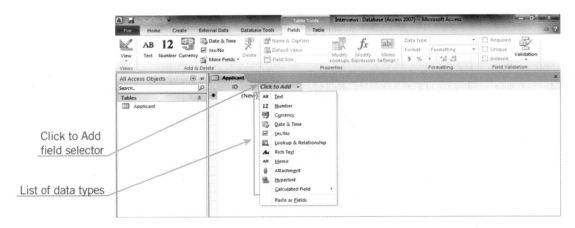

Click to Add field selector

List of data types

FIGURE 2–4   Creating a new field

Step-by-Step 2.3

TIP

You can add field to a table quickly by typing the first letter of the data type name after the Click to Add list opens. For example, typing the letter "t" selects the Text data type, closes the list, and selects the field name.

1. In the datasheet, click the **Click to Add** field selector. Figure 2–4 shows the list that opens.

2. In the list, click **Text**. The list closes, the field's data type is set to Text, and the default field name *Field1* is selected in the field selector.

3. Type **First Name**.

4. Press **Tab**. The field name changes to *First Name*. The Click to Add list opens for the next field in the table.

5. In the list, click **Text**, type **Last Name**, and then press **Tab**. The third field's name and data type are set and the Click to Add list opens for the fourth field.

6. In the list, click **Text**, type **Phone**, and then press **Tab**.

7. In the list for the fifth field, click **Date & Time**, type **Appointment Date**, and then press **Tab**.

8. In the list for the sixth field, click **Number**, type **Job Number**, and then press **Tab**.

9. In the list for the seventh field, click **Text**, type **Notes**, and then press the **down** key. Leave the table open for the next Step-by-Step.

Entering Records in Datasheet View

The First Name, Last Name, Phone, and Notes fields are Text fields that will contain alphanumeric data with less than 255 characters. The Appointment Date field is a Date/Time field that will store dates. To make sure that all job numbers contain only digits, the Job Numbers field has the Number data type. **Figure 2–5** shows the table after creating all the fields.

FIGURE 2–5   Table after creating all the fields

When Access created the table, it created the ID field and assigned it the AutoNumber data type. When you enter a new record in the table, you do not need to type a value in this field. The value *(New)* appears in the ID field. After you enter a field value in the record, Access changes the value *(New)* to a unique value in the ID field automatically.

Step-by-Step 2.4

1. With the ID field for the first record active, press **Tab**.

2. In the First Name field, type **Adam**. Press **Tab**.

3. In the Last Name field, type **Hoover**. Press **Tab**.

4. In the Phone field, type **505-555-7844**. Press **Tab**.

5. In the Appointment Date field, type **9/22/2013**. Press **Tab**.

6. In the Job Number field, type **5492**. Press **Tab**. The insertion point is in the Notes field. Leave the table open for the next Step-by-Step.

Changing a Field's Data Type in Datasheet View

When you need to change the data type for a selected field, you can do so by clicking the Data Type arrow in the Formatting group on the Fields tab. The Notes field has the Text data type, but it needs to use the Memo data type. You can click the Data Type arrow in the Formatting group to display a list of data types for fields, as shown in **Figure 2–6**. Clicking a data type in the list changes the data type for the current field and also closes the list.

The AutoNumber value in your table might be different

Data Type arrow

Notes field is selected

FIGURE 2–6   Data Type list with the Notes field selected

Step-by-Step 2.5

1. With the Notes field for the first record active, click the **Data Type** arrow in the Formatting group on the Fields tab. Figure 2–6 shows the list that opens.

2. In the Data Type list, click **Memo**. The Notes field now uses the Memo data type.

3. Press **Tab**. The first record is complete, and the ID field for the second record is selected. The value "(New)" indicates that this field uses the AutoNumber data type.

4. Use **Figure 2–7** to enter the remaining records in the table. Leave the table open for the next Step-by-Step.

FIGURE 2–7
Records added to the Applicant table

Your numbers in the ID field might be different

Working in Design View

When you are working on a table in Datasheet view, you can change the data type of a field. However, sometimes you need to make certain types of changes to a field that you cannot make in Datasheet view. In **Design view**, you can add, delete, and make changes to the way that fields store data. To change to Design view, click the View button in the Views group on the Fields tab. **Figure 2–8** shows the Applicant table in Design view. Notice that the field names and data types appear in the **design grid** in the top half of the Table window. The bottom half of the Table window is called the **Field Properties pane**. The properties for a field depend on the field's data type. For example, if the selected field in the design grid has the AutoNumber data type, the Field Properties pane displays the properties for an AutoNumber field. If the selected field has another data type, the Field Properties pane displays only those properties for that field's data type.

▶ **VOCABULARY**

Design view

design grid

Field Properties pane

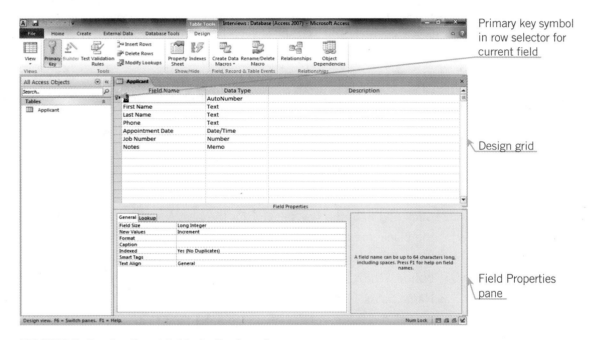

Primary key symbol in row selector for current field

Design grid

Field Properties pane

FIGURE 2–8   Applicant table in Design view

Notice that the row selector for the ID field in Figure 2–8 has a key symbol in it. This key indicates that the field is the table's primary key. To set a table's primary key, click the Primary Key button in the Tools group on the Design tab. This button is a toggle button. For a primary key field, clicking the Primary Key button removes the key symbol from the field. For a field that is not the table's primary key, clicking the Primary Key button adds the key symbol to the field. The row selector for the ID field is also orange. Just like when you select a record selector in a datasheet, the row selector for a selected field in the design grid changes color when the field is selected.

EXTRA FOR EXPERTS

You can open a table directly in Design view from the Navigation Pane. Right-click the table name in the Navigation Pane, and then click Design View on the shortcut menu.

Adding, Deleting, Renaming, and Rearranging Fields in Design View

You can use the options in the Tools group on the Design tab to add and delete fields. You can also drag selected fields to new locations in the design grid. To insert a new field between two existing rows in a table, click the row selector for the row *below* where you want the new field to appear. Then click the Insert Rows button in the Tools group on the Design tab. If you want to add a new field at the end of the table, click in the first empty row in the design grid, and then type the field's name. You can delete a field by clicking the row selector for the field you want to delete, and then clicking the Delete Rows button in the Tools group on the Design tab. To rename a field, edit the field name in the design grid and press Tab. To change a field's data type, click the Data Type box for the field in the design grid. An arrow appears on the right side of the box. Clicking the arrow displays a list of data types so you can click the data type you want from the list. Any changes that you make in Design view are automatically updated in Datasheet view when you save the table.

Step-by-Step 2.6

1. In the Views group on the Fields tab, click the **View** button. The Applicant table opens in Design view, as shown in Figure 2–8.

2. Click the **row selector** for the Last Name field. The field is selected, as indicated by the orange border that surrounds the row.

3. Click and drag the **row selector** for the Last Name field up one row, so the black line appears between the First Name and ID fields. When the black line is between the First Name and ID fields, release the mouse button. The Last Name field now appears between the ID and First Name fields.

4. In the design grid, double-click the word **Appointment** in the Appointment Date field.

5. Type **Appt** and then press the **down** key. The field name changes to *Appt Date*. The Job Number field is selected.

6. With the Job Number field selected, click the **Insert Rows** button in the Tools group on the Design tab. A new row is inserted above the Job Number field.

7. Type **Confirmed** and then press **Tab**.

8. Click the **Data Type** arrow for the Confirmed field. **Figure 2–9** shows the list of data types.

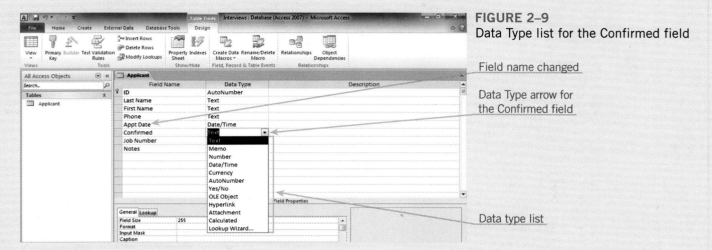

FIGURE 2–9
Data Type list for the Confirmed field

9. In the list, click **Yes/No**.

10. On the Quick Access Toolbar, click the **Save** button 💾. Leave the table open for the next Step-by-Step.

Description

The *Description property* in the design grid is an optional field property that you can use to describe what to enter in the field. When you give your fields descriptive names, it helps you remember the field values to enter in the fields. For example, the Last Name field name easily communicates what field values to enter in the field. When you are entering data in the field, the Description property can remind you what field value to enter, because it appears on the status bar in Datasheet view. For

▶ **VOCABULARY**
Description property

example, **Figure 2–10** shows that the Description property for the Confirmed field in the Applicant table was set to *Has the interview been confirmed?* In this case, the Description property makes it easier to enter the field value. Because this field uses the Yes/No data type, the field value is *Yes* (the check box contains a check mark) if you confirmed the interview; otherwise, the field value is *No* (the check box is empty).

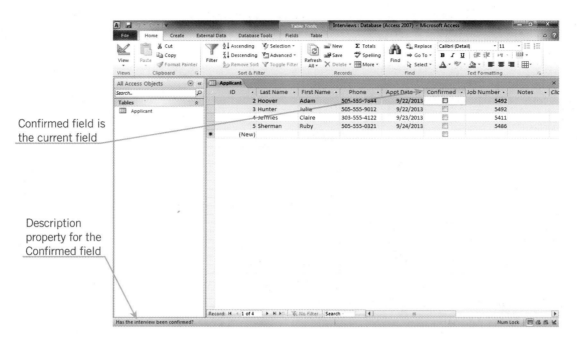

Confirmed field is the current field

Description property for the Confirmed field

FIGURE 2–10 Description property for the Confirmed field

Step-by-Step 2.7

1. Press **Tab**. The insertion point moves to the Description property for the Confirmed field.

2. Type **Has the interview been confirmed?**

3. Press **Enter**. The Description property for the Confirmed field is set, as shown in **Figure 2–11**. When you update certain field properties, the Property Update Options button might appear. If you click this button and then click the update option in the list, you can also update the field property in other database objects that use it. Leave the table open for the next Step-by-Step.

FIGURE 2–11
Confirmed field Description property

Description property

Property Update Options button

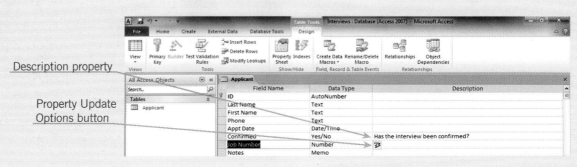

Changing Field Properties in Design View

When you created the fields in the Applicant table in Datasheet view, you assigned each field a name and a data type. When you set a field's data type, the field is given certain properties that help you to define and maintain the data you enter in the field. A *field property* describes a field's contents beyond the field's basic data type, such as the number of characters the field can store or the allowable values that you can enter in the field. For example, **Figure 2–12** shows the field properties for a Text field. Sometimes you won't need to change a field's properties at all. You can view and change field properties in Design view. Remember that the field properties for a field will vary depending on the field's data type.

▶ VOCABULARY
field property
Field Size property

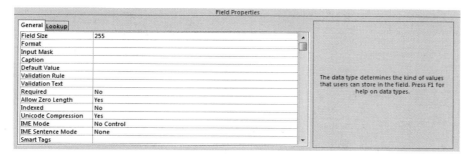

FIGURE 2–12   Field properties for a Text field

Changing the Field Size

The *Field Size property* sets the number of characters you can store in a Text, Number, or AutoNumber field. For Text fields, the default value is 255 characters. This means that every field value must contain 255 or fewer characters. You can change the Field Size property for a Text field to store fewer characters. For example, if you create a field that stores state abbreviations, you might set the Field Size property to two characters, because all state abbreviations contain two characters. This change will ensure that no one can enter a three-character state abbreviation, which would be an incorrect field value. Also, when you decrease the Field Size property, the field requires less disk space to store the field values. All fields are given the default field properties for the data type assigned to them, unless you change the default field properties.

For Number fields, the Field Size property uses a different way of expressing the length. The default Field Size property for a Number field is Long Integer, which stores very large positive and negative whole numbers. Other field sizes for Number fields store numbers with decimals (such as 101.24), positive whole numbers only, and numbers that are less than or equal to 255. You select the field size by evaluating the numbers that you plan to store in the field and choosing the one that takes the smallest amount of disk space. The field size options for Number fields are Byte, Integer, Long Integer, Single, Double, Replication ID, and Decimal.

EXTRA FOR EXPERTS

Always be careful when changing a Field Size property to make sure that you will not lose any data in your fields. If a field value is 30 characters, and you reduce the field size to 20 characters, Access will delete the last 10 characters in the field value for all existing records.

If you have computer programming experience, the available field sizes might be familiar to you. If the options mean nothing to you, don't worry. There is an easy way to select the appropriate field size. If your field stores whole numbers only, use the Integer or Long Integer field size. If your field stores numbers with decimal places, choose the Single or Double field size. To change the Field Size property for a Number field, click in the Field Size box in the Field Properties pane. Click the arrow that appears to display the field size options for a Number field, as shown in **Figure 2-13**, and then click the one you want to use.

The Job Number field is selected and has the Number data type

Arrow on the Field Size box

Field size options in the list that opens

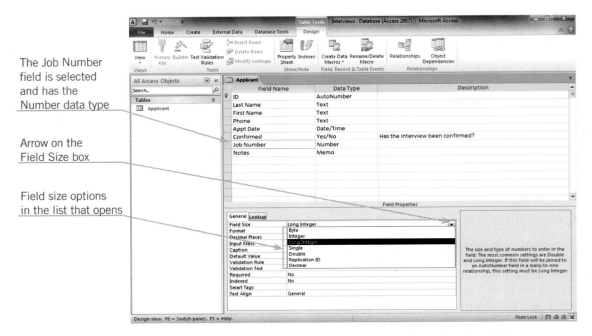

FIGURE 2–13   Setting the Field Size property for a Number field

After you change the Field Size property, Access might open the dialog box shown in **Figure 2–14** to warn you that your changes might affect the data that is already stored in your table. For example, when you change the Field Size property for a Text field from 255 characters to 20 characters, Access decreases the number of characters in the field from 255 to 20. This means that any field values in the table that have 21 or more characters will be changed to 20 characters, resulting in a loss of data. After you change the Field Size property and save the table, you cannot undo your changes.

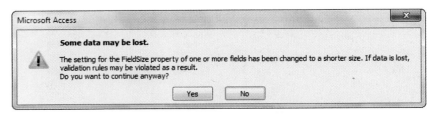

FIGURE 2–14   Dialog box that opens when you save a table after making changes to a field's size

Step-by-Step 2.8

1. In the design grid, click the **Last Name** field.

2. In the Field Properties pane, double-click the value **255** in the Field Size box to select it. Type **20**.

3. In the design grid, click the **First Name** field.

4. In the Field Properties pane, double-click the value **255** in the Field Size box to select it. Type **20**.

5. In the design grid, click the **Phone** field. Double-click the value **255** in the Field Size box in the Field Properties pane. Type **15**.

6. In the design grid, click the **Job Number** field.

7. In the Field Properties pane, click in the **Field Size** box. An arrow appears on the right side of the box.

8. On the Field Size box, click the **arrow**. The list of field size options for Number fields opens.

9. In the Field Size list, click **Integer**. Leave the table open for the next Step-by-Step.

Setting a Field's Format

Use the ***Format property*** to specify how you want Access to display numbers, dates, times, and text. For example, the default format for dates is *10/28/2013*. Using the Format property, you can change the format to *28-Oct-2013* or *Monday, October 28, 2013*. When you set a field's Format property, Access displays the field value using the format you specify, even if it is not stored that way in the table. So, if you enter a date in the table as *10-28-13* but the Format property is set to display the date as *Monday, October 28, 2013*, that's how the date will be displayed.

> ▶ **VOCABULARY**
> **Format property**

> 📧 **EXTRA FOR EXPERTS**
>
> The Format property displays Currency field values with a dollar sign and decimal point. If you enter 10 in a Currency field, Access formats it as $10.00.

Step-by-Step 2.9

1. In the design grid, click the **Appt Date** field.

2. In the Field Properties pane, click in the **Format** box. An arrow appears on the right side of the box.

3. On the Format box, click the **arrow**. In the Format list, click **Short Date**.

4. On the Quick Access Toolbar, click the **Save** button 🖫. The dialog box shown in Figure 2–14 opens.

5. Click **Yes**.

6. In the Views group on the Design tab, click the **View** button. The table is displayed in Datasheet view.

7. Click the **check box** in the Confirmed field for the first record (Adam Hoover). A check mark appears in the check box, indicating a "Yes" response. Notice the Description value on the status bar in the lower-left corner of the screen. (The other changes that you made to the fields in the table aren't readily visible in Datasheet view.)

8. In the Views group on the Home tab, click the **View** button. The table is displayed in Design view. Leave the table open for the next Step-by-Step.

Setting a Field's Default Value

The *Default Value property* enters the same field value in a field every time a new record is added to the table. For example, if most of the customers in a database of names and addresses live in California, you can enter *CA* as the Default Value property for the State field. When you add a new record, the State field will automatically contain the field value *CA*. If you need to change the default value when you enter a new record, select the default value and type a new value.

Using the Required Property

The *Required property* specifies whether you must enter a field value in a record. For example, in an employee database, you might set the Required property for a Phone field to *Yes* so that you must enter a phone number for each employee. If you try to enter a record for a new employee without entering a phone number, Access will open a dialog box similar to the one shown in **Figure 2–15** with an error message that describes why Access will not add the record to the table.

FIGURE 2–15   Dialog box that opens when you don't enter a required field value

When you click in the Required box for a field, an arrow appears on the right side of the box. Clicking the arrow displays the values *Yes* and *No* in a list. The default Required property for most fields is No.

After you change a field's Required property to Yes, the dialog box shown in **Figure 2–16** opens when you save the table. This dialog box opens when you change the Required property because Access will test all of the existing field values in the field to make sure that they contain a field value. When you click Yes, Access will close the dialog box if there are no problems. If problems do exist, Access will help you decide what to do.

FIGURE 2–16   Dialog box that opens when saving a table after setting a required value

Step-by-Step 2.10

1. In the design grid, click the **Notes** field.
2. In the Field Properties pane, click in the **Default Value** box.
3. In the Default Value box, type **Elise McDonnell will be the interviewer.** (Be sure to type the period.)
4. In the design grid, click the **Appt Date** field.
5. In the Field Properties pane, click in the **Required** box. An arrow appears on the right side of the box.
6. In the Required box, click the **arrow**. In the list that opens, click **Yes**.
7. On the Quick Access Toolbar, click the **Save** button 🖫. The dialog box shown in Figure 2–16 opens.
8. Click **Yes**.
9. In the Views group on the Design tab, click the **View** button. Leave the table open for the next Step-by-Step.

After setting the properties for the fields in your table, you can use Datasheet view to enter records in the table.

Step-by-Step 2.11

1. At the top of the Navigation Pane, click the **Shutter Bar Open/Close Button** ⟪. The Navigation Pane closes.

2. In the upper-left corner of the datasheet, click the **datasheet selector**. Double-click the right edge of the **ID** field selector. All columns in the datasheet are resized to best fit.

3. In the Records group on the Home tab, click the **New** button. A new record is added to the table. The ID field is the current field.

4. Press **Tab**, type **Peters**, press **Tab**, type **James**, press **Tab**, and type **970-555-6721**.

5. Press **Tab** five times to skip entering a field value in the Appt Date field and go to the next record. The dialog box shown in Figure 2–15 opens. Because the Required property for the Appt Date field is set to Yes, you must enter a field value in this field.

6. Click **OK**. Click in the Appt Date field, and then type **09/24/13**. Press **Tab**. Notice that the Format property for the Appt Date field changed the field value you entered to the Short Date format, 9/24/2013, even though you entered the field value as 09/24/13.

7. In the Confirmed field, press **spacebar**. Access adds a check mark to the field, which indicates a Yes value.

8. Press **Tab**, and then type **5486** in the Job Number field.

9. Press **Tab**. The Default Value property entered the value in the Notes field automatically.

10. Save the table. On the Access title bar, click the **Close** button ▬ x ▬. Access closes the Applicant table and the Interviews database, and then exits.

SUMMARY

In this lesson, you learned:

■ Creating a database creates a file that stores database objects. You can create a database using a template that creates one or more table, query, form, and report objects. You can also create a database using the Blank database template, which creates a database with an empty table.

■ A field's data type determines the kind of data that you can enter in the field, such as numbers or text, or a combination of numbers and text (also called alphanumeric data).

■ You can create a table in Datasheet view by selecting the data type and typing the field name for each field you plan to use in your table. After entering the fields, you can enter the first record. Access also creates an ID field to serve as the table's primary key. The primary key is the field that contains unique field values for each record in the table.

■ To save a table, click the Save button on the Quick Access Toolbar. Type the table name in the Table Name text box in the Save As dialog box, and then click OK. The table name appears on the tab for the table and also in the Navigation Pane.

■ When you are working in Design view, you can add new fields to a table by clicking the Insert Rows button in the Tools group on the Design tab. After adding a field, type its name and set its data type. You can delete a field from a table by selecting it in the design grid, and then clicking the Delete Rows button in the Tools group. To rename a field, click its name in the Field Name box, and then type the new name. To move a field, click its row selector in the design grid, and then drag it to the new position.

■ A field property describes a field's contents beyond the field's basic data type. The properties you can set for a field depend on the field's data type. You can add an optional Description property to identify the data to enter in a field. You can also change the Field Size property to set the number of characters in a Text field or to select the type of numbers to store in a Number field. The Format property lets you specify how to display numbers, dates, times, and text. When a field uses a commonly entered value, you can set the Default Value property to enter that value in new records automatically. Use the Required property when a field must contain a value.

■ VOCABULARY REVIEW

Define the following terms:

alphanumeric data	Description property	Field Size property
AutoNumber	design grid	Format property
Blank database template	Design view	primary key
data type	Field Properties pane	Required property
Default Value property	field property	template

■ REVIEW QUESTIONS

TRUE / FALSE

Circle T if the statement is true or F if the statement is false.

T   F   **1.**   When you use the Blank database template to create a new database, Access opens a table named *Table1* for you.

T   F   **2.**   A table's primary key might be an AutoNumber field.

T   F   **3.**   A field with the Text data type can store up to 65,535 characters.

T   F   **4.**   To insert a new field in a table in Design view, first click the row above where you want the new field to appear in the design grid.

T   F   **5.**   The Description property is an optional field property that helps users understand what data to enter in a field.

WRITTEN QUESTIONS

Write a brief answer to each of the following questions.

1. What steps do you take to create a new database?

2. How do you create a new field in a table in Datasheet view?

3. How do you change a field's data type in Datasheet view?

4. What is the Field Size property?

5. What is the Format property?

FILL IN THE BLANK

Complete the following sentences by writing the correct word or words in the blanks provided.

1. A table's _____ is the field that contains a unique field value for each record in the table.

2. The _____ data type stores field values with 255 or fewer characters with letters, numbers, spaces, and certain symbols such as an underscore (_).

3. The _____ data type stores numbers that might be used in calculations.

4. The _____ data type adds a unique numeric field value to each record in a table.

5. The bottom half of the Table window in Design view is called the _____ pane.

▪ PROJECTS

If you have a SAM 2010 user profile, your instructor may have assigned an autogradable version of the indicated project. If so, log into the SAM 2010 Web site at *www.cengage.com/sam2010* to download the instruction and start files.

PROJECT 2–1

1. Start Access. Use the Blank database template to create a new database. Store the database in the Access Lesson 02 folder with your Data Files. Use the file name **Music** followed by your initials.

2. Save the table that Access opens using the name **1980s Albums**.

3. In Datasheet view, create three fields in columns 2 through 4. In column 2, create an **Artist** field with the Text data type. In column 3, create a **Title** field with the Text data type. In column 4, create a **Release Year** field with the Number data type.

4. Use **Figure 2–17** to enter three records in the table. (Remember, the ID field value is added automatically. Do not type it. Your ID field values might differ from the ones shown in Figure 2–17.)

FIGURE 2–17

5. Resize all columns in the datasheet to best fit.

6. Save the table. Change to Design view.

7. Change the data type for the Release Year field to Text. Set the Field Size property to **4**.

8. Change the Field Size property for the Artist field to **25**.

9. Change the Field Size property for the Title field to **50**.

10. In Design view, add a new field named **Publisher** to the table so it appears between the Title and Release Year fields. Use the Text data type and change the Field Size property to **30**. Set the Description property to **Label that released the album**.

11. Set the Required property for the Artist field to Yes.

12. Save the table. When the dialog box opens and warns about data loss, click Yes. When the dialog box opens and warns about testing the data with the new rules, click Yes.

13. Change to Datasheet view. Print the datasheet in landscape orientation.

14. Close the table and database, and then exit Access.

SAM PROJECT 2–2

1. Start Access. Use the Blank database template to create a new database. Store the database in the Access Lesson 02 folder with your Data Files. Use the file name **Retail Stores** followed by your initials.

2. Save the table that Access opens using the name **Retailers**.

3. In Datasheet view, create the following fields in columns 2 through 7, being sure to assign the correct data type to each field: **Store Name** (Text), **Address** (Text), **Phone Number** (Text), **Credit Card** (Text), **Date Opened** (Date & Time), and **Outlet Number** (Number).

4. Resize all columns in the datasheet to best fit.

5. Use **Figure 2–18** to enter the first record in the table. (Remember, the ID field value is added automatically. Do not type it. Your ID field value might differ from the one shown in Figure 2–18.)

8. Enter the Description property **Does the store accept credit cards?** for the Credit Card field.

9. Change the Field Size property for the Store Name field to **30**.

10. Change the Field Size property for the Address field to **30**.

11. Change the Field Size property for the Phone Number field to **15**.

12. Move the Outlet Number field so it appears between the Store Name and Address fields.

13. Save the table. When the dialog box opens and warns about data loss, click Yes.

14. Change to Datasheet view. Print the datasheet in landscape orientation.

15. Close the table and database, and then exit Access.

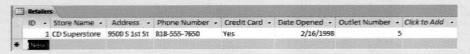

ID	Store Name	Address	Phone Number	Credit Card	Date Opened	Outlet Number	Click to Add
1	CD Superstore	9500 S 1st St	818-555-7650	Yes	2/16/1998	5	

FIGURE 2–18

6. Click the Credit Card field for the first record. Use the Data Type arrow in the Formatting group on the Fields tab to change the data type to Yes/No. When the dialog box opens and warns about data loss, click Yes.

7. Save the table. Change to Design view.

PROJECT 2–3

1. Open the **Company.accdb** database from the Access Lesson 02 folder with your Data Files.

2. Open the **Staff** table in Datasheet view. Change to Design view.

3. Move the Last Name field so it appears between the Employee ID and Title fields.

4. Move the First Name field so it appears below the Last Name field.

5. Change the name of the SS Number field to **SSN**.

6. Delete the Department field from the table. When asked if you want to permanently delete the field, click Yes.

7. Change the data type of the Salary field to Currency.

8. Set the Format property for the Birth Date field to Short Date.

9. Set the Default Value property for the Title field to **Sales Representative**.

10. Change the Employee ID field so it is the table's primary key.

11. Change the Required property for the SSN field to Yes.

12. Set the Description property for the Salary field to **Employee's monthly salary**.

13. Save the table. When asked if you want to test the data with the new rules, click Yes.

14. Change to Datasheet view. In a new record, enter the following field values: Employee ID: **2746**, Last Name: **Wells**, First Name: **Wendy**, Title: **Sales Representative**, SSN: **657-57-1600**, Address: **2610 21st St**, Zip Code: **79832-2610**, Birth Date: **2-15-72**, Salary: **2150**.

15. Print the datasheet in portrait orientation.

16. Close the table and database, and then exit Access.

■ CRITICAL THINKING

ACTIVITY 2–1

Organize a group of contact information that you might have, such as people in your family or in your class. Use the Blank database template to create a database to organize your data. Give the database a name that accurately reflects the data, and add your initials to the end of the file name. Store the database in the Access Lesson 02 folder with your Data Files.

Create and design a table for your data using a table template. To use a table template, close the Table1 table that Access created by clicking its Close button. On the Ribbon, click the Create tab. In the Templates group on the Create tab, click the Application Parts button. In the list that opens, click Contacts.

Open the Contacts table created by the template, click the Home tab on the Ribbon, and then change to Design view. Use Design view to edit, move, add, and delete the fields you want to use to store your data. Save the table.

In Datasheet view, enter at least two records in the table. Print the table. Close the table and exit Access.

ACTIVITY 2–2

In this lesson, you created a new database. When you open a database for the first time, you might see the Security Warning below the Ribbon. Use Access Help to search for information about trusting a database and creating a trusted location. On a sheet of paper, describe a trusted location and how to create a trusted location using Access.

LESSON 3

Creating Queries

■ OBJECTIVES

Upon completion of this lesson, you should be able to:

- Create a query using a Wizard.
- Sort and filter data in a datasheet.
- Create a query in Design view.
- Create relationships in a database.
- Create a query based on more than one table.
- Use operators in a condition in a query.
- Calculate data using a query.

■ VOCABULARY

And operator

AutoFilter

calculated field

common field

condition

expression

filter

Filter By Form

Filter By Selection

foreign key

multitable query

one-to-many relationship

Or operator

query

referential integrity

relationship

Simple Query Wizard

sort

subdatasheet

Total row

The most important feature of a database that you will use is to ask it questions about the data it stores in tables. Extracting information from a database is essential for many businesses to function. In Access, you use a query to extract information from a database. In this lesson, you will learn how to create queries.

Creating a Query with the Simple Query Wizard

A *query* is a database object that lets you ask the database about the data it contains. The result of a query is a datasheet that includes the records you asked to see. You can use a query to see all orders placed after a certain date or all customers who live in a certain zip code. When you specify a certain date or zip code in a query, these specifications are called conditions. A *condition* (also called a *criterion*) is a way of telling the query which data you are interested in seeing. For example, when you ask to see customers living in a certain zip code, the zip code *78001* is a condition. When the condition has two or more parts to it, such as customers who have ordered a specific part and who live in a certain zip code, the two conditions are called *criteria*. You can also create a query that doesn't contain any conditions, but still displays any or all of the fields that you want to see.

A query is based on a table (or on another query), and some queries are based on more than one table (or query). When you say that a query is *based on* a table, it means that the data in the query datasheet is really data that is stored in a table. When you open a query object, you *run* the query. Running a query displays a datasheet that is similar in appearance to the datasheet you see when you open a table. However, the query uses the conditions to display only the records and fields that you asked to see. When you run a query, the data in the table on which the query is based still exists in the table. A query is just another way of viewing the table's data.

An easy way to create a query is to use the *Simple Query Wizard*, which asks you what data you want to see by letting you select options in dialog boxes. To start the Simple Query Wizard, click the Create tab on the Ribbon. The Create tab contains options for creating different database objects. In the Queries group on the Create tab, click the Query Wizard button. The New Query dialog box opens, as shown in **Figure 3–1**.

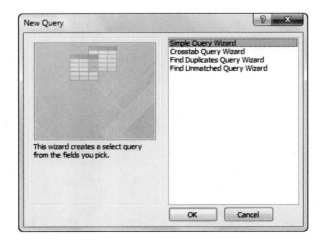

FIGURE 3–1   New Query dialog box

Make sure that the Simple Query Wizard option is selected, and then click OK. The first Simple Query Wizard dialog box opens, as shown in **Figure 3–2**. You use the Tables/Queries arrow in this dialog box to select the table (or query) that contains the data you want your new query to display. After selecting the table (or query) on which to base your new query, you click a field in the Available Fields list box, and then click the Select Single Field button to add one field at a time to the new query. To add all fields to the new query, click the Select All Fields button. When you add a field to a query, the field moves from the Available Fields list box to the Selected Fields list box.

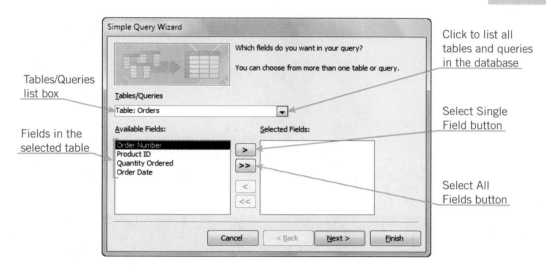

FIGURE 3–2   First Simple Query Wizard dialog box

When you click Next, the second Simple Query Wizard dialog box gives you the option of creating a detail query or a summary query. A *detail query* shows every field in each record. A *summary query* lets you summarize relevant data, such as adding the field values in a column that stores price data. Access gives you the choice of creating a summary query only when the data you selected could be used in calculations.

In the last Simple Query Wizard dialog box, Access suggests a title for your query by using the object name on which the query is based, plus the word "Query," as shown in **Figure 3–3**. You can change the default query title or use the one Access suggests. When you click Finish, the query datasheet is displayed.

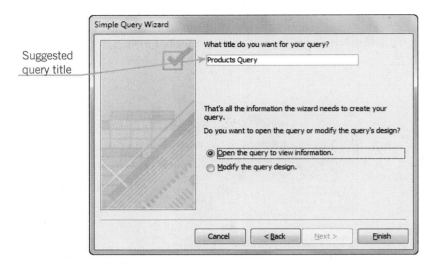

Suggested query title

FIGURE 3–3   Final Simple Query Wizard dialog box

Step-by-Step 3.1

1. Start Access. Open the **Product.accdb** database from the Access Lesson 03 folder where your Data Files are stored.

2. If the Security Warning appears below the Ribbon, click the **Enable Content** button.

3. On the Ribbon, click the **Create** tab.

4. In the Queries group on the Create tab, click the **Query Wizard** button. The New Query dialog box opens, as shown in Figure 3–1.

5. Make sure **Simple Query Wizard** is selected, and then click **OK**. The first Simple Query Wizard dialog box opens, as shown in Figure 3–2. *Table: Orders* is selected in the Tables/Queries list box because it is the first table in the alphabetical list of tables in the database.

6. Click the **Tables/Queries arrow**, and then click **Table: Products**. The fields in the Products table appear in the Available Fields list box.

7. In the Available Fields list box, click **Product Name**, and then click the **Select Single Field** button [>]. The Product Name field moves to the Selected Fields list box, which adds this field to the query.

8. In the Available Fields list box, click **Retail Price**, and then click the **Select Single Field** button . The Retail Price field moves to the Selected Fields list box. The Retail Price field is the second field added to the query.

9. Click **Next**. The second Simple Query Wizard dialog box asks if you want to create a detail query or summary query. Make sure the **Detail** option button is selected.

10. Click **Next**. The final Simple Query Wizard dialog box asks you for a title, as shown in Figure 3–3. The default query title is *Products Query*, which is the name of the table on which the query is based, plus the word *Query*.

> **TIP**
>
> The title you give to a query is also used as the query object name.

11. Select **Products Query** in the text box, and then type **Price List** as the new query title.

12. Make sure that the **Open the query to view information** option button is selected.

13. Click **Finish**. The query datasheet opens, as shown in **Figure 3–4**. The datasheet contains the Product Name and Retail Price fields for 48 records from the Products table. Leave the query open for the next Step-by-Step.

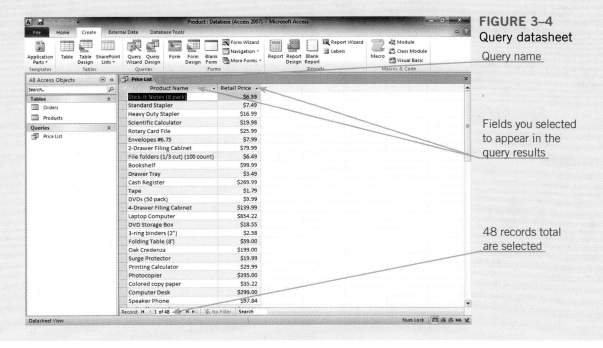

FIGURE 3–4
Query datasheet

Query name

Fields you selected to appear in the query results

48 records total are selected

Sorting Data

When you view a table or query datasheet, the records might not appear in the order that you would like to see them listed. For example, you might want to list customers in alphabetical order or list prices in order from least expensive to most expensive. When you view field values in ascending or descending order from A to Z or from smallest to largest, you apply a *sort* to the field. Sorting a field in *ascending* order arranges records from A to Z, or from smallest to largest. Sorting a field in *descending* order arranges records from Z to A, or from largest to smallest. An easy method to change the way data is sorted is to click any field value in the field you want to sort, and then click the Ascending or Descending buttons in the Sort & Filter group on the Home tab.

▶ **VOCABULARY**
sort

Step-by-Step 3.2

1. In the Retail Price column, click the value in the first row (*$6.59*). The Retail Price field is selected.

2. On the Ribbon, click the **Home** tab.

3. In the Sort & Filter group, click the **Ascending** button 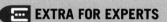. The records are sorted in ascending order by retail price, with the record for the least expensive item, a clipboard priced at $1.29, at the top of the datasheet.

4. In the Sort & Filter group, click the **Descending** button. The records are sorted in descending order by retail price, as shown in **Figure 3–5**, with the record for the most expensive item, a laptop computer priced at $854.22, at the top of the datasheet. Leave the query open for the next Step-by-Step.

■ **EXTRA FOR EXPERTS**

When a field is sorted, an arrow appears on the field selector to indicate the way records are sorted. In Figure 3–5, the Retail Price field selector has a small down arrow to indicate a descending sort order. An ascending sort order displays a small up arrow on the field selector.

FIGURE 3–5
Records sorted in descending order by retail price

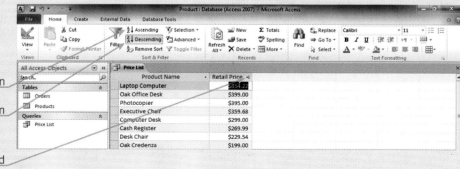

Ascending button
Descending button
Indicates a descending sort order for this field

Filtering Data

When you are viewing a table or query datasheet, you might want to display records that contain a certain value, such as products that have a retail price of $9.99. You can use a filter to view the data in this way. A *filter* temporarily displays records in a datasheet based on the condition that you specify. You can think of a filter as "filtering out" the records that do not match the condition.

You can use different types of filters to display the data you need. When you use *Filter By Selection*, you select a field value (such as *Oak Office Desk*), or part of a field value (such as the just letter *D*) in a datasheet, and then click the Selection button in the Sort & Filter group on the Home tab. A menu opens with a list of options for filtering the field. For numerical data, the options let you filter records that have the same field value as the one you selected, field values that do not equal the selected field value, field values that are less than or equal to or greater than or equal to the selected field value, and in other ways. For fields defined with the Text data type, the options let you filter records that have the same field value, have different field values, contain the field value, or do not contain the field value. Clicking an option in the menu displays only those records in the datasheet that match the filter condition.

You can use *Filter By Form* when you need to display records that contain one or more values based on the values stored in one or more fields. To use Filter By Form, click the Advanced button in the Sort & Filter group on the Home tab. In the menu that opens, click Filter By Form. The datasheet temporarily hides all the records it contains and displays a list box for a selected field, as shown in **Figure 3–6**. Clicking an arrow in a field displays the field's values in a list. When you click a value in the list, you set the filter. Click the Toggle Filter button in the Sort & Filter group on the Home tab to display only the records in the datasheet that match the filter. You can set the filter for one or more fields in the datasheet.

▶ VOCABULARY
filter
Filter By Selection
Filter By Form

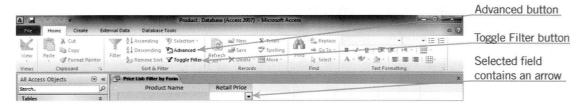

Advanced button

Toggle Filter button

Selected field
contains an arrow

FIGURE 3–6   Price List datasheet after selecting Filter By Form

An easy way to sort and filter data using the same options available in the Sort & Filter group is to use an AutoFilter. An *AutoFilter* is a menu that opens when you click the arrow on the right side of a field selector. The menu contains options for sorting data and clearing any filters that you have already applied. It also contains options for using Filter By Selection and Filter By Form. **Figure 3–7** shows the AutoFilter that opens when you click the arrow on the Product Name field selector and then point to Text Filters. This menu shows the Filter By Selection options for the Product Name field, which has the Text data type.

Click the arrow on the field selector to open the AutoFilter

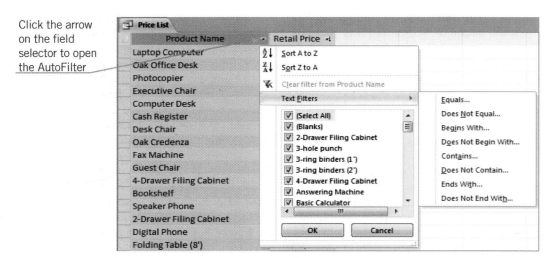

FIGURE 3–7   AutoFilter for the Product Name field (a Text field)

Figure 3–8 shows the AutoFilter that opens when you click the arrow on the Retail Price field selector, and then point to Number Filters. This menu shows the Filter By Selection options for the Retail Price field, which has the Number data type.

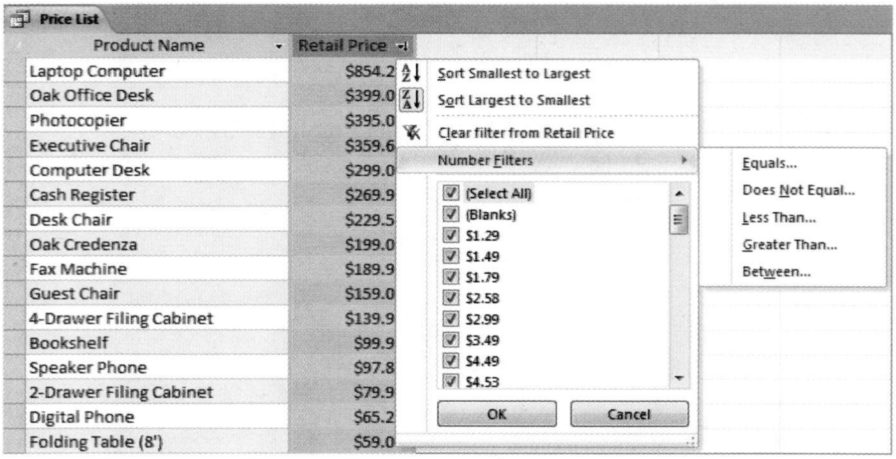

FIGURE 3–8   AutoFilter for the Retail Price field (a Number field)

After applying a filter to a field, clicking the Toggle Filter button in the Sort & Filter group on the Home tab removes the filter and displays all records in the datasheet again. To delete a filter from a query, click the Advanced button, and then click Clear All Filters.

Step-by-Step 3.3

1. Make sure the Retail Price field in the datasheet is sorted in descending order (see Figure 3–5). In the datasheet, click the second value in the Product Name field (*Oak Office Desk*).

2. In the Sort & Filter group on the Home tab, click the **Selection** button, and then click **Contains "Oak Office Desk"**. The filter is applied and one record is displayed in the datasheet.

3. In the Sort & Filter group, point to the **Toggle Filter** button. The Toggle Filter button has a "Remove Filter" ScreenTip because clicking it will remove the filter. Click the **Toggle Filter** button. The filter is removed and all records are displayed.

4. In the Product Name field in the second row in the datasheet, double-click **Desk** to select the word *Desk*.

5. Click the **Selection** button, and then click **Contains "Desk"**. Four records that contain the word *Desk* anywhere in the Product Name field are displayed, as shown in **Figure 3–9**.

Orange Toggle Filter button indicates a filter has been applied

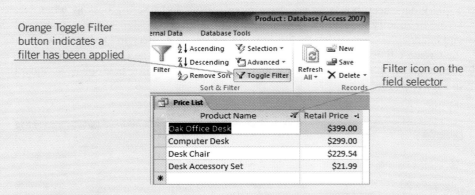

Filter icon on the field selector

FIGURE 3–9
Using Filter By Selection to display records that contain the word "Desk"

6. Click the **Toggle Filter** button. The filter is removed, the filter icon is removed from the Product Name field selector, and the datasheet displays all 48 records. Even though you removed the filter from the records, you need to clear the filter to delete it from the query.

7. In the Sort & Filter group on the Home tab, click the **Advanced** button, and then click **Clear All Filters**.

8. In the Sort & Filter group on the Home tab, click the **Advanced** button, and then click **Filter By Form**. The data in the datasheet is hidden and an arrow appears in the first row in the Product Name field.

9. Click in the first row in the Retail Price field. An arrow appears in the first row for the Retail Price field. (See Figure 3–6.)

10. Click the **arrow** on the Retail Price field. The list that opens displays all of the field values in the Retail Price field. In the list, click **9.99**.

11. Point to the **Toggle Filter** button. The Toggle Filter button has an "Apply Filter" ScreenTip because clicking the button will apply the filter. Click the **Toggle Filter** button. Two records are displayed in the datasheet, both containing the value $9.99 in the Retail Price field.

12. Click the **Toggle Filter** button. The filter is removed and all 48 records appear in the datasheet.

13. Click the **arrow** on the Retail Price field selector. The AutoFilter opens. In the AutoFilter, click **Sort Smallest to Largest**. The values in the Retail Price field are sorted in order from smallest to largest.

14. Click the **Close 'Price List'** button ✖ to close the query. Click **Yes** to save the query. Leave the database open for the next Step-by-Step.

Creating a Query in Design View

Sorting and filtering changes the way that data is displayed in a table or query datasheet. For a table datasheet, using the commands in the Sort & Filter group on the Home tab and the AutoFilter are your only options for applying a sort or filter. For a query datasheet, however, you have more sorting and filtering options when you create or modify a query in Design view. In the Query Design window, you build and change the query using the design grid. To create a query in Design view, click the Create tab on the Ribbon. In the Queries group, click the Query Design button. A new query opens in Design view and the Show Table dialog box opens, as shown in **Figure 3–10**.

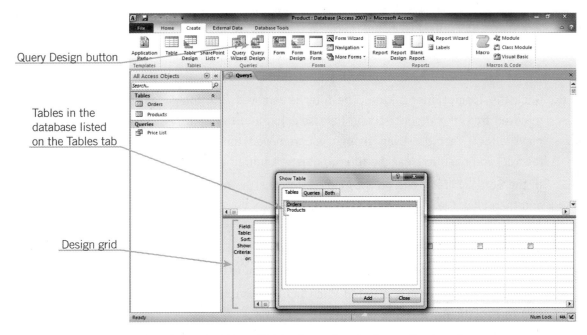

FIGURE 3–10   Show Table dialog box in Query Design view

Because databases often include more than one table, you can select the table in the Show Table dialog box that contains the data you want to see in the query datasheet, and then click Add. After adding a table to the query design, click Close to close the Show Table dialog box. After adding the Orders table to the query design, the fields in the Orders table appear in a field list, as shown in **Figure 3–11**.

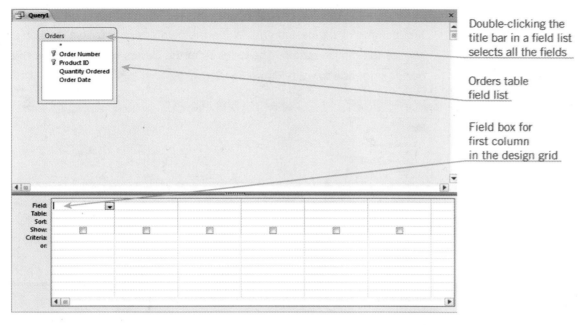

FIGURE 3–11   Orders table field list added to the query design

The Query window in Design view is divided into two parts. The top part of the window shows the field list for the table you included in the query design. The bottom part of the window contains a design grid that allows you to specify the fields to include in the query datasheet, any conditions that you want to use to filter data, and any sort orders you want to use in the query datasheet. Double-click the fields in the table's field list to add them to a query. A query can contain one, some, or all of the fields in the table. You can add the fields in any order to the design grid. To add all of the fields to a query in one step, double-click the table name at the top of the field list to select all the fields, and then drag any field into the first Field box in the design grid.

After creating a query, you can save it by clicking the Save button on the Quick Access Toolbar.

Step-by-Step 3.4

1. On the Ribbon, click the **Create** tab. In the Queries group on the Create tab, click the **Query Design** button. The Query window opens in Design view, and the Show Table dialog box opens on top of the Query window. See Figure 3–10.

2. In the Show Table dialog box, make sure **Orders** is selected. Click **Add**. The Orders table field list is added to the Query window.

3. In the Show Table dialog box, click **Close**. The Show Table dialog box closes. See Figure 3–11.

4. At the top of the Orders table field list, double-click **Orders**. All the fields in the Orders table are selected.

5. In the Orders table field list, drag any selected field to the Field box in the first column of the design grid. When the pointer changes to a ⬚ shape, release the mouse button. The fields from the Orders table appear in the design grid, as shown in **Figure 3–12**.

FIGURE 3–12
Fields added to the design grid

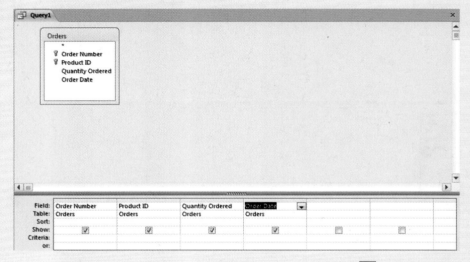

6. On the Quick Access Toolbar, click the **Save** button 🖫. The Save As dialog box opens. The default query name, Query1, is selected.

7. In the Query Name text box, type **Orders List**. Click **OK**. Leave the query open for the next Step-by-Step.

Moving and Sorting Fields in Design View

You can set a sort order for a field using the field's Sort box in the design grid. When you click in a field's Sort box, an arrow appears on the right side of the box. Clicking the arrow displays the Ascending, Descending, and (not sorted) options in a list. Click the Ascending or Descending option to set the sort order. To remove a sort from a field, click the (not sorted) option.

When you need to sort data first based on the values in one field, and then by the values in a second field, you need to set the sort orders for the two fields using the Sort boxes in the design grid. For example, you might sort customer names first by last name and then by first name. To sort on two or more fields, the field that you want to sort first (for example, Last Name) must be to the *left* of the field that you want to sort next (for example, First Name). Sorts on more than one field are applied in left-to-right order, so this is why the first sort field must be to the left of the second sort field in the design grid. You can move a field in the design grid by clicking the bar above the field (see **Figure 3–13**), and then dragging the field to the new location. As you drag the field, a black vertical line shows you where the field will appear when you release the mouse button.

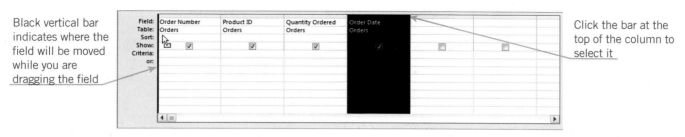

Black vertical bar indicates where the field will be moved while you are dragging the field

Click the bar at the top of the column to select it

FIGURE 3-13 Moving the Order Date field

Step-by-Step 3.5

1. In the design grid, point to the **bar** at the top of the Order Date column so the pointer changes to a ⬇ shape, and then click the **bar**. The field is selected, as shown in Figure 3–13.

2. Point to the **bar** so the pointer changes to a ⬉ shape, and then click and drag the **bar** at the top of the Order Date column to the left. When the black vertical line appears to the left of the Order Number column (see Figure 3–13), release the mouse button. The Order Date field now appears first in the design grid, so it will now appear first in the query datasheet.

3. Click in the **Sort** box for the Order Date field. The Order Date field is deselected, and an arrow appears on the right side of the field's Sort box.

4. Click the **arrow**. A list opens, as shown in **Figure 3–14**.

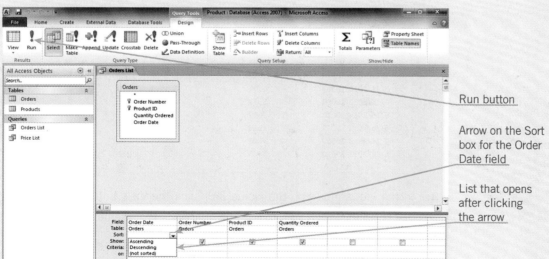

FIGURE 3–14
Sort options for the Order Date field

Run button

Arrow on the Sort box for the Order Date field

List that opens after clicking the arrow

5. Click **Ascending** in the list.

6. Click the right side of the **Sort** box for the Order Number field to display the arrow and the list in one step. Click **Descending**. Leave the query open for the next Step-by-Step.

Running a Query

You can run the query by clicking the Run button in the Results group on the Query Tools Design tab. When you run a query, the results appear in a query datasheet. To return to the query in Design view, click the View button in the Views group on the Home tab. Before running a query, it is a good idea to save it.

Step-by-Step 3.6

1. On the Quick Access Toolbar, click the **Save** button 🖫.

2. In the Results group on the Design tab, click the **Run** button. The query datasheet displays 24 records from the Orders table, with the Order Date field listed first. The records are sorted first in ascending order by the values in the Order Date field, and then in descending order by the values in the Order Number field. See **Figure 3–15**.

FIGURE 3–15
Orders List query datasheet

Date picker →

24 records are selected →

Orders List

Order Date ▾	Order Number ▾	Product ID ▾	Quantity Ordered ▾
1/29/2013 ⊞ 006		1701	1
1/29/2013	10004	1701	2
1/29/2013	10003	1701	4
1/29/2013	10002	1701	10
1/29/2013	10002	5912	1
1/29/2013	10001	1701	1
1/29/2013	10001	1705	1
1/29/2013	10000	1734	2
2/16/2013	10002	3406	3
2/17/2013	10003	3406	1
2/17/2013	10003	5943	2
3/22/2013	10004	5192	1
4/26/2013	10006	5918	10
4/26/2013	10006	5465	6
4/26/2013	10005	5421	1
4/26/2013	10005	3406	3
5/31/2013	10008	1995	10
5/31/2013	10008	2010	2
5/31/2013	10007	1701	1
6/16/2013	10010	5917	2
6/16/2013	10010	2002	6
6/16/2013	10009	1996	1
6/16/2013	10009	2005	1
6/18/2013	10010	5465	2
*			0

TIP

When working with date field values, you might see a date picker like the one shown in Figure 3–15. Clicking this icon opens a calendar. You can enter date values in the field by clicking them on the calendar.

3. In the Views group on the Home tab, click the **View** button. The query is displayed in Design view. Leave the query open for the next Step-by-Step.

Adding a Condition to a Field

You already learned that queries usually contain conditions that help to answer a question about the data in the table. If the question is "Which orders contain an order for Product ID 1701?" then you need to add a condition to the query design before you run it. To add a condition to a field, click in the field's Criteria box, and then type the condition. If the field has the Text or Memo data type, Access will add quotation marks around the condition after you type it and go to another field or run the query. You can type the quotation marks if you like, but it's not necessary to do so.

Step-by-Step 3.7

1. In the design grid, click in the **Criteria** box for the Product ID field.

2. Type **1701**.

3. Press **Tab**. The condition for the Product ID field is set. Because the Product ID field has the Text data type, Access adds quotation marks around the condition.

4. On the Quick Access Toolbar, click the **Save** button 💾.

5. In the Results group on the Design tab, click the **Run** button. The query datasheet displays six records containing orders for Product ID 1701. The records are still sorted first in ascending order by Order Date, and then in descending order by Order Number. See **Figure 3–16**.

Order Date	Order Number	Product ID	Quantity Ordered
1/29/2013	10006	1701	1
1/29/2013	10004	1701	2
1/29/2013	10003	1701	4
1/29/2013	10002	1701	10
1/29/2013	10001	1701	1
5/31/2013	10007	1701	1
*			0

Only six records contain an order for Product ID 1701

6. Click the **Close 'Orders List'** button ✕ to close the query. Leave the database open for the next Step-by-Step.

> **EXTRA FOR EXPERTS**
>
> When you want to run a query and do not need to see the values in a field in the query datasheet, clear the field's Show check box in the design grid. The field is still part of the query design, but its field values will not appear in the query datasheet. To add the field back to the query datasheet, click the field's Show check box to add a check mark to it.

FIGURE 3–16
Orders List query datasheet

Creating Table Relationships

When a database contains more than one table, as most databases do, the feature of the database management system that lets you connect the data in the tables is a relationship. To create a *relationship* between two tables, you must design the tables so they contain a common field. A *common field* is a field that appears in both tables, has the same data type, and contains the same values. A common field is also called a *matching field* because its values must match in the common field in both tables involved in the relationship. The common field usually has the same field name in the related table, but this is not a requirement. When the common field has the same name in both tables, it makes it easier to identify the common field in a relationship.

> ▶ **VOCABULARY**
> **relationship**
> **common field**

When you relate the tables in a database, you can create queries and other objects that display information from more than one table at once. For example, suppose you relate a table containing information about students (student ID number, name, address, and phone number) to a table containing information about classes (class ID number, class name, and room). As designed, these two tables do not have a common field. However, if you add the field from the Student table that contains the student ID number to the Class table, the Student ID field becomes a common field in both tables. After relating the tables, you can use the Student ID field in the Class table to identify the students enrolled in the class. Without this common field, you wouldn't have a way to use a query to display a query that lists the students in each class.

You can create different types of relationships depending on the data used in the tables you are relating. The most common relationship is a one-to-many relationship. (The other types of relationships are one-to-one and many-to-many.) In a **one-to-many relationship**, *one* record in the first table (called the *primary table*) can match *many* (actually, zero, one, or many) records in the second table (called the *related table*). The common field in the related table is called a **foreign key** when it is used in a relationship. In the primary table, the common field is usually the table's primary key.

When you relate tables, Access uses a set of rules to ensure that there are matching values in the common field used to form the relationship, both at the time you create the relationship and as you enter data in the tables after you create the relationship. This set of rules is called referential integrity. **Referential integrity** protects the data in the tables to make sure that data is not accidentally deleted or changed, resulting in inconsistent data. To enforce referential integrity between tables, click the Enforce Referential Integrity check box when creating the relationship. If you break one of the rules when relating tables or entering data into related tables, Access displays a message telling you about the problem and doesn't update the database.

To create a relationship between tables, click the Database Tools tab on the Ribbon. In the Relationships group, click the Relationships button. The Relationships window opens. In the Relationships group on the Relationships Tools Design tab, click the Show Table button. The Show Table dialog box opens. Add the tables to the Relationships window, and then close the Show Table dialog box. The field lists for the tables are added to the Relationships window, in the same way that field lists are added in Query Design view. After adding the field lists, drag the primary key in the primary table to the foreign key in the related table. When you release the mouse button, Access opens the Edit Relationships dialog box, where you select options for relating the tables.

▶ **VOCABULARY**

one-to-many relationship

foreign key

referential integrity

Step-by-Step 3.8

1. On the Ribbon, click the **Database Tools** tab.

2. In the Relationships group, click the **Relationships** button. The Show Table dialog box opens on top of the Relationships window.

3. In the Show Table dialog box, make sure **Orders** is selected, and then click **Add**. Click **Products**, click **Add**, and then click **Close**. The field lists for the Orders and Products tables are added to the Relationships window, and the Show Table dialog box closes.

4. Click and drag the **Product ID** field from the Products field list to the Product ID field in the Orders field list, and then release the mouse button. The Edit Relationships dialog box opens, as shown in **Figure 3–17**.

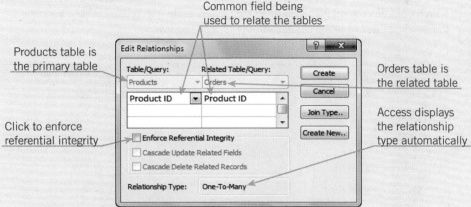

Common field being used to relate the tables

Products table is the primary table

Orders table is the related table

Click to enforce referential integrity

Access displays the relationship type automatically

FIGURE 3–17
Edit Relationships dialog box

5. Click the **Enforce Referential Integrity** check box.

6. Click **Create**. **Figure 3–18** shows the relationship between the tables. A one-to-many relationship has a "1" on the side of the primary table and an infinity symbol on the side of the related table. The key symbol next to a field name in a field list indicates the table's primary key. When you see two keys in a single table, the primary key is the combination of those fields.

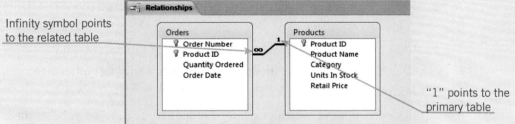

Infinity symbol points to the related table

"1" points to the primary table

FIGURE 3–18
Relationships window after creating a one-to-many relationship

7. In the Relationships group on the Design tab, click the **Close** button. In the dialog box, click **Yes** to save the changes you made. Leave the database open for the next Step-by-Step.

Viewing Related Records

After creating a one-to-many relationship between two tables, you can view the data in the related table by opening the datasheet for the primary table. In the relationship you just created, the Products table is the primary table. **Figure 3–19** shows a column with indicators in each row. Clicking the expand indicator opens a *subdatasheet*, which contains the related records in the Orders table (the related table). You can use the subdatasheet to make changes to the related records.

▶ VOCABULARY
subdatasheet

Collapse indicator

Subdatasheet displays orders for Product ID 1701

Expand indicator

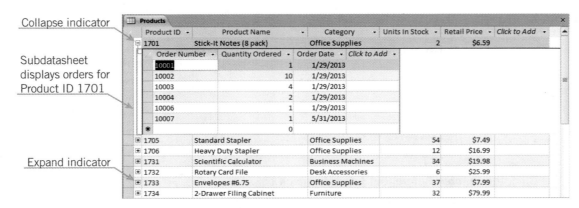

FIGURE 3–19   Subdatasheet in the Products table

Step-by-Step 3.9

1. In the Navigation Pane, double-click the **Products** table. The table opens in Datasheet view.

2. Click the **expand indicator** ⊞ to the left of the record with Product ID 1701. Figure 3–19 shows that there are *many* (six) related records from the Orders table for Product ID 1701.

3. Click the **expand indicator** ⊞ for Product ID 1733. The subdatasheet is empty, which means that there are *zero* related records in the Orders table for Product ID 173 3.

4. Click the **expand indicator** ⊞ for Product ID 1705. The subdatasheet shows that there is *one* related record from the Orders table for Product ID 1705.

5. Click the **collapse indicator** ⊟ to the left of the record with Product ID 1701. The subdatasheet closes.

6. Click the **Close 'Products'** button ⊠ to close the Products table. Leave the database open for the next Step-by-Step.

Creating a Multitable Query

After defining relationships in a database, you can create a query that is based on more than one table. Queries that are based on more than one table are sometimes called *multitable queries*. For example, you might want to view customer information with the orders placed by the customers. To do this, you need data from the table that stores customer information and the table that stores order information.

Creating a query based on more than one table simply requires you to add each table's field list to the query design. After you add two related tables to the query design, a join line shows the relationship between the tables, as shown in **Figure 3–20**. The join line connects the common field used to relate the tables. It also defines the type of relationship by using the "1" to represent the "one" side of the relationship and the infinity symbol to represent the "many" side of the relationship. Keep in mind that you can add the common field to the design grid from either table—after all, the common field contains *matching* values, so it doesn't matter which one you choose.

▶ **VOCABULARY**
multitable queries

EXTRA FOR EXPERTS

When you add a table's field list to the query design, you might not see all the fields in the field list initially if the table contains a lot of fields. You can view the other fields by using the scroll bar that appears on the field list. You can also use the pointer to resize the field list so you can see more fields at once.

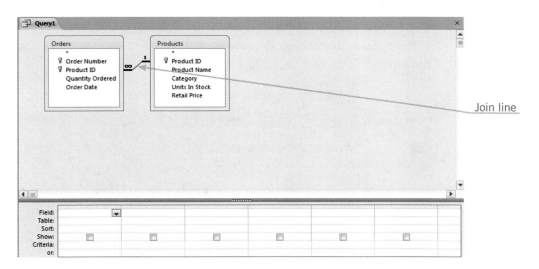

FIGURE 3–20 Joined tables in Query Design view

The skills for adding a table's field list, adding fields to the design grid, sorting fields, and specifying conditions are the same for a multitable query as they are for a query based on a single table.

Step-by-Step 3.10

1. On the Ribbon, click the **Create** tab. In the Queries group on the Create tab, click the **Query Design** button.

2.   In the Show Table dialog box, make sure **Orders** is selected, click **Add**, click **Products**, click **Add**, and then click **Close**. The Query window displays the field lists for the Orders and Products tables. The join line connects the tables using the common field, Product ID. See Figure 3–20.

3.   In the Orders field list, double-click **Order Number**. The Order Number field is added to the first column in the design grid.

4.   In the Products field list, double-click the following fields in the order shown to add them to the second, third, fourth, and fifth columns in the design grid: **Product ID**, **Product Name**, **Units In Stock**, and **Retail Price**.

5.   Click the right side of the **Sort** box for the Product Name field, and then click **Ascending** in the list. (If you don't see the list right away, click the arrow to display it.)

6.   Click in the **Criteria** box for the Units In Stock field. Type **0** (a zero, not the capital letter O), and then press **Tab**.

7.   On the Quick Access Toolbar, click the **Save** button ⊟. In the Save As dialog box, type **Product Prices**, and then click **OK**.

8.   In the Results group on the Design tab, click the **Run** button. **Figure 3–21** shows the query datasheet. Only one item (Oak Office Desk) has a zero in the Units In Stock field, indicating that this product is out of stock.

FIGURE 3–21
Datasheet for a query based on two tables

One record selected with zero units

Field from the Orders table   Fields from the Products table

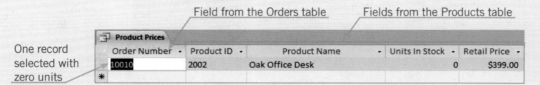

9.   In the Views group on the Home tab, click the **View** button. The query is displayed in Design view. Leave the query open for the next Step-by-Step.

Using Operators in a Condition

The Product Prices query selects records for products that are out of stock (the Units In Stock field value is zero). This is called an *exact match condition* because the records must contain the value 0 in the Units In Stock field to be displayed in the query datasheet. Based on the data in the database, the query selects only one record, for an Oak Office Desk.

Another type of condition that you can create displays a record in the query datasheet when the record matches a range of values. This is called a *range-of-values condition*. For example, you might use a condition to find orders with a Units In Stock value of 2 (an exact match condition) or a Units In Stock value of 5 or more (a range-of-values condition).

To create a range-of-values condition, you need to include a relational operator in the condition. You can use the relational operators listed in **Table 3–1** in a condition.

TABLE 3–1   Relational operators

OPERATOR	DESCRIPTION
>	Greater than
<	Less than
=	Equal to
>=	Greater than or equal to
<=	Less than or equal to
<>	Not equal

You can also use the And or Or operators in a query. The **And operator** selects records that match *all* of two or more conditions in a query. For example, if you want to find records that meet more than one condition, such as employees who earn more than $30,000 a year *and* who have been with the company for less than two years, you can use the And operator. To create a query with the And operator, enter the condition for the first field and the condition for the second field on the *same* Criteria row in the design grid.

The **Or operator** selects records that match *at least* one of two or more conditions in a query. For example, if you want to find records for employees who earn more than $30,000 a year *or* who have been with the company for less than two years, you can use the Or operator. To create a query with the Or operator, enter the condition for the first field in the Criteria row in the design grid and the condition for the second field in the "or" row—a *different* row—in the design grid.

> **VOCABULARY**
> **And operator**
> **Or operator**

Step-by-Step 3.11

1. Select the **0** in the Criteria box for the Units In Stock field, and then press **Delete**.

2. Type **>5** in the Units In Stock Criteria box.

3. Run the query. The datasheet displays 15 records for products that have more than five units in stock.

4. In the Views group on the Home tab, click the **View** button.

5. Click in the **Criteria** box for the Retail Price field, and then type **<20**. Adding this criterion to the query creates an And condition that will select records for products that have a value of less than $20.00 in the Retail Price field and have more than five units in stock. See **Figure 3–22**.

FIGURE 3–22
Query design that uses an And condition

Conditions are in the same Criteria row

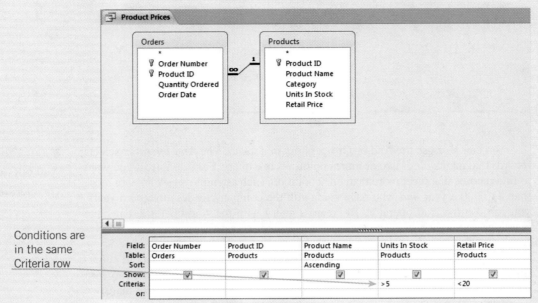

6. Run the query. **Figure 3–23** shows the results of the query with the And condition. Only 8 records match both conditions of having more than five units in stock and a retail price of less than $20.00.

FIGURE 3–23
Datasheet for a query with an And condition

Eight records match both conditions

7. Change to Design view. Select the condition **<20** in the Criteria row for the Retail Price field, and then press **Delete**.

8. Press the **down** key. The insertion point moves to the "or" row for the Retail Price field.

9. Type **<20**. Adding this criterion to the query creates an Or condition that will select records for products that have a value of less than $20.00 in the Retail Price field or have more than five units in stock. **Figure 3–24** shows the query design.

FIGURE 3–24
Query design that uses an
Or condition

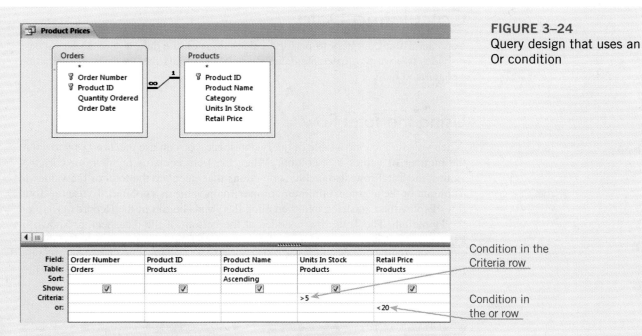

Condition in the
Criteria row

Condition in
the or row

10. Run the query. **Figure 3–25** shows the results of the query with the Or
condition. Only 22 records match either condition of having more than
five units in stock or a retail price of less than $20.00. Leave the query
open for the next Step-by-Step.

FIGURE 3–25
Datasheet for a query with an
Or condition

Order Number	Product ID	Product Name	Units In Stock	Retail Price
10000	1734	2-Drawer Filing Cabinet	32	$79.99
10010	5917	Answering Machine	53	$49.99
10004	5192	Clipboard	32	$1.29
10010	5465	Desk Accessory Set	8	$21.99
10006	5465	Desk Accessory Set	8	$21.99
10006	5918	Digital Phone	57	$65.29
10003	5943	Envelopes #10 (500 count)	11	$11.99
10005	5421	Envelopes (9" x 12") (100 count)	41	$6.49
10008	2010	Fax Machine	15	$189.95
10009	1996	Printing Calculator	221	$29.99
10003	3406	Scissors	6	$4.99
10005	3406	Scissors	6	$4.99
10002	3406	Scissors	6	$4.99
10001	1705	Standard Stapler	54	$7.49
10001	1701	Stick-It Notes (8 pack)	2	$6.59
10007	1701	Stick-It Notes (8 pack)	2	$6.59
10006	1701	Stick-It Notes (8 pack)	2	$6.59
10004	1701	Stick-It Notes (8 pack)	2	$6.59
10003	1701	Stick-It Notes (8 pack)	2	$6.59
10002	1701	Stick-It Notes (8 pack)	2	$6.59
10008	1995	Surge Protector	5	$19.99
10002	5912	Tape Dispenser	44	$5.99

22 records match
either condition

Calculating Data

You can also use a query to perform calculations on the data in a database. Access provides two ways to calculate data using a query: using the Total row and creating a calculated field.

Using the Total Row

▶ **VOCABULARY**

Total row

When you are viewing a table or query datasheet, you can use the **Total row** to count the number of values in a column. When the field contains numbers or currency values, the Total row also includes functions that calculate the total of the values in a column or the average, minimum, or maximum value in a column. To use the Total row, display the datasheet, and then click the Totals button in the Records group on the Home tab. The Total row is added at the bottom of the datasheet, as shown in **Figure 3–26**. When you click in the Total row for a field, an arrow appears on the left side of the field. Clicking the arrow displays a list of functions that you can use in the field. The functions vary based on the field's data type. To hide the Total row, click the Totals button a second time.

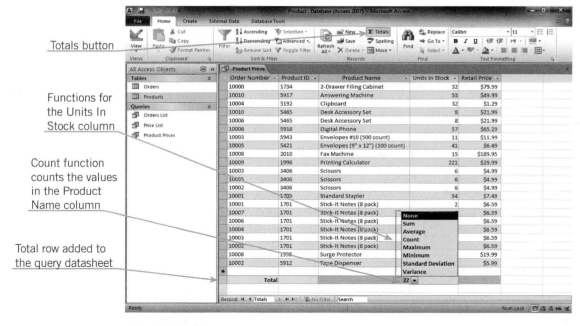

FIGURE 3–26   Total row added to the query datasheet

Step-by-Step 3.12

1. In the Records group on the Home tab, click the **Totals** button. The Total row is added to the datasheet.

2. Click in the **Total** row for the Product Name field. An arrow appears on the left side of the field.

3. Click the **arrow**, and then click **Count**. The Count function counts the number of values in the Product Name column. The value 22 in the Total row indicates that there are 22 products.

4. Click in the **Total** row for the Units In Stock field, and then click the **arrow**. The functions available for the Units In Stock field, which uses the Number data type, appear in the list. See Figure 3–26.

5. In the list, click **Sum**. The Sum function adds the values in the field. The value 611 in the Total row indicates the total number of units in stock.

6. Click in the **Total** row for the Retail Price field, click the **arrow**, and then click **Average**. The Average function calculates the average value and displays $25.77 in the Total row.

7. In the Records group on the Home tab, click the **Totals** button. The Totals row is hidden.

8. Click the **Close 'Product Prices'** button ⊠ to close the query, and then click **Yes** to save it. Leave the database open for the next Step-by-Step.

📼 EXTRA FOR EXPERTS

The Minimum function finds the lowest value in a field. The Maximum function finds the highest value in a field. Two other functions for fields that contain numeric data—Standard Deviation and Variance—are used to compute statistical values.

Creating a Calculated Field in a Query

Because Access can use mathematical operators (+, -, *, and /) to perform calculations on numeric and date data, you do not need to include fields in your tables that store the *result* of a calculation. For example, creating a table with a field that stores a person's age would be considered poor table design because this value changes once a year on a person's birthday. A better table design includes a field that stores a person's birth date. If you need to display a person's age, you can subtract the person's birth date from the current date. The result will always produce the person's age.

To perform a calculation in a query, you add a new field to the query and enter the calculation you need to perform. When a field displays a value that is calculated using other fields in the query, it is called a *calculated field*. The calculation is called an *expression*. In an expression, field names are enclosed in square brackets, which is required when a field name containing spaces is used in an expression. Access uses the expression in the calculated field to display the result in the datasheet. For example, if today's date is June 16, 2013, and your birth date is May 31, 1996, the result of the expression (your age) is 17.

How do you create a calculated field? You can type it directly into an empty column in the design grid for the query in Design view. This method works fine, but it is difficult to read the expression because the default column width in the design grid only displays about 20 characters. For this reason, it's worth the extra step to right-click the empty Field box in the design grid, and then click Zoom on the shortcut menu. The Zoom dialog box provides plenty of space to see your expression as you type it. When you have entered the expression, click OK to close the Zoom dialog box. Then you can run the query as usual.

▶ VOCABULARY
calculated field
expression

📼 EXTRA FOR EXPERTS

When you use a date in a condition, Access puts number signs (#) around the date after you move to another field in the design grid or run the query. For example, when you enter the condition >=9/16/2013, Access changes it to >=#9/16/2013# when you move to another field or run the query.

Step-by-Step 3.13

1. On the Ribbon, click the **Create** tab. In the Queries group on the Create tab, click the **Query Design** button.

2. In the Show Table dialog box, add the **Orders** and **Products** tables to the query design, and then click **Close**.

3. In the Products table field list, double-click the **Product ID** field to add it to the first column in the design grid.

4. In the Products table field list, double-click the **Product Name** field to add it to the second column in the design grid.

5. Add the **Quantity Ordered** field from the Orders table to the third column in the design grid, and then add the **Retail Price** field from the Products table to the fourth column in the design grid.

6. On the Quick Access Toolbar, click the **Save** button 💾. In the Save As dialog box, type **Order Line Totals**, and then click **OK**. The query design is shown in **Figure 3–27**.

FIGURE 3–27
Order Line Totals
query design

Field that you
will enter the
expression into

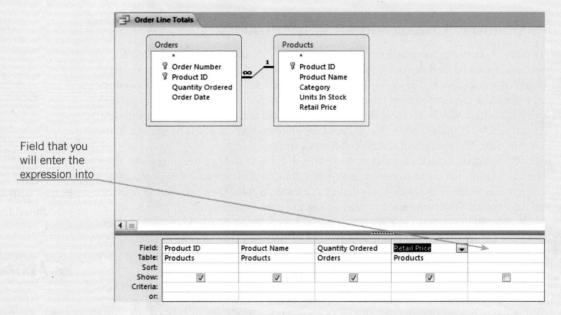

7. Right-click the empty **Field** box to the right of the Retail Price field in the design grid to open the shortcut menu.

8. On the shortcut menu, click **Zoom**. The Zoom dialog box opens.

9. Type **[Quantity Ordered] * [Retail Price]** in the Zoom dialog box, as shown in **Figure 3–28**.

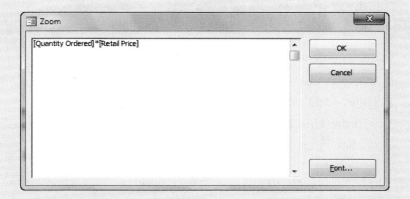

FIGURE 3–28
Expression in the Zoom dialog box

10. Click **OK**. The Zoom dialog box closes. The expression appears in the design grid in the column to the right of the Retail Price field.

11. Save the query. In the Results group on the Design tab, click the **Run** button. The datasheet includes the calculated field, as shown in **Figure 3–29**. Leave the query open for the next Step-by-Step.

FIGURE 3–29
Order Line Totals query datasheet

Order Line Totals				
Product ID ▾	Product Name ▾	Quantity Ordered ▾	Retail Price ▾	Expr1 ▾
1701	Stick-It Notes (8 pack)	1	$6.59	$6.59
1701	Stick-It Notes (8 pack)	10	$6.59	$65.90
1701	Stick-It Notes (8 pack)	4	$6.59	$26.36
1701	Stick-It Notes (8 pack)	2	$6.59	$13.18
1701	Stick-It Notes (8 pack)	1	$6.59	$6.59
1701	Stick-It Notes (8 pack)	1	$6.59	$6.59
1705	Standard Stapler	1	$7.49	$7.49
1734	2-Drawer Filing Cabinet	2	$79.99	$159.98
1995	Surge Protector	10	$19.99	$199.90
1996	Printing Calculator	1	$29.99	$29.99
2002	Oak Office Desk	6	$399.00	$2,394.00
2005	Desk Chair	1	$229.54	$229.54
2010	Fax Machine	2	$189.95	$379.90
3406	Scissors	3	$4.99	$14.97
3406	Scissors	1	$4.99	$4.99
3406	Scissors	3	$4.99	$14.97
5192	Clipboard	1	$1.29	$1.29
5421	Envelopes (9" x 12") (100 count)	1	$6.49	$6.49
5465	Desk Accessory Set	6	$21.99	$131.94
5465	Desk Accessory Set	2	$21.99	$43.98
5912	Tape Dispenser	1	$5.99	$5.99
5917	Answering Machine	2	$49.99	$99.98
5918	Digital Phone	10	$65.29	$652.90
5943	Envelopes #10 (500 count)	2	$11.99	$23.98

Calculated field displays the result of multiplying the Quantity Ordered by the Retail Price for each row

When you create a calculated field in a query, Access gives it a name using the letters "Expr" and a number (in this case, 1) to indicate the first expression in the query. The field name Expr1 isn't meaningful. You can change the name of a calculated field by preceding the expression with the column name you want to use and a colon (such as Order Line Total: [Quantity Ordered] * [Retail Price]). Because you already created the expression, you can edit the field name to replace the default *Expr1* column name with *Order Line Total*.

Step-by-Step 3.14

1. In the Views group on the Home tab, click the **View** button.

2. In the calculated field, double-click **Expr1**. Do not select the colon or any other text in the Field box.

3. Type **Order Line Total** and press **Tab**. **Figure 3–30** shows the revised expression in the last column of the design grid.

FIGURE 3–30
Renaming the calculated field

"Order Line Total" will be the new column heading

Field:	Product ID	Product Name	Quantity Ordered	Retail Price	Order Line Total: [Qua
Table:	Products	Products	Orders	Products	
Sort:					
Show:	✓	✓	✓	✓	✓
Criteria:					
or:					

4. Save and run the query. Double-click the right side of the field selector for the Order Line Total column to resize it to best fit. **Figure 3–31** shows the datasheet with the new calculated field name.

FIGURE 3–31
Query datasheet with the revised calculated field name

New column heading in the resized column

Order Line Totals

Product ID	Product Name	Quantity Ordered	Retail Price	Order Line Total
1701	Stick-It Notes (8 pack)	1	$6.59	$6.59
1701	Stick-It Notes (8 pack)	10	$6.59	$65.90
1701	Stick-It Notes (8 pack)	4	$6.59	$26.36
1701	Stick-It Notes (8 pack)	2	$6.59	$13.18
1701	Stick-It Notes (8 pack)	1	$6.59	$6.59
1701	Stick-It Notes (8 pack)	1	$6.59	$6.59
1705	Standard Stapler	1	$7.49	$7.49
1734	2-Drawer Filing Cabinet	2	$79.99	$159.98
1995	Surge Protector	10	$19.99	$199.90
1996	Printing Calculator	1	$29.99	$29.99
2002	Oak Office Desk	6	$399.00	$2,394.00
2005	Desk Chair	1	$229.54	$229.54
2010	Fax Machine	2	$189.95	$379.90
3406	Scissors	3	$4.99	$14.97
3406	Scissors	1	$4.99	$4.99
3406	Scissors	3	$4.99	$14.97
5192	Clipboard	1	$1.29	$1.29
5421	Envelopes (9" x 12") (100 count)	1	$6.49	$6.49
5465	Desk Accessory Set	6	$21.99	$131.94
5465	Desk Accessory Set	2	$21.99	$43.98
5912	Tape Dispenser	1	$5.99	$5.99
5917	Answering Machine	2	$49.99	$99.98
5918	Digital Phone	10	$65.29	$652.90
5943	Envelopes #10 (500 count)	2	$11.99	$23.98

📧 EXTRA FOR EXPERTS

To change the way values are formatted in a calculated field, select the field in the design grid in Query Design view, and then click the Property Sheet button in Show/Hide group on the Design tab. Click the right side of the field's Format box on the General tab, and then click the desired format. Click the Property Sheet button again to close the Property Sheet.

5. Save the query, and then close it.

6. Click the **Close** button [X] on the Access title bar to close the database and to exit Access.

SUMMARY

In this lesson, you learned:

- A query is a database object that lets you ask the database a question about the data it contains. You can create a query quickly and easily using the Simple Query Wizard, which asks you about the data you want to see and lets you select options in dialog boxes.

- You can change the way data is sorted in a datasheet by applying an ascending or a descending sort order to one of the fields.

- You can use a filter in a datasheet to temporarily display records in a datasheet based on a condition that you specify. Filter By Selection lets you select a field value or part of a field value in a datasheet and then filter out all records that do not match the filter. Filter By Form lets you display records that match a value you select in a field. An AutoFilter opens when you click the arrow on a field selector. You can use an AutoFilter to sort and filter data. You can also move and sort fields in Design view. To run a query, click the Run button in the Results group on the Query Tools Design tab.

- When you need to create a query that uses conditions to select records, create the query in Query Design view.

- Use the Relationships window to create relationships between tables in a database by joining tables with a field that contains matching field values. A one-to-many relationship exists when one record in the primary table matches zero, one, or many records in the related table. Referential integrity is the set of rules that Access uses to protect data in the tables and to make sure that data is not accidentally deleted or changed.

- A multitable query is a query that is based on more than one table.

- When you need to use a query to search for records that match a range of values, use a relational operator in the query design. When you need to select records that match all of two or more conditions in a query, use the And operator by placing the criteria in the same Criteria row in the design grid. When you need to select records that match at least one of two or more conditions in a query, use the Or operator by placing the first condition in the Criteria row and the second condition in the or row in the design grid.

- In Access, you can perform calculations by using the Total row in a datasheet, or by creating a calculated field in the design grid in Query Design view.

■ VOCABULARY REVIEW

Define the following terms:

And operator	Filter By Form	referential integrity
AutoFilter	Filter By Selection	relationship
calculated field	foreign key	Simple Query Wizard
common field	multitable query	sort
condition	one-to-many relationship	subdatasheet
expression	Or operator	Total row
filter	query	

■ REVIEW QUESTIONS

TRUE / FALSE

Circle T if the statement is true or F if the statement is false.

T   F   **1.**   When you sort a field that contains text values in ascending order, data is arranged from A to Z.

T   F   **2.**   Applying a filter is a temporary way of selecting records in a datasheet.

T   F   **3.**   To remove a filter from a datasheet, click the Cancel Filter button.

T   F   **4.**   A common field used to relate tables must have the same field name in the related table.

T   F   **5.**   The >= relational operator selects records that are greater than or equal to the value in the condition.

WRITTEN QUESTIONS

Write a brief answer to each of the following questions.

1. What information do you specify when you run the Simple Query Wizard?

2. What steps do you follow to use Filter By Form in a datasheet?

3. How do you add all fields from a table to the design grid in Query Design view in one step?

4. When a relationship exists between two tables in a database, what name is given to the matching field in the related table?

5. What is a subdatasheet?

FILL IN THE BLANK

Complete the following sentences by writing the correct word or words in the blanks provided.

1. A(n) _____ is a database object that you can use to find answers to questions about the data in a database.

2. When you view field values in ascending or descending order from A to Z or from smallest to largest, you apply a(n) _____ to the field.

3. Applying a(n) _____ to a datasheet temporarily displays records based on the condition that you specify.

4. To display all records in a datasheet after you applied a filter, click the _____ button.

5. To create a relationship between two tables, you must design the tables so they contain a(n) _____ field.

PROJECTS

If you have a SAM 2010 user profile, your instructor may have assigned an autogradable version of the indicated project. If so, log into the SAM 2010 Web site at *www.cengage.com/sam2010* to download the instruction and start files.

PROJECT 3–1

1. Open the **Agents.accdb** database from the Access Lesson 03 folder where your Data Files are stored.

2. Use the Simple Query Wizard to create a query that includes all fields from the Agents table. Name the query **Agents Listing**.

3. Use a button in the Sort & Filter group on the Home tab to sort the records in alphabetical order by Last Name.

4. Use the Affiliation field and Filter By Selection to apply a filter that selects records for agents who do *not* work for Keller McCormack.

5. Remove the filter, and then clear all filters.

6. Use Filter By Form to select records for agents who work for Keller McCormack. Apply the filter, and then change the First Name and Last Name field values in the first row to your first and last names. Print the datasheet in landscape orientation.

7. Remove the filter.

8. Save the query, close the query, and then exit Access.

SAM PROJECT 3–2

1. Open the **Listings.accdb** database from the Access Lesson 03 folder where your Data Files are stored.

2. Create a new query in Query Design view. Add the Agents table field list to the query design.

3. Add all fields from the Agents table to the query design in the order that they appear in the field list.

4. In the design grid, move the Last Name field so it appears between the Agent ID and First Name fields.

5. Sort the records in ascending order first by Last Name, and then in ascending order by First Name.

6. Add a condition to the query design so that only those agents who work for Montglow Real Estate appear in the query datasheet. (The Affiliation field stores the agent's employer.)

7. Save the query as **Montglow Realtors**.

8. Run the query. In the first row, change the Last Name and First Name field values to your last and first names. Print the datasheet in landscape orientation.

9. Close the Montglow Realtors query, and then exit Access.

PROJECT 3–3

1. Open the **Realtors.accdb** database from the Access Lesson 03 folder where your Data Files are stored.

2. In the Relationships window, create a relationship between the Agents and Houses tables. Use the Agent ID field in the primary Agents table and the Agent ID field in the related Houses table as the common field. (Use the scroll bar on the Houses table field list to see the Agent ID field in the list.)

3. Enforce referential integrity in the relationship. Close the Relationships window and save your changes.

4. Create a new query in Query Design view. Add the Agents and Houses field lists to the query design.

5. Add the following fields from the Agents table field list to the design grid in the order listed: Agent ID, Affiliation, and Last Name.

6. Add the following fields from the Houses table field list to the design grid in the order listed: Listing ID, Date Listed, and Price.

7. Save the query as **Listings By Agent**, and then run the query.

8. Change to Design view. Add a condition to the Date Listed field to select properties that were listed after 9/16/2013. Save and run the query.

9. Change to Design view. Change the query design to select records for properties that were listed after 9/16/2013 *and* that have a price that is less than $100,000. Save and run the query.

10. Change to Design view. Change the query design to select records that were listed after 9/16/2013 *or* that have a price that is less than $100,000. Save and run the query. In the first row in the datasheet, change the value in the Last Name field to your last name. Print the datasheet in landscape orientation.

11. Close the Listings By Agent query, and then exit Access.

PROJECT 3–4

1. Open the **Properties.accdb** database from the Access Lesson 03 folder where your Data Files are stored. Close the Navigation Pane.

2. In the Relationships window, create a relationship between the Agents and Houses tables. Use the Agent ID field in the primary Agents table and the Agent ID field in the related Houses table as the common field. (Use the scroll bar on the Houses table field list to see the Agent ID field in the list.)

3. Enforce referential integrity in the relationship. Close the Relationships window and save your changes.

4. Create a new query in Query Design view. Add the Agents and Houses field lists to the query design.

5. Add the following fields from the Agents table field list to the design grid in the order listed: Agent ID, Last Name, and Affiliation.

6. Add the following fields from the Houses table field list to the design grid in the order listed: Listing ID, Bedrooms, Bathrooms, Garages, and Price.

7. Save the query as **Detailed Listings**, and then run the query.

8. Change to Design view. Click in the Field box to the right of the Price field in the design grid. (You might need to scroll the design grid to see the new field.) Open the Zoom dialog box. In the Zoom dialog box, enter the following expression to calculate the estimated real estate commission for each listing: **Price * 0.06**. Save and run the query.

9. In Design view, change the default field name *Expr1* for the calculated field to **Estimated Commission**. Save and run the query. Resize the Estimated Commission field to best fit.

10. Change to Design view. Click the Field box for the Estimated Commission field, and then click the Property Sheet button in the Show/Hide group on the Query Tools Design tab. On the General tab in the Property Sheet, change the Format property to Currency. Click the Property Sheet button again to close the Property Sheet. Save and run the query.

11. Use the Total row in the datasheet to calculate the average price of all properties and the total (sum) of all estimated commissions.

12. In the first row in the datasheet, change the Last Name field value to your first and last names. Print the datasheet in portrait orientation.

13. Save and close the query, and then exit Access.

■ CRITICAL THINKING

ACTIVITY 3–1

You are a realtor with three new clients who are ready to buy homes. List on paper each client's requirements for purchasing a home. For example, Buyer #1 might want a three-bedroom house with a brick exterior and have a budget of $90,000.

Using the **Realtors.accdb** database in the Access Lesson 03 folder where your Data Files are stored, create a query to locate the Listing ID, Address, and other pertinent information for each client. Save the queries using the names **Buyer 1**, **Buyer 2**, and **Buyer 3**. After running each query, print the results in landscape orientation.

ACTIVITY 3–3

In addition to the Simple Query Wizard, Access includes other wizards that can help you create queries. One is the Find Unmatched Query Wizard, which finds records in one table that have no matching records in a second table. For example, this type of query is useful when you need to find students who are not enrolled in any classes, or realtors who have no listings.

Open the **Realtors.accdb** database from the Access Lesson 03 folder where your Data Files are stored. On the Create tab, click the Query Wizard button. In the New Query dialog box, click Find Unmatched Query Wizard, and then click OK. The Find Unmatched Query Wizard starts and opens the first dialog box, in which you select the table that you want to search for unmatched records. Make sure that Table: Agents is selected, and then click Next.

In the second dialog box, choose the table that contains the matching (related) records. Make sure that Table: Houses is selected, and then click Next.

ACTIVITY 3–2

Referential integrity is the set of rules that Access uses to check for valid relationships between tables. It also ensures that related data is not accidentally deleted or changed. Start Access and use Access Help to search for topics about **referential integrity**. In the list of links that opens, click "Guide to table relationships" and read the information in the section entitled "Understanding referential integrity." Determine which conditions must be met before you can enforce referential integrity in a relationship. Write a brief essay that explains the importance of referential integrity in a relational database and identifies some of the problems that referential integrity is designed to prevent and control.

In the third dialog box, choose the fields that contain matching records. (If you also completed Project 3–3 and already created the relationship between the tables, click Next, and then skip to the next paragraph in this activity.) Scroll the Houses field list until you see Agent ID at the bottom of the list, and then click Agent ID. Click the Match Fields button between the field lists. The text *Agent ID < = > Agent ID* appears in the Matching fields box to indicate the matching fields. Click Next.

In the fourth dialog box, click the Select All Fields button to add all fields from the Agents table to the query datasheet. Click Next.

In the final dialog box, click Finish to accept the default query name and display the datasheet. Change the Last Name field value for the first row to your first and last names, print the datasheet, and then close the Agents Without Matching Houses query and the database. Which realtor in the database has no listings?

LESSON 4

Creating and Modifying Forms

■ OBJECTIVES

Upon completion of this lesson, you should be able to:

- Create a form using different form tools.
- Create a form using the Form Wizard.
- Navigate records using a form.
- Use a form to find, replace, update, and delete data.
- Create and modify a form in Layout view.
- Resize and move controls in a form.
- Add an unbound control to a form in Design view.
- Preview and print a form.

■ VOCABULARY

bound control

control

control layout

Datasheet tool

Detail section

Field List pane

Find

form

Form Footer section

Form Header section

Form tool

Form view

Form Wizard

Layout view

Multiple Items tool

record source

Split Form tool

theme

unbound control

In this lesson, you will learn about the different features you can use to create a form to display the data in your database. You will also learn how to navigate and edit records displayed in a form, and use a form to add and delete records.

Creating a Form

▶ **VOCABULARY**

form

record source

Form tool

controls

A *form* is a database object that displays data from one or more tables or queries in a format that has a similar appearance to a paper form. The tables or queries that provide the data to be displayed in a form are called the *record source*. Most database experts agree that users should make all database updates using a form, instead of using table datasheets, because forms provide more control over the way data is displayed, updated, and entered. In addition, most users find that working in a form is easier than working in a table datasheet. The form can contain messages about how to enter data, format data in different ways to call attention to it, and include features that prevent users from updating data that should not be changed.

Creating a Form with the Form Tool

Access includes tools that you can use to create different kinds of forms. After selecting the table or query in the Navigation Pane on which to base the form, click the Create tab on the Ribbon. The different options for creating forms are located in the Forms group on the Create tab. Click the Form button to use the *Form tool*, which creates a simple form that includes all the fields in the selected table or query, uses a simple format, and includes a title with the same name as the table or query on which it is based. **Figure 4–1** shows a form created using the Form tool. Each field in the record source appears in the form. In Figure 4–1, the "Listing ID" text appears in a label, and the field value for the first record (2042) appears in a text box. When fields appear in a form, they appear in *controls*. In this form, the Listing ID label and the Listing ID text box are controls. You can click the buttons on the record navigation bar at the bottom of the Form window to navigate the records in the record source and display them in the form.

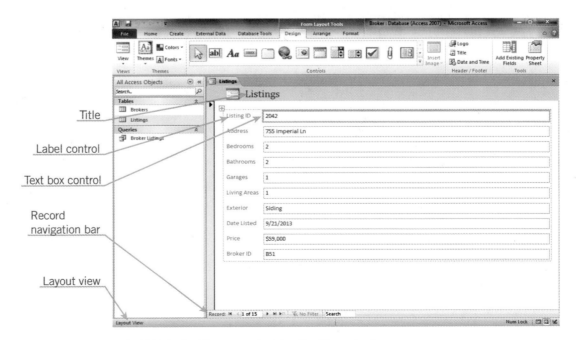

FIGURE 4–1 Form created by the Form tool

When you use a tool to create a form, the form opens in Layout view. In *Layout view*, you can view the controls in the form and data from the record source at the same time. You can also make certain changes to the form's format and appearance, such as resizing a control. When you click a control in Layout view, an orange border appears around the control to indicate that it is selected.

▶ **VOCABULARY**
Layout view
Split Form tool
Multiple Items tool
Datasheet tool

Creating a Form with the Split Form Tool

The *Split Form tool* creates a form using all the fields in the selected table or query and splits the window into two panes, as shown in **Figure 4–2**. To create a split form, click the More Forms button in the Forms group on the Create tab, and then click Split Form. In the top pane, you see a form that is similar to the one created by the Form tool. In the bottom pane, you see a datasheet that contains the form data. The two views are synchronized—when you select a field in the top pane, it is also selected in the bottom pane.

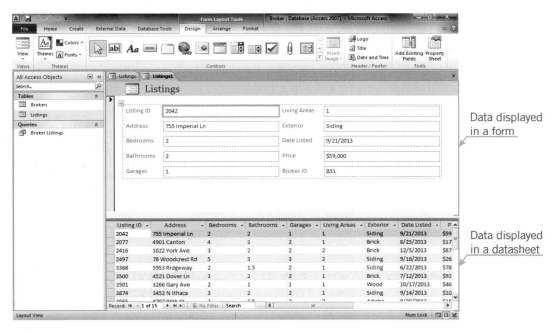

Data displayed in a form

Data displayed in a datasheet

FIGURE 4–2   Form created by the Split Form tool

Creating a Form with the Multiple Items and Datasheet Tools

The *Multiple Items tool* creates a form that lists all the fields in a datasheet format, but using a style that is similar to the form created by the Form tool. The *Datasheet tool* creates a form that looks just like a datasheet. All of these tools create forms quickly and easily. To use the Multiple Items tool or the Datasheet tool, click the More Forms button in the Forms group on the Create tab, and then click Multiple Items or Datasheet in the list.

Step-by-Step 4.1

1. Open the **Broker.accdb** database from the Access Lesson 04 folder where your Data Files are stored.

2. If the Security Warning opens, click the **Enable Content** button.

3. In the Navigation Pane, click the **Listings** table to select it.

4. On the Ribbon, click the **Create** tab. In the Forms group, click the **Form** button. The Form tool creates a form using all the fields in the Listings table and displays the first record in the Listings table. See Figure 4–1.

5. On the Ribbon, click the **Create** tab. In the Forms group, click the **More Forms** button, and then click **Split Form**. Access creates a split form based on the Listings table, as shown in Figure 4–2.

6. On the Ribbon, click the **Create** tab. In the Forms group, click the **More Forms** button, and then click **Multiple Items**. Access creates a multiple items form, which displays the data from the Listings table in a form with a format similar to a datasheet.

7. On the Ribbon, click the **Create** tab. In the Forms group, click the **More Forms** button, and then click **Datasheet**. Access creates a form based on the Listings table that looks like a table or query datasheet.

8. Click the **Close** button ⊠ to close each form that you created. Save each form using the form name that Access suggests. Leave the database open for the next Step-by-Step.

⊞ EXTRA FOR EXPERTS

Table, form, and report objects in the database can have the same name. For example, the Broker database can contain a Listings table and a Listings form. However, you cannot give the same name to a table and a query object in the same database.

▶ VOCABULARY
Form Wizard
theme

Creating a Form with the Form Wizard

When you need to create a simple form quickly, you can use the *Form Wizard*, which helps you create a form by letting you select options in dialog boxes to specify the form's record source and layout. To start the Form Wizard, click the Create tab, and then click the Form Wizard button in the Forms group. The Form Wizard provides four form layouts from which to choose. The Columnar layout displays fields in a stacked column format, with labels to the left of their controls. The Tabular layout displays fields with the labels at the top of a column that contains the field values. The Datasheet layout displays fields in a datasheet format. The Justified layout displays fields across the screen in the order in which they occur. A form's style, also called a *theme*, formats the form and its controls using a predefined color, font, and design scheme. After creating a form with any Form tool, you can use the tools and features in Access to customize the form.

Step-by-Step 4.2

1. On the Ribbon, click the **Create** tab. In the Forms group, click the **Form Wizard** button. The first dialog box of the Form Wizard opens.

2. Click the **Tables/Queries** arrow, and then click **Table: Brokers** in the list. The fields in the Brokers table appear in the Available Fields list box.

3. Click the **Select All** button 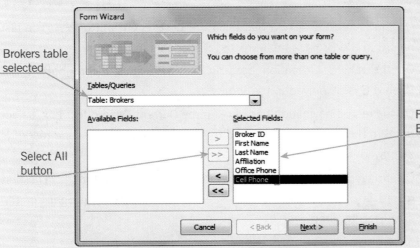 to move all fields to the Selected Fields list box, as shown in **Figure 4–3**.

FIGURE 4–3
Form Wizard dialog box after selecting the table and fields to include

4. Click **Next**. The second Form Wizard dialog box opens.

5. Make sure that the **Columnar** option button is selected, and then click **Next**. In the final dialog box, you enter a title for the form or accept the default name. You'll accept the default name, Brokers.

6. Click **Finish**. The Brokers form appears in Form view, as shown in **Figure 4–4**. The default Office theme is applied to the form. The theme formats the form's colors and fonts. Leave the form open for the next Step-by-Step.

TIP

The default form name is the name of the table or query object on which the form is based.

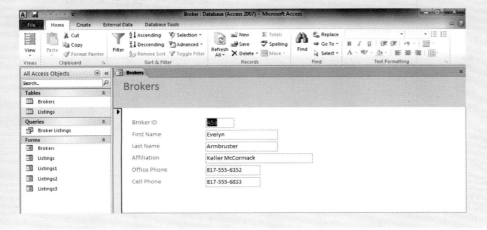

FIGURE 4–4
Brokers form in Form view

Navigating a Form

When you create a form using the Form Wizard, the form opens in Form view. When a form is displayed in *Form view*, you will see each record in the record source, one at a time, in the form. Form view includes a record navigation bar at the bottom of the Form view window that you can use to navigate the records. This record navigation bar has the same buttons with the same functions as the record navigation bar you used to navigate records in a table or query datasheet.

Step-by-Step 4.3

1. On the record navigation bar, click the **Last record** button ▶|. The last record in the Brokers table, record 9, appears in the form.

2. On the record navigation bar, click the **Previous record** button ◀. Record 8 is displayed in the form.

3. On the record navigation bar, click in the **Current Record** text box, select the **8** in the text box, type **2**, and then press **Enter**. The second record is displayed in the form.

4. On the record navigation bar, click the **First record** button |◀. The first record is displayed in the form. Leave the Brokers form open for the next Step-by-Step.

Using a Form to Find and Replace Data

You have used filters and queries to find data in a database. Another option for finding data in a database quickly is to use the *Find* command, which is available when you are using a table or query datasheet, form, or report. When you click the Find button in the Find group on the Home tab, the Find and Replace dialog box shown in **Figure 4–5** opens.

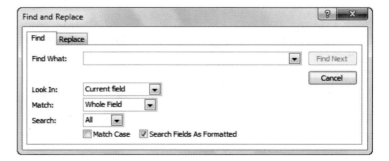

FIGURE 4–5   Find and Replace dialog box

You have several options for finding data, including finding and replacing data. If you select part of a field value in the form (one or more characters or a single word) before clicking the Find button, the selected text appears in the Find What list box automatically. If nothing is selected or more than one word is selected before clicking the Find button, the Find What list box is empty, in which case you type the value you want to find in the list box.

When a field is selected in the form, "Current field" appears in the Look In list box when you open the Find and Replace dialog box. If you want to search the entire table for a matching field value, click the Look In arrow, and then click "Current document." You can use the options in the Match menu to search any part of the field, the whole field, or the start of the field as follows:

- If you type *S* in the Find What list box, and then select the Any Part of Field option in the Match menu, you'll find values that contain the letter *S* anywhere in the value.

- If you select the Whole Field option, you'll find values that contain *only* the letter *S*.

- If you select the Start of Field option, you'll find values that *begin* with the letter *S*.

The Search option lets you search the entire form, or up and down from the location of the insertion point. The two check boxes—Match Case and Search Fields As Formatted—let you search for a matching value that has the same case as the entry in the Find What list box and search for formatted values, respectively. When the Match Case check box is selected, typing *Stars* in the Find What list box will find a record that contains the word *Stars* but will not select a record that contains the word *stars*. To start searching the form for matching records, click Find Next.

If you click the Replace tab in the Find and Replace dialog box, you will see additional options for finding text and replacing it with different text. The only difference is that you type the value that you want to find in the Find What list box and type the value that you want to replace it with in the Replace With list box. **Figure 4–6** shows the Replace tab. Notice the Replace and Replace All buttons. When you start searching the form for matching values by clicking Find Next, you'll find the first matching value. Clicking Replace replaces that instance and resumes searching for the Find What value; clicking Replace All replaces that instance and all others that match.

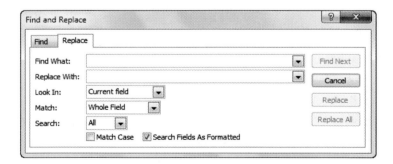

FIGURE 4–6   Replace tab in the Find and Replace dialog box

Step-by-Step 4.4

1. Double-click the word **McCormack** in the Affiliation field in the first record to select it.

2. In the Find group on the Home tab, click the **Find** button. The Find and Replace dialog box opens. Notice that the selected field value *McCormack* in the Affiliation field appears in the Find What list box. See **Figure 4–7**.

FIGURE 4–7
Find and Replace dialog box with selected Find What value

 TIP

If necessary, drag the Find and Replace dialog box to below the Cell Phone field in the form so you can see all the fields in the form.

3. Make sure that the options in your dialog box match the ones shown in Figure 4–7. Click **Find Next**. Because the Match option is set to Whole Field, and there is no field value in the Affiliation field that contains only the word *McCormack*, Access opens a dialog box indicating that it found no matching items.

4. Click **OK** to close the dialog box.

5. Click the **Match** arrow in the Find and Replace dialog box, and then click **Any Part of Field**. Click **Find Next**. The Find command locates the word *McCormack* in the fourth record and selects it.

6. Click **Find Next**. The Find command locates a match in the first record. It displays the first record and selects the word *McCormack* in the record.

7. In the Find and Replace dialog box, click the **Replace** tab.

8. In the Replace With list box, type **Greene**.

9. Click the Look In arrow, click **Current document**, and then make sure the Match value is **Any Part of Field**. Click **Replace**. The word *McCormack* in the first record is replaced with the word *Greene*. The next record containing the Find What value is selected (record 4).

10. Click **Replace**. The word *McCormack* is replaced with the word *Greene* in the fourth record. Click **Replace**. Because record 4 contains the last occurrence of the word *McCormack* in the Affiliation field, a dialog box opens and indicates that Access cannot find any more matches.

EXTRA FOR EXPERTS

When you need to find and replace data, click the Replace button in the Find group on the Home tab. The Find and Replace dialog box opens with the Replace tab activated.

11. Click **OK** to close the dialog box.

12. Click **Cancel** to close the Find and Replace dialog box. Leave the Brokers form open for the next Step-by-Step.

You need to be careful when replacing text because you might accidentally replace text that you didn't intend to change. For example, if you want to replace the word *Green* with the word *Red*, your Find What value is *Green* and your Replace With value is *Red*. When you replace the text, you'll replace the word *Green* with the word *Red* as you intended. However, you'll also change the word *Greenfield* or *Greenley* to *Redfield* and *Redley*, which are changes that you might not intend to make. This is a good reason to use Replace rather than Replace All. With Replace All you do not have the option to choose to replace a specific word. By using Replace, if you find a word that you don't want to replace, click Cancel to skip it.

Using a Form to Update Data

You can also use a form to update the record source, add new records, or delete existing records. Because you can customize a form to display data in different ways, most database experts recommend using a form instead of a table datasheet to make changes. To change a field value, select it and type the new value. To add a new record, click the New button in the Records group on the Home tab to open a blank form, into which you can type the field values for the new record. When you are finished adding the new record, press Tab to move to a new record or close the form.

Step-by-Step 4.5

1. On the record navigation bar, click the **First record** button ⏮ to display the first record.

2. In the form, double-click **Armbruster** in the Last Name field to select it.

3. Type **Arlington** and then press **Tab**. The record is updated.

4. In the Records group on the Home tab, click the **New** button. A blank form is displayed. The insertion point is blinking in the Broker ID text box, ready for you to type the field value.

5. Type **E99** and then press **Tab**. The insertion point moves to First Name field, which is the next text box.

6. Type **Hector** in the First Name text box, and then press **Tab**.

7. Complete the record by typing the values shown in **Figure 4–8**. Remember to press Tab to move to the next field. Do not press Tab after typing the field value in the Cell Phone text box.

FIGURE 4–8
Adding a record in Form view

8. Press **Tab**. Record 10 is added to the Brokers table and a blank form for Record 11 appears.

9. On the Navigation Pane, double-click **Brokers** in the Tables group. The Brokers table opens in Datasheet view. Notice that the record you added, with the Broker ID E99, appears in the datasheet. Leave the Brokers table and the Brokers form open for the next Step-by-Step.

You might be wondering why the record for Hector Marques appears in record 4 in the table, instead of in record 10 as shown in the form. When you use a form to add a record, it is added in a blank form at the end of the record source. However, when you display the datasheet for the table or query on which the form is based, the new record appears in order based on the values in the primary key field. In the Brokers table, the Broker ID field is the table's primary key, and values in this column are alphabetical. That's why record E99 is listed fourth. Hector's record will be record 10 in the form until you close it and then reopen it, and then it will also appear as record 4 in the form.

Using a Form to Delete Data

Access provides two important options when using a form to delete a field value or record. When you click the Delete button in the Records group on the Home tab, you'll delete the selected field value. If you click the Delete button arrow, and then click Delete Record, you'll delete the record that is currently displayed in the form. Be careful when deleting data. You can use the Undo button on the Quick Access Toolbar to restore a deleted field value, but deleting a record permanently deletes it from the record source.

Step-by-Step 4.6

1. Click the **Close 'Brokers'** button ☒ to close the Brokers table.

2. On the record navigation bar for the Brokers form, click the **Previous record** button ◄. Hector's record is still record 10 in the form.

3. Close the Brokers form.

4. Double-click **Brokers** in the Forms group in the Navigation Pane to reopen the form.

5. Navigate to record **4**, which contains Hector's record.

6. Press **Tab** to select the value *Hector* in the First Name text box.

7. In the Records group on the Home tab, click the **Delete** button. The field value in the First Name field is deleted.

8. On the record navigation bar, click the **Previous record** button ◄.

9. On the record navigation bar, click the **Next record** button ►. The First Name field contains no value.

10. On the Quick Access Toolbar, click the **Undo** button ↺. The field value *Hector* is added back to the First Name text box.

11. In the Records group on the Home tab, click the **Delete button arrow**. In the list, click **Delete Record**. The dialog box shown in **Figure 4–9** opens.

12. In the dialog box, click **Yes**. Hector's record is deleted from the Brokers table and is no longer displayed in the form. Notice that the Undo button on the Quick Access Toolbar is not available; you cannot restore a deleted record.

13. Close the Brokers form. Leave the database open for the next Step-by-Step.

> **TIP**
>
> Similar to changing records in a table datasheet, you do not need to save your changes when adding or updating records using a form. You only need to save a form when you change its design.

FIGURE 4–9
Dialog box that opens when you delete a record

Creating and Modifying a Form in Layout View

When you need to create a form to match an existing paper form—or when you need to create a form different from the forms you can create with a form tool or wizard—you can create a form from scratch. To create a new form, click the Create tab on the Ribbon, and then click the Blank Form button in the Forms group. A blank form opens in Layout view, and the Field List pane opens on the right side of the

▶ **VOCABULARY**

Field List pane

control layout

screen. The *Field List pane* contains the tables in the database and displays the fields they contain. When you double-click a field in the Field List pane, Access adds the field to the form. As you add fields to a form in Layout view, Access adds them to a control layout. A *control layout* is a "container" that groups together the controls in a form so that you can change them as a group. You can change the way the controls are arranged by changing the control layout, or you can remove controls from the layout to work with them individually.

The first task is to create a blank form in Layout view, and then to use the Field List pane to add fields to the form.

Step-by-Step 4.7

1. On the Ribbon, click the **Create** tab. In the Forms group, click the **Blank Form** button. A blank form opens in Layout view. The Field List pane opens on the right side of the screen. See **Figure 4–10**.

FIGURE 4–10
Blank form in Layout view

Add Existing Fields button

Field List pane

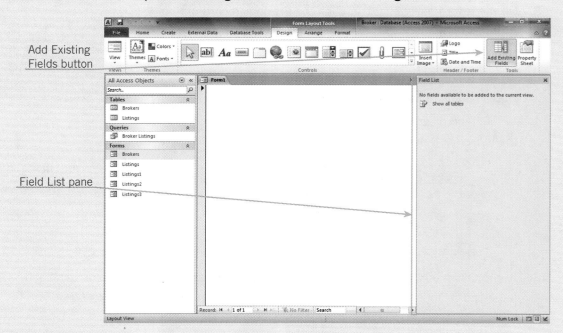

2. If necessary, click **Show all tables** in the Field List pane, and then click the **expand indicator** ⊞ to the left of the Listings table in the Field List pane to see the fields in the table.

3. In the Listings field list, double-click **Listing ID**. The label and text box controls for the Listing ID field are added to the upper-left corner of the form. When you add a field from one table, its related table—in this case, the Brokers table—moves to the "Fields available in related tables" section of the Field List pane. See **Figure 4–11**.

⊦── **WARNING**

If you do not see the Field List pane, click the Add Existing Fields button in the Tools group on the Design tab. If you do not see "Show all tables" in the Field List pane as shown in Figure 4–10, you won't need to click Show all tables in Step 2.

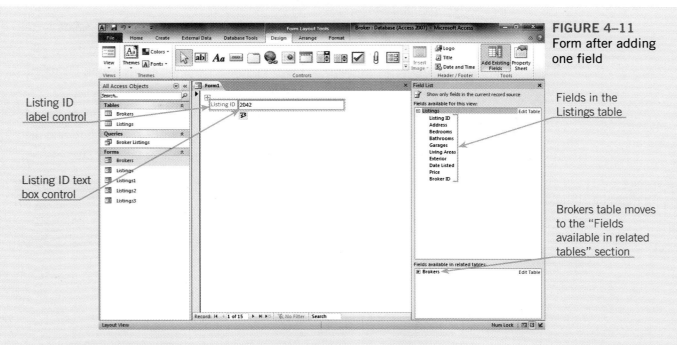

FIGURE 4–11
Form after adding
one field

Listing ID
label control

Listing ID text
box control

Fields in the
Listings table

Brokers table moves
to the "Fields
available in related
tables" section

4. In the Field List pane, in the Listings table, double-click **Address**. The label and text box controls for the Address field are added to the form in the control layout. See **Figure 4–12**.

FIGURE 4–12
Form after adding
two fields

Dotted line indicates
the control layout

5. Double-click the following fields in the Listings table in order listed: **Bedrooms**, **Bathrooms**, **Garages**, **Living Areas**, **Date Listed**, and **Price**.

6. In the Fields available in related tables pane, click the **expand indicator** ⊞ to the left of the Brokers table to display the fields.

7. In the Brokers table in the Fields available in related tables section, double-click the **First Name** field. The Brokers table and its fields move to the top of the Field List pane. The First Name field is added to the form as a combo box control and not as a text box control because this field is in a related table. You can use the Property Update Options button to change it to a text box control.

8. Below the selected First Name control, click the **Property Update Options** button 🖉, and then click **Change to Text Box** in the menu that opens. The First Name control changes to a text box control.

TIP

If you accidentally add the wrong field to the control layout, click the field in the form to select it, and then press Delete.

9. In the Brokers table field list, double-click the following fields in the order listed: **Last Name** and **Cell Phone**.

10. In the Tools group on the Design tab, click the **Add Existing Fields** button to close the Field List pane.

11. On the Quick Access Toolbar, click the **Save** button 🔲 to open the Save As dialog box, type **Listings And Agents** in the Form Name text box, and then click **OK**. See **Figure 4–13**. Leave the form open for the next Step-by-Step.

FIGURE 4–13
Form after adding all fields

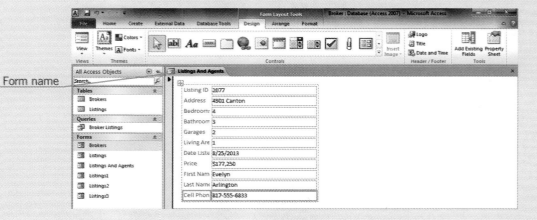

Form name

Adding a Title to a Form and Changing its Format

When you create a form in Layout view, at first it contains one section called the **Detail section**. The form you just created contains a Detail section with controls that display one record at a time. When your form design requires other features, such as a title or a page number, you can add two additional sections to the form. The **Form Header section** displays information at the top of each form, and the **Form Footer section** displays information at the bottom of each form. You can add these sections to a form by clicking a tool in the Header/Footer group on the Form Layout Tools Design tab. When you add a control to one of these sections, the Form Header and Form Footer sections are added to the form as a pair, even when you add a control to the form that appears in only one of the two sections.

You can add two types of controls to a form. A **bound control** is connected to a field in the record source and is used to display, enter, and update data. An **unbound control** is not connected to a record source and is used to display information, lines, rectangles, and pictures.

Figure 4–13 shows the Header/Footer group on the Design tab in Layout view, which includes buttons that add different types of controls to a form. For example, clicking the Logo button adds a picture to a form, and clicking the Title button adds a title control in the Form Header section.

To add a title to a form, which adds an unbound control to the form, click the Title button in the Header/Footer group on the Design tab. Access will add the Form Header and Form Footer sections to the form and add a title control to the Form Header section. The default form title is the form's name. Because you already saved the form as "Listings And Agents," this is the form title that will be added when you add a title control to the form. You can edit the title by clicking and editing text just like you would in a document. You can also change the default font size, color, and style of the title text using the buttons in the Font group on the Format tab.

Step-by-Step 4.8

1. In the Header/Footer group on the Design tab, click the **Title** button. Access adds the Form Header and Form Footer sections to the form, and adds a title control to the Form Header section. (You won't see the Form Footer section until you change to Design view because it's empty.) The text in the title control is "Listings And Agents," which is the same as the form's name.

2. Click the **Format** tab, and then in the Font group, click the **Bold** button **B**. The title is formatted in bold. The text is deselected, and the title control is selected, as indicated by its orange border shown in **Figure 4–14**.

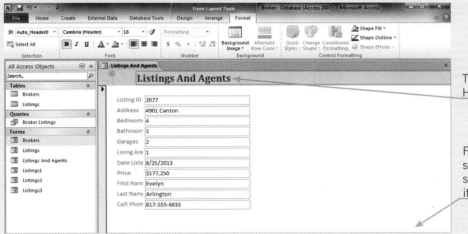

FIGURE 4–14
Title control added to form

Title added to Form Header section

Form Footer section is empty, so you can't see it in Layout view

3. With the title control still selected, click the **Font Color arrow** in the Font group. A gallery of colors opens.

4. In the gallery, click the **Dark Red** color (the first color in the last row of the Standard Colors section). The gallery closes and the text in the title control is formatted as dark red.

5. Click to the left of the letter "A" in the word "And" in the title to position the insertion point, press **Delete**, and then type **a**. The title changes to "Listings and Agents." Leave the form open for the next Step-by-Step.

> **TIP**
>
> A form can have a different name and title. The form's name is "Listings And Agents," and the form's title is "Listings and Agents."

Resizing a Control in a Form

When you add controls to a form, you might need to adjust their widths to display the values they contain correctly. For the Listings And Agents form, the text box controls are much wider than the data they contain. When you resize controls in a control layout in Layout view, reducing the width of *one* control reduces all the widths of all *other* controls in the control layout at the same time. When resizing the controls, be sure to resize them with the longest data value displayed in the form, so you don't accidentally resize a control too narrowly and limit what users can see. You can resize a control by dragging its edge to a new location. You can also resize a control precisely. As you resize a control, the status bar displays the width of the control in characters and lines. By watching the lower-left corner of the status bar as you resize a control, you can specify the width of the control using an exact number of characters.

Step-by-Step 4.9

1. Use the record navigation bar to display record **11** in the form. This record contains the longest Address field value in the record source.

2. Click the **Address** text box to select it. An orange border appears around the text box. A dotted outline surrounds all the controls in the control layout.

3. Point to the right edge of the Address text box control. When the pointer changes to a ⟷ shape, press and hold the mouse button and slowly drag the right edge of the Address text box control to the left. When the Characters value on the left side of the status bar is 16, as shown in **Figure 4–15**, release the mouse button. Because all of the text boxes in the form are part of a control layout, they are all resized to the same size.

FIGURE 4–15
Resizing the text box controls in a control layout

Pointer on Address text box control

Record 11 contains the longest Address field value

Status bar indicates number of lines and characters while resizing

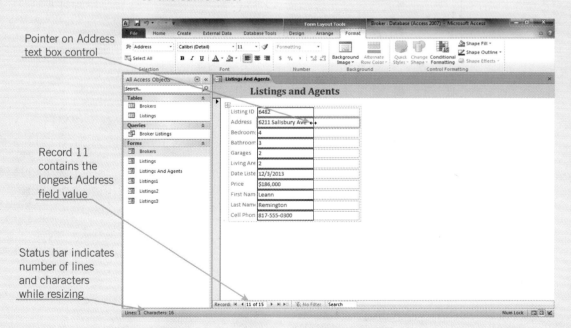

4. Save the form. Leave the form open for the next Step-by-Step.

Moving a Control in a Form

When controls are grouped in a control layout, moving one control moves all the selected controls in the group. When you need to move one or more controls in a form, you'll need to select and then remove them from the control layout first. To select one control, you click it. To select a group of controls, click the first control, press and hold down Shift, click the other controls, and then release Shift. Some people call this "Shift-Click" because you hold down Shift while clicking the other controls. To remove one or more selected controls from a control layout, right-click the control to open the shortcut menu, point to Layout, and then click Remove Layout.

Step-by-Step 4.10

1. Click the **First Name** text box (which contains the value *Leann*) to select it. An orange border appears around the text box.

2. Press and hold down **Shift**.

3. Click the **Last Name** text box, click the **Cell Phone** text box, and then release **Shift**. **Figure 4–16** shows the three selected controls.

FIGURE 4–16
Selected controls in a form

4. Right-click one of the selected controls to open the shortcut menu, point to **Layout**, and then click **Remove Layout**. The selected controls are removed from the control layout. An orange border appears around the three text box controls for the First Name, Last Name, and Cell Phone fields, and the dotted border is removed from the fields on the form.

5. Press and hold **Shift**, click the **First Name**, **Last Name**, and **Cell Phone** labels, and then release **Shift**. The three label controls and text box controls are selected, with an orange border around each control.

TIP

If you move the controls to the wrong location, click the Undo button on the Quick Access Toolbar, and then repeat Steps 6 and 7.

6. Point to the **First Name** label so the pointer changes to a ✛ shape.

7. Click and drag the selected controls to the top of the form, so the top left corner of the outline of the controls is to the right of and aligned with the top of the Listing ID controls, as shown in **Figure 4–17**, and then release the mouse button to move the selected controls.

FIGURE 4–17
Controls removed from control layout and moved to new position

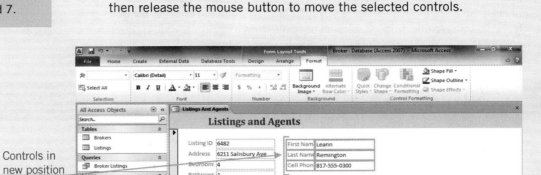

8. Save the form.

9. On the Ribbon, click the **Design** tab.

10. In the Themes group, click the **Themes** button. A gallery of themes opens. When you point to a theme in the gallery, its name appears in a ScreenTip and the form displays a Live Preview of the theme's fonts and colors.

11. Point to the **Apothecary** theme, which is the first theme in the second row of the Built-In section. Notice that the colors and fonts in the form change to show a Live Preview of this theme.

12. Point to the **Equity** theme, which is the third theme in the fourth row in the Built-In section, and notice the changes in the form.

13. Click the **Equity** theme to apply it to the form and close the Themes gallery.

14. In the Views group on the Design tab, click the **View** button. The form is displayed in Form view. See **Figure 4–18**. Leave the form open for the next Step-by-Step.

FIGURE 4–18
Form with Equity theme applied to it

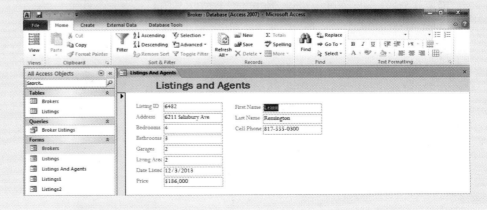

Adding an Unbound Control to a Form in Design View

Some changes that you need to make to a form require you to work in the third form view, Design view. In Design view, you see the controls that you added to the form on a grid, as shown in **Figure 4–19**. Unlike when working in Layout view, the controls do not display data from the record source. You must be in Design view to add controls such as lines, rectangles, and labels to a form. You add controls to the form by clicking the button for the desired control in the Controls group on the Design tab, and then clicking to position the control in the form. Another difference when working in Design view is that you see the Form Header, Detail, and Form Footer sections in the form. Each section contains a section bar at the top that you can click and select. You adjust the size of a section by clicking the bottom edge of the section and dragging it up or down to change its height. When you do not see a grid below a section, like the Form Footer section shown in Figure 4–19, the section height is set to zero. To expand a section, click the bottom edge of the section bar and then drag the border down to the desired height. You can see the position of objects in Design view as you are moving them, and you can position controls precisely by looking at the horizontal and vertical rulers that appear on the top and left sides of the form.

> **EXTRA FOR EXPERTS**
>
> To delete a control from a form, click the control to select it, and then press Delete.

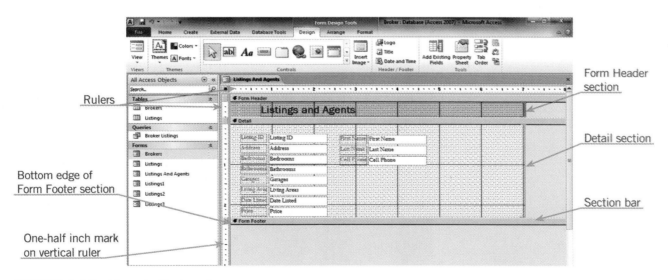

FIGURE 4–19   Form in Design view

Step-by-Step 4.11

1. Right-click the **Listings And Agents** object tab, and then click **Design View** on the shortcut menu. The form is displayed in Design view, as shown in Figure 4–19.

2. Point to the bottom edge of the Form Footer section so the pointer changes to a ✛ shape, and then drag the section bar down until the outline of the bottom edge of the section bar is at the one-half inch mark on the vertical ruler. Release the mouse button. The height of the Form Footer section increases, as shown in **Figure 4–20**.

FIGURE 4–20
Form Footer section with increased height

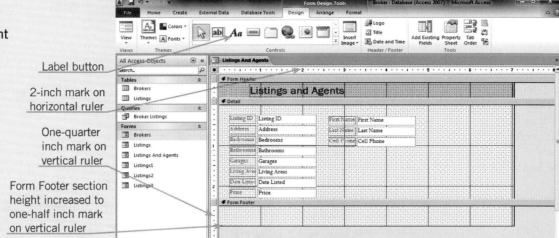

Label button

2-inch mark on horizontal ruler

One-quarter inch mark on vertical ruler

Form Footer section height increased to one-half inch mark on vertical ruler

3. In the Controls group on the Design tab, click the **Label** button. The Label tool is selected. When you move the pointer over the form, it changes to a ⁺A shape.

4. Move the ⁺A pointer into the Form Footer section so the plus sign in the pointer is at the 2-inch mark on the horizontal ruler and the one-quarter-inch mark on the vertical ruler, and then click. **Figure 4–21** shows the label control added to the Form Footer section. The insertion point is blinking inside the control, which will expand in size when you start typing.

FIGURE 4–21
Form Footer section with label control added

Label control

Listings And Agents

Form Header

Listings and Agents

Detail

Listing ID	Listing ID		First Name	First Name
Address	Address		Last Name	Last Name
Bedrooms	Bedrooms		Cell Phone	Cell Phone
Bathrooms	Bathrooms
Garages	Garages
Living Area	Living Areas
Date Listed	Date Listed
Price	Price

Form Footer

5. Type your first and last names, and then press **Enter**.

6. Save the form.

7. In the Views group on the Design tab, click the **View** button. The form is displayed in Form view, and the label control in the Form Footer section displays your name. Leave the form open for the next Step-by-Step.

Previewing and Printing a Form

You can preview and print a form. To preview a form, click the File tab to display Backstage view, click Print on the navigation bar, and then click Print Preview. Each record in the record source appears in a miniature version of the form, one after the other, on the page. To print all records in the form, click the File tab, click Print on the navigation bar, and then click Print to open the Print dialog box. Make sure the All option button is selected, and then click OK.

To print the form with the current record displayed, you must be in Form view and navigate to the desired record. Click the File tab, click Print on the navigation bar, and then click Print. The Print dialog box opens. Click the Selected Record(s) option button, and then click OK.

Step-by-Step 4.12

1. Click the **File** tab to display Backstage view, click **Print** on the navigation bar, and then click **Print Preview**. The form is displayed in Print Preview.

2. Use the buttons on the page navigation bar to display each page of the form. Notice that each record appears in a form, and the forms for each record are stacked on top of each other. The form's title, "Listings and Agents," appears once at the top of the first page, and your name appears once after the last form on the last page.

3. In the Close Preview group on the Print Preview tab, click the **Close Print Preview** button.

4. Navigate to record **3** in the form.

5. Click the **File** tab, click **Print** on the navigation bar, and then click **Print**. In the Print dialog box, make sure your printer is selected in the Name box, click the **Selected Record(s)** option button, and then click **OK**. The current record in the form is printed.

6. Close the **Listings And Agents** form.

7. Close the database, and then exit Access.

SUMMARY

In this lesson, you learned:

- A form is a database object that displays data from a record source. You can create a form using a form tool or wizard, or you can create a blank form from scratch.

- You can use the record navigation bar in Form view to navigate the records displayed in a form.

- The Find command is used to locate records in a table or query datasheet, form, or report. When finding data in a form, you need to identify the text to find, the field in which to search (or to search the entire form), the type of search to conduct (whole field, any part of field, or start of field), the desired case of the search text, and the direction to search or to search the entire form. You can also find and replace data using the Replace tab in the Find and Replace dialog box.

- You can use a form to update records or to add and delete records. When you make changes to data in a form, the changes are made in the record source on which the form is based.

- You can create a blank form and add fields to it by double-clicking the fields in the Field List pane in Layout view. When you add fields to a form, they are added to the form as controls in a control layout. You can resize and change the controls in a control layout as a group. You can also remove controls from a control layout so you can work with them individually.

- When you create a form in Layout view, the form has one default section, called the Detail section, that contains the controls that display the data in a form. Two other sections, which are added when the form's design uses controls that appear in these sections, are the Form Header section and the Form Footer section. The Form Header section usually contains the form's title, and the Form Footer section might contain labels that describe the form.

- You can add two types of controls to a form. A bound control is connected to a field in the record source and is used to display, enter, and update data. An unbound control is not connected to a record source and is used to display information, lines, rectangles, and pictures.

- You can preview and print all the records in a form, or you can use the Print dialog box to print only selected records in a form.

◼ VOCABULARY REVIEW

Define the following terms:

bound control	form	Layout view
control	Form Footer section	Multiple Items tool
control layout	Form Header section	record source
Datasheet tool	Form tool	Split Form tool
Detail section	Form view	theme
Field List pane	Form Wizard	unbound control
Find		

REVIEW QUESTIONS

TRUE / FALSE

Circle T if the statement is true or F if the statement is false.

T　F　**1.**　The table or query on which a form is based is called a record source.

T　F　**2.**　The Multiple Items tool creates a form that displays a form and a datasheet in separate panes.

T　F　**3.**　Many database experts agree that updates to the data in a database should be made using forms.

T　F　**4.**　When you click the Delete button in the Records group on the Home tab, the record displayed in Form view is deleted.

T　F　**5.**　When you add fields to a form in Layout view, the fields are added to a control layout.

WRITTEN QUESTIONS

Write a brief answer to each of the following questions.

1. The Find and Replace dialog box offers three options to help you match data in a form when searching the database. What are these three options and what do they do?

2. If you delete a record using a form, is it possible to undo the action? Why or why not?

3. How do you add fields to a blank form in Layout view?

4. When working in Layout view, how do you remove a field from a control layout in a form?

5. What is the difference between a bound control and an unbound control?

FILL IN THE BLANK

Complete the following sentences by writing the correct word or words in the blanks provided.

1. The _____ creates a simple form that includes all the fields in the selected table or query, uses a simple format, and includes a title with the same name as the record source.

2. When you add a field to a form in Layout view, the field's label and text box are added to the form in an object called a(n) _____.

3. When a form is displayed in _____ view, you can view the controls in the form and data from the record source at the same time.

4. The _____ creates a form using all the fields in the selected table or query and splits the window into two panes.

5. The _____ creates a form that looks just like a datasheet.

■ PROJECTS

If you have a SAM 2010 user profile, your instructor may have assigned an autogradable version of the indicated project. If so, log into the SAM 2010 Web site at *www.cengage.com/sam2010* to download the instruction and start files.

PROJECT 4–1

1. Open the **Recreation.accdb** database from the Access Lesson 04 folder with your Data Files.

2. Use the Form tool to create a form based on the Class table. Save the form as **Class Listing**.

3. Apply the Angles theme to the form.

4. Navigate the records in the record source until you find the record that has the longest field value in the Class Name text box.

5. Resize the width of the text boxes so the longest Class Name field value is displayed correctly.

6. Select the text box control for the Teacher ID field and then remove it from the control layout.

7. Select the Teacher ID label and text box controls, and then move them to the right of the Class ID text box, so the bottom edges of the Class ID and Teacher ID controls are aligned.

8. Change the text in the title control to **Class Listing**. Press Enter.

9. Change to Form view, and then navigate to record 8. Change the field value in the Location text field to your first and last names.

10. Print record 8.

11. Use the Class Listing form to add a new record using the following information: Class ID: **201**, Class Name: **Masters Swimming**, Location: **Swim Center**, Start Date: **6/1/2013**, End Date: **6/30/2013**, Fee: **100.00**, and Teacher ID: **12910**.

12. Save and close the form, close the Recreation database, and then exit Access.

SAM PROJECT 4–2

1. Open the **Teacher.accdb** database from the Access Lesson 04 folder with your Data Files.

2. Use the Split Form tool to create a form based on the Teacher table. Save the form as **Teacher Split Form**.

3. In the datasheet, select the First Name column value for the second record. Type your first name. Press Tab, and then type your last name in the Last Name column for record 2.

4. Change the text in the title control to **Teacher Information**, and then change the font style to italic. Save and close the form.

5. Use the Multiple Items tool to create a form based on the Class table. Save the form as **Class Information**.

6. In Layout view, resize the columns in the Class Information form so that each column is just wide enough to display the widest field value it contains.

7. Change the text in the title control to **Class Information**. Then change the font style to bold and the font color to Dark Blue (last row, column 9 in the Standard Colors gallery).

8. Change to Design view. Click below the Form Footer section to deselect any selected controls. Increase the height of the Form Footer section so it is one-half inch. Add a label to the Form Footer section at the 3-inch mark on the horizontal ruler and the one-quarter-inch mark on the vertical ruler. Type your first and last names in the label control.

9. Save the Class Information form, and then change to Form view.

10. Preview the Class Information form. Print the page in landscape orientation.

11. Close the Class Information form, close the Teacher database, and then exit Access.

PROJECT 4–3

1. Open the **Class.accdb** database from the Access Lesson 04 folder with your Data Files.

2. Create a blank form and save it as **Teachers And Classes**.

3. Add the following fields from the Class table to the form in the order listed: Class ID, Class Name, Location, Start Date, End Date, and Fee.

4. Use the Teacher table field list to add the Teacher ID field to the form, use the Property Update Options button to change the Teacher ID control to a text box control, and then add the following fields from the Teacher table to the form in the order listed: First Name, Last Name, and Phone. Close the Field List pane.

5. Select the Class ID label control, and then drag its right edge to the *right*, so that the text in all of the label controls in the control layout is fully visible.

6. Select the Teacher ID, First Name, Last Name, and Phone text box controls, and then remove them from the control layout.

7. Select the label and text box controls for the Teacher ID, First Name, Last Name, and Phone fields, and then move them to the right of the Class ID, Class Name, Location, and Start Date fields so the top of the Teacher ID text box is aligned with the top of the Class ID text box.

8. Add a title control to the form and use the default title.

9. Apply the Essential theme to the form.

10. Save the form and change to Design view.

11. Increase the height of the Form Footer section to one-half inch. Then add a label to the Form Footer section at the 2-inch mark on the horizontal ruler and the one-quarter-inch mark on the vertical ruler that contains your first and last names.

12. Save the form and change to Form view.

13. Navigate to record 9 in the form (Class ID 123). Change the End Date field value to **6/30/2013**. Print record 9.

14. Close the Teachers And Classes form, close the Class database, and then exit Access.

▪ CRITICAL THINKING

ACTIVITY 4–1

Open the **Broker.accdb** database from the Access Lesson 04 folder with your Data Files. Use the Form Wizard to create a form based on the Broker Listings query. Include all fields from the Broker Listings query in the form, view the data by broker in a form with a subform, use a Tabular layout, and use the name **Brokers Form** for the main form and **Listings Subform** for the subform. Click Finish. The form opens in Form view. Use the buttons on the record navigation bar at the bottom of the Form window to scroll through the records. How is the data in the subform related to the data in the main form? Explain your answer.

Display record 5 in the main form, change the field values in the Last Name and First Name fields to your last and first names, and then print record 5. Close the form, close the Broker database, and then exit Access.

ACTIVITY 4–2

Open the **Broker.accdb** database from the Access Lesson 04 folder with your Data Files. Open the **Listings** form in Layout view, examine the form's contents, and then change to Design view. Drag the bottom edge of the Detail section down approximately one inch to increase the height of this section. In the Controls group on the Design tab, click the Text Box button. Move the pointer to the Detail section, and click the plus sign in the pointer at the 4-inch mark on the horizontal ruler, approximately two rows of grid dots below the Broker ID text box control. A text box control and attached label are added to the form. Click in the text box control (which contains the word *Unbound*), and then type =[Price]*0.06 and press Enter. Click the label control (which contains the word *Text* and a number) to select it, double-click the text in the label control to select it, and then type **Commission**. Click the text box control (which contains the expression you entered), click the Property Sheet button in the Tools group on the Design tab to open the Property Sheet, click the All tab (if necessary), and then set the Format property to Currency. Close the Property Sheet, save the form, and then change to Form view. What kind of text box control did you create? What value is displayed in the Commission text box? Close the Listings form, close the Broker database, and then exit Access.

LESSON 5

Creating and Modifying Reports

■ OBJECTIVES

Upon completion of this lesson, you should be able to:

- Create a report using the Report tool, the Label Wizard, and the Report Wizard.
- Modify a report in Layout view.
- Modify a report in Design view.
- Add a line, label, and picture to a report.
- Move a control in a report.
- Resize a report.

■ VOCABULARY

grouping level

Label Wizard

Line tool

Print Preview

read-only

report

report selector

Report tool

Report Wizard

In this lesson, you will learn how to create and modify reports that display the data from the tables in your database in a format that you can print.

Creating a Report Using the Report Tool

A *report* is a database object that displays data from one or more tables or queries in a format that has an appearance similar to a printed report. Just as with forms, the tables or queries that contain the data used in a report are called the record source. You can use a report to create a formatted list of information or to summarize information in different ways. You can even use reports to print form letters and mailing labels.

Access includes tools that you can use to create different kinds of reports. After selecting the table or query in the Navigation Pane on which to base the report, click the Create tab on the Ribbon. The different options for creating reports are located in the Reports group on the Create tab. The *Report tool* quickly creates a simple report that includes all the fields in the selected table or query, uses a columnar format, formats the report using a theme, and includes a title with the same name as the record source. A report's theme formats the report and its controls using a predefined color, font, and design scheme. In addition, Access adds the current date and time at the top of the report and a page number at the bottom of the report. **Figure 5–1** shows a report created using the Report tool. The record source for the report is the Teacher table. Each field in the Teacher table appears in the report. When fields appear in a report, they appear in controls. For example, in this report, the Teacher ID label and the records shown below the labels appear in controls.

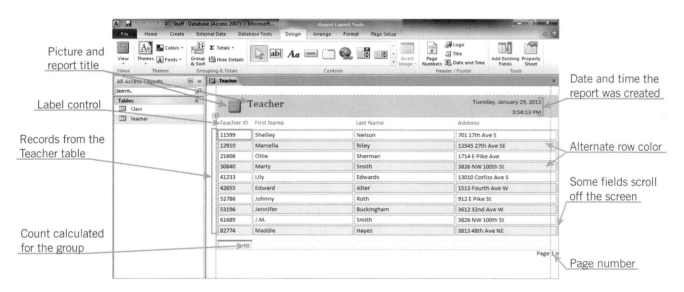

FIGURE 5–1   Report created using the Report tool

When you use the Report tool to create a report, the report opens initially in Layout view. In Layout view, you can view the controls in the report and data from the record source at the same time. In Layout view, you can make certain types of changes to the report's format and appearance, such as resizing a control. When you click a control in Layout view, an orange border appears around it to indicate that the control is selected.

Step-by-Step 5.1

1. Open the **Staff.accdb** database from the Access Lesson 05 folder where your Data Files are stored.

2. If the Security Warning opens, click the **Enable Content** button.

3. In the Navigation Pane, click the **Teacher** table to select it.

4. On the Ribbon, click the **Create** tab.

5. In the Reports group, click the **Report** button. Access creates a report using all the fields in the Teacher table, and formats it using the default Office theme. See Figure 5–1.

6. On the Quick Access Toolbar, click the **Save** button 🖫. Save the report as **Teacher List**.

7. Click the **Close 'Teacher List'** button ☒ to close the report. Leave the database open for the next Step-by-Step.

> **■ EXTRA FOR EXPERTS**
>
> Click the Themes button in the Themes group on the Design tab, and then point to a theme in the gallery to preview the theme, or click a theme to apply it.

The data in a report is ***read-only***, which means that you can view it but you cannot change it. If you need to make changes to the data in a report, close the report, and then open the record source on which the report is based. After making changes in the record source, the new data will be updated automatically when you open the report again.

> **▶ VOCABULARY**
> read-only
> **Label Wizard**

Creating a Report Using the Label Wizard

The *Label Wizard* lets you create a report that you can use to print standard or custom labels. To create labels, select the record source in the Navigation Pane, click the Create tab on the Ribbon, and then click the Labels button in the Reports group. Then use the Label Wizard dialog boxes to select the label you are using; to choose the font name, style, size, and color to use when printing the labels; to select the fields to include from the record source and their arrangement when printed on the labels; to select an optional sort order; and to choose a name for the report. **Figure 5–2** shows a report of mailing labels, printed three labels across the page and sorted in alphabetical order by the values in the Last Name field.

> **TIP**
>
> You can use the buttons in the Data group on the Print Preview tab to save the data in the report in another file format, such as a Microsoft Word document.

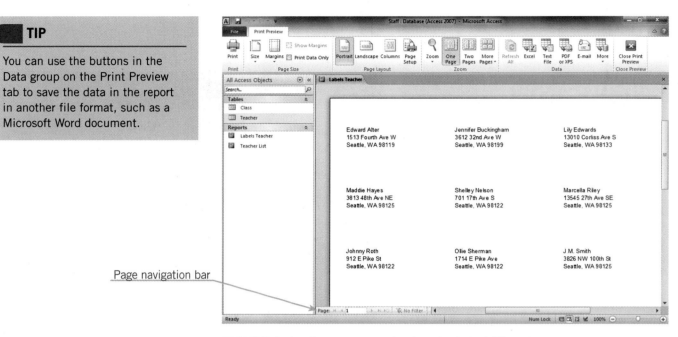

Page navigation bar

FIGURE 5–2   Report created using the Label Wizard

> ▶ **VOCABULARY**
> **Print Preview**

When you use a wizard to create a report, the report opens in *Print Preview*. When a report contains more than one page, you can click the buttons on the page navigation bar at the bottom of the Print Preview window to view additional pages in the report. You can also use the options on the Print Preview tab to change the page layout or zoom settings for the report.

Step-by-Step 5.2

1. In the Navigation Pane, make sure the **Teacher** table is selected.

2. On the Ribbon, click the **Create** tab. In the Reports group, click the **Labels** button. The Label Wizard starts and opens the first dialog box, in which you choose the type of label. See **Figure 5–3**.

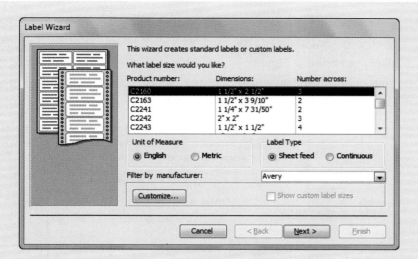

FIGURE 5–3
Using the Label Wizard to choose
a label

3. Make sure that **Avery** is selected in the Filter by manufacturer list box and
    that **C2160** is selected in the Product number column, and then click
    Next. **Figure 5–4** shows the second Label Wizard dialog box, in which you
    specify the font name, size, weight, and color that you want to use.

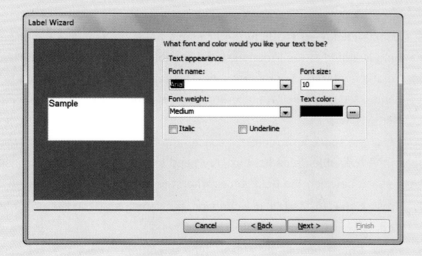

FIGURE 5–4
Using the Label Wizard to choose
the font

4. Make sure that the settings in your dialog box specify the Font name **Arial**, the Font size **10**, the Font weight **Medium**, and the Text color **black**, as shown in Figure 5–4, and then click **Next**. The third dialog box contains the Available fields list box, which contains the fields in the record source you selected. See **Figure 5–5**.

FIGURE 5–5
Using the Label Wizard to add fields to the label

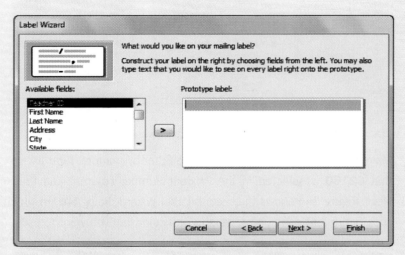

5. Double-click **First Name** in the Available fields list box. The First Name field is added to the Prototype label section. Notice that the First Name field is enclosed in curly brackets. This is how Access indicates a field name used in a label. An insertion point appears to the right of the First Name field.

6. Press the **spacebar** to insert a space, and then double-click **Last Name** in the Available fields list box. You need to press the spacebar to insert a space between the field values when they are printed on the label.

7. Press **Enter** to start a new line on the label, and then double-click **Address**.

8. Press **Enter**, double-click **City**, type a **comma**, press the **spacebar**, double-click **State**, press the **spacebar**, and then double-click **Zip**. **Figure 5–6** shows the completed prototype of the label.

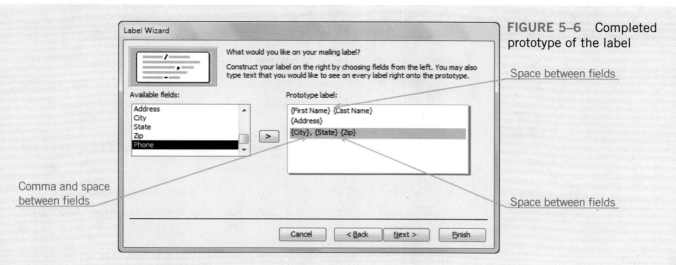

FIGURE 5–6   Completed prototype of the label

9. Make sure that your prototype label matches the one shown in Figure 5–6, and then click **Next**.

10. In the Available fields list box in the fourth dialog box, double-click **Last Name** to add it to the Sort by list box. The labels will be printed in alphabetical order based on the values in the Last Name field.

11. Click **Next**. In the final dialog box, make sure **Labels Teacher** appears in the text box and that the **See the labels as they will look printed** option button is selected, and then click **Finish**. Refer back to Figure 5–2, which shows the report in Print Preview.

12. Click the **Close 'Labels Teacher'** button ⊠ to close the Labels Teacher report.

13. Close the Navigation Pane. Leave the database open for the next Step-by-Step.

Creating a Report Using the Report Wizard

When you need to create a customized report quickly, you can use the *Report Wizard*, which asks you about the report you want to create and lets you select options in dialog boxes to specify the report's record source and layout. Another option for a report is to select a grouping level. A *grouping level* organizes data based on one or more fields. For example, in a customer report, you might choose to group records using the State field so the records will be listed by the state in which customers live. You can also choose an optional sort order for the report, so records in one or more fields are sorted in ascending or descending order. The layout options for reports are Stepped, Block, and Outline, which arrange data in different ways. You can also choose the page orientation for the report (portrait or landscape). When you use the Report Wizard to create a report, Access applies the default theme for the database to the report.

▶ **VOCABULARY**
Report Wizard
grouping level

Step-by-Step 5.3

TIP

After using the Report Wizard or the Report tool to create a report, you can use the tools and features in Access to customize the report.

1. On the Ribbon, click the **Create** tab. In the Reports group, click the **Report Wizard** button. The Report Wizard starts and opens the first dialog box, in which you choose the record source for the report and the fields to print in the report.

2. Click the **Tables/Queries** arrow, and then click **Table: Class** in the list. The fields for the Class table appear in the Available Fields list box.

3. Double-click the following fields in the order listed to add them to the Selected Fields list box: **Class ID**, **Class Name**, **Location**, **Start Date**, and **Fee**.

4. Click the **Tables/Queries** arrow, and then click **Table: Teacher** in the list. The fields for the Teacher table appear in the Available Fields list box.

5. Double-click the following fields in the order listed to add them to the Selected Fields list box below the selected Fee field from the Class table: **Teacher ID**, **First Name**, and **Last Name**.

6. Click **Next**. The dialog box shown in **Figure 5–7** asks how you want to view your data. Leave the Report Wizard open for the next Step-by-Step.

FIGURE 5–7
Report Wizard dialog box that asks how you want to view your data

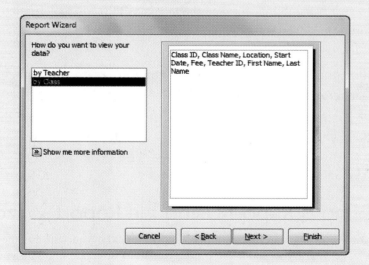

The dialog box shown in Figure 5–7 opens because you added fields from two related tables to the report's design. The sample page on the right of the dialog box illustrates how the data will be grouped in the report if it is grouped by the selected option (in this case, data is grouped by the Class table). You can also choose to group data by the Teacher table. In this case, you'll see the teacher's ID, first name, and last name and the classes each teacher has in a group. After selecting a grouping option based on a table, you can use the next dialog box to add an additional grouping level to the report by choosing a field.

Step-by-Step 5.4

1. In the dialog box, click **by Teacher**. The sample page changes to show the data grouped by teacher. See **Figure 5–8**.

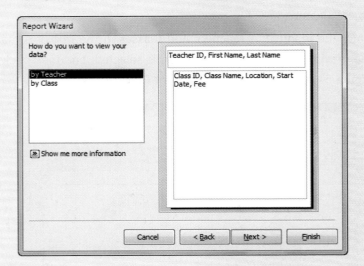

FIGURE 5–8
Report Wizard dialog box that shows data grouped by teacher

2. Click **Next**. You won't add an additional grouping level field to the report.

3. Click **Next**. A dialog box opens and asks if you want to add a sort order to the report. The default sort order, Ascending, is already set. To change to descending sort order, click the Ascending button to change it to Descending.

4. Click the **arrow** on the first text box, click **Class Name** in the list, and then click **Next**. The next dialog box requests information about the layout and page orientation that you would like to use in the report. A preview of the selected Stepped layout appears on the left side of the dialog box, as shown in **Figure 5–9**.

TIP

You cannot sort data in a report using a field that is already used to group records.

Sample report layout using the selected options →

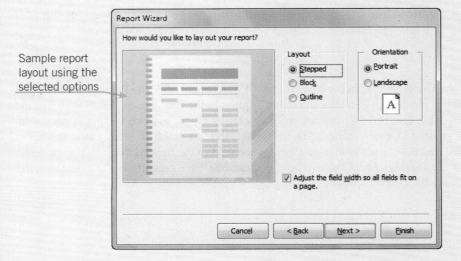

FIGURE 5–9
Report Wizard dialog box that requests page layout information

5. Click the **Block** option button to view a sample of this layout.

6. Click the **Outline** option button to view a sample of this layout.

7. Click the **Landscape** option button, click the **Block** option button, and then click **Next**. The final dialog box lets you accept the default report title or enter a new one. The report title you enter will also be the report object's name.

8. Enter the report title **Teachers And Classes** in the text box, make sure the **Preview the report** option button is selected, and then click **Finish**. **Figure 5–10** shows the report in Print Preview.

FIGURE 5–10
Report created using the Report Wizard

Report pages use landscape orientation

Teacher with four classes

Teacher with one class

Some of the page scrolls off the screen

Layout View button

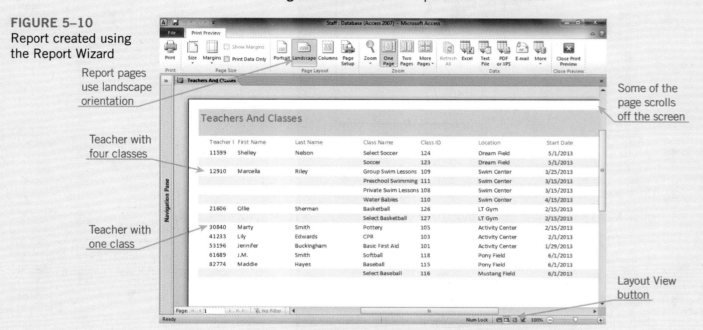

9. Use the horizontal scroll bar to scroll the report so you can see the right side of the page.

10. In the Zoom group on the Print Preview tab, click the **Zoom button arrow**, and then click **Fit to Window**. Leave the report open for the next Step-by-Step.

The report created by the Report Wizard opens in Print Preview because you chose the default "Preview the report" option in the final dialog box. Notice that the report is grouped by teachers, with the classes taught by each teacher appearing in a group with each teacher's ID, first name, and last name. In many cases, the report will need some adjustments to display the data in the desired manner. For example, in the Teachers And Classes report, you can resize the columns in the report to better fit the data they display.

Modifying a Report in Layout View

Most developers use reports to provide on-screen displays or paper printouts of data in the database. An easy way to create a report is to use the Report Wizard to specify the report's record source, fields, grouping and sorting levels, layout, and name. However, if you find that the Report Wizard doesn't create the *exact* report that you need, you can use Layout view to make adjustments. When you close the report in Print Preview, Access displays the report in Design view. To change directly to Layout view, click the Layout View button on the status bar.

When the controls in a report exceed the page width that you selected for the report, you can usually resize the fields to make them fit on the page. Controls in reports are grouped in control layouts, just like they are in forms. When resizing a control in Layout view, you can use the outline of the control as you drag it with the pointer to see the actual width of the control. You can also look at the status bar to see the control's width in characters and size a control exactly.

> **⌨ EXTRA FOR EXPERTS**
>
> You can remove a control from a control layout in a report just like you can for a form. Display the report in Layout view, click the control to select it, right-click the control to open the shortcut menu, point to Layout, and then click Remove Layout.

Step-by-Step 5.5

1. On the status bar, click the **Layout View** button ⊞. The report is displayed in Layout view, as shown in **Figure 5–11**. (If the Field List pane opens when you change to Layout view, click the Add Existing Fields button in the Tools group on the Design tab to close it.)

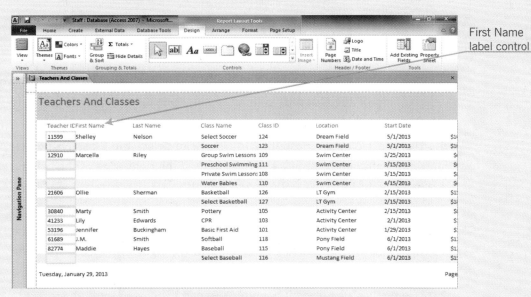

First Name label control

FIGURE 5–11
Teachers And Classes report in Layout view

2. Click the **First Name** label control (at the top of the column) to select the control, press and hold **Shift**, click the first text box control in the First Name column (which contains the field value *Shelley*) to select it, and then release **Shift**. The entire First Name column is selected, with an orange border around the label control and each text box control in the column. You'll resize this column from the left side, so the column size decreases. This will also add some space between the Teacher ID and First Name columns, so you can resize the Teacher ID column later.

3. Point to the left edge of the **First Name** label control. When the pointer changes to a ↔ shape, click and slowly drag the left edge of the **First Name** label control to the right, which decreases the size of the First Name column from the left side. When the lower-left corner of the status bar shows the width as 10 characters, release the mouse button. **Figure 5–12** shows the resized First Name column. Because the label and all of the text boxes in the column are part of a control layout, they are all resized to 10 characters wide.

FIGURE 5–12
Resized First Name column

4. Use the technique described in Steps 2 and 3 to select and resize the left side of the **Class ID** column to the right to decrease its width to 8 characters.

5. Use the technique described in Step 2 to select the **Class Name** column, and then use the ↔ pointer to drag the right edge of the column to the right to increase the column width to 20 characters.

6. Use the technique described in Step 2 to select the **Teacher ID** column (the first column in the report), and then use the pointer to resize the right side of the **Teacher ID** column to the right to increase its width to 10 characters.

7. Use the horizontal scroll bar on the Report window to scroll the report to the right so you can see the Fee column, use the technique described in Step 2 to select the **Fee** column, and then use the pointer to resize the right side of the **Fee** column to the left to decrease its width to 10 characters. **Figure 5-13** shows the report with the resized columns. Leave the report open for the next Step-by-Step.

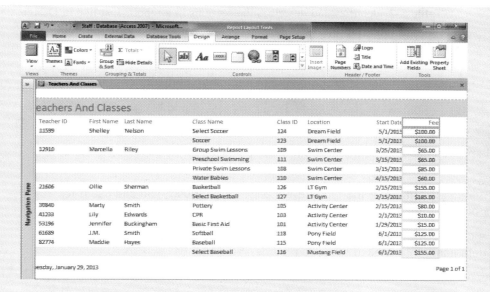

FIGURE 5–13
Report with resized columns

Modifying a Report in Design View

Similar to working with forms, there are certain types of changes for reports that you must make in Design view. When you view a report in Design view, you see the different sections of the report.

Step-by-Step 5.6

1. On the Quick Access Toolbar, click the **Save** button 🔲 to save the changes to the report.

2. On the status bar, click the **Design View** button 📐. The report is displayed in Design view, as shown in **Figure 5–14**. Leave the report open for the next Step-by-Step.

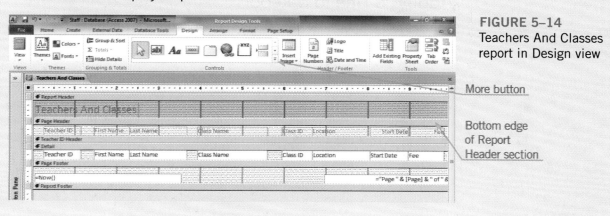

FIGURE 5–14
Teachers And Classes report in Design view

More button

Bottom edge of Report Header section

Table 5–1 identifies and describes the sections in a report. Just like in Design view for forms, you can adjust the height of a section by dragging its bottom edge up or down, and you can select a section in a report by clicking its section bar.

TABLE 5–1   Report sections

SECTION	DESCRIPTION
Report Header	This section is printed once at the top of the first page of the report, and usually includes the report title.
Page Header	Because this section is printed at the top of every page of the report, you can use it to print a title or other information that is required on every page.
Group Header	This section is printed at the beginning of each new group of records. The section name includes the field name that is used to group records.
Detail	This section is printed once for each row in the record source and contains the main body of the report.
Group Footer	This section is printed at the end of each group of records and usually includes summary options, such as totals. The section name includes the field name that is used to group records.
Page Footer	Because this section is printed at the bottom of every page of the report, you can use it to include page numbers or other information that you want to print at the bottom of every page.
Report Footer	This section is printed once at the bottom of the last page of the report, and usually includes summary information for the entire report, such as grand totals.

The Controls group on the Design tab for a report looks similar to the Controls group that you see in Design view for a form. To add a control to a report, click the button in the Controls group (or click the More button in the Controls group to display buttons not shown on the Ribbon), and then click the desired location in which to add the control in the report.

Adding a Line to a Report

The *Line tool* lets you draw a line in a report. Adding lines to a report makes it easier for users to identify the report sections and also adds visual interest. To insert a line, click the More button in the Controls group on the Design tab, and then click the Line button. Move the pointer to the report, position the plus sign in the pointer where you want the line to begin, and then click and drag the pointer to the location where you want the line to end. When you release the mouse button, the line will appear in the report. To draw a straight line, press and hold Shift while drawing the line. You can use the horizontal and vertical rulers at the top and left side of the report in Design view to help you draw a line on the report, or to position other controls on the report.

Step-by-Step 5.7

1. Point to the bottom edge of the **Report Header** section. When the pointer changes to a ✛ shape, click and drag the **Report Header** section down to the ¾-inch mark on the vertical ruler.

2. In the Controls group on the Design tab, click the **More** button ⏷ to open the Controls gallery, and then click the **Line** button (second row, third button).

3. Move the pointer to the **Report Header** section. Position the plus sign in the ⁺⟍ pointer at the ½-inch mark on the vertical ruler and in the first column of grid dots (just below the "T" in the Teachers And Classes title).

4. Press and hold **Shift**. Hold down the left mouse button, and then drag the pointer to the 9.5-inch mark on the horizontal ruler. Release the mouse button, and then release **Shift**. A line appears in the Report Header section, as shown in **Figure 5–15**.

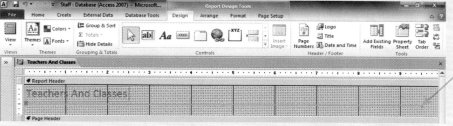

FIGURE 5–15
Line in Report
Header section

Selected line
control

5. On the Ribbon, click the **Format** tab.

6. In the Control Formatting group, click the **Shape Outline** button, point to **Line Thickness**, and then point to the fourth line style in the list. Notice that the ScreenTip identifies the line thickness as "3 pt," which indicates a line thickness of three points.

7. Click the line with the ScreenTip "3 pt."

TIP

To change the style of a selected line, click the Shape Outline button, point to Line Type, and then click one of the line styles.

8. Click the **Report Header** section bar to deselect the line control. **Figure 5–16** shows the line with the thickness you selected.

FIGURE 5–16
Report Header section with line added

Line with 3 pt thickness

Label control will be added here

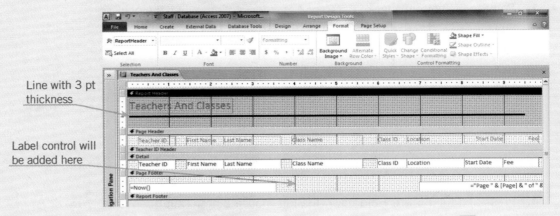

9. On the Quick Access Toolbar, click the **Save** button 🖫 to save the report. Leave the report open for the next Step-by-Step.

Adding a Label Control to a Report

You can add new controls to a report by using the tools in the Controls group. Just like when used in forms, you can add text to a report by adding it in the label control. You can delete a control from a report in Design view by clicking it to select it and then pressing Delete. If the selected control is part of a control layout, you'll need to remove it from the control layout first, or you'll delete all controls in the control layout.

Step-by-Step 5.8

1. On the Ribbon, click the **Design** tab.

2. In the Controls group, click the **Label** button (third button from the left).

3. Move the pointer to the Page Footer section. Move the plus sign in the ⁺A pointer to the 4-inch mark on the horizontal ruler, in the fourth row of grid dots from the top of the Page Footer section. (Refer to Figure 5–16 for this location, if necessary.) Click to insert the label control, which is a very narrow box that contains the insertion point.

4. Type your first and last names, and then press **Enter**. The insertion point is removed from the label control, which now has an orange border to show that it's still selected.

5. On the Quick Access Toolbar, click the **Save** button 🖫 to save the report.

TIP

Point to a button in the Controls group to display its name in a ScreenTip.

6. On the status bar, click the **Print Preview** button. **Figure 5–17** shows the report with the line and label controls added to it. Leave the report open for the next Step-by-Step.

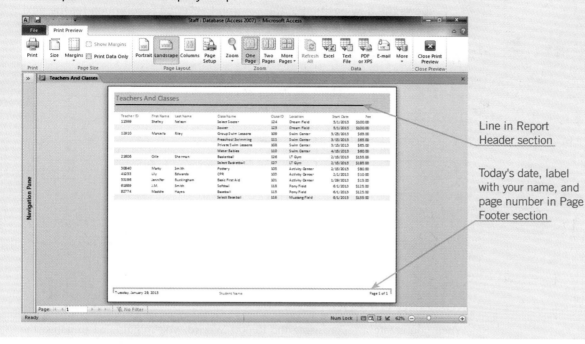

FIGURE 5–17
Teachers And Classes report in Print Preview

Line in Report Header section

Today's date, label with your name, and page number in Page Footer section

Moving a Control in Design View

The report's controls all fit on the page, but the control in the Page Footer section, which was added by the Report Wizard and contains the page number, is not aligned with the data on the report. You can drag a control to position it better on the page.

Step-by-Step 5.9

1. On the status bar, click the **Design View** button.

2. In the Page Footer section, click the control on the right, which contains the text that begins =*"Page "* &. The control is selected when it has an orange border.

3. Point to the top edge of the selected control so the pointer changes to a shape.

4. Drag the selected control to the left, so the left edge of the control is at the 6.25-inch mark on the horizontal ruler and the bottom edge of the control is at the bottom of the Page Footer section. **Figure 5–18** shows the new position of the control. Leave the report open for the next Step-by-Step.

FIGURE 5–18
Control in new position

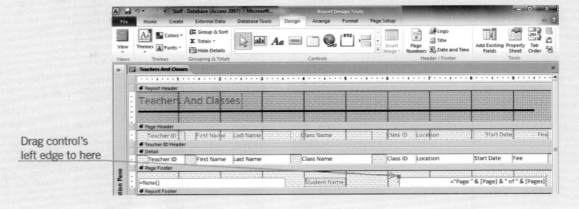

Drag control's left edge to here

Resizing a Report

When you create a report using the Report Wizard, you might need to adjust the report's width to eliminate blank pages. You know that you need to make this change when you switch to Print Preview and get an error message that tells you that your report contains blank pages or when you see blank pages in the report.

To resize a report, you can position the pointer on the report's right edge in Design view so it changes to a ✛ shape, and then click and drag the report's right edge to the left to reduce the report's width. Another way to resize a report is to use the **report selector**, which appears in the upper-left corner of the report, where the horizontal and vertical rulers intersect. When you see a small, green triangle on the report selector, clicking the report selector displays the Error Checking Options button, which you can click to open a shortcut menu with options for correcting the error. When the report contains blank pages, the shortcut menu contains options to edit the report margins, or remove extra report space. To resize the report to fit its controls, click the Remove Extra Report Space option.

The controls for the Fee field are just past the 9.5-inch mark on the horizontal ruler. To practice resizing the report, you'll use the pointer to increase the report's width, and then you'll use the report selector and the Error Checking Options button to resize the report to fit the controls it contains.

▶ **VOCABULARY**
report selector

Step-by-Step 5.10

1. Use the horizontal scroll bar to scroll the report to the right, so you can see the right edge of the report and the 13-inch mark on the horizontal ruler.

2. Point to the right edge of the report so the pointer changes to a ✛ shape, and then click and drag the report's right edge to the right. When the report's edge is at the 13-inch mark on the horizontal ruler, release

the mouse button. The report is resized to 13 inches wide. Notice that the report selector now displays a small, green triangle, indicating that the report contains an error. See **Figure 5-19**. (If you do not see the green triangle, follow the instructions in the Tip box on this page.)

Report selector with green triangle indicates an error

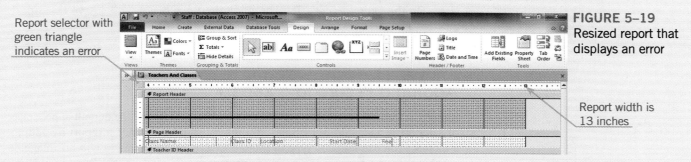

FIGURE 5–19
Resized report that displays an error

Report width is 13 inches

3. On the status bar, click the **Print Preview** button 🔍. A dialog box opens and indicates that some pages may be blank.

4. Click **OK**. The dialog box closes, and the report appears in Print Preview. Notice that the Next Page button on the page navigation bar is active, indicating that the report contains one or more additional pages.

5. On the page navigation bar, click the **Next Page** button ▶. The second page of the report is blank, except for the default colors used in the report.

6. On the status bar, click the **Design View** button to display the report in Design view.

7. Click the **report selector**. The Error Checking Options button ◈ appears below the report selector.

8. Click the **Error Checking Options** button ◈. **Figure 5–20** shows the shortcut menu that opens after you click the button.

> **TIP**
>
> If you do not see the green triangle shown in Figure 5-19, save and close the report, click the File tab on the Ribbon, click Options in the navigation bar, click Object Designers, scroll down the page, click the Enable error checking check box, click OK, open the report in Design view, and close the Navigation Pane.

Report selector

Error Checking Options button

Remove Extra Report Space option

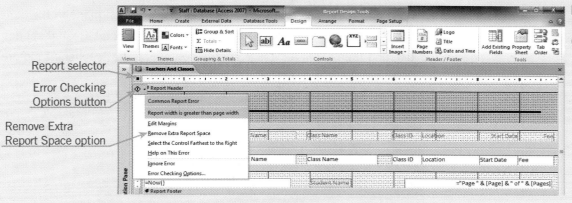

FIGURE 5–20
Error Checking Options shortcut menu

9. On the shortcut menu, click **Remove Extra Report Space**. The report's width is reduced to fit the controls it contains. You can see the right edge of the report now, just to the right of the controls at or around the 9.75-inch mark on the horizontal ruler.

10. On the Quick Access Toolbar, click the **Save** button 🖫. Leave the report open for the next Step-by-Step.

Adding a Picture to a Report

Reports are usually printed or viewed on the screen. Although the default appearance of a report is adequate, sometimes you might want to enhance a report by adding a picture. You can add any type of picture to a report, including a clip-art image, a graphic that you create using another program, or a digital image. To add a picture to a report, click the Insert Image button in the Controls group on the Design tab, and then click Browse. In the Insert Picture dialog box, browse to and select the file that contains the picture you want to insert in the report. After selecting the file, click OK. The pointer changes shape when you move it over the report. Click the plus sign in the pointer in the upper-left corner where you want to insert the picture. An image control is added to the report. You can use the sizing handles on the selected image control to resize the picture to the desired size and shape. You can also drag the selected image control to reposition it in the report.

Step-by-Step 5.11

1. In the Controls group on the Design tab, click the **Insert Image** button, and then click **Browse**. The Insert Picture dialog box opens.

2. Browse to the **Access Lesson 05** folder with your Data Files.

3. Click the **Teacher.gif** file to select it, and then click **OK**. The Insert Picture dialog box closes.

4. Position the plus sign in the ⁺🖾 pointer at the 4-inch mark on the horizontal ruler and one row of grid dots below the Report Header section bar, and then click. An image control containing the Teacher.gif picture is inserted in the report, as shown in **Figure 5–21**.

FIGURE 5–21
Image control
added to report

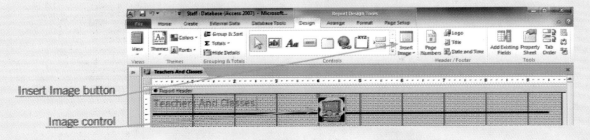

Insert Image button

Image control

5. Drag the selected image control to the right in the Report Header section so that the right edge of the image control is at the **right edge** of the report. There should be one row of grid dots above the picture. **Figure 5–22** shows the image control in the new location.

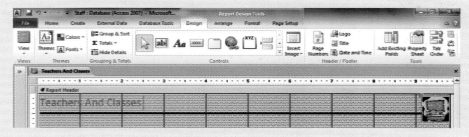

FIGURE 5–22
Image control moved to new location

6. On the Quick Access Toolbar, click the **Save** button.
7. On the status bar, click the **Print Preview** button. **Figure 5–23** shows the completed report.

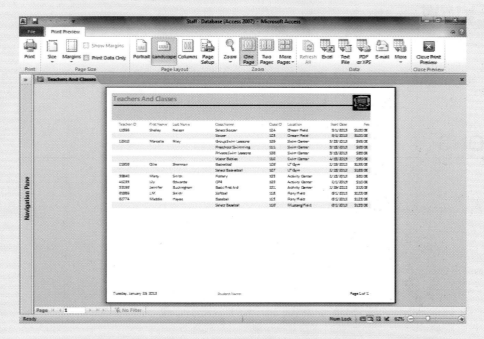

FIGURE 5–23
Completed report in Print Preview

8. In the Close Preview group on the Print Preview tab, click the **Close Print Preview** button.
9. Close the Teachers And Classes report.
10. Click the **Close** button on the Access title bar to exit Access.

SUMMARY

In this lesson, you learned:

- A report is a database object that displays data from one or more tables or queries in a format that has an appearance similar to a printed report. You can use the Report tool or the Report Wizard to create a report. You can also use the Label Wizard to create a report that is used to print labels.

- When used in a report, a field that is used as a grouping level organizes data into groups. You can also choose to sort data within the groups based on a field.

- When working in Layout view, you can resize the controls in a control layout by selecting the control and dragging its edge to increase or decrease its width.

- You can use Design view to change the height of a report section. You can also add a line, label, or picture to a report. You can change the location of a control in a report by dragging it to a new location.

- When a report contains blank pages, drag the right edge of the report to resize the report, or click the report selector to select the report, click the Error Checking Options button, and then click the Remove Extra Report Space option on the shortcut menu to resize the report.

VOCABULARY REVIEW

Define the following terms:

grouping level	Print Preview	report selector
Label Wizard	read-only	Report tool
Line tool	report	Report Wizard

REVIEW QUESTIONS

TRUE / FALSE

Circle T if the statement is true or F if the statement is false.

T   F   **1.** When you use the Report tool to create a report, you can base it on two or more tables.

T   F   **2.** When a report is displayed in Layout view, you can use it to change the data the report contains.

T   F   **3.** When you use the Report Wizard to create a report, you can base it on one or more tables.

T   F   **4.** If you want to print something only at the bottom of the last page of a report, add the content in the Page Footer section.

T   F   **5.** To draw a straight line in a report, press and hold down Shift while you draw the line.

WRITTEN QUESTIONS

Write a brief answer to each of the following questions.

1. List the steps for using the Report tool to create a report based on a table.

2. List the steps for using the Label Wizard to create a report based on a table.

3. What information might you include in the Report Header section of a report?

4. How do you use the report selector to resize a report that contains one or more blank pages when the report selector contains a small, green triangle on it?

5. Which button in the Controls group on the Design tab do you use to add a picture to a report?

FILL IN THE BLANK

Complete the following sentences by writing the correct word or words in the blanks provided.

1. The _____ creates a simple report that includes all the fields in the selected table or query, uses a simple columnar format, formats every other row in the report with a gray color, and includes a title with the same name as the record source.

2. The _____ creates a report that you can use to print standard or custom labels.

3. The data in a report is _____, which means that you can view it but you cannot change it.

4. A(n) _____ organizes data in a report based on one or more fields.

5. The _____ section is printed once at the bottom of the last page of the report, and usually includes summary information for the entire report, such as grand totals.

■ PROJECTS

If you have a SAM 2010 user profile, your instructor may have assigned an autogradable version of the indicated project. If so, log into the SAM 2010 Web site at *www.cengage.com/sam2010* to download the instruction and start files.

PROJECT 5–1

1. Open the **Sales.accdb** database from the Access Lesson 05 folder with your Data Files.

2. Use the Report tool to create a report based on the Brokers table.

3. In Layout view, resize each column so that it is just wide enough to display the longest value in the column.

4. In Design view, add a label control at the top of the Report Footer section and at the 4-inch mark on the horizontal ruler. Type your first and last names in the label control.

5. Use the report selector and the Error Checking Options button to resize the report to remove extra report space.

6. Save the report using the name **Brokers**.

7. Display the report in Print Preview. Change the page orientation to landscape. Make sure that the report is displayed on a single page. If necessary, display the report in Layout view or Design view and make any required adjustments. Save the report, and then close it.

8. Use the Report tool to create a report based on the Listings table.

9. In Layout view, resize each column so that each column is just wide enough to display the longest value in the column.

10. In Design view, add a label control at the top of the Report Footer section and at the 1-inch mark on the horizontal ruler. Type your first and last names in the label control.

11. Use the report selector and the Error Checking Options button to resize the report to remove extra report space.

12. Save the report using the name **Listings**.

13. Display the report in Print Preview, change to landscape orientation, and make sure that it is displayed on a single page. If necessary, display the report in Layout view or Design view and make any required adjustments. Save the report if you make any changes, and then close it.

14. Close the database and exit Access.

PROJECT 5–2

1. Open the **Supplies.accdb** database from the Access Lesson 05 folder with your Data Files.

2. Use the Report tool to create a report based on the Products table.

3. In Layout view, resize each column so that each column is just wide enough to display the longest value in the column. Scroll down the page and check to be sure that all values in each column are displayed.

4. In Design view, add a label control at the top of the Report Footer section and at the 1-inch mark on the horizontal ruler. Type your first and last names in the label control.

5. Click the control in the Report Footer section that displays a sum of the values in the Retail Price field and remove it from the control layout.

6. Press Delete to delete the control in the Report Footer section that displays a sum of the values in the Retail Price field.

7. Delete the image control to the left of the Products title.

8. Insert the **Office.gif** file as a picture in the Report Footer section of the report, so the upper-left corner of the picture is at the 6-inch mark on the horizontal ruler and at the top of the Report Footer section.

9. Use the pointer to resize the report so its right edge is aligned with the controls that display the date and time in the Report Header section.

10. Save the report using the name **Products**.

11. Preview the report. If necessary, display the report in Layout view or Design view and make any required adjustments. Save the report, and then print it.

12. Close the database, and then exit Access.

PROJECT 5–3

1. Open the **Agencies.accdb** database from the Access Lesson 05 folder with your Data Files.

2. Use the Report Wizard to create a new report based on the Brokers and Listings tables.

3. Add the following fields from the Brokers table to the report in the order listed: Affiliation, Broker ID, First Name, Last Name, Office Phone, and Cell Phone.

4. Add the following fields from the Listings table to the report in the order listed: Price, Address, and Date Listed.

5. View the data by brokers.

6. Use the Affiliation field as a grouping level. (Click the Affiliation field, and then click the $\boxed{>}$ button.)

7. Sort the data in ascending order by Price.

8. Choose the Stepped layout and the Landscape orientation.

9. Use the report title **Brokers And Listings** and choose the option to preview it.

10. In Layout view, resize each column so that the column is just wide enough to display the longest value in the column. (*Hint*: You might need to resize some columns from the left and others from the right. Resize the columns so they are closer together by first resizing columns that are far apart from the left, and then from the right.)

11. Change to Print Preview and make sure that all the data in the main body of the report fits on one page. If necessary, return to Layout view and continue resizing the columns.

12. Add a label control anywhere in the Report Header section that contains your first and last names. Press Enter after typing your name, and then move the label control so its right edge is aligned at the 10-inch mark on the horizontal ruler and at the top of the Report Header section.

13. Save and preview the report.

14. Close the report, close the database, and exit Access.

■ CRITICAL THINKING

ACTIVITY 5–1

Open the **Sales.accdb** database from the Access Lesson 05 folder with your Data Files. Open the Brokers report that you created in Project 5-1 in Print Preview. Why does the label control that contains your name print above the page number? What change would you need to make to print your name below the page number? Write your answer on a sheet of paper. Your answer should be specific to the Brokers report. Close the report, close the database, and exit Access.

ACTIVITY 5–3

In this lesson, you learned how to use the Label Wizard to create labels that you might use to address envelopes or packages. What other uses can you think of for creating labels from a database? On a sheet of paper, give one example of the kind of labels that you might need and how you would use Access to create a record source and print the labels.

ACTIVITY 5–2

Open the **Sales.accdb** database from the Access Lesson 05 folder with your Data Files. Open the Listings report that you created in Project 5-1 in Print Preview. A line and a number appear at the bottom of the Price column. What does the number represent? What do you call this? What was used to create this number? You used the Report tool to create the Listings report. Why do you think that the Report tool added this number to the report? Write your answer on a sheet of paper. Your answer should be specific to the Listings report. Close the report, close the database, and exit Access.

LESSON 6

Integrating Access

■ OBJECTIVES

Upon completion of this lesson, you should be able to:

- Import data from other programs into an Access database.
- Export data from an Access database to other programs.
- Prepare a form letter for merging with a data source.
- Merge a form letter with a data source.
- Edit a data source to print specific form letters.

■ VOCABULARY

comma-separated values (CSV)

data source

delimited data

delimiter

export

form letter

import

main document

merge field

In this lesson, you will learn how to use Access to import and export data from other programs and to create form letters.

Importing and Exporting Data

Sometimes you might find that you need to use the data stored in an Access database in another program. For example, a friend or coworker who does not have Access might request information from you. You can share the information with them by saving it in another file format. When you save data in another file format, you *export* the data from the database. You can export data to many other formats, including a Word document, an Excel workbook, or a text file. Access also exports data to another Access database, another database format, or an HTML document (which creates a Web page).

> ▶ **VOCABULARY**
> **export**
> **import**

You might also find yourself in a situation where you need to add data stored in a different format to an Access database. Instead of entering the records one at a time, you can *import* the data into the database. When you import data, you copy it from another Access database, an Excel workbook, a text file, or another compatible file format into an existing or new table in the current database. Importing saves you time and effort by adding records to a new or existing table automatically. Fortunately, Access includes features that make it easy to import and export data to and from a database.

Importing and Exporting Documents

When you need to export data from a database table to a Word document, select the table in the Navigation Pane, click the External Data tab on the Ribbon, click the More button in the Export group, and then click Word. When you export the data, it will be saved as an RTF file, which stands for Rich Text Format. Most word processors, including Word, can open files with the .rtf file extension.

Step-by-Step 6.1

1. Open the **School.accdb** database from the Access Lesson 06 folder where your Data Files are stored.

2. If the Security Warning opens, click the **Enable Content** button.

3. Click the **Student** table in the Navigation Pane to select it. On the Ribbon, click the **External Data** tab.

4. In the Export group, click the **More** button, and then click **Word**. The Export – RTF File dialog box opens, as shown in **Figure 6–1**.

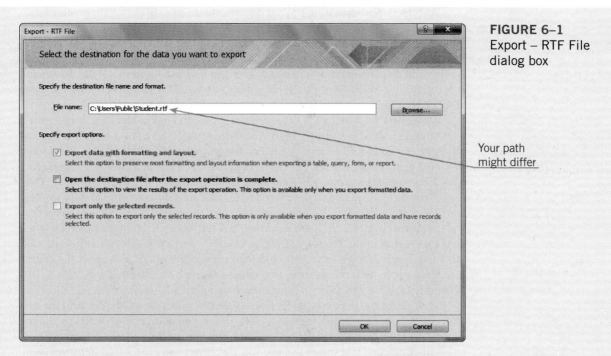

FIGURE 6–1
Export – RTF File
dialog box

Your path
might differ

5. Click **Browse** and navigate to the drive and folder where your Data Files
    are stored, open the **Access Lesson 06** folder, and then click **Save** in the
    File Save dialog box to close it.

6. Click the **Open the destination file after the export operation is complete**
    check box to add a check mark to it.

7. Click **OK** to export the data. Word starts and opens the Student.rtf file
    that you created. The data appears in a table format when viewed in
    Word. See **Figure 6–2**.

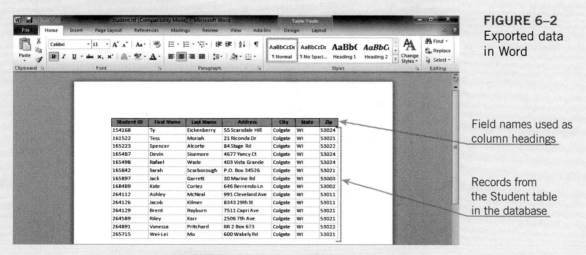

FIGURE 6–2
Exported data
in Word

Field names used as
column headings

Records from
the Student table
in the database

8. Click the **Close** button ![Close button] on the Word title bar to close Word.

9. Click **Close** to close the Export – RTF File dialog box. (You do not need to
    save the export steps.) Leave the database open for the next Step-by-Step.

You can import data from a Word document into an existing database table when the data has the same number of columns and the same *type* of data as the database table. For example, if the Access table has a field that is defined using the Number data type, you cannot import text data (containing letters) into the field. In this case, Access will display an error message. When you import data from a Word document, it is usually best to store it in a Word table. The Word table must contain the same number of columns as the database table.

When data is stored in another format, you can import the data and create a new table in a database in one step. When importing data from a text file, the data might be stored in a file format called ***comma-separated values (CSV)***. Most word processing, spreadsheet, and database programs can read and save CSV files. In a CSV file, commas separate the field values in each record in the data source. When data is formatted using comma separators, it is called ***delimited data*** and the comma is called a ***delimiter***. A paragraph mark indicates the end of a record. To import data and create a new table, click the External Data tab on the Ribbon, and then click the Text File button in the Import & Link group. Browse to and select the file that contains the data you want to import, and then choose the option to import the source data into a new table in the current database. Follow the steps in the Import Text Wizard to create a new table in the database using the file name of the text file.

Most programs have converters to separate the values in a CSV file into the columns of a worksheet or the cells of a table. When you convert a CSV file to another format, the program removes the commas that separate the field values. If there are quotation marks around text values in a text file, the conversion process also removes them.

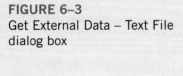

VOCABULARY
comma-separated values (CSV)
delimited data
delimiter

Step-by-Step 6.2

1. In the Import & Link group on the External Data tab, click the **Text File** button. The Get External Data – Text File dialog box opens, as shown in **Figure 6–3**.

FIGURE 6–3
Get External Data – Text File dialog box

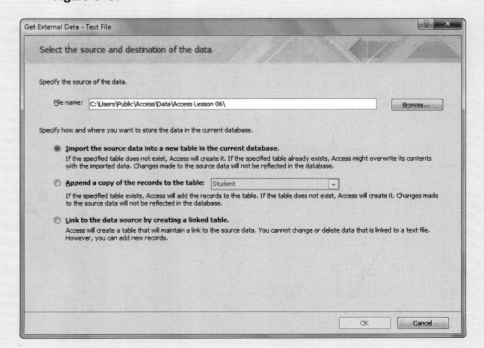

2. Click **Browse**. If necessary, navigate to and open the **Access Lesson 06** folder, click **Student.txt** to select it in the File Open dialog box, and then click **Open**.

3. Make sure that the **Import the source data into a new table in the current database** option button is selected, and then click **OK**. The Import Text Wizard starts and opens the first dialog box, as shown in **Figure 6–4**.

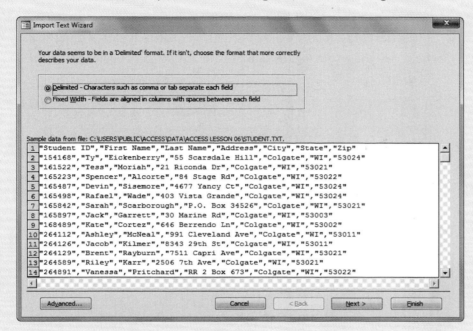

FIGURE 6–4
First Import Text Wizard dialog box

4. Make sure that the **Delimited** option button is selected, and then click **Next**. The second dialog box requests information about the delimiter that separates the fields in the data source, as shown in **Figure 6–5**.

Click this check box to use the values in the first row as field names

First row of text file contains field names

Each row will become one record

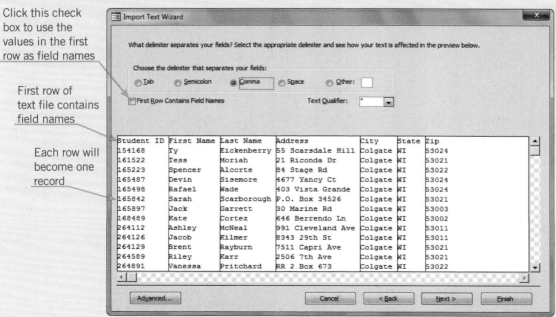

FIGURE 6–5
Second Import Text Wizard dialog box

5. Make sure that the **Comma** option button is selected, and then click the **First Row Contains Field Names** check box to add a check mark to it. If you don't identify the first row as containing field names, the field names will be added in a record, instead of as field names.

6. Click **Next**. The third dialog box asks you about the data types you want to use for each field. If you do not choose any data types for the fields, Access assigns the Text data type to each field.

7. Click **Next**. The fourth dialog box lets you set or create a primary key field, as shown in **Figure 6–6**. Leave the Wizard open for the next Step-by-Step.

FIGURE 6–6
Fourth Import Text Wizard
dialog box

Recall that the primary key field stores unique values for each record in a table. The Student ID field already contains unique field values, so you can use the arrow on the list box to the right of the "Choose my own primary key" option button to select the Student ID field as the table's primary key. You can also choose not to set a primary key, or you can let Access create a primary key. If you select the option for Access to create a primary key, Access creates a field named ID at the beginning of the table and assigns it the AutoNumber data type.

Step-by-Step 6.3

1. Click the **Choose my own primary key** option button. Because the Student ID field is the first field in the table, it is selected automatically in the list box.

2. Click **Next**. The final dialog box asks you for a table name.

3. In the Import to Table text box, type **Student Word**, and then click **Finish**.

4. Click **Close** in the Get External Data – Text File dialog box to close it. (Do not save the import steps.)

5. In the Navigation Pane, double-click **Student Word** to open the table. Leave the Student Word table open for the next Step-by-Step.

The table contains the imported data. The field names are from the first row of the text file because you chose the option to use the values in the first row as the field names. All the fields in the table have the Text data type because you didn't set them to other data types using the Import Text Wizard. The Text fields have the default properties as well, which includes a default Field Size property of 255 characters. If you need to customize this table, you could change to Design view and reevaluate the data types and field properties for each field so they use the settings you need.

Importing and Exporting Workbooks

When you need to export data from a database table to an Excel workbook, click the External Data tab on the Ribbon, and then click the Excel button in the Export group. When you export the data, it will be saved in Excel format, with each field in the table stored in a worksheet column and each record in the table stored as a row in the worksheet.

 EXTRA FOR EXPERTS

You can export data from a database to a specific version of Excel by selecting a different file format in the Export – Excel Spreadsheet dialog box. The default file format is Excel Workbook (*.xlsx).

Step-by-Step 6.4

1. In the Export group on the External Data tab, click the **Excel** button. The Export – Excel Spreadsheet dialog box opens, as shown in **Figure 6–7**.

FIGURE 6–7
Export – Excel Spreadsheet
dialog box

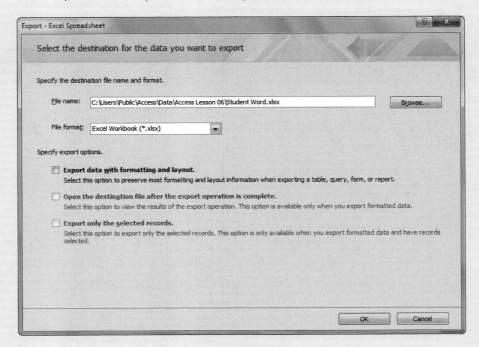

2. If the path to the Access Lesson 06 folder with your Data Files does not appear in the File name text box, click **Browse**, navigate to and open the **Access Lesson 06** folder, and then click **Save** in the File Save dialog box.

3. Click the **Export data with formatting and layout** check box to add a check mark to it.

4. Click the **Open the destination file after the export operation is complete** check box to add a check mark to it.

5. Click **OK**. Excel starts and opens the file that contains the data you exported. See **Figure 6–8**.

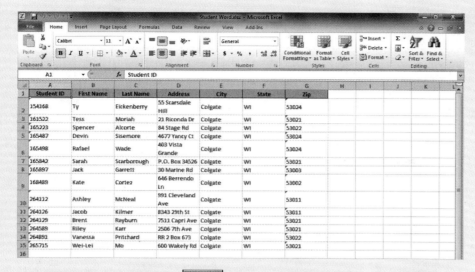

FIGURE 6–8
Excel worksheet with the exported data

6. Click the **Close** button on the Excel title bar to close Excel.

7. Click **Close** to close the Export – Excel Spreadsheet dialog box. (Do not save the export steps.)

8. Click the **Close 'Student Word'** button to close the Student Word table. Leave the database open for the next Step-by-Step.

You can also import data stored in a workbook into a new or existing database table. When you use the data in a workbook to add records to a database table, the columns in the worksheet must be the same as the fields in the database and contain the same type of data. When you need to create a new table using the data in a workbook, the Import Spreadsheet Wizard guides you through the process.

Step-by-Step 6.5

1. In the Import & Link group on the External Data tab, click the **Excel** button. The Get External Data – Excel Spreadsheet dialog box opens.

2. Click **Browse**, if necessary navigate to and open the **Access Lesson 06** folder, click **Student Excel.xlsx**, and then click **Open**.

3. Make sure that the **Import the source data into a new table in the current database** option button is selected. See **Figure 6–9**.

FIGURE 6–9
Get External Data – Excel
Spreadsheet dialog box

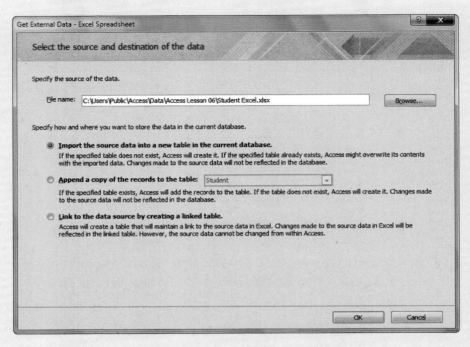

4. Click **OK**. The Import Spreadsheet Wizard dialog box opens, as shown in **Figure 6–10**.

FIGURE 6–10
First Import
Spreadsheet Wizard
dialog box

Click this check box to use the values in the first row as field names

First row of worksheet contains field names

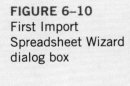

Each row will become one record

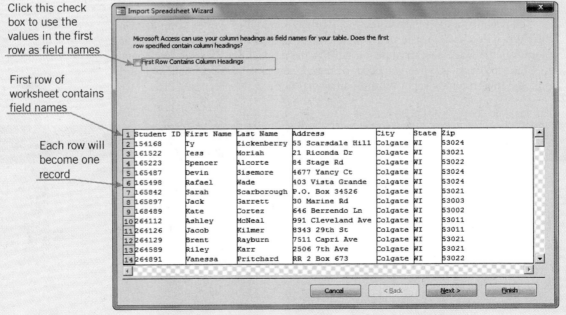

5. Click the **First Row Contains Column Headings** check box to add a check mark to it, and then click **Next**. The second dialog box lets you set data types for fields. As when importing a text file, you can set the data types now or do so after creating the table. If you choose not to change the data types, Access will assign the Text data type and the default property settings for Text fields to all fields in the table.

6. Click **Next**. The third dialog box asks you about the table's primary key.

7. Click the **Choose my own primary key** option button. Make sure that **Student ID** appears in the list box to the right of the Choose my own primary key option button, and then click **Next**. The final dialog box asks you for the table name.

8. In the Import to Table text box, type **Student Excel**, and then click **Finish**.

9. In the Get External Data – Excel Spreadsheet dialog box, click **Close**. (Do not save the import steps.)

10. In the Navigation Pane, double-click **Student Excel** to open the table in Datasheet view. The table contains the data that was stored in the columns and rows in the Excel workbook.

11. Click the **Close 'Student Excel'** button ☒ to close the Student Excel table. Leave the database open for the next Step-by-Step.

TECHNOLOGY CAREERS

Databases are helpful in the sales business. Salespersons can create a database to store detailed information about their customers. They can then create queries and filters to search the database for specific information. They can also use the database to create reports, form letters, and mailing labels.

Creating Form Letters

Another way to integrate Access and Word is to create form letters. A *form letter* is a document that includes codes that insert information from a data source. The *data source* might be information stored in a Word document, an Excel workbook, an Access database, or another file format. When you merge the data source with the form letter, one letter is created for each record in the data source. In this case, the form letter is also called the *main document*. Form letters are used to customize letters and other documents. When used with a data source, Word does the work of addressing letters or customizing forms, so you don't need to type the information directly and create each letter individually.

For example, suppose a fourth grade teacher wants to send a letter to the parents of students in her class to welcome them to the new school year. Instead of typing each recipient's name, mailing address, salutation (such as Dear Mr. and Mrs. Peterson), and child's name in each letter and printing it, the teacher can create a form letter with the basic information she wants to include in the letter. Then the teacher can create a data source that stores the mailing address and student information for each child in her class. When she merges the main document with the data source, Word creates letters using the specific address and student information from each record in the data source. All the teacher needs to do is set up the process and load the printer with paper.

Creating a Form Letter

A form letter is a document that you create using Microsoft Word and that contains codes to tell Word where to insert the fields in records in the data source. The codes are the same as the field names used in the data source. When you insert the codes in a main document, they are called *merge fields*. When you insert a merge field in a Word document, the field name is enclosed in double angle brackets. For example, the merge field for a First Name field is displayed as <<First_Name>> in the Word document. When you merge the main document and the data source, Word replaces <<First_Name>> with the First Name field value in the first record of the data source, and inserts the first name.

You can use any document as a form letter, including documents that you create from scratch or a template. You can start a mail merge from Word or from Access. To start a mail merge using Access, open the database that contains the data source for the form letters, and then click the data source (table or query) in the Navigation Pane to select it. Click the External Data tab on the Ribbon. In the Export group, click the Word Merge button. The Microsoft Word Mail Merge Wizard starts and asks if you want to link your data to an existing document or create a new document. If you click the option to use an existing document, and then click OK, the Select Microsoft Word Document dialog box opens. Use the options to browse to and select the document, and then click Open. Word starts and opens the document you selected, and sets the data source to the object you selected in the database. If you choose the option to create a new document, and then click OK, Word starts and opens a new document. In either case, after Word starts, the Mailings tab is selected on the Ribbon and the Mail Merge task pane opens on the right side of the window, as shown in **Figure 6–11**.

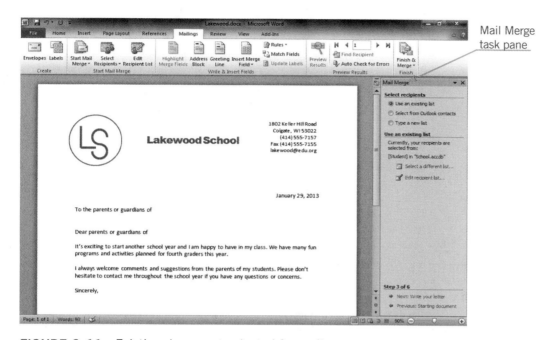

FIGURE 6–11   Existing document selected for mail merge

You can type or edit content in the document and use the tools in Word to make any changes to the letter, such as changing the font style or adding pictures. If you are creating a document from scratch, the first step is to select the type of document you are creating (letter, e-mail message, envelope, label, or a directory). For a form letter, choose the Letters option button. The second step asks you to select the document you want to use or to create a new document. After making your selection, click the Next: Select recipients link at the bottom of the Mail Merge task pane to select the data source.

In the third step, shown in Figure 6–11, you select the data source that contains the records for the recipients. This data source might be an existing list, an Outlook contact, or data that you type. When you start the mail merge from Access, Word sets the data source for you automatically.

If you want to merge all the records in the data source, you don't need to do anything else. If you want to merge selected records in the data source, click the Edit recipient list link in the Mail Merge task pane to open the Mail Merge Recipients dialog box, shown in **Figure 6–12**. The name of the data source appears in the first column, and the fields in the data source appear in columns to the left of the Data Source column. In Figure 6–12, the data source is an Access database.

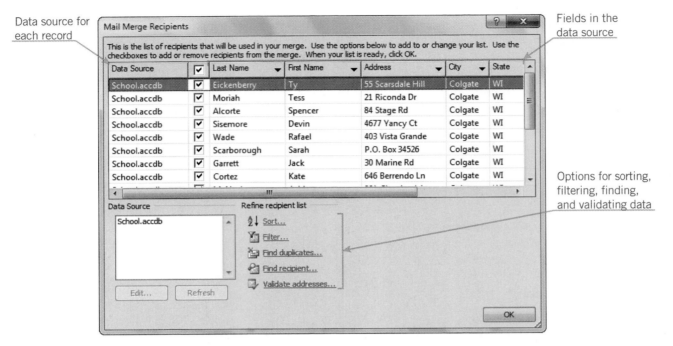

FIGURE 6–12   Mail Merge Recipients dialog box

A check box is shown to the left of the first field for each record; a check mark indicates that the record will be merged. If you want to remove a record from the mail merge, clear its check box. Also notice the "Refine recipient list" section, which provides options for sorting and filtering data, finding duplicate records, locating a specific recipient, and validating addresses. You can use these options when you need to change how letters are merged when you complete the mail merge. For example, if you want to print form letters in alphabetical order based on a specific field, you can click the Sort link to open the Filter and Sort dialog box with the Sort Records tab selected, as shown in **Figure 6–13**. To sort on a specific field, click the Sort by list arrow, and then select the field that you want to sort. Figure 6–13 shows that the mail merge will be sorted in ascending order based on the values in the Last Name field.

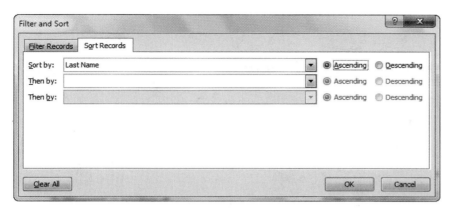

FIGURE 6–13   Sort Records tab in the Filter and Sort dialog box

You can also filter records by clicking the Filter link in the Refine recipient list section in the Mail Merge Recipients dialog box, which opens the Filter and Sort dialog box with the Filter Records tab selected. To create a filter, use the Field list arrow to select the field to filter, use the Comparison list arrow to choose the filter operator, and then type a value in the Compare to text box. **Figure 6–14** shows a filter to select records with the last name *Cortez*.

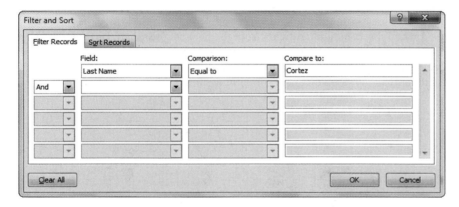

FIGURE 6–14   Filter Records tab in the Filter and Sort dialog box

When you click OK to close the Filter and Sort dialog box, you'll apply the new settings to the form letters. However, the changes you make are not reflected in the data source. Click OK to close the Mail Merge Recipients dialog box, and then click the Next: Write your letter link at the bottom of the Mail Merge task pane. If necessary, make any changes to the content of the letter, just like you would in any other document.

Word provides several options for adding merge fields to a document. You can use the Address block link in the Mail Merge task pane to add an address to the letter in the location of the insertion point. You can also add merge fields individually at the location of the insertion point by clicking the Insert Merge Field button in the Write & Insert Fields group on the Mailings tab. If you click the Address block link in the Mail

Merge task pane, the Insert Address Block dialog box opens and shows a preview of the address information that you will be inserting, as shown in **Figure 6–15**.

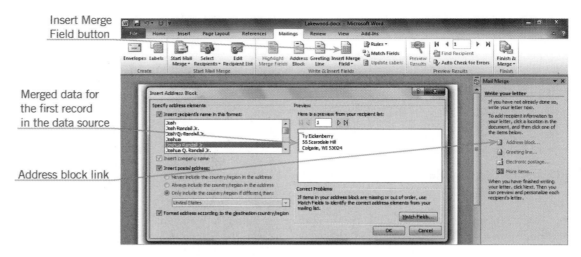

FIGURE 6–15   Insert Address Block dialog box

If the preview of the address block is correct, click OK. (If it is incorrect, click Match Fields to make adjustments.) After inserting the address block, it appears as <<AddressBlock>> in the main document.

You can insert individual fields from the data source wherever necessary in the main document. For example, you can include a first name in the middle of a sentence to customize the content. **Figure 6–16** shows the first and last names added to the salutation and the first name inserted in the first sentence of the first paragraph.

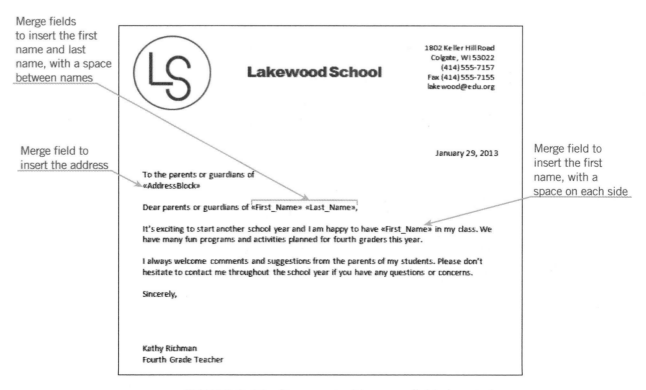

FIGURE 6–16   Document with merge fields inserted

Be careful when inserting fields individually—you will need to type any surrounding punctuation, such as inserting a space between field names so the first and last names print as "Riley Karr" instead of as "RileyKarr" and typing a comma or colon after the salutation.

After adding the merge fields to the letter, click the Next: Preview your letters link at the bottom of the Mail Merge task pane. The main document displays one letter for each record in the data source. **Figure 6–17** shows the first letter. Notice that the <<AddressBlock>> merge field was replaced by the address information for Ty Eickenberry. Ty's first and last names replaced the <<First_Name>> and <<Last_Name>> fields in the salutation. Ty's first name replaced the <<First_Name>> field in the first sentence of the first paragraph. If you click the next and previous buttons in the Preview your letters section of the Mail Merge task pane, you'll see the next and previous records as they will appear in the final letter.

TIP

If you don't want to print the letter for the currently displayed record, click Exclude this recipient in the Mail Merge task pane.

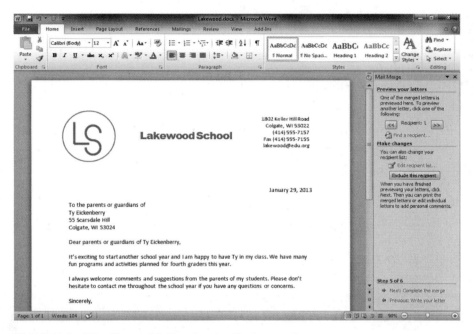

FIGURE 6–17   Merged letter for the first record

After verifying that your form letters are correct, click the Next: Complete the merge link at the bottom of the Mail Merge task pane. Click the Print link in the Merge section of the Mail Merge task pane to print the letters.

Step-by-Step 6.6

1. In the Navigation Pane, click the **Student** table to select it as the data source.

2. In the Export group on the External Data tab, click the **Word Merge** button. The Microsoft Word Mail Merge Wizard dialog box opens.

3. If necessary, click the **Link your data to an existing Microsoft Word document** option button, and then click **OK**. The Select Microsoft Word Document dialog box opens.

4. If necessary, navigate to and open the **Access Lesson 06** folder, click **Lakewood.docx**, and then click **Open**. The Select Microsoft Word Document dialog box closes. Word starts and opens the document you selected.

5. If necessary, click the **Lakewood.docx** program button on the taskbar to switch to Word.

6. If necessary, click the **Maximize** button 🔲 on the Word title bar to maximize the program window. (See Figure 6–11.) Leave Word open for the next Step-by-Step.

Because you started the mail merge from Access, the Mail Merge task pane opens with the Step 3 of 6 task displayed. The data source is already set to the Student table in the School database because you selected the data source in Access.

Step-by-Step 6.7

1. At the bottom of the Mail Merge task pane, click the **Next: Write your letter** link. The Step 4 of 6 Mail Merge task pane is displayed.

2. In the document, click the blank line below the paragraph that contains the text *To the parents or guardians of*.

3. In the Mail Merge task pane, click the **Address block** link. The Insert Address Block dialog box opens. (See Figure 6–15.) Make sure the settings in your dialog box match the ones shown in Figure 6–15, and then click **OK**. The <<AddressBlock>> field is added to the document.

4. In the document, click to the right of the line that contains the text *Dear parents or guardians of*. In the Write & Insert Fields group on the Mailings tab, click the **Insert Merge Field button arrow**. In the list, click **First_Name**.

5. Press the **spacebar**.

6. In the Write & Insert Fields group on the Mailings tab, click the **Insert Merge Field button arrow**. In the list, click **Last_Name**.

7. Type a comma.

8. In the first paragraph of the document, click after the space following the word *have* in the first sentence. Click the Insert Merge Field button arrow, and then click **First_Name** to insert the First Name field in the sentence.

9. Press the **spacebar** and make sure that the <<First_Name>> field that you just inserted has a space on each side of it, so the text will be merged correctly.

10. At the bottom of the Mail Merge task pane, click the **Next: Preview your letters** link. The data source is merged with the letter. (See Figure 6–17.)

11. In the Mail Merge task pane, click the ⟩⟩ button to display the next merged letter.

12. In the Mail Merge task pane, click the ⟨⟨ button to display the previous merged letter.

13. At the bottom of the Mail Merge task pane, click the **Next: Complete the merge** link. The Mail Merge task pane displays options to merge the letters or to edit individual letters.

14. On the Quick Access Toolbar, click the **Save** button 🖫. Leave Word open for the next Step-by-Step.

Editing the Recipient List

The default setting for a mail merge is to merge all the records in the data source. If you only need to merge certain records, you can set a filter or choose specific records individually.

Step-by-Step 6.8

1. At the bottom of the Mail Merge task pane, click the **Previous: Preview your letters** link. The Step 5 of 6 Mail Merge task pane is displayed. (See Figure 6–17.)

2. In the Mail Merge task pane, click the **Edit recipient list** link. The Mail Merge Recipients dialog box opens. (See Figure 6–12.)

3. Click the **check box** next to the Data Source column heading at the top of the column of check boxes. The check marks are removed from all check boxes.

4. Click the **check box** to the left of the record for Rafael Wade to add a check mark to it.

5. Click **OK** to close the Mail Merge Recipients dialog box.

6. In the Preview your letters section of the Step 5 of 6 Mail Merge task pane, click the ▶▶ button to display the next record. Because you set the mail merge to merge only one record, there are no "next" letters.

7. On the Quick Access Toolbar, click the **Save** button 🔲.

8. Click the **Close** button ❌ on the Word title bar to close Word.

9. Click the **Close** button ❌ on the Access title bar to close the Student database and Access.

SUMMARY

In this lesson, you learned:

- You can import and export data from a database and use it in other programs. When importing data, you can append records to an existing table or create a new table. When appending records to an existing table, the data source must have the same number of fields and contain the same type of data as the existing table.

- Delimited data contains commas or other separators to separate the fields in a data source. When the delimiter is a comma, the data is called comma-separated values (CSV). Access, Excel, and other programs can read and process CSV files.

- A form letter is a document that includes codes that merge information from a data source. The data source might be information stored in a Word document, an Excel workbook, an Access database, or another file format. When you merge the data source with the form letter, one letter is merged for each record in the data source.

- A merge field tells Word where to insert data from the data source.

- To merge certain records from a data source in a form letter, edit the recipient list by applying a filter or by selecting individual records.

■ VOCABULARY REVIEW

Define the following terms:

comma-separated values (CSV)   delimiter   import
data source   export   main document
delimited data   form letter   merge field

■ REVIEW QUESTIONS

TRUE / FALSE

Circle T if the statement is true or F if the statement is false.

T   F   1.   When importing data from a Word document into an existing Access database table, the Word document data must contain the same number of columns and type of data as the database table.

T   F   2.   When importing data into a database using the Import Text Wizard, you cannot specify a primary key for a new table.

T   F   3.   When importing data into a new database table, the fields will have the default property settings for a Text field unless you choose new data types for the fields.

T   F   4.   When creating a mail merge in Word, the data source must be a table in an Access database.

T   F   5.   You can insert a merge field anywhere in a form letter.

WRITTEN QUESTIONS

Write a brief answer to each of the following questions.

1. List three file formats that you can use to import data into a database.

2. List three file formats that you can use to export data from a database.

3. In a comma-separated values file, what is the delimiter that separates fields? What is the delimiter that separates records?

4. How do you insert a merge field into a Word document?

5. Describe the steps to insert the city, state, and zip code fields from a data source in a letter. Use the field names City, State, and Zip in your answer. The data should be printed on a single line in the format *City, State Zip*.

FILL IN THE BLANK

Complete the following sentences by writing the correct word or words in the blanks provided.

1. When you save database data in another file format, you _____ the data from the database.

2. When you _____ data into a database, you copy it from another Access database, an Excel workbook, a text file, or another compatible file format into an existing or new table in the current database.

3. A paragraph mark, comma, or space character are examples of _____ that might be used in a text file that you are importing into Access.

4. When you insert a merge field into a Word document, the field name is enclosed in _____.

5. To insert a merge field into a Word document, click the _____ button in the Write & Insert Fields group on the Mailings tab.

◼ PROJECTS

If you have a SAM 2010 user profile, your instructor may have assigned an autogradable version of the indicated project. If so, log into the SAM 2010 Web site at *www.cengage.com/sam2010* to download the instruction and start files.

PROJECT 6–1

1. Open the **Inventory.accdb** database from the Access Lesson 06 folder where your Data Files are stored.

2. Choose the option to import data from an Excel workbook.

3. Choose the Products.xlsx file in the Access Lesson 06 folder as the data source.

4. Choose the option to import the source data into a new table in the current database.

5. Complete the steps in the Import Spreadsheet Wizard and accept the default settings. The first row in the data source contains column headings. Choose the Product ID field as the table's primary key. In the last dialog box, enter **Products** in the Import to Table text box.

6. If necessary, close the Get External Data – Excel Spreadsheet dialog box without saving the import steps.

7. Close the database and exit Access.

PROJECT 6–2

1. Open the **Items.accdb** database from the Access Lesson 06 folder where your Data Files are stored.

2. Select the Products table, and then choose the option to export data from the Products table to a text file.

3. Click Browse and set the destination for the exported text file to the Access Lesson 06 folder. Click OK in the Export – Text File dialog box. The delimiter is a comma and the first row contains field names. Do not save the export steps.

4. Import the data in the Products.txt file in the Access Lesson 06 folder into a new table in the Items database. The delimiter is a comma and the first row contains field names. Do not set the data types for any of the fields. Choose the Product ID field as the table's primary key. Change the default table name to **Products Import**.

5. If necessary, close the Get External Data – Text File dialog box without saving the import steps.

6. Close the database and exit Access.

PROJECT 6–3

1. Open the **InfoTech.accdb** database from the Access Lesson 06 folder where your Data Files are stored.

2. Select the Employee table in the Navigation Pane, and then start a mail merge using the Abbott.docx document in the Access Lesson 06 folder.

3. In the main document, on the second line below the date, insert an address block.

4. On the line that contains the word *Dear*, type a space, insert the First_Name field, and then type a comma.

5. Preview the letters.

6. Exclude Donna Abbott from the mail merge by displaying her record and using a button in the Mail Merge task pane.

7. Save the document and close Word.

8. Close the database and exit Access.

PROJECT 6–4

1. Open the **InfoTech.accdb** database from the Access Lesson 06 folder where your Data Files are stored.

2. Select the Employee table in the Navigation Pane, and then start a mail merge using the Sales.docx document in the Access Lesson 06 folder.

3. In Word, set a filter to select only those records that have the field value *Sales* in the Department field in the data source.

4. Sort the records in alphabetical (ascending) order by Last Name.

5. On the second line below the date, insert an address block.

6. On the line that contains the word *Dear*, type a space, insert the First_Name field, and then type a comma.

7. Preview the letters.

8. Save the document and close Word.

9. Close the database and exit Access.

CRITICAL THINKING

ACTIVITY 6–1

One of the data types you can use in an Access table is the Attachment data type, which lets you store a file created in another program as part of a record in a table. You can save files in many different file formats, including files created with Office 2010 programs and files created by graphics programs.

Start Access, and then use Access Help to learn more about the Attachment data type by searching using the text "Attach files to records." Click the "Attach files and graphics to the records in your database" link, and then read the page that opens. On a sheet of paper, answer the following questions.

1. When a Word document is attached to a record in a database table, which program displays the document when you open it from Access?

2. Are there any rules for naming attachments stored in a database table? If so, what are the rules?

3. Can you attach a file with any filename extension using the Attachment data type? Explain your answer.

ACTIVITY 6–2

Start Access and use the Blank database template in the Available Templates section to create a new database named **Swimming.accdb** in the Access Lesson 06 folder with your Data Files. Close the default table that opens (Table1). Import the data in the Clubs.txt text file in the Access Lesson 06 folder into a new table in the Swimming database. The delimiter is a comma and the first row contains field names. Do not change the data types of any fields. Choose the Club Code field as the table's primary key. Import the data into a new table named **Clubs**. Do not save the import steps.

Import the data in the Officials.xlsx Excel workbook in the Access Lesson 06 folder into a new table in the Swimming database. The first row contains column headings. Do not change the data types of any fields. Choose the Official ID field as the table's primary key. Import the data into a new table named **Officials**. Do not save the import steps.

Create a relationship between the primary Clubs table and the related Officials table, using the Club Code field. Choose the option to enforce referential integrity. Save and close the Relationships window.

Use the Simple Query Wizard to create a query that includes the Club Code and Club Name fields from the Clubs table and the First Name, Last Name, and Position fields from the Officials table. Use the query name **Club Officials**.

Export the data in the Club Officials query to an Excel workbook named **Club Officials.xlsx** in the Access Lesson 06 folder.

You created a new database and imported data from a text file and a workbook into the database to create two new tables. You related the tables using a common field, and then created a query that includes data from both tables. Finally, you exported the data in the query to an Excel workbook.

How could you continue improving the database that you created? (*Hint:* Think about the fields in the tables and their data types and field properties.) When other swim teams need to add officials to the database, what advice would you give them about sending their data to you? (*Hint:* Consider the rules you learned about importing data into existing tables.)

Close the database and exit Access.

ACCESS UNIT REVIEW

Introductory Microsoft Access

■ REVIEW QUESTIONS

TRUE / FALSE

Circle T if the statement is true or F if the statement is false.

T   F   **1.**   A database is a collection of objects that store, retrieve, display, and summarize data.

T   F   **2.**   A field's data type stores the field's name.

T   F   **3.**   A query always contains a condition.

T   F   **4.**   Forms are always based on queries.

T   F   **5.**   You cannot edit the data displayed in a report.

WRITTEN QUESTIONS

Write a brief answer to each of the following questions.

1. What data type would you choose for a field that stores numeric data that you will use in calculations?

2. What field property do you use to change the number of characters that a Text field can store?

3. What is a filter?

4. Describe how to delete a record using a table datasheet.

5. Define the term *comma-separated values* and explain how a CSV file is used when importing data into an Access database.

FILL IN THE BLANK

Complete the following sentences by writing the correct word or words in the blanks provided.

1. A(n) _____ allows you to store, retrieve, analyze, and print information stored in a database.

2. Use the _____ data type to automatically add a unique value to a field in a table as you enter new records.

3. A(n) _____ is a menu that opens when you click the arrow on the right side of a field selector, and contains options for sorting data in the field.

4. The "container" that groups together the controls in a form so that you can change them as a group is called a(n) _____.

5. To create a simple report using all of the fields in a table or query, first select the table or query in the Navigation Pane, and then click the _____ button in the Reports group on the Create tab.

■ PROJECTS

PROJECT AC 1

1. Open the **Favorites.accdb** database from the Access Unit Review folder where your Data Files are stored.

2. Open the **Stores** table in Design view.

3. Move the Hours field so it appears between the Specialty and Credit Cards fields.

4. Insert a new field between the Hours and Credit Cards fields. Use the field name **Last Visit** and assign the field the Date/Time data type. Change the field's Format property to Short Date.

5. Change the Field Size property for the Specialty field to 30.

6. Change the data type of the Credit Cards field to Yes/No, and then change the Format property to Yes/No.

7. Change the Required field property for the Name field to Yes.

8. Set the Store ID field so it is the table's primary key.

9. Save the table, click Yes twice in the dialog boxes warning about data loss and data integrity rules, change to Datasheet view, and then resize the columns in the datasheet to best fit.

10. Enter today's date in the Last Visit field for the Electronics Plus record.

11. Change the Specialty field value for the Electronics Plus record to your first and last names.

12. Preview the datasheet, and then print it in landscape orientation. Save and close the Stores table.

13. Compact and repair the database.

14. Close the database, and then exit Access.

PROJECT AC 2

1. Open the **Dining.accdb** database from the Access Unit Review folder where your Data Files are stored.

2. Open the **Restaurants** table in Design view.

3. Change the Restaurant ID field so it is the table's primary key.

4. Change the Field Size property for the Name field to **30**, and change its Required property to Yes.

5. Change the Format property of the Last Visit field to Short Date.

6. Change the data type of the Reservations field to Yes/No, and then change the Format property to Yes/No.

7. Change the data type of the Meal Cost field to Currency.

8. Save the table, click Yes twice in the dialog boxes warning about data loss and data integrity rules, and then change to Datasheet view.

9. In Datasheet view, change the Format property for the Last Visit field to Long Date. Resize the Last Visit column to best fit.

10. Preview the datasheet, print it in landscape orientation, and then save and close the table.

11. Close the database, and then exit Access.

PROJECT AC 3

1. Open the **Personnel.accdb** database from the Access Unit Review folder where your Data Files are stored.

2. In the Relationships window, create a relationship using the Employee ID field in the primary Employees table and the Employee ID field in the related Personal Data table. Choose the option to enforce referential integrity. Save your changes, and then close the Relationships window.

3. Use the Simple Query Wizard to create a query based on the Employees and Personal Data tables. Include the following fields in the order listed from the Employees table in the query: Employee ID, First Name, and Last Name. Include the following fields in the order listed from the Personal Data table in the query: Title, Department, Date of Birth, and Salary.

4. Choose the option to create a detail query and use the query title **Employee Data**.

5. In the query datasheet, sort the records from smallest to largest using the Salary field.

6. Filter the records so that only those employees working in the Marketing department are displayed.

7. Use the Total row to calculate the average salary for employees working in the Marketing department.

8. In the record with Employee ID 1007, change the First Name and Last Name field values to your first and last names.

9. Preview and print the Employee Data query in landscape orientation, and then save and close the Employee Data query.

10. In Query Design view, create a new query using the Employees and Personal Data tables. Add the Employee ID, First Name, and Last Name fields from the Employees table to the query design. Then add the Salary field from the Personal Data table to the query design.

11. Use a condition to select the records for only those employees with salaries greater than $2,000.

12. Save the query as **High Salaries**, and then run the query.

13. In the record with Employee ID 1099, change the First Name and Last Name field values to your first and last names.

14. Preview and print the High Salaries query, and then close the High Salaries query.

15. Close the database, and then exit Access.

PROJECT AC 4

1. Open the **Meals.accdb** database from the Access Unit Review folder where your Data Files are stored.

2. Use the Form tool to create a form based on the Restaurants table.

3. Resize the width of the text boxes in the control layout in the form to 23 characters.

4. Apply the Angles theme to the form.

5. Change the form title to **My Favorite Restaurants**.

6. Change to Form view and delete the record with the Restaurant ID SAL2.

7. Display the record with the Restaurant ID TON1 in the form. Change the Name field value to your first and last names. Print the form for this record only.

8. Save the form using the name **My Favorite Restaurants**.

9. Close the form, close the database, and then exit Access.

PROJECT AC 5

1. Open the **Price.accdb** database from the Access Unit Review folder where your Data Files are stored.

2. Use the Report Wizard to create a report based on the Products table. Include all fields in the report.

3. Group the report by Category and sort the records in ascending order based on the Retail Price field.

4. Choose the Block layout and Landscape orientation.

5. Change the report title to **Products By Category**, and then choose the option to preview the report.

6. Change to Layout view. Resize each column so that it is just wide enough to display the longest value in the column. Scroll down the page to check and make sure that the field values in each column are completely visible.

7. Change to Design view and move the text box control that contains the page number to the left, so its right edge is at the 9.75-inch mark on the horizontal ruler.

8. Save the report, preview the report, and then print it.

9. Close the report, close the database, and then exit Access.

■ SIMULATION

You work at the newly renovated Java Internet Café. The café serves coffee and pastries and offers clients the opportunity to use the café's computers and Wi-Fi to gain Internet access. In addition to free wireless access, seven computers are set up on tables in quiet areas of the café. The café has many regular early morning customers who grab a cup of coffee and a pastry and then use one of the computers to check e-mail and browse the Internet before going to work or school.

The café charges a $10 monthly fee for Internet service. All membership fees for March were due on March 1. A few members have not paid their monthly fees. Your manager asks you to send out a reminder letter to customers with outstanding balances.

JOB AC 1

1. Open the **Java.accdb** database from the Access Unit Review folder where your Data Files are stored.

2. Open the **Members** table in Datasheet view.

3. Scott Payton just paid his membership fee for March. Update his record to show his $10 payment.

4. The café has a new member who paid her $10 dues for April. Use the following information to add the record for Halie Shook to the Members table:
   Member ID: **hsht**
   Title: **Ms.**
   First: **Halie**
   Last: **Shook**
   Address: **1290 Wood Crest Ln**
   City: **Boulder**
   State: **CO**
   Zip: **80302**

5. Close the Members table.

6. Merge the records in the Members table with the **Reminder.docx** letter in the Access Unit Review folder where your Data Files are stored.

7. Edit the recipient list so letters are merged only for those clients who have not paid their dues for March. (*Hint:* Use a filter to select records for members who have March field values equal to 0 (zero). Use the Mail Merge Recipients dialog box to remove Halie Shook from the recipient list (she was not a member in March and should not receive a letter).

8. On the second line below the date field, add an address block.

9. On the second line below the address block you just inserted, add a greeting line in the format *Dear Mr. Stanley* followed by a comma.

10. Preview the merged letters.

11. Change the manager's name (Trace Green) in the closing to your first and last names. Exclude the first and second recipients and print the third recipient's letter only.

12. Save the document and close Word.

13. Close the database, and then exit Access.

JOB AC 2

You need to create mailing labels so you can mail the member statements for April.

1. Open the **Java.accdb** database from the Access Unit Review folder where your Data Files are stored.

2. Use the Label Wizard to create mailing labels for the Members table.

3. Use the Avery C2160 label and accept the default font settings. Add the Title, First, and Last fields on the first line of the label, separated by spaces; add the Address field on the second line of the label; and the City, State, and Zip fields on the last line of the label. There should be a comma and space between the City and State fields and a space between the State and Zip fields.

4. Save the report as **Labels Members**, and then preview it.

5. Close the report, close the database, and exit Access.

Estimated Time for Unit:
17.5 hours

ADVANCED

MICROSOFT ACCESS UNIT

LESSON 7

Enhancing Table Design

■ OBJECTIVES

Upon completion of this lesson, you should be able to:

- Create an input mask.
- Enter data in an input mask field.
- Set validation rules.
- Enter data into a field with a validation rule.
- Set a lookup property.
- Select field values from a list.
- Use the Lookup Wizard to set lookup properties.
- Select data from a list with multiple columns.
- Create a calculated field in a table.

■ VOCABULARY

Expression Builder

expression

input mask

list box

operator

placeholder

validation rule

Introduction

Microsoft Access is a powerful database application that lets you store, organize, and manipulate vast amounts of data. You should already be familiar with the primary objects that comprise a database: tables, forms, and reports. In these advanced lessons, you'll learn more about each of these objects plus other features that help you manage and control your database records.

In this lesson, you will learn about the various enhancements you can add to tables, such as an input mask. An input mask is a pattern created for a data type, such as (XXX) XXX-XXXX for a telephone number, so that it is entered correctly into a field with the parentheses and the dash. You will also learn about applying validation rules to data so that a message box appears if the data is entered incorrectly. You will then learn how to add lookup properties to a table so that you can select the values you need for a field from a list. You will set lookup values using the Lookup Wizard to display two columns of data in a list, and finally, you will create a calculated field in a table for the purpose of showing actual calculations between fields in the table.

Creating an Input Mask

An *input mask* is a pattern for common types of data entered in a field. Access includes several input mask formats, such as phone numbers, Social Security numbers, and ZIP codes.

For example, if you need to enter phone numbers using the format (XXX) XXX-XXXX, typing the parentheses and the dash each time you enter a phone number might get tiresome. Instead, you can apply the Phone Number input mask; then all you need to type are the numbers. The input mask inserts the parentheses and hyphen in the correct positions for you.

To create an input mask, you must be in Design view. Select the field for which you want to create the input mask, and then click in the Input Mask text box in the Field Properties pane. After you create the input mask, Access will ask if you want to save the values with the symbols, such as the parentheses and a dash in a phone number. If your computer has plenty of disk space, it should be okay to save the values with the symbols.

You may also select the placeholder for your input mask field. A *placeholder* appears in a field before the value is entered. The default placeholder is the underscore. The placeholder simply identifies that an input mask is assigned to the field in the table. In the next Step-by-Step, you will add an input mask to the Phone and Cell Phone fields in an Access table.

EXTRA FOR EXPERTS

To save a database with a different name and in another location, you first open the database, then click the File tab and select Save Database As. Select the location where you want to save the file, and then in the File name text box, type the name for the database before clicking the Save button.

Step-by-Step 7.1

1. Open the **Student Teams** file from the drive and folder where your Data Files are stored. Save the database as **Student Teams Database**, followed by your initials.

2. In the Navigation pane, double-click **tblStudent** to open the table. Notice that the Phone and Cell Phone fields include telephone numbers.

3. On the Home tab, click the **View** button arrow in the Views group and then click **Design View**. The table is displayed in Design view, as shown in **Figure 7–1**.

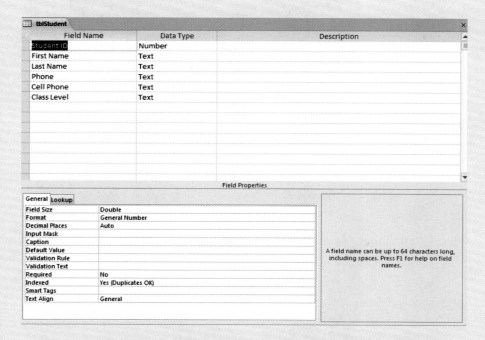

FIGURE 7–1
tblStudent in Design view

4. Click in the **Phone** field name, and then click in the **Input Mask** field in the Field Properties pane, as shown in **Figure 7–2**. Notice that the Build button appears to the right side of the Input Mask field.

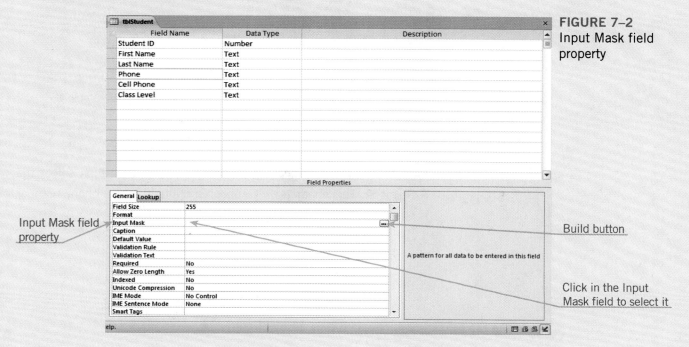

FIGURE 7–2
Input Mask field property

5. Click the **Build** button. The Input Mask Wizard dialog box opens, as shown in **Figure 7–3**.

FIGURE 7–3
Input Mask Wizard dialog box

Phone Number input mask

6. In the Input Mask Wizard dialog box, verify that **Phone Number** is selected, and then click the **Next** button to display the next Input Mask Wizard window. The second window of the Input Mask Wizard dialog box shows options for adding placeholders, as shown in **Figure 7–4**.

FIGURE 7–4
Input Mask Wizard dialog box with placeholder options

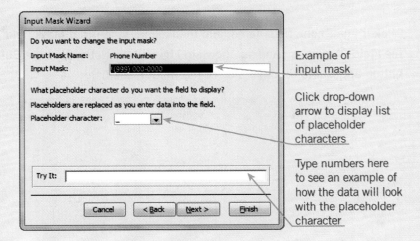

Example of input mask

Click drop-down arrow to display list of placeholder characters

Type numbers here to see an example of how the data will look with the placeholder character

7. Click the **Placeholder character** drop-down arrow, and then select the # character. This character will appear in the field until a phone number is entered.

8. Click in the **Try It** text box to the left of the first #, and then type **5551234567**. A sample of how the telephone number will look when data is entered into the field is shown in **Figure 7–5**.

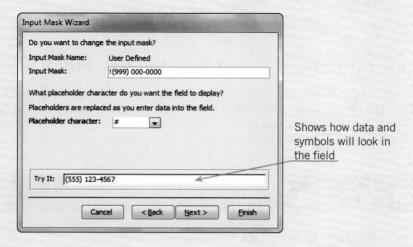

Shows how data and symbols will look in the field

FIGURE 7–5
Input Mask Wizard dialog box with telephone number sample

9. Click **Next** to go to the next window of the Input Mask Wizard. The next window lets you select whether or not you want to store the symbols with the telephone numbers.

10. Click the **With the symbols in the mask, like this** option button to select it, and then click **Next**. The parentheses and dashes will be stored with the telephone numbers. The final Input Mask Wizard window appears, stating that you have completed all the information needed for the input mask. See **Figure 7–6**.

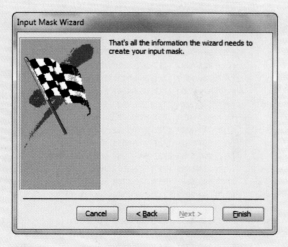

FIGURE 7–6
Final Input Mask Wizard dialog box window

11. Click **Finish** to close the Input Mask Wizard dialog box, then click the **Save** button on the Quick Access toolbar to save the changes to the table.

12. Repeat Steps 4 through 11 to create an Input Mask Wizard for the **Cell Phone** field.

13. Click the **Save** button to save changes to the table.

14. In the Views group, click the **View** button arrow and then click **Datasheet View**. Leave the database and table open for the next Step-by-Step.

Entering Data Into an Input Mask Field

After the input mask is created, placeholders appear in the fields until the values are entered. The format in the input mask, such as parentheses and a dash for a telephone number, will display as you enter new records. In this next exercise, you will enter a new record that includes two phone numbers in fields with the input mask.

Step-by-Step 7.2

1. On the Home tab, click the **New** button in the Records group.

2. In the Student ID field, type **67690** and then press **Tab**.

3. In the First Name field, type **John** and then press **Tab**.

4. In the Last Name field, type **Hernandez** and then press **Tab**.

5. In the Phone field, type **7175559876** and then press **Tab**. Notice that the telephone number symbols appeared automatically.

6. In the Cell Phone field, type **7175552466** and then press **Tab**. Compare your screen to **Figure 7–7**.

FIGURE 7–7
Data entered into fields with input masks

Student ID	First Name	Last Name	Phone	Cell Phone	Class Level
23423	Michael	Lemley	(717) 897-9879	(717) 579-8544	Freshman
23468	Matthew	Couric	(717) 987-9834	(717) 543-2100	Sophmore
23480	Kathy	Reid	(717) 325-4997	(717) 579-8310	Junior
23483	Corey	Graham	(717) 789-7987	(717) 654-8791	Junior
23487	Tai	Zejecka	(717) 879-8797	(717) 653-4687	Sophmore
23648	Mary	Moldrem	(717) 548-7214	(717) 351-2000	Senior
23749	Jeanie	Lowry	(717) 987-9797	(717) 8791-222	Freshman
24324	Bill	Melendez	(717) 787-9787	(717) 249-5312	Freshman
28349	Robbie	Littleton	(717) 987-8979	(717) 247-6555	Senior
28374	Todd	Verde	(717) 554-8765	(717) 645-7987	Sophmore
34248	David	Miller	(717) 234-5612	(717) 542-1032	Junior
34872	Jimmy	White	(717) 531-5671	(717) 246-8798	Junior
56346	Sue	Silverberg	(717) 543-2012	(717) 802-1546	Sophmore
56757	Terry	Kennsington	(717) 635-3154	(717) 864-0123	Senior
57723	Sharon	Stevens	(717) 315-4651	(717) 267-4955	Freshman
66723	Judith	Gonzalez	(717) 213-5795	(717) 798-4321	Freshman
67237	Steven	Ellis	(717) 213-5791	(717) 549-8800	Senior
67634	Alice	Grittner	(717) 354-9873	(717) 246-7841	Senior
67678	Kirstie	Allison	(717) 810-4657	(717) 249-2465	Junior
67686	Candace	Mendosa	(717) 214-6327	(717) 549-8713	Senior
67690	John	Hernandez	(717) 555-9876	(717) 555-2466	Freshman

Input mask places the symbols in the data when it is entered

7. In the Class Level field, type **Freshman** and then press **Enter**.

8. Save your work, close the table, and then close the database.

Set Validation Rules

You can increase accuracy and efficiency of data entry by setting validation rules. *Validation rules* are rules that need to be met before the data can be entered. For example, in a company, if the highest hourly wage paid to employees is $50 per hour, you can enter an expression in the validation rule that the dollar amount entered needs to be equal to or less than 50.

The validation rule is entered as an expression in the Expression Builder. The *Expression Builder* is where you type, or build, the expression. An *expression* is an arithmetic formula that performs a calculation. Using the above example, you would enter the expression <=50. **Table 7–1** shows examples of expressions.

TABLE 7–1   Examples of Expressions

EXPRESSION	WHAT IT MEANS
>=900	Data entered needs to be greater than or equal to 900.
[Retail Price]>[Cost]	The value in the Retail Price field needs to be greater than the value in the Cost field. Notice that field name needs to be placed in square brackets.
>#6/30/2014#	Date entered needs to be after June 30, 2014. Notice that the date needs to be between two pound signs.

When you set a validation rule for a field, you have the option to create a message that displays the validation rule to the person entering the data. The message appears when data entered into the field does not meet the validation rule. Using the hourly wage example, if a dollar amount greater than 50 is entered in the field, the message might be something like "Hourly rates cannot exceed $50." In the next exercise, the manager at Pacific Sales requires that all sales personnel make at least $40,000 in sales every month. You will enter a validation rule that displays a message if the sales amount is less than $40,000.

Step-by-Step 7.3

1. Open the **Pacific Sales** file from the drive and folder where your Data Files are stored. Save the database as **Pacific Sales Database**, followed by your initials.

2. In the Navigation pane, double-click **Sales Data** to open the table. Review the sales amounts.

3. On the Home tab, click the **View** button arrow, and then click **Design View**.

4. Click in the **Sales** field.

5. Click in the **Validation Rule** field in the Field Properties pane, and then compare your screen to **Figure 7–8**.

FIGURE 7–8
Field Properties pane with Validation Rule field selected

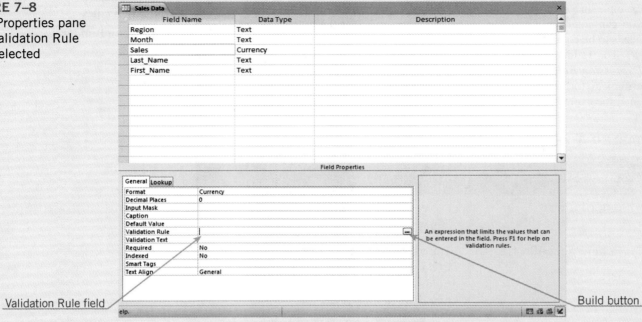

6. Click the **Build** button located on the right side of the Validation Rule field.

7. In the Expression Builder text box, type **>=40000**. See **Figure 7–9**.

FIGURE 7–9
Expression Builder dialog box

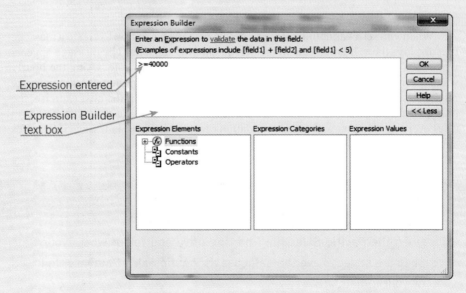

8. Click **OK**. Next, you will enter the text that appears in the message box when the data entered does not meet the rule.

9. Click in the **Validation Text** field in the Field Properties pane, and then type **Sales need to be at least $40,000**, as shown in **Figure 7–10**.

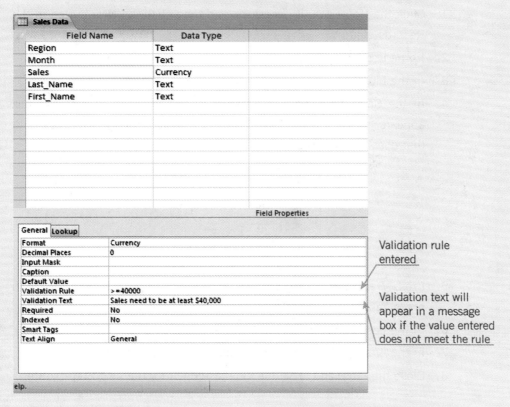

FIGURE 7–10
Validation rule and message

Validation rule entered

Validation text will appear in a message box if the value entered does not meet the rule

10. On the Quick Access toolbar, click the **Save** button. A message box may appear indicating that Data integrity rules have been changed and existing data will be tested for the new rule.

11. Click **Yes**, if necessary.

12. In the Views group, click the **View** button arrow and then click **Datasheet View**. Keep the file open for the next Step-by-Step.

Add Data Into a Field with a Validation Rule

When a validation rule is created, data entered into the field must meet the rule requirements. In the next exercise, you will enter a record with a field that has a validation rule. You will first enter the data incorrectly to see the message, and then you will reenter the data correctly.

Step-by-Step 7.4

1. Click the **Home** tab, if necessary, and then click the **New** button in the Records group.

2. In the Region field, type **West** and then press **Tab**.

3. In the Month field, type **April** and then press **Tab**.

4. In the Sales field, type **39450** and then press **Tab**. A message box appears, as shown in **Figure 7–11**. You realize that you entered data that does not pass the rule.

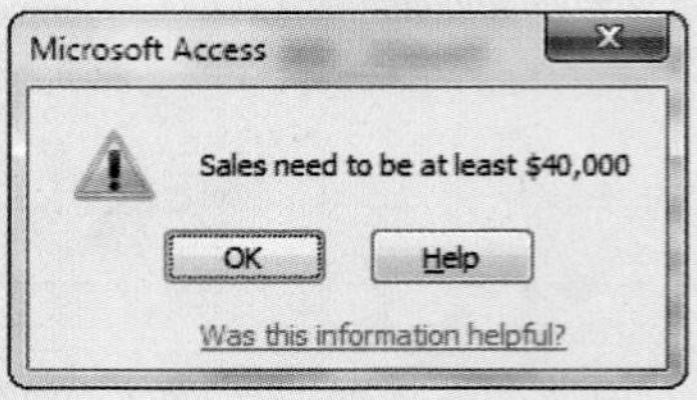

FIGURE 7–11
Message box displays validation rule

5. Press **Backspace** until 39450 is deleted, type **49450**, and then press **Tab**.

6. In the Last Name field, type **Johnson** and then press **Tab**.

7. In the First Name field, type **Jerome** and then press **Enter**.

8. Close the table and leave the database open for the next Step-by-Step.

Setting a Lookup Property

A lookup property offers a list of values that you can select. The list of values can be from another field or in a query. You can also create your own list of lookup values. When the field or list of values appears, you simply select the value you want entered into the selected field. Setting lookup properties can help prevent data entry errors.

> **VOCABULARY**
> **list box**

You can set lookup properties in the Lookup tab in the Field Properties pane, or you can use the Lookup Wizard to take you step by step through the process. You can select whether you want the lookup property to be in the form of a text box, list box, or combo box. A text box is used when you want to enter data. A *list box* lets you select more than one value, and a combo box lets you enter a value or select a value from a list. In the following exercise, you will setup lookup properties in the Lookup tab of the Field Properties pane.

Step-by-Step 7.5

1. In the Navigation pane, double-click **Region** to open the Region table. Notice that this table contains the four sales regions.

2. Close the table.

3. Right-click the **Sales Data** table, and then select **Design View** from the shortcut menu.

4. Click the **Region** field, and then click the **Lookup** tab in the Field Properties pane. See **Figure 7–12**.

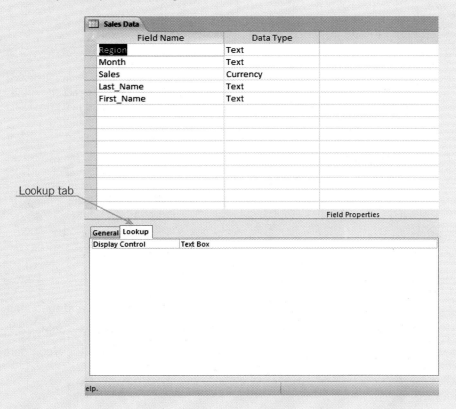

FIGURE 7–12
Lookup tab in the Field Properties pane

5. Click the **Display Control** drop-down arrow, and then click **List Box**. Several settings for List Box appear in the Field Properties pane, as shown in **Figure 7–13**. These settings help you define how the list should function. The Table/Query option is already selected as the Row Source Type. Since you will be creating the list from a field in a table, this option is correct. Next, you will enter Region table as the Row Source.

FIGURE 7–13
Lookup tab showing field properties for List Box

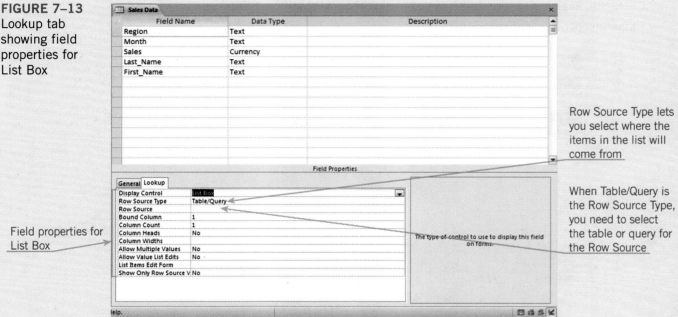

Row Source Type lets you select where the items in the list will come from

When Table/Query is the Row Source Type, you need to select the table or query for the Row Source

Field properties for List Box

6. Click in the **Row Source** field, click the **drop-down arrow**, and then click **Region**. The List Box will now display data from the Region table.

7. Click the **Region** field in the Field Name column, and then compare your screen to **Figure 7–14**.

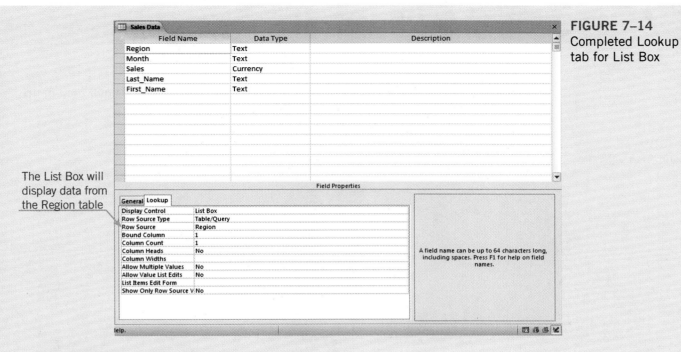

The List Box will display data from the Region table

FIGURE 7–14
Completed Lookup tab for List Box

8. Click the **Save** button on the Quick Access toolbar.

9. In the Views group, click the **View** button arrow and then click **Datasheet View**.

10. Leave the table open for the next Step-by-Step.

Selecting Field Values From a List

After you set the lookup properties for a field, a drop-down arrow will appear in the field when it is selected. You click the drop-down arrow to display the list. Then, you choose the value that you want entered into the field from the list. In the following exercise, you will enter data into a field from the list.

Step-by-Step 7.6

1. In the Records group, click the **New** button to start a new record.

2. In the new record, click the **drop-down arrow** in the **Region** field to display the list for regions, as shown in **Figure 7–15**.

FIGURE 7–15
Region field with list

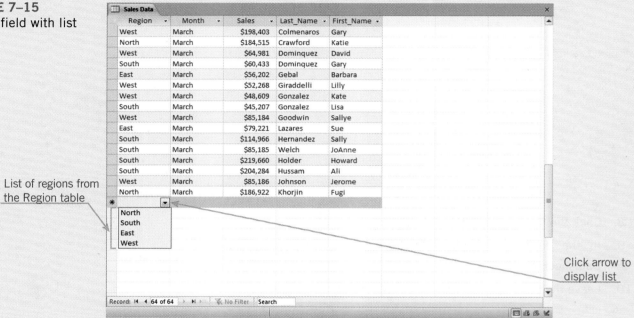

List of regions from the Region table

Click arrow to display list

3. Click **East** and then press **Tab**.

4. In the Month field, type **April** and then press **Tab**.

5. In the Sales field, type **53982** and then press **Tab**.

6. In the Last Name field, type **Gebal** and then press **Tab**.

7. In the First Name field, type **Barbara** and then press **Enter**.

8. Save your work, close the table, and then close the database.

Using the Lookup Wizard to Set Lookup Properties

When you create lookup properties in the Lookup pane, your selections are limited, such as selecting the entire table. However, you may find that you need to create lookup properties with additional options. For example, you may have a field that has product numbers, such as **PK-SWSM**. Just looking at the product number, you may not recognize the product. But if you have the product description displayed in the column next to the product number, you will be able to identify the product, such as **PK-SWSM Puppy Sweater – Small**. To have more than one field appear in the list, you need to create lookup properties using the Lookup Wizard.

In the next exercise, you will set lookup properties with two descriptions using the Lookup Wizard.

Step-by-Step 7.7

1. Open the **P & K Industry** file from the drive and folder where your Data Files are stored. Save the database as **P & K Industry Database**, followed by your initials.

2. Double-click the **Products** table to view the data, look at the Item Number and Description fields, and then close the table.

3. Double-click the **Sales Order** table to view the data. Notice how the Item Number and Description fields are in this table as well.

4. In the Views group, click the **View** button arrow and then click **Design View**.

5. Click in the field next to **Item Number** in the Data Type column.

6. Click the **Data Type** drop-down arrow, and then select **Lookup Wizard** from the Data Type menu. The first dialog box for the Lookup Wizard opens, as shown in **Figure 7–16**.

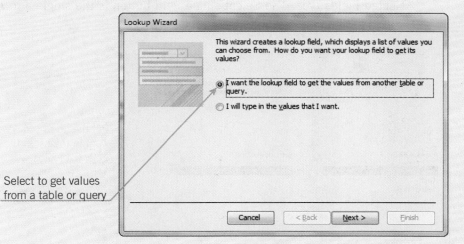

Select to get values from a table or query

FIGURE 7–16
First window in the Lookup Wizard dialog box

7. Verify that the **I want the lookup field to get the values from another table or query** option button is selected, then click **Next**. The second window of the Lookup Wizard dialog box appears, as shown in **Figure 7–17**. The Products table should be selected.

FIGURE 7–17
Second window in the Lookup Wizard dialog box

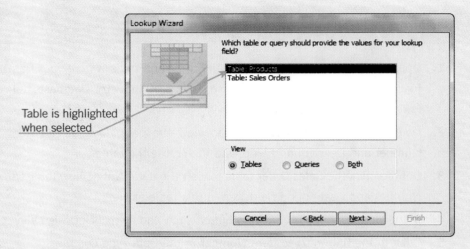

Table is highlighted when selected

8. Click **Next** to select the fields you want in the lookup field.

9. Verify that the **Item Number** field is selected, and click the **Select single field** button to move this field from the Available Fields area to the Selected Fields area. The Select single field button is the single arrow button in the dialog box, as shown in **Figure 7–18**.

FIGURE 7–18
Third window in the Lookup Wizard dialog box

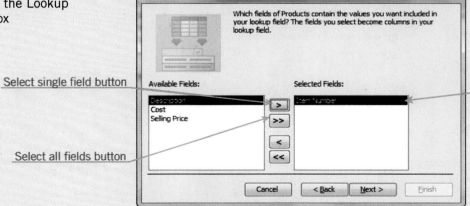

Select single field button

Select all fields button

Put the fields you want in the list in the Selected Fields area

10. Verify that the **Description** field is selected, click the **Select single field** button, then click **Next** to view the fourth window of the Lookup Wizard dialog box.

11. Click the **down arrow** to the left of Ascending, select **Item Number** to sort the data by this field, and then click **Next**. The fifth window of the Lookup Wizard dialog box is displayed, as shown in **Figure 7–19**.

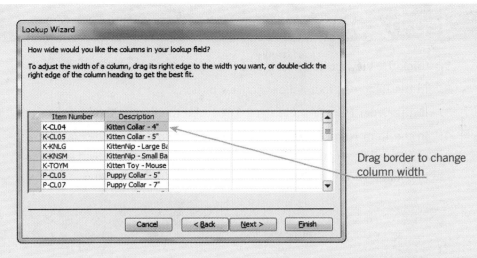

FIGURE 7–19
Fifth window in the Lookup
Wizard dialog box

12. Place the mouse pointer over the right border of the **Item Number** heading, then drag to the left to decrease the size of this field to display all of the description. Place your mouse pointer over the left border of the **Description** heading, and then drag to the right to increase the size of this field. In the next window, you will select the field that contains the value you want stored in the table.

13. Click **Next**. You want to store the Item Number in the Item Number field, so you leave this option selected.

14. Click **Next**, and then type **Item Number** in the *What label would you like for your lookup field?* text box. When you enter data, Item Number will appear at the top of the list.

15. Click **Finish**. A message box appears letting you know that the table needs to be saved so the relationship between the Item Number fields in the Sales Orders table and the Products table can be created. When these tables are related, you can select an item from the Products table and it will be entered into the Sales Products table.

16. Click **Yes** and remain in this screen for the next Step-by-Step.

Selecting Data From a List with Multiple Columns

Using the Lookup Wizard to set lookup properties allows you to have more than one column of data appear in the list. Having more than one column of data helps you identify the correct value to select. Even though two columns are displayed in the list, data from only one field is entered into the field when you select an item. For the following exercise, you will enter a record and in the field with the lookup properties, you will display the list with multiple columns before you make a selection.

Step-by-Step 7.8

1. Click the **View** button arrow, and then click **Datasheet View**.

2. In the Records group, click the **New** button.

3. In the **Order Number** field, type **1061** and then press **Tab**.

4. In the **Item Number** field, click the **drop-down arrow** to display the list of options as shown in **Figure 7–20**. Notice that even with the changes in column width, you still cannot view all of the information.

FIGURE 7–20
List with multiple
columns

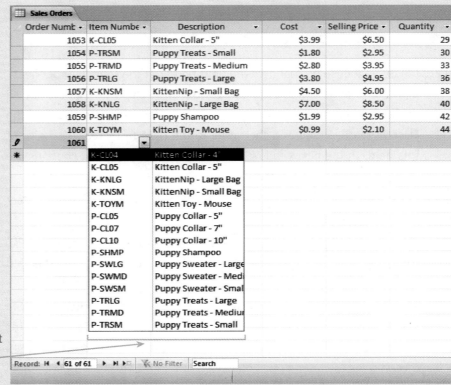

Multiple columns
help identify correct
product numbers

5. Click **P-SWSM Puppy Sweater - Small**, and then press **Tab**.

6. In the Description field, type **Puppy Sweater - Small** and then press **Tab**.

7. In the Cost field, type **6.65** and then press **Tab**.

8. In the Selling Price field, type **9.50** and then press **Tab**.

9. In the Quantity field, type **15**, and then press **Enter**.

10. Close the table and leave the database open for the next Step-by-Step.

Creating a Calculated Field in a Table

Access 2010 has a new feature that allows you to create a calculated field in a table. If you have two fields in a table, such as Quantity and Selling Price, you can multiply the values in these two fields and show the result in the calculated field in the table. And, if an amount in either of these fields changes, the result in the calculated field will show the new result.

Using a calculated field saves you time by printing reports directly from the table rather than needing to create a query to perform the calculation and then display a report from the query.

You create the calculated field using the Expression Builder. The Expression Builder displays the fields from the table. You will then select fields that you want to be calculated. In addition, you will choose the operators that you want to use. *Operators* are the mathematical characters—such as plus (+), minus (–), multiplication (*), and division (/)—that determine the type of calculation in the expression. In the next exercise, you will create a calculated field in the Sales Orders table.

▶ **VOCABULARY**
operators

Step-by-Step 7.9

1. Right-click the **Sales Orders** table, and then click **Design View** from the shortcut menu.

2. Click in the field under Quantity in the Field Name column, and then type **Order Total**.

3. Press **Tab**, and then click the **Data Type** drop-down arrow to display a list of the data types, as shown in **Figure 7–21**.

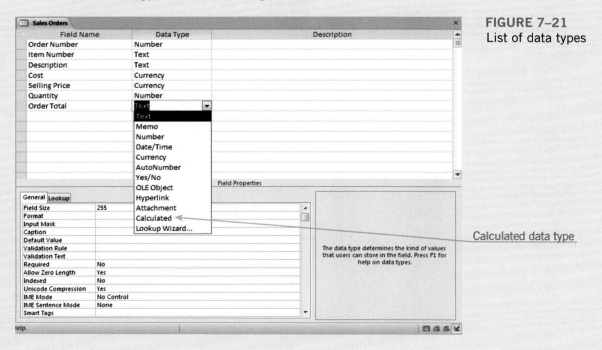

FIGURE 7–21
List of data types

Calculated data type

4. Click **Calculated**. The Expression Builder dialog box opens, as shown in **Figure 7–22**.

FIGURE 7–22
Expression Builder dialog box for Calculated field

Select the table to display the fields in the Expression Categories area

Click Operators to display available operators in the Expression Values area

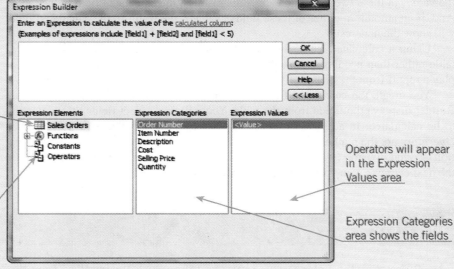

Operators will appear in the Expression Values area

Expression Categories area shows the fields

5. In the Expression Categories section, double-click **Quantity** to move it up to the top expression box.

6. In the Expression Elements section, click **Operators** to display the operators in the Expression Values area.

7. Double-click ***** in the Expression Values area. An asterisk is the symbol for multiplication.

8. Click **Sales Orders** in the Expression Elements area to redisplay the table fields in the Expression Categories area.

9. In the Expression Categories area, double-click **Selling Price** to move it into the top expression box. Compare your screen to **Figure 7–23**.

FIGURE 7–23
Completed Expression Builder dialog box

Expression for Calculated field

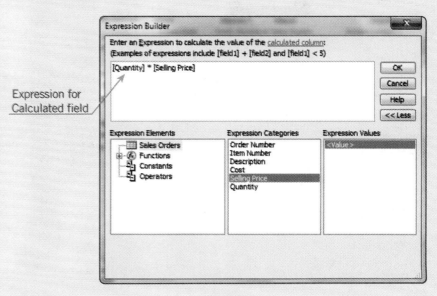

10. Click **OK** to close the Expression Builder dialog box.

11. Click the **Save** button on the Quick Access toolbar.

12. In the Views group, click the **Datasheet View** button. Review the results of the calculated field. See **Figure 7–24**. Notice how the Order Total field displays the Quantity multiplied by the Selling Price.

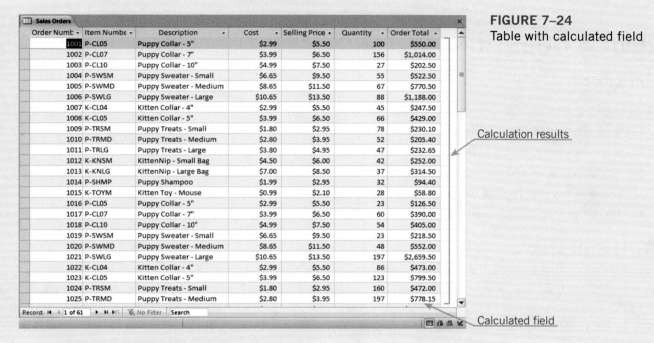

FIGURE 7–24
Table with calculated field

Calculation results

Calculated field

13. Close the table and then close the database.

SUMMARY

In this lesson, you learned:

- An input mask improves the accuracy of the data entered, such as automatically adding symbols like parentheses and a dash in a telephone number field.

- After an input mask is created for a field, just the values need to be typed into the field, not the symbols.

- Validation rules prevent inaccurate data from being entered into a field.

- Setting a lookup property in the Lookup tab in the Field Properties pane creates a list from which values can be selected.

- After lookup properties are set up for a field, you simply need to click a value from a list to select it.

- Using the Lookup Wizard to set lookup properties allows you to have more than one column of information in the list.

- A calculated field can be added to a table to perform calculations on fields in the table.

■ VOCABULARY REVIEW

Define the following terms:

Expression Builder   list box   validation rule
expression   operator
input mask   placeholder

■ REVIEW QUESTIONS

TRUE / FALSE

Circle T if the statement is true or F if the statement is false.

T   F   **1.**   If the expression >=900 is entered as a validation rule, the data entered into the field needs to be greater than or equal to 900.

T   F   **2.**   In Access, you can create a calculated field in a table.

T   F   **3.**   Validation rules are rules that need to be passed before the data can be entered in a field.

T   F   **4.**   Setting lookup properties can help prevent data entry errors.

T   F   **5.**   The default placeholder for input masks is the underscore.

FILL IN THE BLANK

1. A(n) _____ is an arithmetic formula that performs a calculation.

2. A(n) _____ improves the accuracy of the data entered, such as automatically adding symbols like dashes in a Social Security number field.

3. A(n) _____ is a pattern for certain types of data entered in a field.

4. After you set up the lookup properties for a field, a(n) _____ will appear in the field when it is selected.

5. You can add _____ properties to a field to display data from another table in a list from which you can make a selection.

WRITTEN QUESTIONS

Write a brief answer to the following questions.

1. Explain how the expression [Retail Price]>[Cost] would be used in a validation rule.

2. Explain the benefit of using the Lookup Wizard versus entering lookup properties in the Lookup pane.

3. When a person enters data that does not pass a validation rule, what can you do that will help them understand the problem with their data?

4. Give an example of placeholders for an input mask in a field for zip codes.

5. Explain the purpose of a calculated field in a table.

■ PROJECTS

If you have a SAM 2010 user profile, your instructor may have assigned an autogradable version of the indicated project. If so, log into the SAM 2010 Web site at *www.cengage.com/sam2010* to download the instruction and start files.

PROJECT 7–1

1. Open the **Division Sales** file from the drive and folder where your Data Files are stored. Save the database as **Division Sales Database**, followed by your initials.

2. Create a lookup property for the Division field in the Sales Data table that creates a list box using the Divisions table. The list created from the Divisions table should only have one field or column displayed.

3. After you create the lookup property, switch to Datasheet view.

4. Enter the following record:

   Division: **Division 3**

   Month: **April**

   Sales: **55190**

   Last_Name: **Welch**

   First_Name: **JoAnne**

5. Close the table and then close the database.

SAM PROJECT 7–2

1. Open the **Internet Sales** file from the drive and folder where your Data Files are stored. Save the database as **Internet Sales Database**, followed by your initials.

2. Create an input mask for the Social Security field.

3. Use the # symbol as the placeholder in the input mask, and store the symbols with the data.

4. View the changes in Datasheet view.

5. Enter the following record into the table:

   First Name: **Emily**

   Last Name: **Manz**

   SSN: **555220987**

   Address: **1612 East Loop**

   City: **Cortez**

   State: **CO**

   ZIP: **81321**

6. Close the table and then close the database.

PROJECT 7–3

1. Open the **Pet Sales** file from the drive and folder where your Data Files are stored. Save the database as **Pet Sales Database**, followed by your initials.

2. Create a calculated field in the table with the field name **Order_Total.**

3. The calculated field will need to multiply Selling Price by Quantity.

4. Save the table.

5. Switch to Datasheet view to review the results.

6. Close the table and then close the database.

■ CRITICAL THINKING

ACTIVITY 7–1

As the new division manager, you want to enhance the table design in the company's sales database. Open the **Sales** database from the drive and folder where your Data Files are stored, and then save it as **Sales Database**, followed by your initials. Create a calculated field that shows the price difference between the Selling Price field and the Cost field. Name the field **Markup**. View the table results in Datasheet view. Close the database.

ACTIVITY 7–2

Think of a Lookup field you could use in a database table for your personal use. For example, think of a table that includes a weekly sports schedule. The table might include weeks identified as Week 1, Week 2, Week 3, and so on. Or, you might also have a table that has all the names of the coaches.

LESSON 8

Using Advanced Queries

■ OBJECTIVES

Upon completion of this lesson, you should be able to:

- Create a parameter query.
- Run a parameter query.
- Prepare a table for action queries.
- Use an append query.
- Change data with an update query.
- Use wildcards in a query.
- Use parameters and wildcards in a query.
- Create a crosstab query.

■ VOCABULARY

action query

append

criterion

parameter

wildcard character

Introduction

Queries are operations that let you locate specific information in tables. You use a query to ask Access a question. When you run the query, the answer is displayed. In this lesson, you will explore parameter queries, which ask you to enter search data each time you run the query. You will also learn how to prepare a table for action queries. Action queries, such as an append query or an update query, make changes to the records in a table. An append query adds records from one table and puts them in another table. An update query actually changes records in a table based on the information you enter. Finally, you'll discover the advantages of crosstab queries, which rearrange the data in a table or query into another format.

Creating a Parameter Query

Parameter queries increase efficiency by providing a single query that you may use many times with a different criterion each time the query runs. *Parameter* means to vary. *Criterion* refers to the specific information you are searching for. For example, in a large table of customers, you might need to search for an individual customer. Rather than creating a query for each customer, you can create a parameter query, which allows you to enter a new criterion each time you run the query. And, when tables are related, which means they have a common field, you can display information from more than one table.

To create a parameter query, you enter a "prompt" in the Criteria cell of the desired field. This prompt appears above the text box where you type the search criterion and lets you know the type of information you need to enter. When you save the query, you add *qry-* before the query name to easily recognize it as a query in a list. For example, if you have a table and a query with the same name, you can easily spot the query because it will have the *qry-* before the name.

▌ **VOCABULARY**

parameter

criterion

Step-by-Step 8.1

1. Open the **Book Sales** file from the drive and folder where your Data Files are stored. Save the database as **Book Sales Database**, followed by your initials. You will now create a parameter query to look up an employee by their Employee ID number.

2. Click the **Create** tab, and then click the **Query Design** button in the Queries group to display the Query Design window.

3. In the Show Table dialog box, click **Sales Department** to select it, if necessary, and then click **Add**. The Sales Department table is now added to the Query Design window.

4. Click the **Sales Orders** table, and then click **Add**.

5. Click the **Close** button to close the Show Table dialog box. If you want to increase the size of the tables in Query Design window to see all of the fields, place the mouse pointer over the bottom of the table field list and drag down until you see the entire list of fields. Compare your screen to **Figure 8–1**.

Relationship with
Employee ID fields

Multiple tables
in query

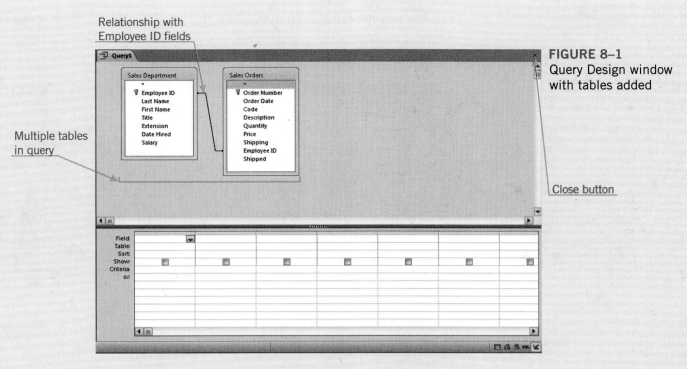

FIGURE 8–1
Query Design window
with tables added

Close button

6. In the Sales Department table, double-click the following fields to add them to the design grid in the order shown: **Employee ID**, **First Name**, and **Last Name**.

7. In the Sales Orders table, double-click the following fields to add them to the design grid in the order shown: **Order Number** and **Description**. Next, you will create a calculated field.

8. Right-click the empty field to the right of the Description field in the design grid to display the shortcut menu, and then click **Zoom**. See **Figure 8–2**.

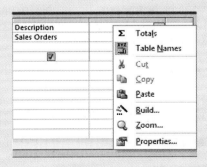

FIGURE 8–2
Shortcut menu

9. Type **Order Total:[Quantity]*[Price]** in the Zoom dialog box. The text before the colon is what will appear at the top of column, and the information after the colon is the expression.

10. Click **OK** to close the Zoom dialog box. Next, you will enter the parameter, which will appear in the message box as a prompt.

11. Click in the **Criteria** cell in the Employee ID field, and then type **[Enter Employee ID]**. The text you type in the square brackets will appear as the title for the parameter dialog box. See **Figure 8–3**.

FIGURE 8–3
Query design grid with a parameter

Parameter entered in square brackets in the Criteria field

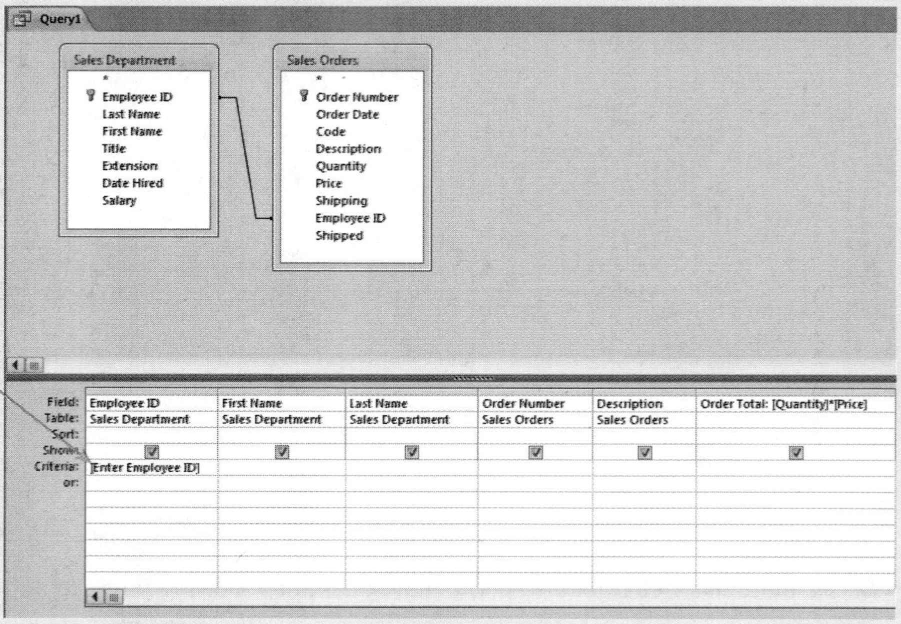

12. Save the query as **qry-Employee Sales**. Leave the query open for the next Step-by-Step.

Running a Parameter Query

After you create a parameter query, you will need to run the query so that it displays the message box where you enter the criterion. Each time you run the query, you can type a different criterion in the text box. Being able to run a query to provide the same or different criterion each time you run it saves time because a new query does not have to be created for each new search criterion.

You run a query by clicking the Run button on the Design tab, clicking the View button in the Results group, or double-clicking the query in the Navigation pane.

Step-by-Step 8.2

1. On the Ribbon, click the **Query Tools Design** tab and then click the **Run** button in the Results group. The Enter Parameter Value dialog box opens, as shown in **Figure 8–4**.

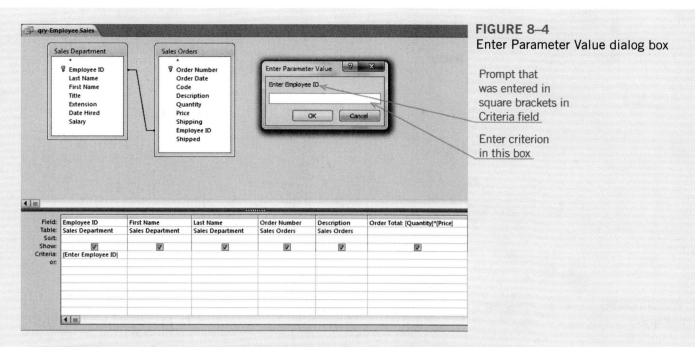

FIGURE 8–4
Enter Parameter Value dialog box

Prompt that
was entered in
square brackets in
Criteria field

Enter criterion
in this box

2. Type **N175** to display the sales results for John Carroll, and then click
   OK. See **Figure 8–5**.

FIGURE 8–5
Datasheet for
query with
parameter

Records for
Employee ID number
N175 displayed

Employee ID	First Name	Last Name	Order Nt	Description	Order Total
N175	John	Carroll	1028	Advanced Presentations	$498.75
N175	John	Carroll	2028	Advanced Presentations	$498.75
N175	John	Carroll	2029	Advanced Publishing	$1,596.00
N175	John	Carroll	3015	Computer Artist	$750.00
N175	John	Carroll	3019	Advanced Databases	$1,236.90
N175	John	Carroll	3023	Advanced Computers	$1,236.90
N175	John	Carroll	3028	Advanced Presentations	$498.75

Record: ◄ ◄ 1 of 7 ► ►I ►☀ ☀ No Filter   Search

3. On the Ribbon, click the **Home** tab and then click the **View** button in
   the Views group to return to the Query Design window.

4. On the Ribbon, click the **Query Tools Design** tab and then click the **Run**
   button in the Results group.

5. Type **N550** and then press **Enter** to display the sales results for Kelly Gordon.

6. Close the query by clicking the **Close** button in the upper-right corner of the query window. Next, you will run the query.

7. In the Navigation pane, double-click the **qry-Employee Sales** query. The Enter Parameter Value dialog box opens.

8. Type **N440** and then press **Enter** to display the sales results for Karen Lopez.

9. Close the query. Leave the database open for the next exercise.

Preparing a Table for Action Queries

▶ **VOCABULARY**

action query

An *action query* makes changes to the records in a table. For example, you can use an update action query to instantly update all the employee salaries in a table by five percent. Since the records in the table are changed as soon as you run the query, you cannot undo the changes. To protect the data in the table, it is best to make a copy of the table before you run the query. Then, if the query does not work as you expected, you have the copy of the table with the correct data to continue working.

Before you run an action query, you will want to compare the fields in the tables. Records may not be added correctly if the fields in the two tables do not match. For example, one table may have one less field than the other table. It is always best to check the data types and fields in both tables before you run the query. In this lesson, you will check the data types in both tables and then make a copy of a table.

Step-by-Step 8.3

1. In the Navigation pane, click once on the **Sales Orders** table to select it.

2. On the Ribbon, click the **Home** tab, and then click the **Copy** button in the Clipboard group.

3. Click the **Paste** button. The Paste Table As dialog box opens, as shown in **Figure 8–6**.

FIGURE 8–6
Paste Table As dialog box

Selecting the Structure and Data option button copies everything about the table, including the table structure and records

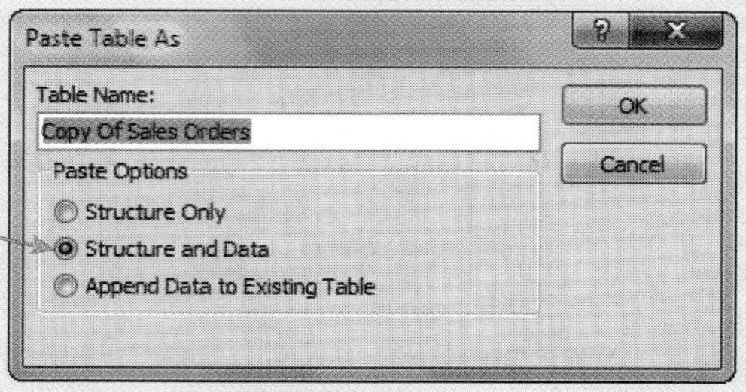

4. In the Paste Table As dialog box, verify that the **Structure and Data** option button is selected, and then click **OK**. The copied table will now serve as a backup of the table in case an error occurs in an action query.

5. Open the **Sales Orders** table and the **April Sales** table in Design View, as shown in **Figure 8–7**.

Click the table tabs to view the information for the tables

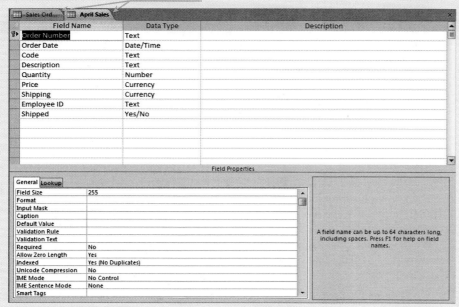

FIGURE 8–7
Opened tables in Design view

6. Click the **Sales Orders** tab and the **April Sales** tab to review the data types in each table. Each table does have the same data types for the fields.

7. Close the Sales Orders and April Sales tables.

Using an Append Query

An append query moves data from one table to another table. The word **append** means to add. When you use an append query, you add the table that has the records you want added to another table. Then, you need to add the fields to the query design

▶ **VOCABULARY**
append

grid for the fields that will contain the data to be appended to another table. To add all of the fields at one time, you can double-click the table name title to select all of the fields. The fields will be highlighted and selected, as shown in **Figure 8–8**.

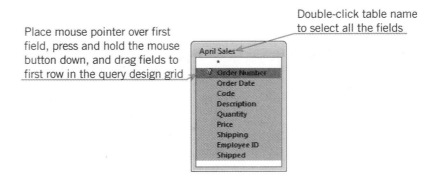

Place mouse pointer over first field, press and hold the mouse button down, and drag fields to first row in the query design grid

Double-click table name to select all the fields

FIGURE 8–8   Table with all fields selected

Then, you place the mouse pointer over the first field in the highlighted fields, press and hold down the mouse button, and drag them to the first row in the query design grid.

When you click the Append button, you will need to select the table where the records will be added. A new row will appear in the query design grid, as shown in **Figure 8–9**.

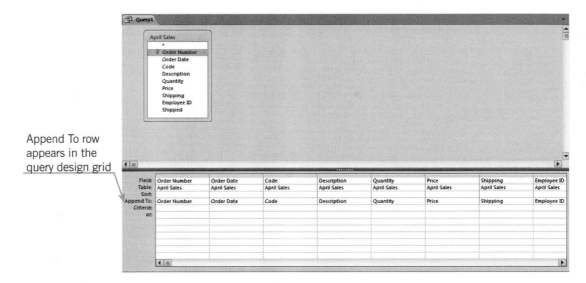

Append To row appears in the query design grid

FIGURE 8–9   Append query window

When you run the query, the records are instantly added. At this point, you should not save the query because doing so may cause the query to accidentally run again. The records would then be added for a second time. Next, you will use an append query.

Step-by-Step 8.4

1. On the Ribbon, click the **Create** tab and then click the **Query Design** button in the Queries group.

2. Double-click **April Sales** in the Show Table dialog box to place it in the Query Design window, and then click the **Close** button to close the Show Table dialog box.

3. Double-click the **April Sales** title in the Table Field List title bar. Place your mouse pointer over the first field in the list of selected fields, then press and hold the left mouse button down and drag the fields to the first row in the query grid.

4. If necessary, click the **Query Tools Design** tab and then click the **Append** button in the Query Type group. The Append dialog box opens, as shown in **Figure 8–10**.

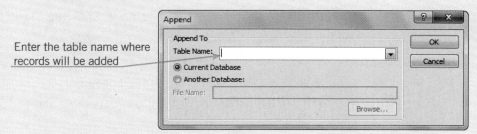

Enter the table name where records will be added

FIGURE 8–10
Append dialog box

5. In the Append dialog box, click the **Table Name** drop-down arrow and then click **Sales Orders** from the list. Click **OK** and then compare your screen to **Figure 8–11**.

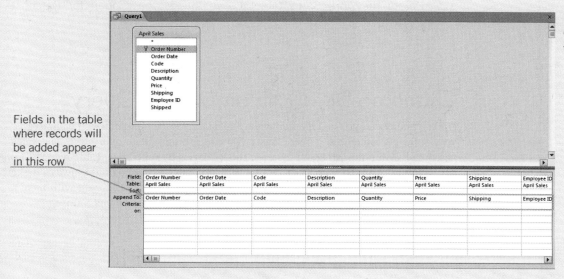

Fields in the table where records will be added appear in this row

FIGURE 8–11
Query Design window for append query

6. On the Query Tools Design tab, click the **Run** button in the Results group. A message box appears stating that you are about to append thirty rows of data, as shown in **Figure 8–12**.

FIGURE 8–12
Append message box

Check the number of records

7. Click **Yes**. Note that if you were to click the Run button again, all of the records in the April Sales table would be added to the Sales Orders table for a second time. To prevent this action from accidentally happening, you will first check to see if the records were added to the Sales Orders table and then close the query without saving it.

8. In the Navigation pane, double-click the **Sales Orders** table to open it. Scroll down in the table to review the orders for April. Click the **Close** button to close the Sales Orders table.

9. Click the **Close 'Query1'** button to close the query.

10. Click **No** so the query is not saved. Since the append query was successful, you can now delete the Copy Of Sales Orders table and the April Sales table.

11. In the Navigation pane, right-click **Copy Of Sales Orders** table, click **Delete** from the shortcut menu, and then click **Yes** to confirm the deletion.

12. Delete the **April Sales** table. Leave the database open for the next exercise.

Changing Data with an Update Query

Update queries let you change field values in a table. For example, if you want to give your sales personnel a 6 percent raise, you can use an update query to locate sales personnel within the table and increase their salaries by 6 percent. Table records are permanently changed when you run the update query, so you should always make a copy of the table before running the query. In this next exercise, you will make a copy of the Sales Department table and then give the sales personnel a raise.

Step-by-Step 8.5

1. Click once on the **Sales Department** table to select it. On the Home tab, click the **Copy** button and then click the **Paste** button. Verify that the **Structure and Data option button** is selected in the Paste Table As dialog box, and then click **OK**.

2. Double-click the **Sales Department** table to open it. Notice that the salary for Sally Loyal is $54,800. Also notice that there are nine Sales Reps. Keep this amount in mind so you can check the results of the updated data. Click the **Close 'Sales Department'** button to close the table.

3. On the Ribbon, click the **Create** tab and then click the **Query Design** button in the Queries group.

4. Double-click the **Sales Department** table in the Show Table dialog box to place it in the Query Design window, and then close the Show Table dialog box.

5. Double-click the **Title** field and the **Salary** field to move them to the query design grid.

6. Click the **Query Tools Design** tab, and then click the **Update** button in the Query Type group.

7. Click in the **Criteria** field in the Title field, and then type **Sales Rep**.

8. Click in the **Update To** field under Salary, and then type **[Salary]*1.03**. This calculation will give the sales representatives a 3 percent raise. Compare your screen to **Figure 8–13**.

FIGURE 8–13
Query Design window for an update query

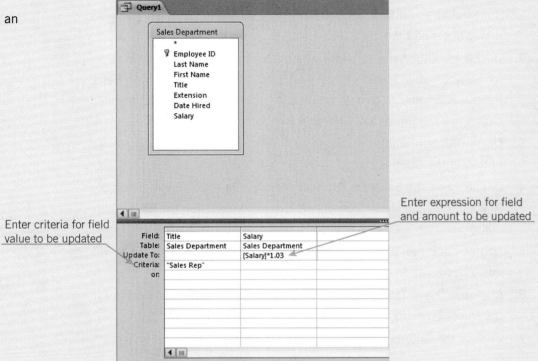

Enter criteria for field value to be updated

Enter expression for field and amount to be updated

9. Click the **Run** button in the Results group, and then click **Yes** in the message box that follows.

10. In the Navigation pane, double-click the **Sales Department** table to open it. Notice that the salary for Sally Loyal is $56,444. Her salary shows the 3 percent increase ($54,800 * 1.03 = $56,444).

11. Click the **Close 'Sales Department'** button to close the Sales Department table. Now that you have checked to see that the update query was successful, you will close the query without saving it.

12. Click the **Close 'Query1'** button to close the query. Click **No** to close the query without saving the changes.

13. Since the query successfully updated salaries for the Sales Reps, you can delete the copy you made. Right-click the **Copy of Sales Department** table, click **Delete** from the shortcut menu, and then select **Yes** in the message box.

Using Wildcards in a Query

A **wildcard character** is a character, such as an asterisk, that you can use to represent incomplete or unknown information. For example, you may know that a person's last name begins with Del, but you do not know how to spell the rest of it. In a query, you can search for the person by typing del*. The asterisk is the wildcard character. The wildcard character lets Access know that it should look for any last name that starts with Del. The query result may show people with last names of Delagarza, Delaware, or Del Gado. In other words, any person's last name that starts with Del will be displayed, regardless of what comes after Del.

You can use a wildcard character with letters or numbers in any order. For example, if you type *del*, Access will find last names such as Adelgo, Delagarza, Del Gado, and Begedel. Access looks at what is between the asterisks and returns an answer. In other words, it will not matter what comes before or after the del; any last name with del will be displayed. In this next exercise, you will use wildcards to look for various book titles.

Step-by-Step 8.6

1. On the Ribbon, click the **Create** tab and then click the **Query Design** button in the Queries group.

2. Double-click **Sales Orders** in the Show Table dialog box to add the table to the Query Design window, and then close the Show Table dialog box.

3. Double-click the **Order Number**, **Order Date**, **Description**, **Quantity**, and **Price** fields to add them to the query design grid. Next, you will use wildcards to see how many database books were ordered.

4. Click in the **Criteria** field under the Description column.

5. Type ***database*** and then press **Enter**. Notice that Access automatically adds the word Like and quote marks around the criteria. Compare your screen to **Figure 8–14**.

FIGURE 8–14
Query design grid using wildcards

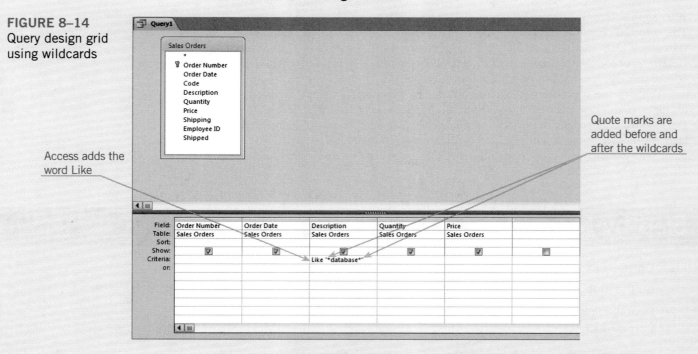

6. Click the **Run** button to view the results as shown in **Figure 8–15**.

FIGURE 8–15
Query datasheet with wildcard results

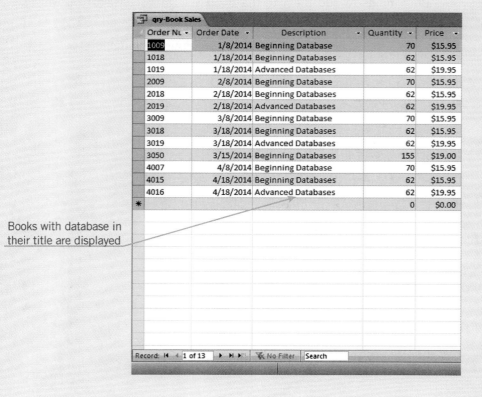

7. Click the **View** button in the Views group to return to the Query Design window. Clicking the View button will toggle you between the two windows.

8. Click the **Save** button on the Quick Access toolbar, and then type **qry-Book Sales** in the Query Name text box in the Save As dialog box.

9. Click **OK**. Remain in Query Design window for the next Step-by-Step.

Using Parameters and Wildcards in a Query

You learned that using parameters in a query displays a message box where you can type different search criteria each time you run the query. In addition, you discovered that wildcards can be used instead of exact text or numbers when looking for data. For added flexibility, Access allows you to use parameters and wildcards in the same query. Using both parameters and wildcards allows you to enter only the criterion that you are sure of in the provided message box. In this next exercise, you will use a parameter and wildcards in the same Criteria field.

Step-by-Step 8.7

1. Click in the **Criteria** field under the Description column, and then press **Delete** or **Backspace** to delete the criteria.

2. In the Criteria cell, type **Like "*" & [Enter search text] & "*"**. Entering a parameter with wildcards lets you enter a word or a few letters of your search term. In this example, you are looking for any books that contain "publish" in their title. Notice that you cannot see the entire Description field, as shown in **Figure 8–16**. In the next step, you will increase the width of this field.

FIGURE 8–16
Query with criteria entered

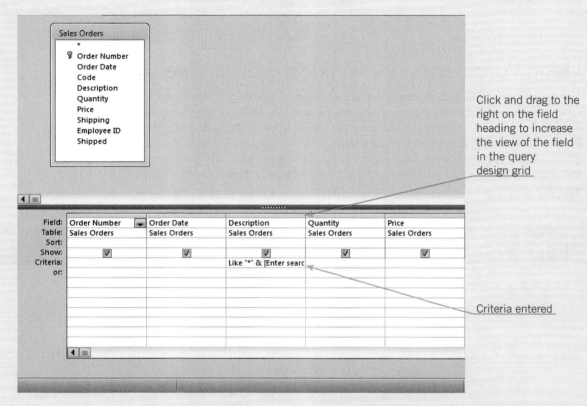

Click and drag to the right on the field heading to increase the view of the field in the query design grid

Criteria entered

3. Place the mouse pointer on the right side of the bar above the Description field name, and drag to the right to increase the width of the field in the query design grid so you can see all of the criteria. See **Figure 8–17**.

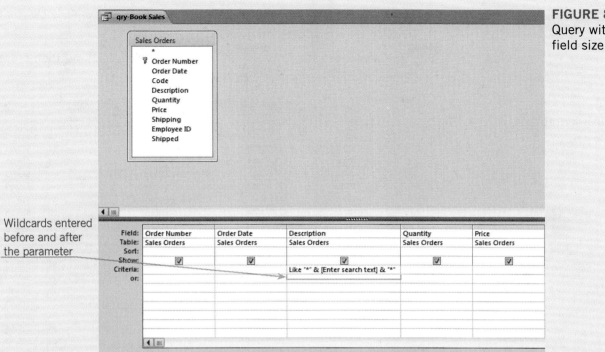

FIGURE 8–17
Query with increased field size

Wildcards entered before and after the parameter

4. Click the **Save** button.
5. Click the **Run** button. The Enter Parameter Value dialog box opens.
6. In the Enter Parameter Value dialog box, type **publish**, and then click **OK**. The Query datasheet shows the results for all books that contain "publish" in their title. See **Figure 8–18**.

Order Nu ▾	Order Date ▾	Description ▾	Quantity ▾	Price ▾
1010	1/12/2014	Beginning Publishing	80	$15.95
1011	1/12/2014	Advanced Publishing	80	$19.95
1012	1/12/2014	Desktop Publishing for Beginners	115	$19.95
1020	1/21/2014	Beginning Publishing	55	$15.95
1021	1/21/2014	Advanced Publishing	55	$19.95
1025	1/28/2014	Desktop Publishing for Beginners	95	$19.95
2010	2/12/2014	Beginning Publishing	80	$15.95
2011	2/12/2014	Advanced Publishing	80	$19.95
2012	2/12/2014	Desktop Publishing for Beginners	215	$19.95
2020	2/21/2014	Beginning Publishing	55	$15.95
2021	2/21/2014	Advanced Publishing	55	$19.95
2025	2/28/2014	Desktop Publishing for Beginners	95	$19.95
2029	2/12/2014	Advanced Publishing	80	$19.95
2030	2/12/2014	Desktop Publishing for Beginners	215	$19.95
3010	3/12/2014	Beginning Publishing	80	$15.95
3011	3/12/2014	Advanced Publishing	80	$19.95
3012	3/12/2014	Desktop Publishing for Beginners	315	$19.95
3020	3/21/2014	Beginning Publishing	55	$15.95
3021	3/21/2014	Advanced Publishing	55	$19.95
3025	3/28/2014	Desktop Publishing for Beginners	95	$19.95
3029	3/12/2014	Advanced Publishing	80	$19.95
3030	3/12/2014	Desktop Publishing for Beginners	215	$19.95
3051	3/15/2014	Beginnina Publishing	193	$15.95
4008	4/14/2014	Beginning Publishing	80	$15.95
4009	4/14/2014	Advanced Publishing	80	$19.95

Record: 1 of 31   No Filter   Search

FIGURE 8–18
Query datasheet for publish criteria

Books with publish in their title are displayed

7. Click the **View** button to return to the Query Design window.

8. Click the **Run** button. You want to find book sales for all books that include the word "presentations".

9. Type **present** in the Enter Parameter Value dialog box, and then press **Enter**. Compare your screen to **Figure 8–19**.

FIGURE 8–19
Query datasheet for present criteria

Order Nu ▾	Order Date ▾	Description	▾	Quantity ▾	Price ▾
1007	1/7/2014	Beginning Presentations		62	$15.95
1008	1/7/2014	Advanced Presentations		62	$19.95
1013	1/13/2014	Beginning Presentations		34	$15.95
1014	1/13/2014	Advanced Presentations		34	$19.95
1026	1/29/2014	Beginning Presentations		50	$15.95
1027	1/29/2014	Advanced Presentations		50	$19.95
1028	1/30/2014	Advanced Presentations		25	$19.95
2007	2/7/2014	Beginning Presentations		62	$15.95
2008	2/7/2014	Advanced Presentations		62	$19.95
2013	2/13/2014	Beginning Presentations		34	$15.95
2014	2/13/2014	Advanced Presentations		34	$19.95
2026	2/28/2014	Beginning Presentations		50	$15.95
2027	2/28/2014	Advanced Presentations		50	$19.95
2028	2/28/2014	Advanced Presentations		25	$19.95
2031	2/13/2014	Beginning Presentations		34	$15.95
2032	2/13/2014	Advanced Presentations		34	$19.95
3007	3/7/2014	Beginning Presentations		62	$15.95
3008	3/7/2014	Advanced Presentations		62	$19.95
3013	3/13/2014	Beginning Presentations		67	$15.95
3014	3/13/2014	Advanced Presentations		67	$19.95
3026	3/28/2014	Beginning Presentations		50	$15.95
3027	3/28/2014	Advanced Presentations		50	$19.95
3028	3/28/2014	Advanced Presentations		25	$19.95
3031	3/13/2014	Beginning Presentations		67	$15.95
3032	3/13/2014	Advanced Presentations		67	$19.95

Record: 1 of 34   No Filter   Search

Books with present in their title are displayed

10. Click the **Close 'qry-Book Sales'** button to close the query.

11. Close the database.

Creating a Crosstab Query

A crosstab query rearranges data in a table or query so that it appears in another format. Typically records in a table appear in rows, and the columns display the information for the field. Crosstab queries let you arrange the information you want to place in the rows and columns. Crosstab queries also calculate a Sum, Avg, Count, or other type of calculation that you choose for numerical data. The completed crosstab query displays the data in a spreadsheet-like format.

Step-by-Step 8.8

1. Open the **Healthcare Training** file from the drive and folder where your Data Files are stored. Save the database as **Healthcare Training Database**, followed by your initials.

2. On the Ribbon, click the **Create** tab and then click the **Query Wizard** button in the Queries group. The New Query dialog box opens, as shown in **Figure 8–20**.

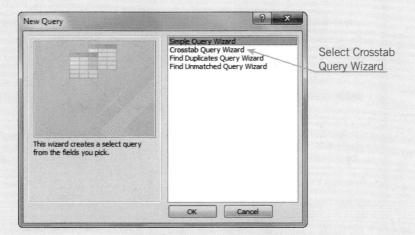

FIGURE 8–20
New Query dialog box

3. Double-click **Crosstab Query Wizard** in the New Query dialog box. The first window of the Crosstab Query Wizard opens. See **Figure 8–21**.

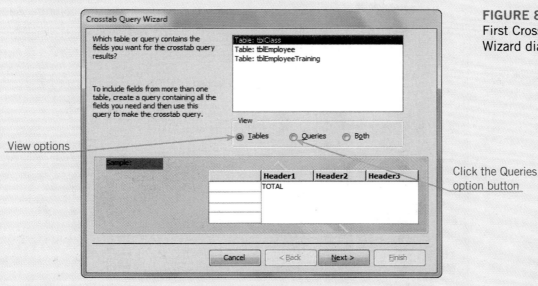

FIGURE 8–21
First Crosstab Query Wizard dialog box

4. Click the **Queries** option button in the View section of the dialog box.

5. Verify that **qry-TrainingCostAndDate** is selected, and then click the **Next** button. Next, you will click the field you want for the row headings.

6. Click **Description** for the row headings so that you can see the description for each class. Then, click the **Select Single Field** button. Compare your screen to **Figure 8–22**.

FIGURE 8–22
Description field selected for row headings

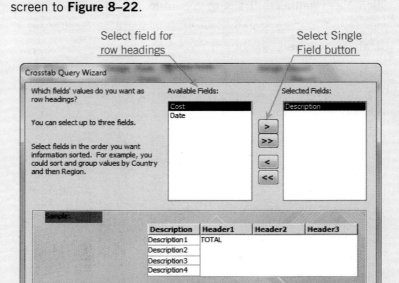

7. Click **Next**. You will now select the field for the column headings.

8. Click **Date**, and then click **Next.** You will be asked how you want the date to be displayed, such as by year, quarter, or month.

9. Click **Year** as the interval for the grouping for the Date column. See **Figure 8–23**.

FIGURE 8–23
Year selected as grouping for Date

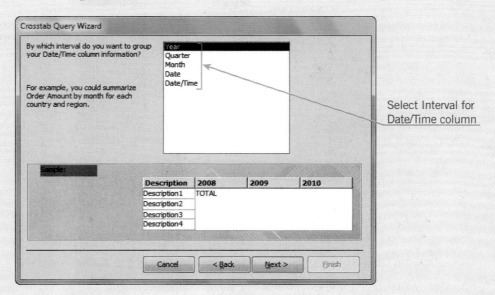

10. Click **Next**.

11. Click **Sum** in the Functions area to view the total cost for the classes. See **Figure 8–24**.

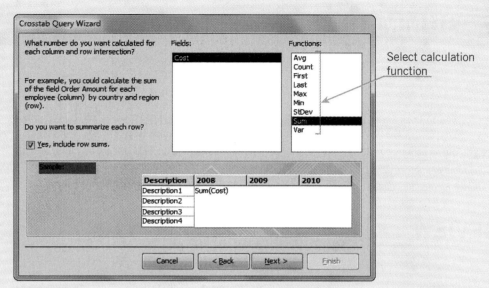

FIGURE 8–24
Sum selected to view total costs

Select calculation function

12. Click **Next**.

13. Delete the existing text in the text box below "What do you want to name your query?", type **qry-ClassCostAnalysis**, and then click **Finish**. The Crosstab query datasheet appears, as shown in **Figure 8–25**. Notice that the icon that appears before the crosstab query is different than for a select query.

Description	Total Of Cos	2011	2012	2013	2014
Adult CPR Recertification	$100.00	$40.00	$30.00	$20.00	$10.00
Child/Infant CPR	$15.00				$15.00
Child/Infant CPR Recertification	$50.00	$20.00		$20.00	$10.00
First Aid	$15.00	$15.00			
Nutritional Supplements	$25.00		$25.00		
Yoga	$50.00		$50.00		

Record: 1 of 6   No Filter   Search

FIGURE 8–25
Results of crosstab query

14. Click the **Close** button to close qry-ClassCostAnalysis. Then click the **Close** button on the Access title bar to close the database and exit Access.

SUMMARY

In this lesson, you learned:

■ Parameter queries display a dialog box for you to enter information each time you run the query.

■ It is best to make a copy of a table before you run an action query.

■ An append query can add records from one table to another table.

■ Using an update query lets you quickly change records in a table.

■ Using wildcards in queries allows for the flexibility of not knowing a complete phrase or spelling.

■ Using both parameters and wildcards allows you to enter only the criteria that you are sure of in the provided message box.

■ A crosstab query places data in a spreadsheet-like format.

VOCABULARY REVIEW

Define the following terms:

action query   criterion   wildcard character
append   parameter

REVIEW QUESTIONS

TRUE / FALSE

Circle T if the statement is true or F if the statement is false.

T   F   **1.**   If you want to add records from one table to another table, you use a parameter query.

T   F   **2.**   A wildcard, such as an asterisk, can be used in searches when you do not know the exact spelling of a person's last name.

T   F   **3.**   It is safe to run an action query that makes changes to records in a table without first making a copy of the table.

T   F   **4.**   Append queries increase efficiency by providing a single query that you may use many times with various criteria each time the query runs.

T   F   **5.**   Parameters and wildcards cannot be used in the same query on the same Criteria row.

FILL IN THE BLANK

1. A(n) _____ query rearranges data in a table or a query so that it appears in another format.

2. A(n) _____ query can instantly update several records in a table at one time.

3. _____ means to vary.

4. _____ is the data you are searching for.

5. If you are not certain of the exact spelling of a person's last name, you could use a(n) _____ in the query.

WRITTEN QUESTIONS

Write a brief answer to the following questions.

1. Explain what you should do with a table before you run an action query that makes changes to the table.

2. Explain the difference between an update query and an append query.

3. Explain the process for creating a crosstab query.

4. Give examples of when you could use an action query. Use different examples than those used in this lesson.

5. Explain the word and characters that are added in a Criteria cell when you use a wildcard.

◼ PROJECTS

If you have a SAM 2010 user profile, your instructor may have assigned an autogradable version of the indicated project. If so, log into the SAM 2010 Web site at *www.cengage.com/sam2010* to download the instruction and start files.

PROJECT 8–1

1. Open the **Pet Supplies** file from the drive and folder where your Data Files are stored. Save the database as **Pet Supplies Database**, followed by your initials.

2. Create an update query that finds the records in the Inventory table whose *Product ID* field begins with **4**. Update the *Reorder Point* field to **10**. (*Hint*: Use the criteria of 4* in the *Product ID* field.)

3. Save the query as **Qry-Product 400 Reorder Change**. Close the query.

4. Open the Inventory table and view the changes. Sort the Inventory table by the *Product ID* field. Print the table.

5. Close the query and then close the database file.

$\overset{\Lambda}{\text{SAM}}$ PROJECT 8–2

1. Open the **Atlantic Sales** file from the drive and folder where your Data Files are stored. Save the database as **Atlantic Sales Database**, followed by your initials.

2. Create a parameter query for the Sales Data table. In the Design window, add the Region, Month, Sales, Last_Name, and First_Name fields to the query grid. Since each field in the table will be included in the query, think of a quick way to put each field in the query grid.

3. Enter a prompt in the Region field that will prompt the user to enter a region.

4. Sort the query in ascending order by the Last Name field, and then add another sort in ascending order to the First Name field.

5. Save the query as **Qry-Sales by Region**.

6. Run the parameter query using West as the criterion. Adjust the column widths if necessary. Print the query results.

7. Run the query using the North and the East parameters. Print the results of each query.

8. Close the query and the database file.

PROJECT 8–3

1. Open the **Teams** file from the drive and folder where your Data Files are stored. Save the database as **Teams Database**, followed by your initials.

2. Create a parameter query with wildcards that search tblStudent for students' last names in the Last Name field. The query should be able to search for a student's last name based on the first letter of the student's last name. The query should also display all of the fields from the table.

3. Save the query as **Qry-Student Search**.

4. Run the query and search for any student's last name that begins with Lo.

5. Print the results of the query.

6. Close the query and the database file.

■ CRITICAL THINKING

ACTIVITY 8–1

Open the **Regional Sales** file from the drive and folder where your Data Files are stored, and then save the database as **Regional Sales Database** followed by your initials.

You are a new database administrator for a company in Massachusetts. When you review the Access database, you realize that the sales for January and February are in a table named Sales Data. However, the person entering the sales data created a new table for the March sales. You decide to correct this data by adding the records from the March Sales table into the Sales Data table.

ACTIVITY 8–2

As a professor at Collinsborough Community College, you're going to give a presentation to your Access class on the various types of action queries. Write a brief summary of the types of action queries discussed in this lesson and give an example of when you would use each query.

LESSON 9

Using Advanced Form Features

■ OBJECTIVES

Upon completion of this lesson, you should be able to:

- Understand the importance of consistent form design.
- Apply a theme to a form.
- Add a logo.
- Create command buttons.
- Add a new field to an existing form.
- Create a combo box.
- Size and align a control.
- Use a combo box in a new record.
- Add a calculated control.
- Change tab order.

■ VOCABULARY

calculated control

combo box

command button

live preview

logo

tab order

theme

Introduction

In this lesson, you will learn the importance of using a consistent design for all the forms in a database. A consistent design can be created with the use of themes. Themes add borders and colors to forms. You will also learn how to add command buttons to forms. A command button can be clicked to move within a form or to open another form. Then, you will add a new field to an existing form. A combo box that displays a list of options will also be created in the form. You will then add a calculated control that calculates the total of fields in a form. And, finally, you will change the order of how you move between the fields in a form, called the tab order.

Understanding the Importance of Consistent Form Design

Most people use forms to enter and retrieve data. If all the forms in your database share the same design, users will have an easier time using the forms. When designing forms, you will want to decide what color scheme, fonts, and general layout to use. Because users expect to find similar features in the same location on each form, consistency in design will simplify the data entry. Visually appealing forms make working in the database more enjoyable and efficient.

When designing forms, pay close attention to key features, such as titles, field organization, form layout, and error prevention. The form title should clearly identify the purpose of the form, such as *Customer Order Form*. Fields should be arranged in a meaningful order, such as First Name, Last Name, Street Address, City, State, and ZIP. The form layout should have a professional appearance and minimal graphics, so that the focus remains on the data. You can also reduce the chance of errors if you add features that let the user select information from a list rather than typing the data into a field. After you decide on a design for the form, you may want to write down the features in a check list so that you can look at the list each time you create a form. By using a list, you can ensure that the forms share the same design.

Applying a Theme to a Form

Themes are preset designs that include borders, background colors, shading, and graphic effects. Themes can be applied to an entire form to give it an attractive and professional appearance. Several themes are available with Access 2010, and each theme has a specific look. If you apply a theme to a form in a database, it is automatically applied to all forms in the database. If you make a change to a theme, such as changing the theme colors, all of the forms in the database will be updated with the new appearance. Using themes is a quick way to design forms and ensures consistency among them.

Themes are available in the Themes gallery on the Ribbon. If you move your mouse pointer over a theme in the Themes gallery, it is temporarily applied to the form so that you can see how your form would look with that theme applied. This feature is called *live preview*. In this next exercise, you will apply a theme to one form and then open another form in the database to see that the theme is applied to both forms.

Step-by-Step 9.1

1. Open the **Internet Sales** file from the drive and folder where your Data Files are stored. Save the database as **Internet Sales Database**, followed by your initials.

2. Open the **Employees** form and the **Regional Sales** form to view the formatting. Then, close both forms by clicking the **Close** button ☒ located in the upper-right corner of the form.

3. Right-click the **Employees** form, then click **Design View** from the shortcut menu to open it in Design view. The form will appear as shown in **Figure 9–1**. Next, you will look at the Themes gallery.

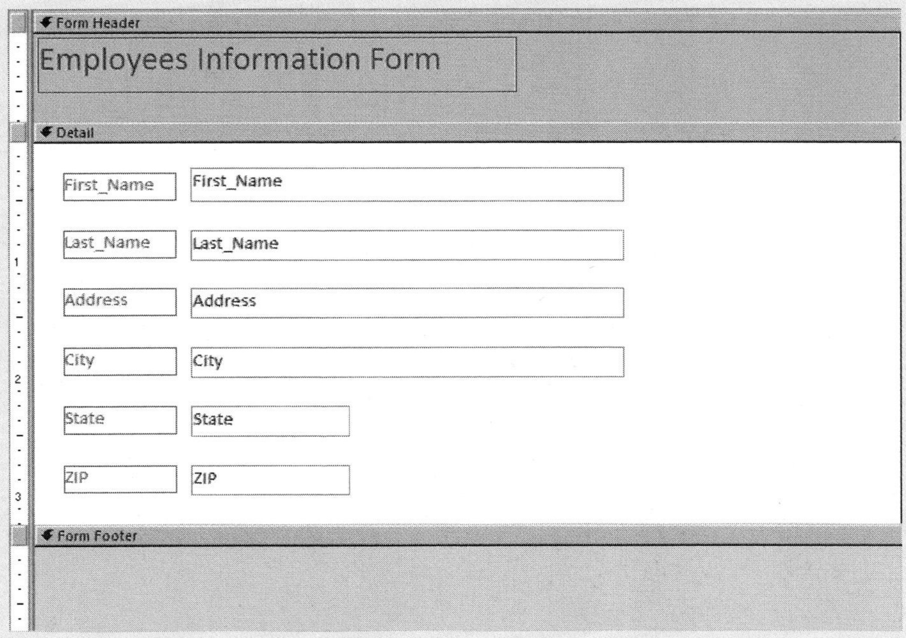

FIGURE 9–1
Employees form in Design view

4. On the Ribbon, click the **Design** tab and then click the **Themes** button in the Themes group. The Themes gallery opens, as shown in **Figure 9–2**.

FIGURE 9–2
Themes gallery

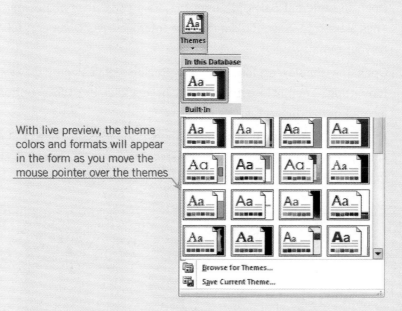

With live preview, the theme colors and formats will appear in the form as you move the mouse pointer over the themes

5. Move your mouse pointer over the themes. The live preview feature shows you how the form will appear with the various themes applied.

6. Scroll down in the Themes gallery, and then click **Solstice**. The themes are listed alphabetically in the gallery. Notice the background color applied to the heading.

7. Click the **Save** button 🖫 on the Quick Access toolbar to save the change made to the form.

8. Open the **Regional Sales** form and notice that the Solstice theme is also applied to this form. See **Figure 9–3**.

Solstice theme colors display in the
Form Header and in the Detail section

Region	Month	Sales	First_Name	Last_Name
East	January	$138,639.00	Michael	Cavillo
West	February	$59,616.00	Michael	Cavillo
West	March	$52,268.00	Michael	Cavillo
West	January	$42,798.00	Brian	Conlee
East	February	$72,680.00	Brian	Conlee
South	March	$219,660.00	Brian	Conlee
South	January	$49,802.00	Connie	Dominguez
South	February	$105,473.00	Connie	Dominguez
South	March	$204,284.00	Connie	Dominguez
West	February	$90,994.00	Elaine	Estes
West	March	$198,403.00	Elaine	Estes

FIGURE 9–3
Regional Sales form in
Design view

9. Close both forms and leave the database open for the next Step-by-Step.

Adding a Logo

Another way you can add consistency to forms is to add a logo. A *logo* is a graphic or picture that can be placed in a form. A logo usually represents a company name or identity. Placing the logo in the same area in each form gives them a consistent look that helps users feel comfortable using the form. In this next exercise, you will add a logo to each form. You will then modify the logo by changing its properties using the Property Sheet pane. The Property Sheet pane displays all of the properties for a selected object.

▶ **VOCABULARY**
logo

Step-by-Step 9.2

1. Open the **Regional Sales** form in Design view.
2. Click anywhere in the Form Header section. You will now add a logo to the Form Header.

3. On the Design tab, click the **Logo** button in the Header / Footer group. The Insert Picture dialog box opens, as shown in **Figure 9–4**.

FIGURE 9–4
Insert Picture
dialog box

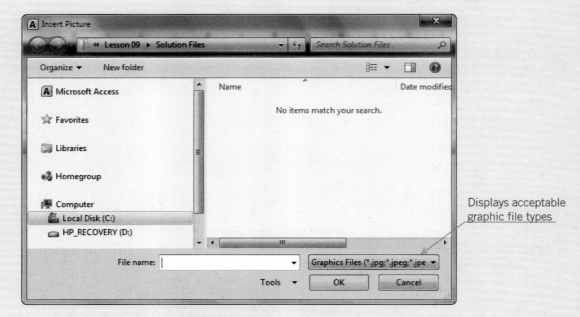

Displays acceptable
graphic file types

4. Navigate to the drive and folder where your Data Files are stored. Click the **Internet Sales Logo** file, and then click **OK**. The logo is automatically placed in the upper-left corner of the Form Header and remains selected, as shown in **Figure 9–5**. A dashed border appears next to the logo to prevent its size from being changed. In the next step, you will remove this border so you can resize the logo.

Dashed border that
automatically appears
around the logo

FIGURE 9–5
Logo placed in Form Header

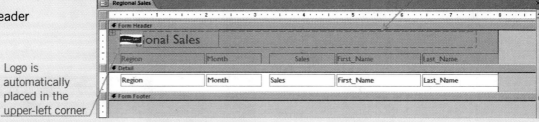

Logo is
automatically
placed in the
upper-left corner

5. Click the **dashed border** to select it and then press the **Delete** key to delete the border.

6. Click the **logo** to select it. Place the mouse pointer over the logo and when you see the pointer change to a four-headed arrow, press and hold the mouse button, then drag it to the right of the Regional Sales title, as shown in **Figure 9–6**. Next, you will resize the graphic.

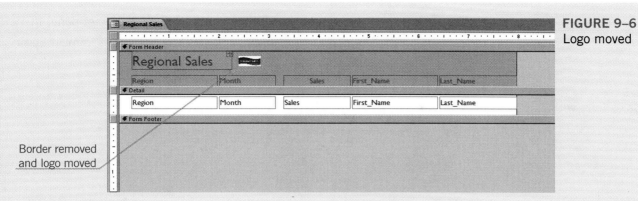

FIGURE 9–6
Logo moved

Border removed
and logo moved

7. Place the mouse pointer over the lower-right corner of the logo and then when the mouse pointer becomes a double-sided diagonal arrow, click and drag down and to the right to increase the size of the logo so that it resembles **Figure 9–7**. You will now change the alignment of the logo so that it will be on the right side of the label in the Report Header.

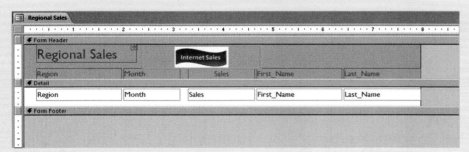

FIGURE 9–7
Logo resized

8. Click the **Property Sheet** button in the Tools group. The Property Sheet pane appears on the right side of the window.

9. If necessary, on the Property Sheet pane, click the **Format** tab, click the **Picture Alignment** property, click the **drop-down arrow** on the right to display the picture alignment options as shown in **Figure 9–8**, and then click **Top Left**.

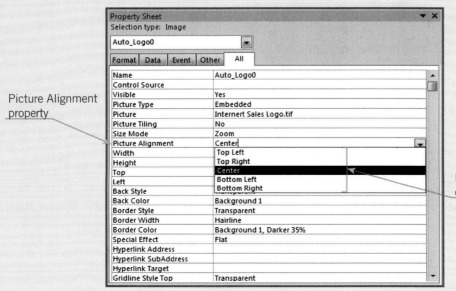

FIGURE 9–8
Picture Alignment options

Picture Alignment
property

Picture Alignment
options

10. Click the **Property Sheet** button to close the Property Sheet pane, then click the **View** button in the Views group to display the form in Form view. See **Figure 9–9**.

FIGURE 9–9
Regional Sales form with logo

11. Click the **Save** button and then close the form. For design consistency, you will now add the same logo to the Employees form.

12. Open the Employees form in Design view. Add the Internet Sales logo to the form header, then compare your screen to **Figure 9–10**.

FIGURE 9–10
Employees form with logo

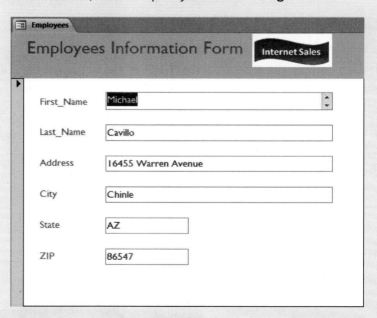

EXTRA FOR EXPERTS

You may see gridlines and dots appear on your form in Design view. If you want to hide the dots and gridlines, right-click in the section where they are, and then click Grid from the shortcut menu. Repeat the same step to show dots and gridlines.

13. Click the **Save** button. Leave the Employees form open for the next Step-by-Step.

Creating Command Buttons

One way to make forms easier to use is to include command buttons. A ***command button*** is a button that users can click to perform common tasks, such as moving to the next record in a form or adding a record. These buttons are known as record navigation and record operation command buttons. Record navigation refers to moving within the records in a form, such as going to the next record or to the previous record. Record operation options let you add a command button with a task, such as adding a new record. Both record navigation and record operation work with the records within a form. Even though Access offers its own navigation buttons in the document window, command buttons make navigating easier.

To create a command button, you choose the appropriate button on the Ribbon and then drag the mouse pointer that appears into the shape of a button. Command buttons can be made from text or graphics to indicate the purpose of the button. In this next exercise, you will create a command button using the Command Button Wizard, and you will create three command buttons in the Detail section of the form.

▶ **VOCABULARY**
command button

Step-by-Step 9.3

1. If necessary, switch to Design view. You are going to add a command button to the right side of the form.

2. Place the mouse pointer over the right border in the Detail section and then drag to the right until you are at the **7.5 inch mark** on the ruler, as shown in **Figure 9–11**. This will make room for the command button.

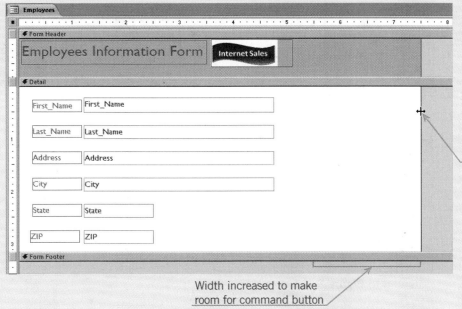

FIGURE 9–11
Increasing the width of the Employees form

Pointer shape when resizing

Width increased to make room for command button

3. Click the **Button** button 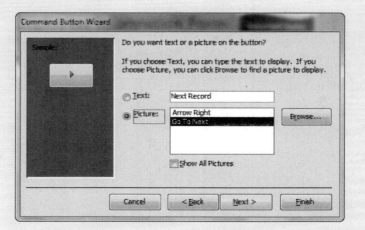 in the Controls group. Place your mouse pointer in the right side of the Detail section and then drag out the shape of a button. The Command Button Wizard dialog box opens, as shown in **Figure 9–12**. Notice that Record Navigation is selected in the Categories box.

FIGURE 9–12
Command Button Wizard
dialog box

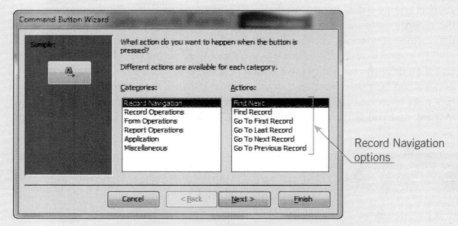

4. Click the **Go To Next Record** action and then click **Next**. The next window of the Command Button Wizard dialog box appears, as shown in **Figure 9–13**. Next, you will choose to have text to appear on the button and enter the button text.

FIGURE 9–13
Next window of the Command
Button Wizard dialog box

5. Click the **Text** option button, click in the text box before the words Next Record text, type **Go to**, and then press **[Spacebar]**. Compare your screen to **Figure 9–14**.

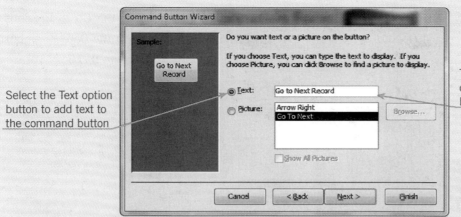

FIGURE 9–14
Choosing the Text option button

Select the Text option button to add text to the command button

Text that will appear on the command button

6. Click **Next**, accept the default name in the text box, and then click **Finish**. The completed command button appears on the form, as shown in **Figure 9–15**.

FIGURE 9–15
Form with command button

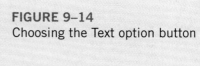

Command button

7. Using the Command Button Wizard, create a command button that moves to the previous record using the text **Go to Previous Record** on the button. Next, you will add a command button that uses record operations.

8. Click the **Button** button 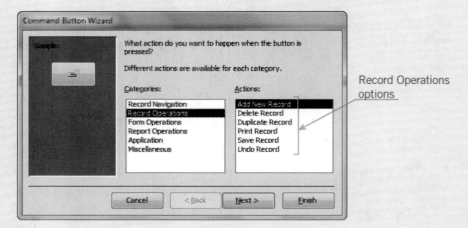, draw a button under the Go to Previous Record button, and then click **Record Operations** in the Categories box of the Command Button Wizard dialog box. See **Figure 9–16**.

FIGURE 9–16
Record Operations category

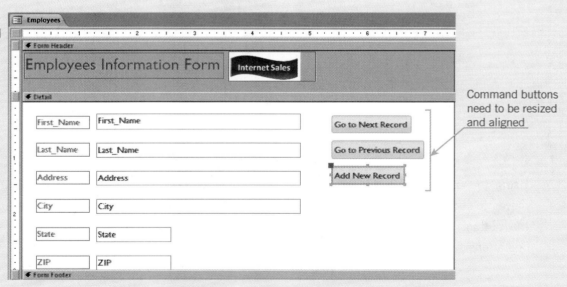

9. Click **Next**, click between the words *Add* and *Record* in the text box, and then type **New**, as in "*Add New Record*".

10. Click **Next**, and then click **Finish**. Your form should appear similar to **Figure 9–17**. In the next step, you will select all of the buttons in order to resize and align them.

FIGURE 9–17
Form with command buttons

11. Verify that the **Add New Record** button is still selected, press and hold the **Shift** key, click the **Go to Next Record** button, and then click the **Go to Previous Record** button so that all three buttons are selected. *Note*: You can also draw a selection marquee around all three command buttons to select them.

12. On the Ribbon, click the **Arrange** tab, click the **Size/Space** button in the Sizing & Ordering group, and then click **To Widest** to increase the size of the buttons to the size of the widest button. You will now evenly distribute the space between the buttons.

13. Click the **Size/Space** button in the Sizing & Ordering group, and then click **Equal Vertical**.

14. Click the **Align** button, and then click **Left** to align the left side of each button. Click outside the buttons to deselect them. See **Figure 9–18**.

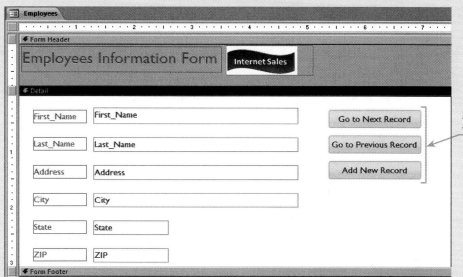

FIGURE 9–18
Command buttons aligned and resized

Aligned with equal vertical spacing

15. Switch to Form view and then click each of the command buttons to verify that they are working correctly. Save and close the form, and leave the database open for the next Step-by-Step.

Adding a New Field to an Existing Form

After you create a form, you may find that additional fields need to be added to the form. For example, you may have created a form that displays sales information with the name of an employee that made the sale. Now, you decide that you want to add the employee identification number field to the form to make it easier to locate records for that employee.

Since the form is already created, the fields are in alignment and have equal spacing between them. When you add a new field, you will need to align the new field with the other fields. A form field has two parts: the label and the text box. The label typically appears on the left side of the field and identifies the information in the field. The text box displays the actual information from the table. In this next exercise, you will add a field to an existing form and then align the field.

Step-by-Step 9.4

1. Open the **Regional Sales** form in Design view. Increase the form width by dragging the right edge of the form to the right about one inch.

2. On the Design tab, click the **Add Existing Fields** button in the Tools group to display the Field List pane, as shown in **Figure 9–19**. Then, click the **Show all tables** link at the top of the Field List pane.

FIGURE 9–19
Field List pane

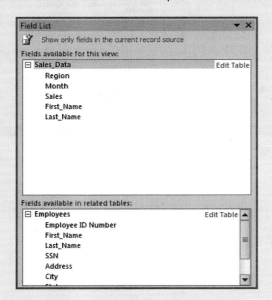

3. Click the **plus sign** next to Employees, right-click the **Employee ID Number** field to display the shortcut menu, as shown in **Figure 9–20**, and then click **Add Field to View**.

FIGURE 9–20
Field List shortcut menu

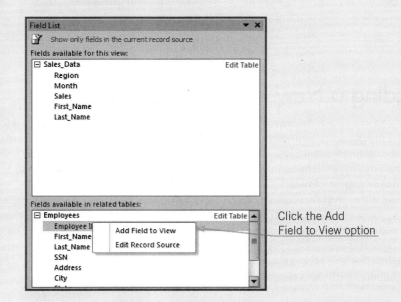

Click the Add
Field to View option

4. Click the **Add Existing Fields** button in the Tools group to close the Field List pane. Notice that the new field is located at the bottom of the Detail section as shown in **Figure 9–21**. In this next step, you will move the field.

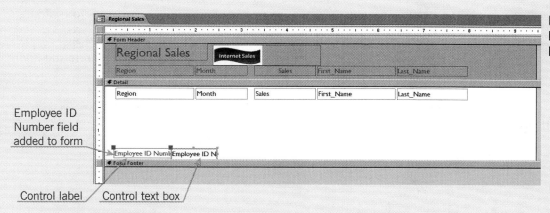

FIGURE 9–21
Form with new field in Design view

Employee ID Number field added to form

Control label   Control text box

5. Select the **Employee ID Number** text box and drag it to the right side of the form next to Last_Name.

6. Right-click the **Employee ID Number** field label and click **Cut**. Click in the Form Header section, right-click, and then select **Paste**. Drag the **Employee ID Number** field label to the right of the Last_Name label.

7. Click the **View** button arrow in the Views group, and then click **Form View**. Notice that the field is not in alignment with the other fields, as shown in **Figure 9–22**. Next, you will align the field.

Employee ID
Number field

FIGURE 9–22
Form with new field in Form view

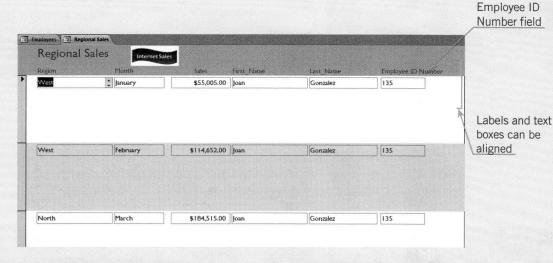

Labels and text boxes can be aligned

8. Click the **View** button arrow in the Views group, then click **Design View**.

9. Click outside the field to deselect it. You will now align the fields.

10. Click the label on the right side and increase the width by dragging the right selection handle to the right. You will now select each of the field labels to align them.

11. Select each of the field labels, click the **Arrange** tab, click the **Align** button, and then click **Bottom**.

12. Click the **Employee ID Number** text box, and then select each of the text boxes for the fields.

13. Click the **Align** button and click **Top**. To decrease the size of the Detail section, click at the top of the Form Footer section bar and drag it upward until only the fields are displayed, and then switch to the Form view. Your form should appear similar to **Figure 9–23**.

FIGURE 9–23
Form view displays new field

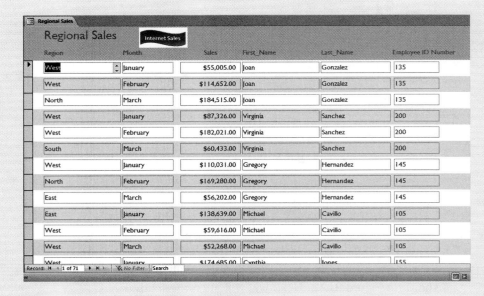

14. Save and close the form, then close the database.

Creating a Combo Box

A *combo box* displays a list of values and lets you select one from the list. This feature adds efficiency to the data entry process. Rather than typing information in a field, you simply select the value you want from a list. Selecting the value rather than typing it in the field helps decrease the chance of making typographical errors.

As with a command button, you can use a control wizard to add a combo box to a form. Like other wizards, a control wizard asks a series of questions and then uses your answers to create the combo box control in a form.

Step-by-Step 9.5

1. Open the **Pets Unlimited** file from the drive and folder where your Data Files are stored. Save the database as **Pets Unlimited Database**, followed by your initials.

2. Open the **Purchases** form in Design view to view the form. Notice that the form just has Product ID, Price, and Quantity fields, but not the Product Description field. See **Figure 9–24**. You will add a combo box for the Product Description field to the form.

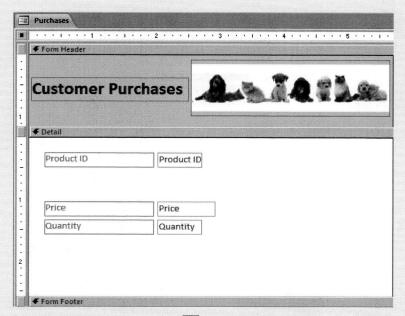

FIGURE 9–24
Purchases form

3. Click the **Combo Box** button 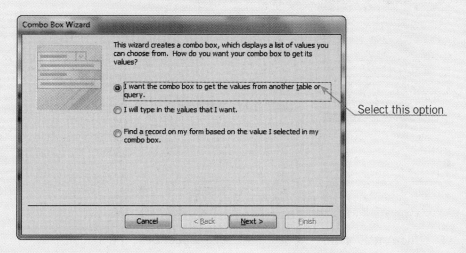 in the Controls group, then place your mouse pointer under the Product ID text box and click. The Combo Box Wizard dialog box opens, as shown in **Figure 9–25**.

FIGURE 9–25
Combo Box Wizard dialog box

4. Verify that the **I want the combo box to get the values from another table or query** option button is selected, and then click **Next**. In the next window, click **Table: Inventory** as shown in **Figure 9–26**. Click **Next**. You will now select the field from the table that you want for the combo box.

FIGURE 9–26
Select table option

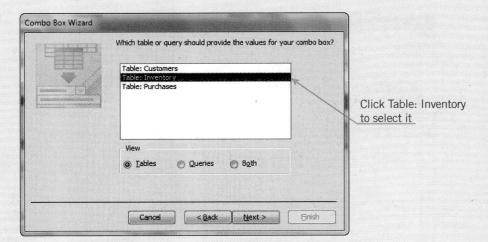

Click Table: Inventory to select it

5. Click the **Product Description** and then click the **Select Single Field** button to move the field to the Selected Fields box on the right, as shown in **Figure 9–27**. This field will store the data selected from the combo box list. Click **Next**. You will select the sort order for the field in the next step.

FIGURE 9–27
Select field for combo box

Select Single
Field button

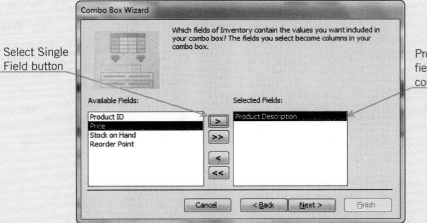

Product Description
field selected for
combo box

EXTRA FOR EXPERTS

To change from ascending order to descending order in any of the Wizard dialog boxes, you click the Ascending button. Then, the word Descending appears on the button.

6. Click the first drop-down arrow, click **Product Description** to display it in ascending alphabetical order, and then click **Next**. You will now increase the size of the column so that all of the text in the field is displayed.

7. Place your mouse pointer over the right edge of the **Product Description** column heading and drag to the right to increase the size of the column, as shown in **Figure 9–28**. Click **Next**.

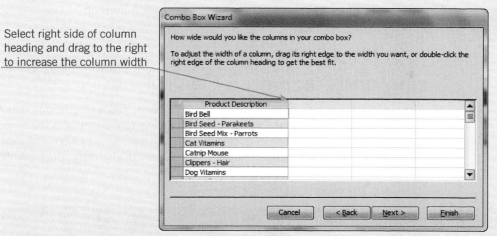

Select right side of column heading and drag to the right to increase the column width

FIGURE 9–28
Column heading adjustment

8. Verify that the **Remember the value for later use** option button is selected, and then click **Next**. Product Description is shown as the column label.

9. Click **Finish**. The completed combo box appears in the form. Compare your screen to **Figure 9–29**. You will now add a control source to the combo box so that it will display the product descriptions.

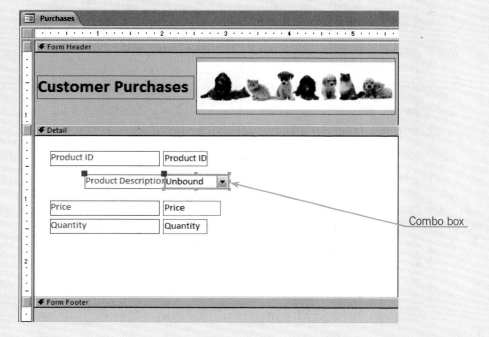

FIGURE 9–29
Combo Box placed in form

Combo box

10. With the combo box selected, click the **Property Sheet** button in the Tools group.

11. If necessary, click the All tab and in **Control Source**, click the drop-down arrow, and then click **Product Description**.

12. Click the **Property Sheet** button to close the Property Sheet pane.

13. Save the form and keep it open for the next Step-by-Step.

Sizing and Aligning a Control

After you add a control, such as a combo box, to a form, you will probably want to align it with the fields in the form. Access makes aligning controls in the form a simple process. You select the controls and fields that you want to align and then choose the desired alignment options on the Ribbon. You can also resize the controls so that they look consistent with the fields.

Step-by-Step 9.6

1. Drag the **Product Description** label to the left so it is aligned approximately with the other field labels. You will now change the font color.

2. Press and hold the **Shift** key, and then click on each of the other field labels.

3. Click the **Home** tab, click the **Font Color** button arrow in the Text Formatting group, click **Black, Text 1**, and then click the **Bold** button **B**. Next, you will arrange the labels so that they are equally spaced.

4. With the field labels selected, click the **Arrange** tab, click the **Size/Space** button in the Sizing & Ordering group, and then click **Equal Vertical**. You will now align the labels to the left.

5. Click the **Align** button in the Sizing & Ordering group, and then click **Left** to align the field labels left. Next, the text boxes need to be aligned.

6. Click the **Product ID** field text box and then while pressing and holding the **Shift** key, click each of the field text boxes.

7. Click the **Align** button in the Sizing & Ordering group, and then click **Left** to align the field labels left.

8. Click the **Arrange** tab, click the **Size/Space** button in the Sizing & Ordering group, and then click **Equal Vertical**. Compare your screen to **Figure 9–30**.

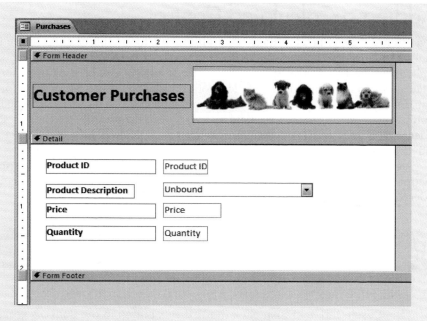

FIGURE 9–30
Completed form with combo box

9. Click the **Design** tab, and then click the **View** button in the Views group. You can now see how the form appears after the changes.

10. Save the form and leave it open for the next Step-by-Step.

Using the Combo Box in a New Record

A combo box makes it easy to add information into a new record. Normally, you type data into a field. However, with a combo box, you simply click the combo box arrow and select an option from the list. By selecting an option from the combo box list and not typing lengthy text, you increase the accuracy of the information.

Step-by-Step 9.7

1. Click the **Home** tab on the Ribbon.

2. Click the **New** button in the Records group, click in the **Product ID field**, and then type **486**.

3. Click the **Product Description** arrow to display the product descriptions, and then click **Flea Collar – Cats**.

4. Press **Tab**. Notice that when you pressed Tab, you were not moved to the Price field. You will correct this order of movement later. If necessary, you may need to move back to the field with Product ID number 486. Click in the Price field, and then type **3.21**.

5. Press **Enter** to move to the **Quantity** field, type **50**, and then press **Enter**.

6. Save the form and leave the database open for the next Step-by-Step.

Adding a Calculated Control

▶ **VOCABULARY**
calculated control

You can add a control that contains a calculation to a form. This calculation can be addition, subtraction, multiplication, division or one of the many other calculations available in the Expression Builder. A *calculated control* can be used to perform calculations on the values in other fields. For example, you may have an order form that has a quantity field and a price field. Adding a calculated control, you could multiply the value in the quantity field by the value in the price field to display the order total. If the values in the fields are changed, the calculated control recalculates and displays the new values.

Just like adding a new field to an existing form, you will need to align this control. In this next exercise, you will add a calculated control that displays an order total.

Step-by-Step 9.8

1. Verify that the Purchases form is open and switch to in Design view, click the **Design** tab, and then click the **Text Box** button in the Controls group.

2. Click under the Quantity field, as shown in **Figure 9–31**.

FIGURE 9–31
Form with Text Box control

3. With the text box selected, click the **Design** tab and then click the **Property Sheet** button in the Tools group. You will now open the Expression Builder to enter the calculation.

4. On the Property Sheet pane, click the **Control Source** property and then click the **Build** button ⌐⋯⌐. The Expression Builder dialog box opens.

5. To start the calculation, type = (equal sign) in the expression box. Next, you will add a field to the calculation.

6. In the Expression Elements area on the left side, double-click **Pets Unlimited Database**, click the plus sign next to **Forms**, click the plus sign next to **Loaded Forms**, and then click **Purchases**. You should now see the fields and labels for the Purchases form displayed in the Expression Categories area.

7. Double-click the **Price** field to place it in the Expression box at the top.

8. Type *. The asterisk option is used for multiplication.

9. In the Expression Categories area, double-click the **Quantity** field. See **Figure 9–32**.

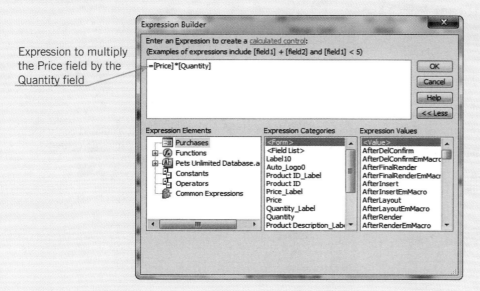

Expression to multiply
the Price field by the
Quantity field

FIGURE 9–32
Completed Expression
Builder dialog box

10. Click **OK**. In the Property Sheet pane, click in the Format box, click the arrow on the right to display the formats, and then click **Currency**.

11. Align and distribute the labels and text boxes using the Size/Space button options and the Align button options.

12. Click once on the field label for the calculated control and then click again. Your insertion point appears in the label. Delete the existing text and then type **Total**.

13. Add bold formatting to the **Total** label, and change the font color to Black, Text 1. Compare your screen to **Figure 9–33**.

FIGURE 9–33
Calculated control in the form

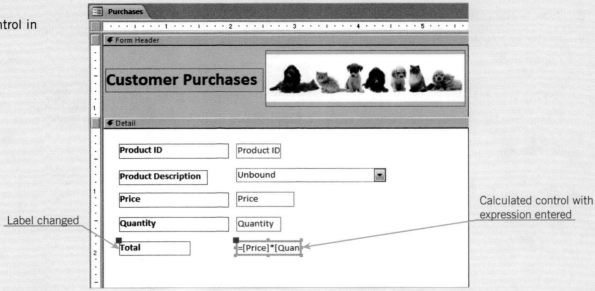

Label changed

Calculated control with expression entered

14. Save the form and leave it open for the next Step-by-Step.

Changing Tab Order

► **VOCABULARY**
tab order

Tab order is the order of movement in a record when you press the Tab key. Pressing the Tab key moves you from one field to another in a form. The tab order in a form should flow logically, such as from the top of the form to the bottom. However, if you add a new field or calculated control to a form, the tab order within the record changes. For example, if you add a new field between two existing fields, Access recognizes the new field and places it as the last tab stop in the form rather than between the fields where it was placed. In this case, you would be entering data into fields at the bottom of the record and then moving back to the top of the form to enter data into a new field. This movement would break the logical order of entering data into the form.

The tab order can be changed in Design view by selecting the Tab Order button in the Tools group of the Design tab. Then you simply click the Auto Order button and the tab order is instantly reordered based on how the fields are located in the form. In this next exercise, you will change the tab order in a form.

Step-by-Step 9.9

1. Switch to Design view, if necessary.

2. Click the **Design** tab, and then click the **Tab Order** button in the Tools group. The Tab Order dialog box opens, as shown in **Figure 9–34**.

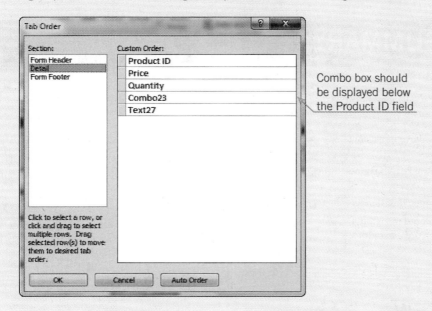

FIGURE 9–34
Tab Order dialog box

Combo box should be displayed below the Product ID field

3. Click the **Auto Order** button. The tabs are now arranged as they are in the form, as shown in **Figure 9–35**.

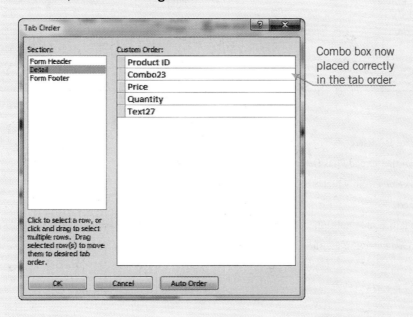

FIGURE 9–35
Tab Order rearranged

Combo box now placed correctly in the tab order

4. Click **OK**.

5. Save your work.

6. Click the **View** button to switch to Form view.

7. Press **Tab** to move through each of the fields. You can now move in the order of the fields.

8. Close the form and then close the database.

SUMMARY

In this lesson, you learned:

- It is important for every form in a database to have consistent formatting.

- Applying a theme to a form in the database makes changing the form's appearance quick and uniform.

- A logo can be added to a form to enhance design consistency.

- Command buttons can be added to forms for record navigation, such as moving to the next record, and for record operations, such as adding a new form.

- A new field can be added to an existing form.

- A combo box displays a list of values for a field.

- You can size and align controls easily.

- Adding a new record that has a combo box makes data entry easier and more efficient.

- A calculated control can be added to perform calculations on fields in a form.

- The tab order is how you move from one field to another in a form.

■ VOCABULARY REVIEW

calculated control	live preview	theme
combo box	logo	
command button	tab order	

■ REVIEW QUESTIONS

TRUE / FALSE

Circle T if the statement is true or F if the statement is false.

T   F   **1.** A new field cannot be added to a form that already has fields aligned in the form.

T   F   **2.** A command button displays a list of values from which you can make selections.

T   F   **3.** The tab order in a form can be changed.

T   F   **4.** A calculated control can be added to a form that multiplies the values in one field by the values in another field.

T   F   **5.** A logo can be placed in each form in a database in the same position, such as the Form Header, for design consistency.

FILL IN THE BLANK

1. A(n) _____ can be added to a form to perform a calculation.

2. A(n) _____ displays a list of values for a field.

3. To make the process of moving to the next record in a form or adding a new record easier, you can add _____ .

4. For format and design consistency, you can add a(n) _____ to a form.

5. If you add a new field between two existing fields, you will probably need to change the _____ so the navigation between records is logical.

WRITTEN QUESTIONS

Write a brief answer to the following questions.

1. Describe the importance of design consistency between all the forms in a database.

2. Explain the difference between a combo box and a command button.

3. Explain how themes make changing formats in forms easier and help to maintain consistency between the forms.

4. Describe how you would add a calculated control to a form.

5. Explain all the steps necessary for adding a new field into an existing form.

■ PROJECTS

If you have a SAM 2010 user profile, your instructor may have assigned an autogradable version of the indicated project. If so, log into the SAM 2010 Web site at *www.cengage.com/sam2010* to download the instruction and start files.

PROJECT 9-1

1. Open the **Coastal Sales** file from the drive and folder where your Data Files are stored. Save the database as **Coastal Sales Database**, followed by your initials.

2. Apply the Hardcover theme to the Sales Data form.

3. Move the Last Name field to the bottom of the form, and then move the First Name field above the Last Name field.

4. Realign the labels and text boxes.

5. Add equal vertical spacing between the fields.

6. Change the tab order for the fields.

7. Save and close the database.

SAM PROJECT 9-2

1. Open the **Animal Supply Industry** file from the drive and folder where your Data Files are stored. Save the database as **Animal Supply Industry Database**, followed by your initials.

2. Add two command buttons to the **Orders Form**: one to go to the next record and another to add a new record. (*Hint*: You will need to increase the width of the form.)

3. Align and size the command buttons.

4. Add a calculated control under the quantity field that multiplies the Selling Price values by the values in the Quantity field. Use currency formatting for the calculated control.

5. Change the calculated control label to Order Total.

6. Adjust the alignment, spacing, and formatting of the calculated control as necessary to match the other labels and text boxes in the form.

7. View the form in Form view and test the command buttons.

8. Save and close the database.

PROJECT 9-3

1. Open the **Book Sales** file from the drive and folder where your Data Files are stored. Save the database as **Book Sales Database**, followed by your initials.

2. In the Book Orders form, add the Shipping field to the form below the Price field.

3. Realign and adjust the spacing for the fields.

4. Use Auto Order in the Tab Order dialog box to change the tab order.

5. Save and close the database.

■ CRITICAL THINKING

ACTIVITY 9-1

You are the new database administrator for the Healthcare Training Company. Open the **Healthcare Training** file from the drive and folder where your Data Files are stored and save the database as **Healthcare Training Database**, followed by your initials. Upon inspection of the Employee Information Form, you notice that the fields are not in a logical order. You decide to change the order of the fields to present a more logical flow. You then adjust the alignment and the tab order. When complete, save the form and close the database.

ACTIVITY 9-2

A database is a great way to track an extracurricular activity. Think of a form you can create for a sport that you play or for a school club, such as chess team or student government. You will need to think of the fields you want in the form and how to align them. Think of the formats, fonts, graphics, and colors that you want to use for the form in the database. Apply a theme to the form and then view it in Design view. Feel free to create additional forms for your database, if necessary. Make any necessary adjustments to the form(s) or layout. Save the database as **My Form** and then close Access.

LESSON 10

Adding Advanced Features to Reports

■ OBJECTIVES

Upon completion of this lesson, you should be able to:

- Create a report from a parameter query.
- Add formatting and a theme to a report.
- Change a control property.
- Add a calculated control to a report.
- Add conditional formatting to a control.
- Add a subreport to a report.
- Create a summary report.
- Add a chart to a report.

■ VOCABULARY

calculated control

chart

conditional formatting

subreport

ADVANCED   Microsoft Access Unit

Introduction

In this lesson, you will learn to take creating reports to an advanced level. First, you will create a report based on a parameter query, which will require that you enter parameter data before the report will be displayed. Then, you will add a theme to a report, which applies the theme formats to each report in the database. You will change the properties of a report control as well as add a calculated control to a report. In addition, you will add a subreport to an existing report. Finally, you will create a report with summary information and then add a chart to the report.

Creating a Report from a Parameter Query

Basing a report on a parameter query is useful if you need to run multiple reports that display similar information. For example, you may want to see a report for all of your customers who live in Texas. You may also want to see another report for all of your customers who live in California. If you create a report from a parameter query, you could enter Texas as the parameter value for the first report and California as the parameter value for the second report. By using a report based on a parameter query, you do not need to create several reports; you just need to create one report.

As you know, a parameter query displays a message box for you to enter parameter data each time you run the query. When a report is based on a parameter query, each time you open the report, the message box appears. You need to enter data before the report will be displayed. When you enter the parameter data, the report appears showing the information based on the parameter value.

You can also add grouping options to the report. For example, if you want to group your customers by region, such as the North, South, East, and West, you can add a grouping named Region. Then, when you enter a parameter, the report will display with the data grouped by region. In this next exercise, you will create a report based on a parameter query and add grouping to the report.

Step-by-Step 10.1

1. Open the **Computer Sales** file from the drive and folder where your Data Files are stored. Save the database as **Computer Sales Database**, followed by your initials. Next you will open a query in Design view.

2. In the Navigation pane, right-click **qry-Monthly Sales** and then click **Design View** to view the query, as shown in **Figure 10–1**. Notice the Month field contains a parameter that will ask for the month for sale when the query runs.

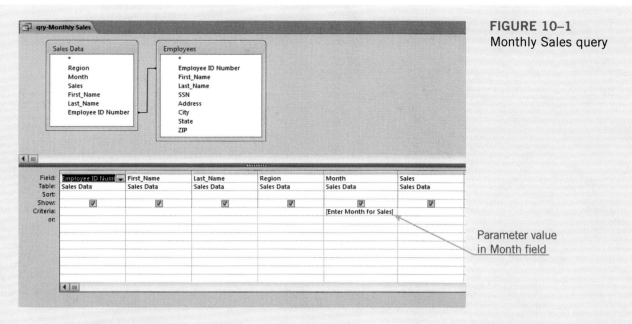

FIGURE 10–1
Monthly Sales query

Parameter value
in Month field

3. Click the **Close** button to close the query.

4. Verify that qry-Monthly Sales is highlighted in the Navigation pane, click the **Create** tab on the Ribbon, and then click the **Report Wizard** button in the Reports group. The Report Wizard will take you through the steps of creating a report.

5. Double-click the following fields in the order they appear to add them to the Selected Fields list box: **First_Name**, **Last_Name**, **Region**, **Month**, and **Sales**, as shown in **Figure 10–2**.

FIGURE 10–2
Report Wizard dialog box

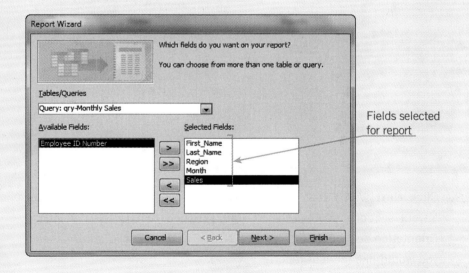

Fields selected
for report

6. Click **Next**, then double-click the **Region** field to add a grouping level. Compare your screen to **Figure 10–3**.

FIGURE 10–3
Report grouping

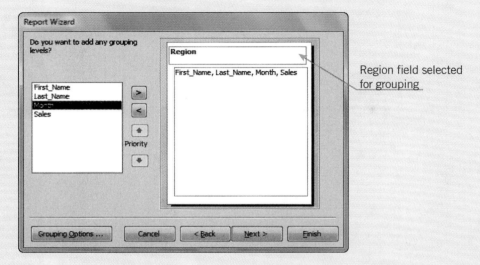

Region field selected for grouping

7. Click **Next**, click the **drop-down arrow** in the first sort box, and then click **Month**.

8. Select **Last_Name** for the next sort box and **First Name** for the third sort box, as shown in **Figure 10–4**.

FIGURE 10–4
Fields selected for sorting

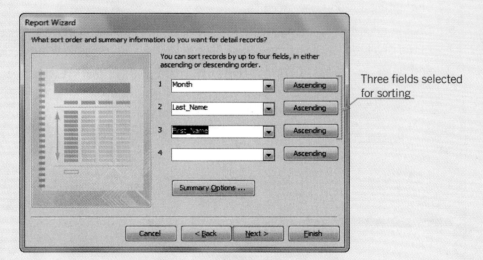

Three fields selected for sorting

9. Click **Next**. Verify that the **Stepped** option button is selected in the Layout section and that the **Portrait** option button is selected in the Orientation section, and then click **Next**. The wizard asks you what title you would like for your report.

10. Click in the text box, delete the existing text, type **Monthly Sales Report**, and then click **Finish**.

11. The Enter Parameter Value dialog box opens, as shown in **Figure 10–5**.

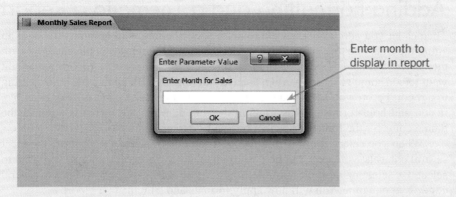

Monthly Sales Report

Enter month to
display in report

FIGURE 10–5
Enter Parameter Value dialog box

12. Type **March** and then click **OK**. The report with March sales is displayed, as shown in **Figure 10–6**. Notice that the sales amounts need to be assigned a currency format. You will add this format after you apply themes. To view more of the report, click the **Close Shutter Bar** button on the Navigation pane.

FIGURE 10–6
Monthly Sales Report

Region	Month	Last_Name	First_Name	Sales
East				
	March	Farris	Vincent	157463
	March	Farris	Vincent	157463
	March	Hernandez	Gregory	56202
	March	Latour	Dominque	78717
	March	Lightford	Darnell	79221
North				
	March	Gonzalez	Joan	184515
	March	Thompson	Rachel	186922
South				
	March	Conlee	Brian	219660
	March	Domingez	Connie	204284
	March	Farris	Louis	85185
	March	Farris	Louis	85185

13. Save the report.

14. Click the **Close Print Preview** button in the Close Preview group at the far right side of the Print Preview tab. Clicking Close Print Preview takes you into Design view. Next you will add some basic formatting and a theme to the report.

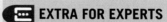

EXTRA FOR EXPERTS

To reopen the Navigation pane, you can click the Open Shutter Bar button.

Adding Formatting and a Theme to a Report

Themes let you add borders, background colors, shading, and graphic effects to an entire report at one time. If you change the theme, all the reports in the database with themes are changed at the same time. Before you add a theme to a report, you might want to add some basic formatting, such as bolding text. By adding basic formatting to a report before you apply a theme, the theme formats are enhanced. For example, if you add bold formats to the fonts in the report, when the theme is applied, the theme color for the fonts will be in a bolder, or darker, font color.

When you select controls in a report, you click to select the control. To select several controls, you press and hold Shift and then click on each control you want to select. By selecting multiple controls, you have the ability to apply formats to several controls at one time. You will now apply formats and a theme to a report.

Step-by-Step 10.2

1. Place the mouse pointer in the **vertical** ruler on the left side of the report to the left of the labels in the Page Header to display the selector arrow, as shown in **Figure 10–7**. Then, click to select all of the Page Header labels.

FIGURE 10–7
Selector arrow in ruler

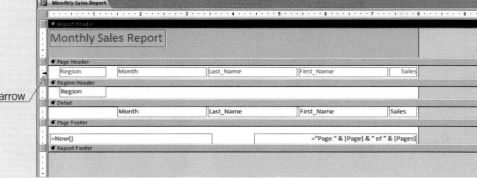

Selector arrow

2. On the Ribbon, click the **Home** tab and then click the **Bold** button **B** in the Text Formatting group.

3. Click the **Font Color** button arrow and then click **Red, Accent 2** in the top row of the Theme Colors group.

4. Click in the **vertical** ruler to the left of the Report Header label, press and hold the **Shift** key, and then click in the ruler to the left of the Region Header label and the Detail labels.

5. Click the **Home** tab, click the **Bold** button **B** in the Text Formatting group, click the **Font Color** button arrow, and then click **Red, Accent 2**.

6. Deselect all, and then click the **Report Header** label to select it.

7. Drag the **right middle selection handle** to the right to resize the Report Header label so that your screen resembles **Figure 10–8**.

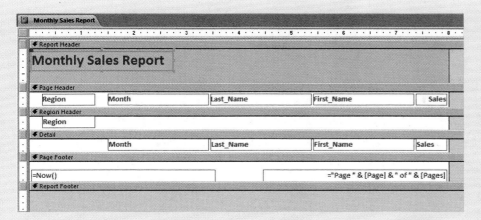

FIGURE 10–8
Labels formatted and resized

8. Click the **report selector** in the upper-left corner of the report where the horizontal and vertical rulers intersect. When the report selector is selected, it appears with a dark square . You have selected the entire report in order to apply a theme.

9. Click the **Design** tab, and then click the **Themes** button arrow in the Themes group to display the Themes gallery, as shown in **Figure 10–9**. Notice how the report formats change as you move the mouse pointer over the themes.

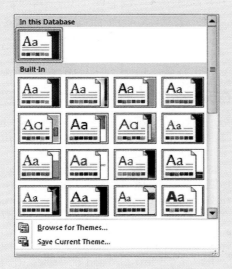

FIGURE 10–9
Themes gallery

10. Click the **Verve** theme to apply the theme to the report and then, if necessary, increase the size of the Report Header label.

11. Save the report, click the **View** button arrow, and then click **Report View**. In the Enter Parameter Value dialog box, type **March**, click **OK**, and then compare your screen to **Figure 10–10**.

FIGURE 10–10
Report with Verve theme applied

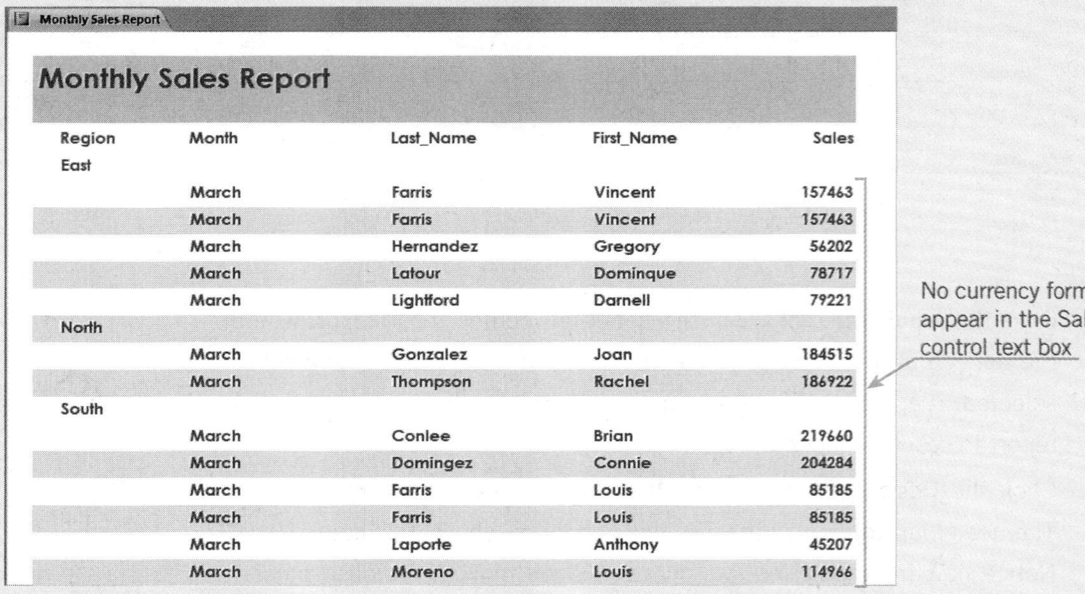

Region	Month	Last_Name	First_Name	Sales
Monthly Sales Report				
Region	Month	Last_Name	First_Name	Sales
East				
	March	Farris	Vincent	157463
	March	Farris	Vincent	157463
	March	Hernandez	Gregory	56202
	March	Latour	Dominque	78717
	March	Lightford	Darnell	79221
North				
	March	Gonzalez	Joan	184515
	March	Thompson	Rachel	186922
South				
	March	Conlee	Brian	219660
	March	Domingez	Connie	204284
	March	Farris	Louis	85185
	March	Farris	Louis	85185
	March	Laporte	Anthony	45207
	March	Moreno	Louis	114966

No currency formats appear in the Sales control text box

12. Switch back to Design view. Leave the report open for the next Step-by-Step.

Changing a Control Property

The controls in a report have multiple properties that can be changed once they are added to the report. For example, if you include a control that shows sales data, the data will appear as a number in the report. However, you might want the data to appear with a currency format. The currency format places the dollar sign and commas in the control. You can also have the data display decimal places. By changing the properties of a control, the data will make more sense to the people who look at the report. For example, the sales amount of 1156789 does not make as much sense as seeing the data displayed as $1,156,789.

A control has two parts, the label and the text box. The label typically appears either above or to the left of the text box and describes what is in the field. The text box displays the actual data from the table. When you change control formats, you will typically be changing the text box when the data is displayed. In this next exercise, you will change the properties for a control.

Step-by-Step 10.3

1. Click the **Sales** text box in the Detail section, and then click the **Property Sheet** button to open the Property Sheet pane

2. On the Property Sheet pane, click the **All** tab if necessary, as shown in **Figure 10–11**. Notice that no formats appear in the Format box.

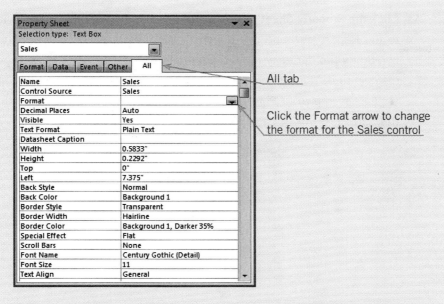

FIGURE 10–11
Property Sheet pane for
Sales text box

All tab

Click the Format arrow to change
the format for the Sales control

3. Click in the **Format** field, and then click the **drop-down arrow** to display
the format options, as shown in **Figure 10–12**.

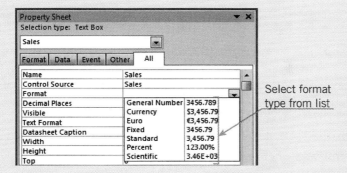

FIGURE 10–12
Format options

Select format
type from list

4. Click the **Currency** option to add a dollar sign, commas, and decimal
places to the control.

5. Click the **Property Sheet** button to close the Property Sheet pane. Switch to the Report view and use **March** as the parameter value. Notice that by adding the currency format, your control may not be wide enough to display all of the numbers and format; instead, number signs (#) may appear, as shown in **Figure 10–13**. You will now increase the width of the Sales text box in Layout view.

FIGURE 10–13
Sales text box
needs to be wider

Sales control may
not be wide enough
to display entire
sales amount

6. Click the **View** button arrow, and then click **Layout View**.

7. Click the top **Sales** text box, place the pointer over the left side of the control, and when the pointer turns into a double-headed arrow, drag to the left to increase the size of the control until the numbers and their formatting appear, as shown in **Figure 10–14**.

■ EXTRA FOR EXPERTS

To move a control in Design view, you can select the control, press and hold the Ctrl key, and then press the arrow keys to move the control right, left, up, or down.

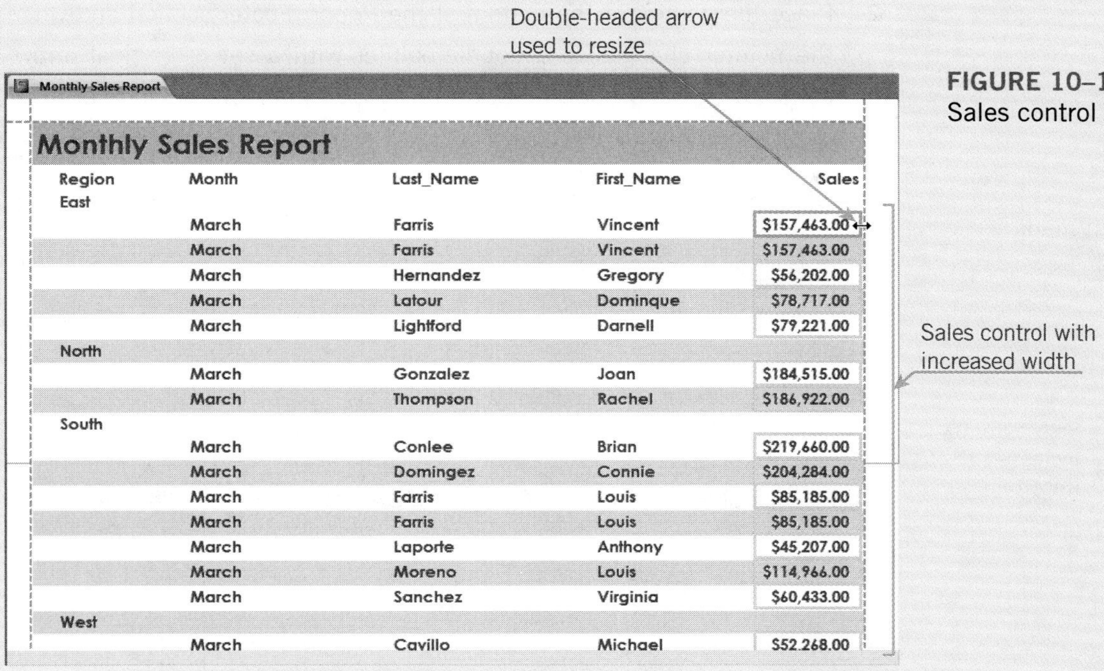
Double-headed arrow used to resize
Monthly Sales Report
Monthly Sales Report
Region Month Last_Name First_Name Sales
East
March Farris Vincent $157,463.00
March Farris Vincent $157,463.00
March Hernandez Gregory $56,202.00
March Latour Dominque $78,717.00
March Lightford Darnell $79,221.00
North
March Gonzalez Joan $184,515.00
March Thompson Rachel $186,922.00
South
March Conlee Brian $219,660.00
March Domingez Connie $204,284.00
March Farris Louis $85,185.00
March Farris Louis $85,185.00
March Laporte Anthony $45,207.00
March Moreno Louis $114,966.00
March Sanchez Virginia $60,433.00
West
March Cavillo Michael $52,268.00
Sales control with increased width

FIGURE 10–14
Sales control with increased width

8. Save the report and leave it open for the next Step-by-Step.

Adding a Calculated Control to a Report

After you create a report, you might want to add a control that will calculate some of the data in the report. For example, you might have data in a report that shows monthly sales for each employee. However, you would also like to show the total sales for the month. A ***calculated control*** lets you use functions to add a calculation to a report.

By adding a calculated control in the report footer, the total of the sales will be displayed at the end of the report. After you add the control, you can format it. In this next exercise, you will add a calculated control that adds all of the sales data in the report.

VOCABULARY
calculated control

Step-by-Step 10.4

1. Switch to **Design** view. Since you want the calculated control in the Report Footer, you will increase the size of the footer.

2. Place the pointer at the bottom of the Report Footer section and when the pointer changes to a double-pointer with a set of vertical arrowheads, drag the section down to the ½ inch mark on the vertical ruler, as shown in **Figure 10–15**.

FIGURE 10–15
Report Footer at ½ inch mark

Selector arrow to increase size of Report Footer

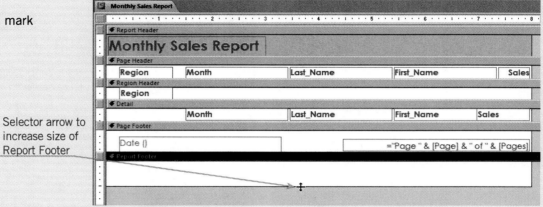

3. On the Design tab, click the **Text Box** button in the Controls group then, in the Report Footer section, click below the Sales text box, as shown in **Figure 10–16**.

FIGURE 10–16
Report Footer with Text Box control

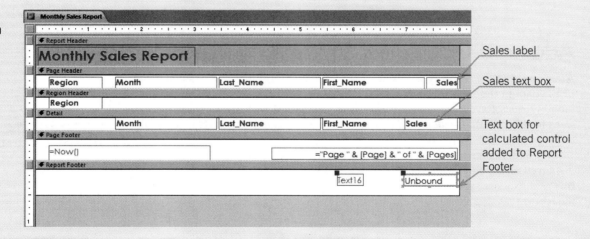

Sales label

Sales text box

Text box for calculated control added to Report Footer

4. Click the **Property Sheet** button to display the Property Sheet pane, click the **Control Source** field, and then click the **Build** button on the right side to display the Expression Builder dialog box, as shown in **Figure 10–17**. You will now create the expression that will show the total amount for the Sales control.

Expression will be
entered in this box

FIGURE 10–17
Expression Builder dialog box

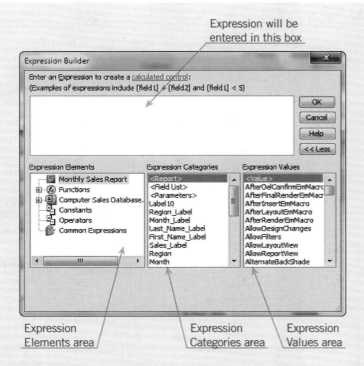

Expression
Elements area

Expression
Categories area

Expression
Values area

5. Click **Operators** in the Expression Elements list, and then double-click the **Equal** sign (=) in the Expression Values list.

6. Click the **plus sign** to the left of Functions in the Expression Elements list, and then click **Built-In Functions**. Scroll down in the Expression Values list and double-click **Sum**. You will need to replace <<expression>> with the Sales text box value.

7. In the Expression box, click **<<expression>>** to highlight it. The Sales text box needs to be selected and added to the expression.

8. In the Expression Elements list, click **Monthly Sales Report** located above the Functions option.

9. In the Expression Categories list, scroll down and double-click **Sales**. The completed expression should appear as shown in **Figure 10–18**. You will now add the currency format to the calculated control.

FIGURE 10–18
Completed Expression
Builder dialog box

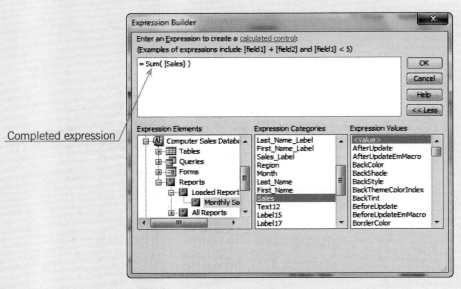

Completed expression

10. Click **OK** to close the Expression Builder dialog box. On the Property Sheet pane, click in the **Format** field, click the **drop-down** arrow, and then click **Currency**.

11. Click the **Property Sheet** button to close the Property Sheet pane, and then replace the text in the label for the text box with **Total**, as shown in **Figure 10–19**.

    You will now apply formatting to the text box and label.

FIGURE 10–19
Control with
Expression added

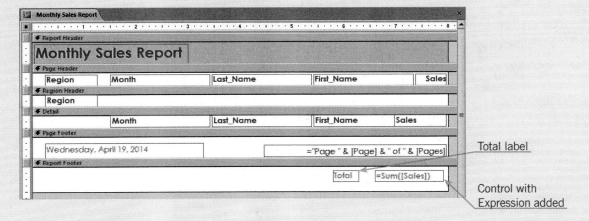

Total label

Control with
Expression added

12. Click any label in the Detail section to select it, click the **Home** tab, double-click the **Format Painter** button in the Clipboard group, and then click the **label** and **text box** in the Report Footer. Click the **Format Painter** button again to turn this feature off.

13. Switch to **Layout** view, type **March** for the parameter value, and then view the results. Increase the size of the calculated control text box so that all the numbers and symbols appear, as shown in **Figure 10–20**.

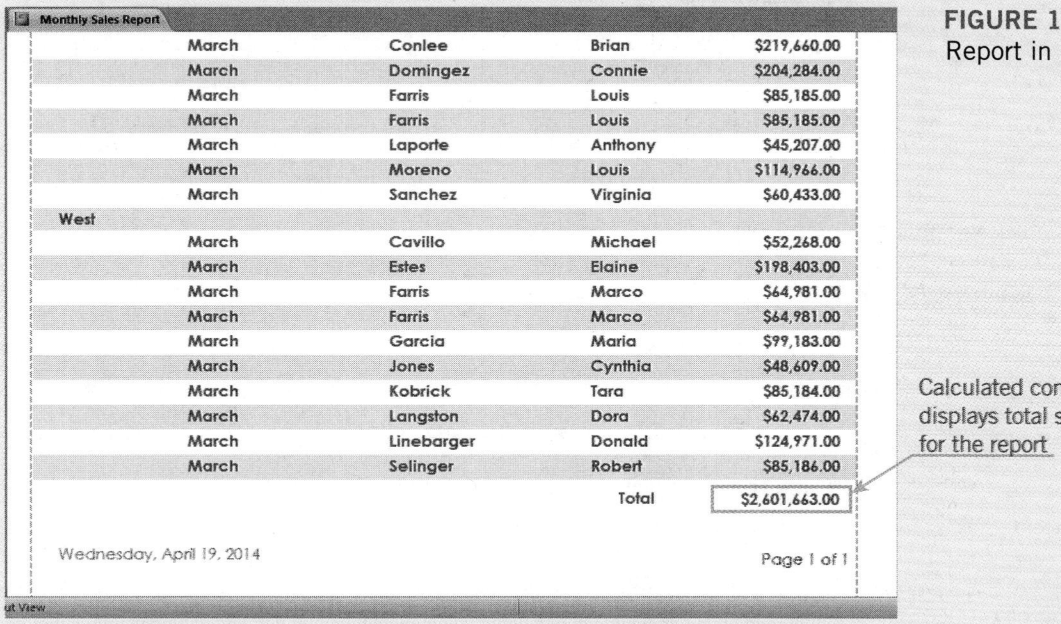

Monthly Sales Report			
March	Conlee	Brian	$219,660.00
March	Domingez	Connie	$204,284.00
March	Farris	Louis	$85,185.00
March	Farris	Louis	$85,185.00
March	Laporte	Anthony	$45,207.00
March	Moreno	Louis	$114,966.00
March	Sanchez	Virginia	$60,433.00
West			
March	Cavillo	Michael	$52,268.00
March	Estes	Elaine	$198,403.00
March	Farris	Marco	$64,981.00
March	Farris	Marco	$64,981.00
March	Garcia	Maria	$99,183.00
March	Jones	Cynthia	$48,609.00
March	Kobrick	Tara	$85,184.00
March	Langston	Dora	$62,474.00
March	Linebarger	Donald	$124,971.00
March	Selinger	Robert	$85,186.00
		Total	$2,601,663.00

Wednesday, April 19, 2014   Page 1 of 1

FIGURE 10–20
Report in Layout view

Calculated control displays total sales for the report

14. Save the report and leave it open for the next Step-by-Step.

Adding Conditional Formatting to a Control

Conditional formatting allows you to add formatting features to the data based on criteria you specify. In other words, the appearance of the data will differ from one record to another depending on whether the value in the control meets criteria that you specify. You can use conditional formatting to have a different background color, font style, or text color appear in a control so that its values are emphasized when they meet a certain condition. If the value of the control no longer meets the condition, the default formatting for the control will be applied. You can specify up to three conditions for a field. In this next exercise, you will have formatting applied to a control if its value is less than $75,000.

▶ **VOCABULARY**
conditional formatting

Step-by-Step 10.5

1. Switch to **Design** view.
2. In the Detail section, click the **Sales** text box.

3. On the Ribbon, click the **Format** tab and then click the **Conditional Formatting** button in the Control Formatting group. The Conditional Formatting Rules Manager dialog box opens, as shown in **Figure 10–21**.

FIGURE 10–21
Conditional Formatting
Rules Manager dialog box

Click New Rule button
to start entering a
conditional formatting rule

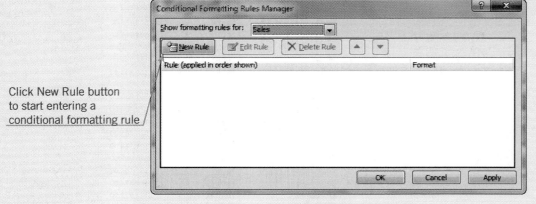

4. Click the **New Rule** button. The New Formatting Rule dialog box opens, as shown in **Figure 10–22**.

FIGURE 10–22
New Formatting Rule dialog box

Click arrow to select
format cells option

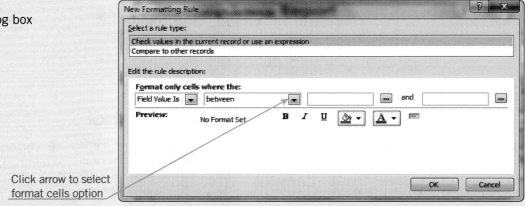

5. Click the **drop-down arrow** next to *between* to display the possible options for the rule description, as shown in **Figure 10–23**, and then click **less than**.

FIGURE 10–23
Options for the rule description

Select format
cells option

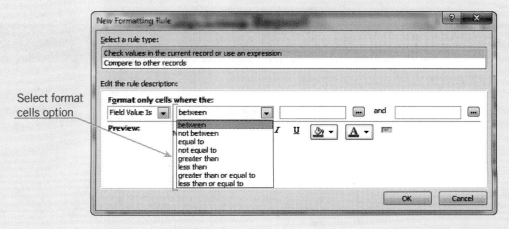

6. Click in the text box to the right and then type **75000**. Entering this amount will select any amount less than $75,000. Next you will add the formatting to the condition so that it will appear in a dark blue when the condition is met.

7. In the Edit Formatting Rule dialog box, click the **Bold** button **B**, click the **Font Color** button arrow, and then click **Dark Blue** (the fourth color in the top row). The completed Edit Formatting Rule dialog box is shown in **Figure 10–24**.

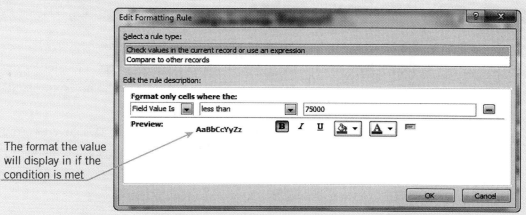

The format the value will display in if the condition is met

FIGURE 10–24
Completed conditional formatting rule

8. Click **OK** to close the Edit Formatting Rule dialog box, click **Apply**, and then click **OK** to close the Conditional Formatting Rules Manager dialog box.

9. Click the **Home** tab, click the **View** button arrow, and then click **Report View**. Display the results for March. Notice that the amounts less than $75,000 appear in a bold dark blue format. See **Figure 10–25**.

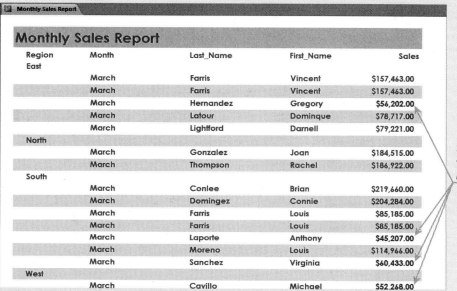

FIGURE 10–25
Report in Layout view

Shows conditional format when condition is met

10. Save and close the report.

Adding a Subreport to a Report

▶ **VOCABULARY**
subreport

After you create a report, you may want to display additional information located in another table in the report as well. *Subreports* are reports you create and then embed in another report. The easiest way to add a subreport to a report is with SubReport Wizard. The wizard takes you step by step through the process of adding a subreport. As you work through the wizard, you will be asked to define a link between the two reports. The link needs to be a common field between the two tables. In this next exercise, you will add a subreport to an existing report.

Step-by-Step 10.6

1. On the Navigation pane, right-click **qry-Employee Sales,** and then select **Design View** to view the query. Notice that a parameter is located in the Employee ID Number field that will prompt you to enter an Employee ID Number. Close the query.

2. Right-click **Employee Sales Report** and then select **Design View**. You will now add a subreport that displays employee contact information.

3. Place the pointer over the bottom of the Report Footer section and drag down to 1½" on the vertical ruler. See **Figure 10–26**.

FIGURE 10–26
Report Footer extended
for subreport

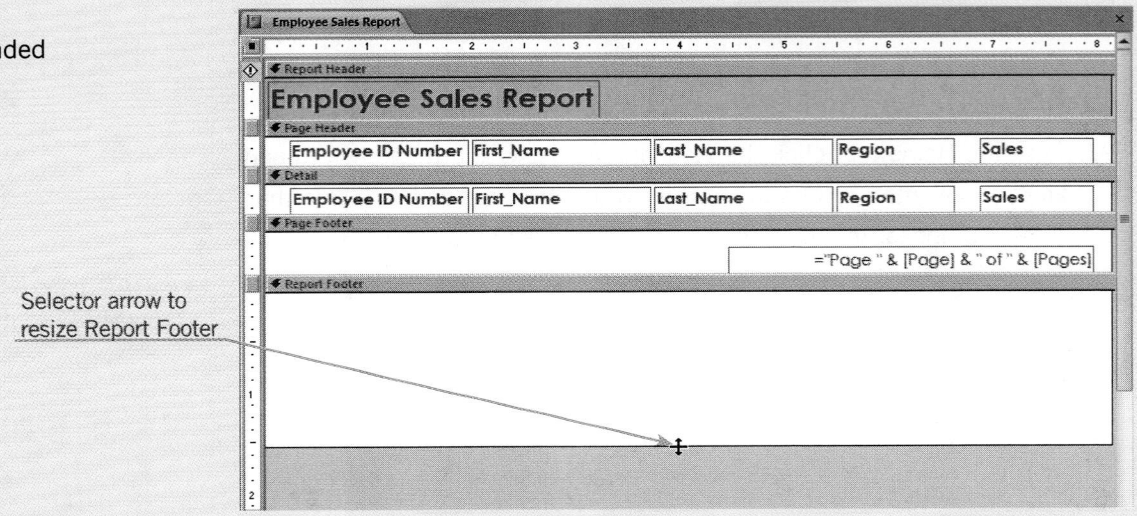

Selector arrow to
resize Report Footer

4. In the Controls group, click the **More** button, then click the **Subform/ Subreport** button 🔳.

5. Draw an outline under the controls in the Report Footer section that extends the width of the Report Footer section and is about 1" in depth. See **Figure 10–27**. When you release the mouse button, the SubReport Wizard dialog box opens, as shown in **Figure 10–28**.

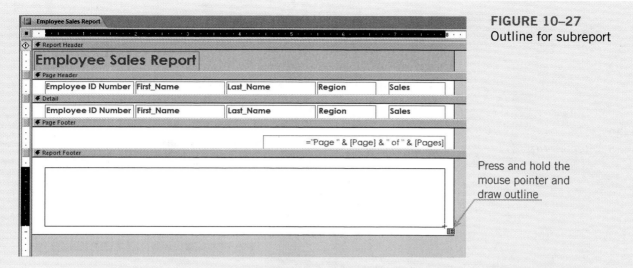

FIGURE 10–27
Outline for subreport

Press and hold the
mouse pointer and
draw outline

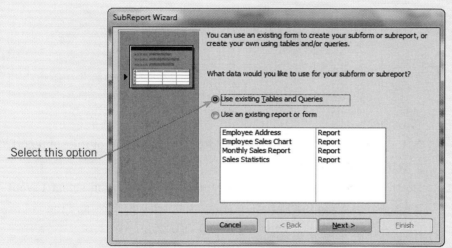

FIGURE 10–28
SubReport Wizard dialog box

Select this option

6. Verify that the **Use existing Tables and Queries** option button is selected, and then click **Next**.

7. Verify that **Table:Employees** is chosen as the table to choose fields from and then double-click **Employee ID Number**, **Address**, **City**, **State**, and **ZIP** to place these fields in the Selected Fields box. Click **Next**. See **Figure 10–29**. Access recognized the link between the report and subreport as the Employee ID Number field, which is the correct link.

FIGURE 10–29
Define link in SubReport Wizard

Select field that links between
report and subreport

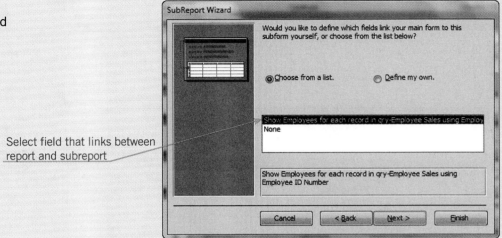

8. Click **Next**.
9. In the name box, type **Employee Address** for the name of the subreport, and then click **Finish**.
10. On the Home tab, click the **View** button arrow and then select **Layout View**. Type **145** in the Enter Parameter Value dialog box, and then click **OK**. Compare your screen to **Figure 10–30**.

FIGURE 10–30
Report and
subreport
in Layout view

Subreport heading
needs to be deleted

Subreport needs to
be realigned

Subreport will be
resized so that it is
even with the report
controls

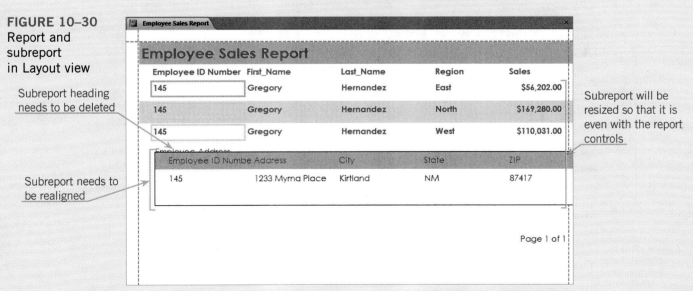

11. Click the **subreport heading**, and then press **Delete** since you do not need it.

12. Place the pointer over the right edge of the subreport and drag left, or right, until it is aligned with the right edge of the Sales control, as shown in **Figure 10–31**.

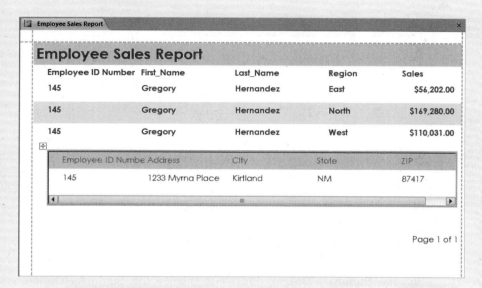

FIGURE 10–31
Subreport realigned

13. Save and close the report. Notice that Employee Address appears as a report in the Navigation pane. Both reports and subreports are displayed in the Reports group.

Creating a Summary Report

If you know ahead of time that you want to have calculations in a report, you can select them as you create the report using the Report Wizard. You can select the Sum, Avg, Min, and Max functions to display in the report. By adding these functions to a report, you might see trends in the data that you may not have seen if these functions were not in the report. For example, you may have sales data that is grouped by regions, such as East and West. Then, you can look at the sales in these regions and the sales person who made the maximum, or highest, sales. You will then see who the top sales people are in your organization.

When you create a summary report, you select the summary options in the Summary Options dialog box. You are given the choices of Sum, Avg, Min, and Max. You can select one, several, or all of the functions. In the next exercise, you will create a summary report for the sales in each region.

Step-by-Step 10.7

1. Click the **Sales Data** table in the Navigation pane to select it, click the **Create** tab, and then click **Report Wizard** in the Reports group.

2. Double-click **Region** and **Sales** to move these fields over to the Selected Fields box, and then click **Next**.

3. Verify that **Region** is selected, click the **Single Field** arrow button to create a grouping level, and then click **Next**. Notice the Summary Options button in this dialog box, as shown in **Figure 10–32**.

FIGURE 10–32
Report Wizard dialog box with Summary Options button

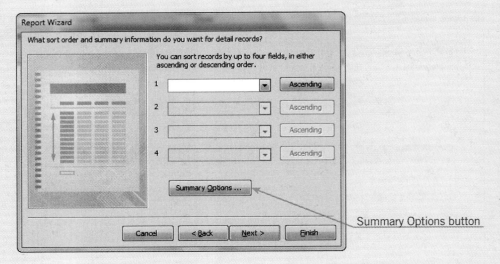

4. Click the **Summary Options** button to display the Summary Options dialog box, as shown in **Figure 10–33**.

FIGURE 10–33
Summary Options dialog box

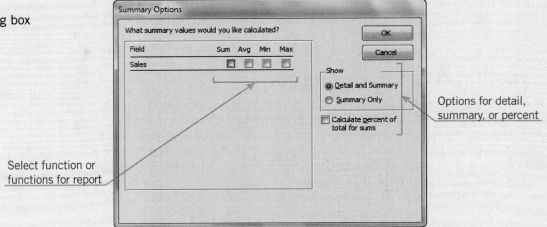

5. Click the **Sum**, **Avg**, **Min**, and **Max** check boxes.

6. In the Show section, click the **Summary Only** option button, and then click **OK**.

7. Click **Next,** verify that the **Stepped** option button is selected, and then click **Next**.

8. Type **Sales Statistics** as the name of the report, and then click **Finish**. A preview of the report opens. Notice that you will need to adjust the width of the Sum, Avg, Min, and Max controls.

9. Click the **Close Print Preview** button 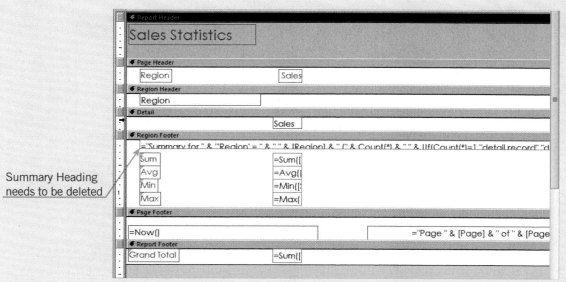 in the Close Preview group on the Ribbon, click the **View** button arrow, select **Design View**, and then compare your screen to **Figure 10–34**. Next, you will delete the summary heading in the Region Footer section.

FIGURE 10–34
Sales Statistics
report

Summary Heading
needs to be deleted

10. In the Region Footer section, click the **Summary** heading and press **Delete**. You will now resize the text boxes.

11. Switch to the **Layout** view. To select the four function text boxes, choose any region, press and hold the **Shift** key, and click each of the text boxes. Then, place the pointer over the right side of one of the selected text boxes and drag to the right to increase the width of each text box. Next, you will add currency formatting to the text boxes.

12. With the function text boxes selected, click the **Format** tab and then click the **Apply Currency Format** button in the Number group. Switch to Design view. Select the =Sum([Sales]) text box in the Report Footer and then click the **Apply Currency Format** button.

13. Press and hold the **Ctrl** key, click in the vertical margin next to all of the objects, click the **Format** tab, and then click the **Bold** button **B**. Click the **Font Color** button arrow, click **Pink, Accent 2**, click the **Design** tab, click the **Themes** button arrow, and then click **Verve**.

14. Switch to Layout view and resize the Sales controls again, if necessary. Then switch to **Report** view, compare your screen to **Figure 10–35**, then save and close the report.

FIGURE 10–35
Final Sales Statistics report

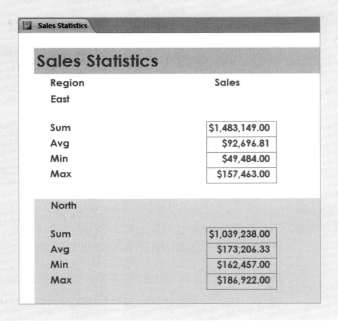

Adding a Chart to a Report

▶ VOCABULARY
chart

A **chart** is a graphical display of data. Charts are a great solution for presenting data in Access graphically. Charts are simple to make and format. Access offers formatting features that you can apply to a chart to make it a professional representation of the data. In this lesson, you will learn how to add a chart to a report.

Step-by-Step 10.8

1. Open the **Employee Sales Chart** report in Design view.

2. Select and delete all of the controls in the Page Footer. Then, place the pointer at the top of the Report Footer section and drag up until the Page Footer section heading is against the Report Footer section heading.

   To make room for the chart, you will increase the size of the Report Footer.

3. Place the pointer over the bottom of the Report Footer and drag down to the 4" mark on the vertical ruler.

4. Click the **More** button ⊡ in the Controls group, and then click the **Chart** button 📊.

5. Draw an outline about the same size as the Report Footer section. The Chart Wizard dialog box opens.

6. Click the **Queries** option button and then click **Queries: qry-Employee Sales**, as shown in **Figure 10–36**.

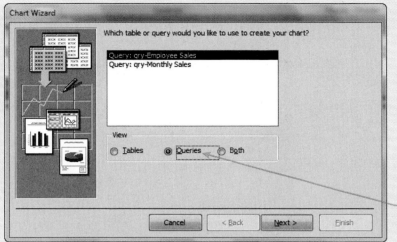

FIGURE 10–36
Chart Wizard dialog box

7. Click **Next**, then double-click the **Employee ID Number** field and then the **Sales** field to move them to the Fields for Chart area.

8. Click **Next**, then click the **3-D Column Chart**, as shown in **Figure 10–37**.

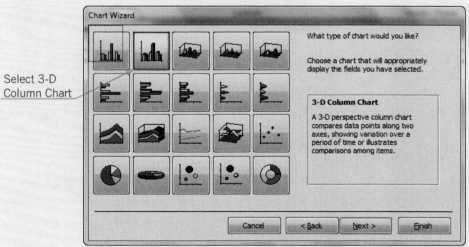

FIGURE 10–37
Select chart type

9. Click **Next** and preview the chart, as shown in **Figure 10–38**. Next, you will change SumOfSales in the chart to Sales.

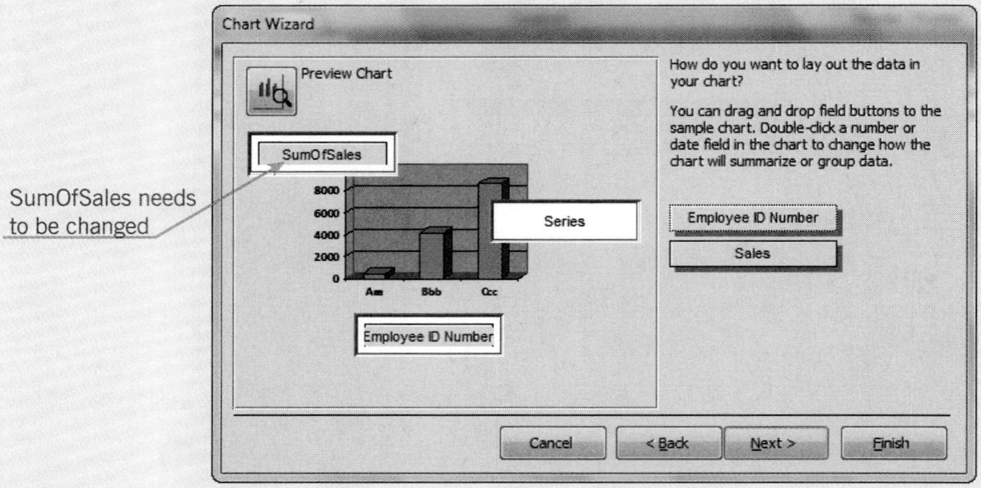

FIGURE 10–38
Preview Chart

SumOfSales needs to be changed

10. Double-click **SumOfSales** to display the Summarize dialog box. See **Figure 10–39**. Click **None** and then click **OK**.

FIGURE 10–39
Summarize dialog box

11. Click **Next**. Select **Employee ID Number** for both the Report Fields and the Chart Fields, and then click **Next**.

12. Type **Sales Data** for the chart title, and then click **Finish**.

13. Switch to Report view and view the report and chart for Employee ID number 145. You will then be prompted to enter the parameter again for the chart. After you enter 145 again, the chart should appear as shown in **Figure 10–40**.

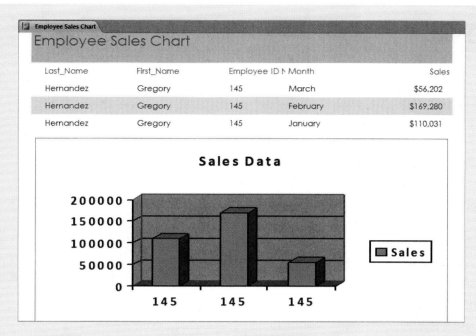

FIGURE 10–40
Report with chart

14. Save the report, and then close the database.

SUMMARY

In this lesson, you learned:

■ When you create a report from a parameter query, you will be prompted for data each time you open the report.

■ Adding a theme to a report adds text formats, borders, and shading to the report.

■ Control properties can be easily changed so that data displayed in the control is properly formatted.

■ If you want to total all the data in a report, you can add a calculated control to a report.

■ Adding conditional formatting to a control displays the data in a different format if a certain condition is met.

■ A report can be added to an existing report using the subreport feature.

■ Creating a summary report lets you create reports that can find Sum, Avg, Min, and Max values for the data.

■ Adding a chart to a report lets you display the data graphically.

■ VOCABULARY REVIEW

calculated control   conditional formatting   subreport
chart

◼ REVIEW QUESTIONS

TRUE / FALSE

Circle T if the statement is true or F if the statement is false.

T   F   **1.**   Charts can only be added to the Detail section of the report.

T   F   **2.**   Conditional formatting will display the control data in a different format if certain criteria are met.

T   F   **3.**   A calculated control lets you apply calculations to the data in the report and display the results in the control.

T   F   **4.**   Adding a theme to a report applies text colors and shading to the report based on the theme you select.

T   F   **5.**   When creating a summary report, you can only choose two functions.

FILL IN THE BLANK

1. A(n) _____ can be added to a report to perform a calculation using data in the report.

2. To display specific data in a report, such as for a certain region, you can base the report on a(n) _____.

3. A report that is added to an existing report is called a(n) _____.

4. If you want sales data greater than $80,000 to appear in a unique format, you can add _____ to the control.

5. To add a graphical display of the data to a report, you can add a(n) _____.

WRITTEN QUESTIONS

Write a brief answer to the following questions.

1. Describe the benefits of conditional formatting and give an example.

2. Explain how to add a chart to a report.

3. Explain the benefits of adding a subreport to a report.

4. Describe the steps necessary to change the property of a control from a number format to a currency format with two decimal places.

5. Explain the benefits of a summary report.

PROJECTS

If you have a SAM 2010 user profile, your instructor may have assigned an autogradable version of the indicated project. If so, log into the SAM 2010 Web site at *www.cengage.com/sam2010* to download the instruction and start files.

PROJECT 10–1

1. Open the **Pacific Sales** file from the drive and folder where your Data Files are stored. Save the database as **Pacific Sales Database**, followed by your initials.

2. In the Sales Data Report, resize the controls so that all of the sales data is displayed.

3. Add a calculated control to the report footer that shows a grand total for all the sales in the report. Be sure to align and size the calculated control in the report. (*Hint*: You might need to use the alignment buttons in the Sizing & Ordering group on the Arrange tab.)

4. Change the text in the label to **Grand Total**.

5. Change the control property for the calculated control to Currency with no decimal places.

6. Save the report.

7. Close the database.

PROJECT 10–3

1. Open the **Pet Supplies** file from the drive and folder where your Data Files are stored. Save the database as **Pet Supplies Database**, followed by your initials.

2. Create a report based on the parameter query qry-Customer Sales. Include all of the fields in the query in the report.

3. Sort by Production Description and then by Quantity.

4. Use the Tabular layout.

5. Use Sales by Customer ID for the title.

6. Run the report for Customer ID Number 5. Notice that you need to change the alignment of the Customer ID control so that the data is displayed under the label. Also notice that you need to increase the size of the Product Description label and text box.

7. Realign and resize the Customer ID and the Product Description controls.

8. Save the report.

9. Run the report again for Customer ID Number 5 to be certain the alignment and sizing are correct.

10. Print the report.

11. Close the report and then close the database.

SAM PROJECT 10–2

1. Open the **Regional Sales** file from the drive and folder where your Data Files are stored. Save the database as **Regional Sales Database**, followed by your initials.

2. Open the Sales Data Report in Design view. Then, add a conditional formatting rule to the Sales control that displays sales amounts greater than or equal to $150,000 in a Dark Red, bold font.

3. View the report in Report view to be certain the conditional formatting is working correctly.

4. Save the report.

5. Print the report.

6 Close the database.

CRITICAL THINKING

ACTIVITY 10–1

You are the new database administrator for the Book Sales company. Open the **Book Sales** database and then save it as **Book Sales Database**, followed by your initials. Create a professional report named **High Volume Sales Orders** that will display the Sales Orders. To help management make decisions on sales, the report should display sales figures in another format when the total is greater than $2,000. When complete, save the report, print the report, and close the database.

ACTIVITY 10–2

Think of how you could use conditional formatting in a report that displays sporting events. The report consists of dates, teams, and scores. Write down your thoughts and how you would present this report to a coach.

LESSON 11

Creating and Running Macros

■ OBJECTIVES

Upon completion of this lesson, you should be able to:

- Review macro security settings.
- Record a macro.
- Run a macro.
- Edit a macro.
- Create a macro to open and print reports.
- Run a macro with multiple actions.
- Create an embedded macro.
- View and run an embedded macro.

■ VOCABULARY

argument

code

comment

embedded macro

filter

macro

run

virus

Introduction

A macro automates common, repetitive tasks you perform in Access, thereby saving valuable time. In this lesson, you will learn about macros and potential viruses. Then, you will learn how to create and run macros. To run a macro means to have it perform a programmed, automated task. You will also learn how to make changes to a macro and how to add a macro to a button that can be clicked to run the macro.

Understanding Macros

A *macro* is a series of actions that you want Access to perform. Macros automate repetitive tasks, such as opening forms, printing reports, and running queries. Rather than doing a set of instructions repeatedly to perform the same task, you can save time and ensure accuracy by creating a macro that performs those actions for you.

When you create a macro, Excel records the selections you make using buttons and commands on the Ribbon as well as the keystrokes you use. Visual Basic for Applications (or VBA) is the program used to create macros. VBA is a programming language that is embedded into applications such as Excel.

When a macro is being recorded, all of the selections you make are translated into code. *Code* is simply the macro actions formatted in easy-to-read sentences, just like text in a book. Before you record a macro, it is important to review and understand macro security settings.

Reviewing Macro Security Settings

Macros are susceptible to virus attacks. A *virus* is a computer program that is designed to reproduce itself by attaching to other programs in a computer. Viruses can cause extreme damage to data on your computer. If a virus attaches itself to a macro, it can cause damage when you run the macro. To help protect your data from the corruption caused by a virus hidden in a macro, you can set one of four macro security levels in Access: *Disable all macros without notification*, *Disable all macros with notification*, *Disable all macros except digitally signed macros*, and *Enable all macros*. The Disable all macros with notification option is the default setting unless you choose another. **Table 11–1** explains each setting in detail.

TABLE 11–1   Macro security level options

MACRO SECURITY LEVEL OPTIONS	DESCRIPTION
Disable all macros without notification	Disables harmful content, but does not notify you.
Disable all macros with notification	Harmful content will be disabled and a notification appears on the Message Bar, just below the Ribbon, letting you know that the macro is disabled unless you click the Enable Content button on the Message Bar.
Disable all macros except digitally signed macros	Only macros that are digitally signed and come from a trusted source will be executed.
Enable all macros	Allows all macros to run and does not offer any protection.

As a best practice, you should set the security level in Access to Disable all macros with notification or Disable all macros except digitally signed macros. In the next Step-by-Step, you will view the macro settings currently set for Access.

Step-by-Step 11.1

1. Open the **Supplies for Happy Pets** file from the drive and folder where your Data Files are stored. Save the database as **Supplies for Happy Pets Database**, followed by your initials.

2. Click the **File** tab on the Ribbon, then click the **Options** button. The Access Options dialog box opens, as shown in **Figure 11–1**. You choose macro security level settings in the Trust Center section of the Access Options dialog box.

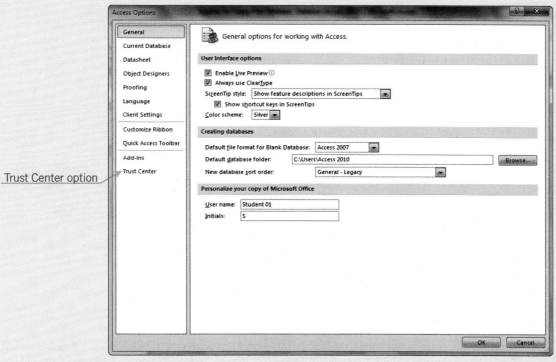

Trust Center option

FIGURE 11–1
Access Options dialog box

3. In the Access Options dialog box, click **Trust Center** on the left and then click the **Trust Center Settings** button on the right.

4. Click **Macro Settings** on the left to display the macro settings, as shown in **Figure 11–2**. Notice that the default setting is selected. If your screen does not match Figure 11–2, select the Disable all macros with notification option. Now that you have viewed the settings, you will close the dialog boxes.

FIGURE 11–2
Trust Center dialog box

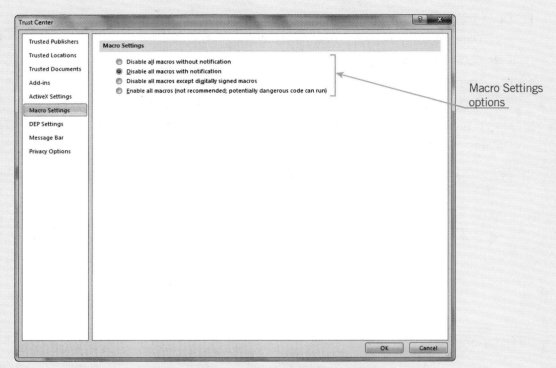

5. In the Trust Center dialog box, click **OK**.
6. In the Access Options dialog box, click **OK**.

Creating a Macro

A macro is used to remember and perform repetitive tasks. Unlike other Microsoft Office products, such as Microsoft Excel and Microsoft Word, which typically create macros by recording keystrokes as you work, you create an Access macro in the Macro window. To create a macro, you open the Macro window by clicking the Create tab and then clicking the Macro button in the Macros & Code group. In the Macro window, you select actions. Actions perform tasks, such as opening a form. You can select an action using one of several methods. First, you can click the Add New Action arrow in the Macro window, and then scroll through the list until you see the action you want and click on the option. You can also type the action name in the Search box in the Action Catalog to find the action. Another option is to click the plus sign in front of a folder in the Action Catalog to display the actions stored in the folder. The Macro window is shown in **Figure 11–3**.

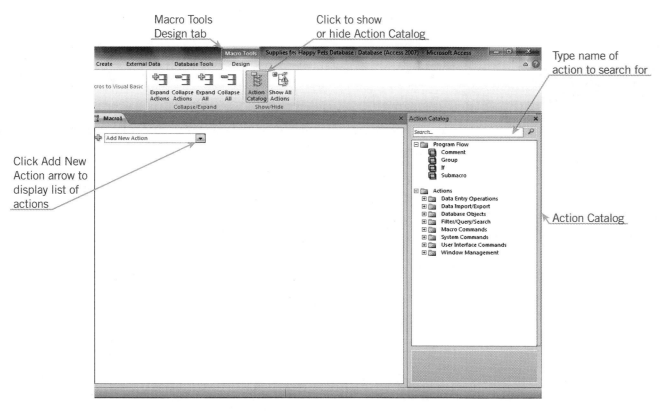

FIGURE 11–3 Macro window for creating macros

After you select an action, Access displays the argument(s) below the action. *Arguments* are the additional information that Access needs based on the chosen action. An example of a completed macro is shown in **Figure 11–4**.

▶ **VOCABULARY**
arguments

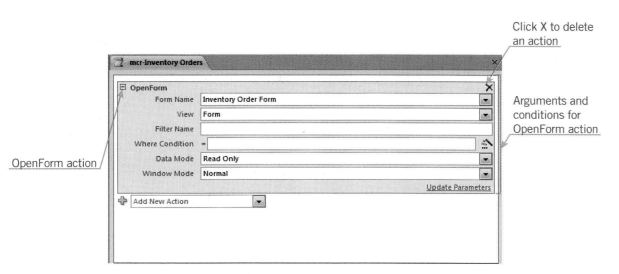

FIGURE 11–4 Macro window with completed macro

While the process for creating macros might sound difficult, it is very easy. In the next Step-by-Step, you will create a macro that opens a form in Read Only view.

Step-by-Step 11.2

1. In the Navigation pane, locate the **Inventory Order Form** and open it to view the contents, as shown in **Figure 11–5**, then, close the form. You will create a macro that opens a form.

FIGURE 11–5
Inventory Order Form

Product ID	Product Description	Price	Stock on Hand
150	Wonder Diet - Dogs	$11.92	560
162	Nail Trimmer - Small	$11.03	205
230	Wonder Diet - Cats	$6.26	256
245	Flea Shampoo	$5.62	658
301	Clippers - Hair	$25.37	56
318	Silkie Shampoo	$7.86	632
323	Linatone for Coats	$17.56	248
326	Dog Vitamins	$15.63	77
340	Nail Trimmer - Large	$17.66	963
347	Rawhide Bone - Small	$3.90	145
349	Bird Bell	$15.24	65
358	Lory Nectar - Small	$5.00	25
415	Bird Seed - Parakeets	$8.74	36
417	Cat Vitamins	$14.90	79
486	Flea Collar - Cats	$3.21	130
532	Groomer Brush	$17.24	985
547	Rawhide Bone - Medium	$5.24	452

Record: 1 of 27   No Filter   Search

2. Click the **Create** tab, and then click the **Macro** button in the Macros & Code group. The Macro window opens. You will now select an action for the macro.

3. Click the **Add New Action** arrow, scroll through the list, and then click **OpenForm**. See **Figure 11–6**. Next, you will select the arguments for this macro.

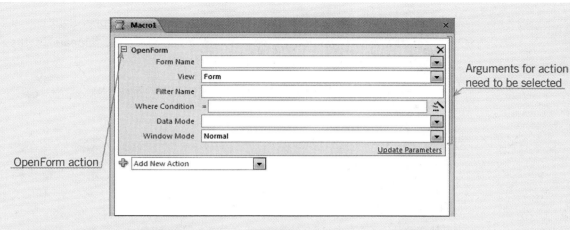

FIGURE 11–6
Macro window with
OpenForm action

Arguments for action
need to be selected

OpenForm action

4. Click the **Form Name** arrow, and then click **Inventory Order Form**. You will now change the data mode for this form to Read Only so that no changes can be made to the form when it is opened.

5. Click the **Data Mode** arrow, and then click **Read Only**. Compare your screen to **Figure 11–7**.

Macro opens Inventory
Order Form in Read
Only mode

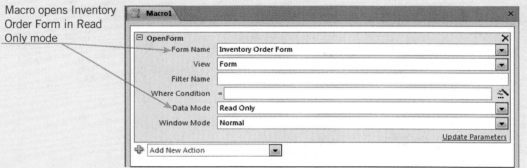

FIGURE 11–7
Macro window with action
and arguments

6. Click the **Save** button on the Quick Access toolbar. The Save As dialog box opens, as shown in **Figure 11–8**. Access names each macro consecutively, so your macro number may differ from the figure.

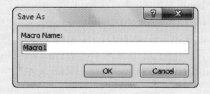

FIGURE 11–8
Save As dialog box for macros

7. Type **mcr-Inventory Orders** in the Macro Name text box, and then click **OK**.

8. Close the macro by clicking the **Close** button in the upper-right corner of the Macro window. A new object group, Macros, appears in the Navigation pane, as shown in **Figure 11–9**.

FIGURE 11–9
Navigation pane with
Macros group

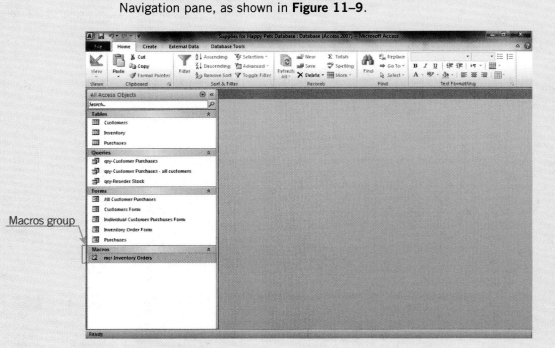

Macros group

9. Leave the database open for the next Step-by-Step.

Running a Macro

After you create and save a macro, you need to *run* the macro in order to have it perform the recorded steps. You can run the macro in three ways:

- In the Navigation pane, right-click the macro name, and then click Run on the shortcut menu.
- On the Database Tools tab, click the Run Macro button in the Macro group, select the macro in the Run Macro dialog box, and then click the OK button.
- On the Macro Tools Design tab, click the Run button in the Tools group. This tab appears when you have the macro opened in Design view. The macro that is currently open will run when you click the Run button.

When you run a macro, Access performs the actions listed in the Macro window one after the other. You will now use the three methods mentioned to run the macro that will open the Inventory Order Form in Read Only view.

Step-by-Step 11.3

1. Click the **Database Tools** tab, and then click the **Run Macro** button in the Macro group. The Run Macro dialog box opens, as shown in **Figure 11–10**. Notice that an arrow appears next to the Macro Name text box. The arrow provides a list of all the macros in the database.

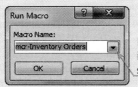

If there is more than one macro in the database, click arrow and select macro from list

FIGURE 11–10
Run Macro dialog box

2. Verify that mcr-Inventory Orders appears in the Macro Name text box, and then click **OK** to run the macro. The Inventory Order Form opens.

3. Click in any text box, such as the Stock on Hand text box, and try to make changes. Notice that changes cannot be made to the form since the form was opened in Read Only mode.

4. Close the form. You will now run the macro by right-clicking the macro in the Navigation pane.

5. In the Macros object group in the Navigation pane, right-click **mcr-Inventory Orders**. The shortcut menu appears, as shown in **Figure 11–11**.

Click the Run command

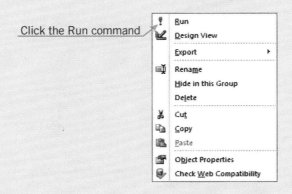

FIGURE 11–11
Shortcut menu for macros

6. Click **Run**. Try to make changes to the data displayed in the form.

7. Close the form.

8. Right-click **mcr-Inventory Orders** in the Navigation pane, and then click **Design View** on the shortcut menu. The Design tab becomes active on the Ribbon.

9. Click the **Run** button in the Tools group.

10. Close the form, but keep the database open for the next Step-by-Step. You will now learn how to edit a macro.

Editing a Macro

To edit a macro, you work in the Macro window as you did when you created the macro. When you edit a macro, you can add comments, add new actions, and add additional arguments to an existing action. Because macros often need to be changed, it is a good idea to include a comment for each macro action. A *comment* is explanatory text that you can add to a macro that does not affect the way the macro is executed. By adding comments, you can explain the purpose of each action, which is helpful when you are reviewing or editing the macro. Comments appear in green in the macro window, making them easy to identify.

Additional arguments, such as filters, can be added to an action. A *filter* displays only certain records based on certain criteria. The filter in a macro is typically based on a query in the database. For example, you may have a query that has criteria entered on a "Stock on Hand field" of less than or equal to 50 (<=50). By adding the filter, the report will only display data for fields with Stock on Hand less than or equal to 50. You will now edit the macro by adding a comment and a filter based on a query.

▶ **VOCABULARY**
comment
filter

Step-by-Step 11.4

1. Right-click the **qry-Reorder Stock** query, and then click **Design View** to view the query. Notice that the criteria in the Stock on Hand field is less than or equal to 50, as shown in **Figure 11–12**. Then, close the query.

FIGURE 11–12
qry-Reorder Stock in Design view

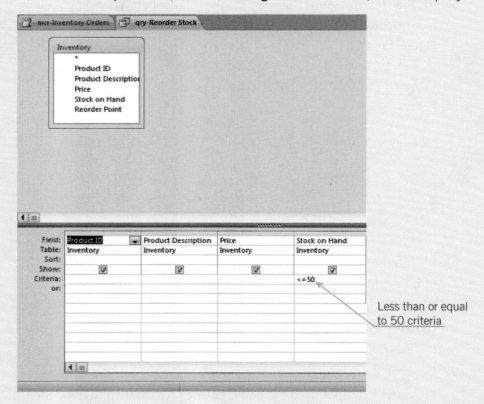

Less than or equal to 50 criteria

2. Click the **Design** tab, and then, if necessary, click the **Action Catalog** button in the Show/Hide group to hide the Action Catalog. By hiding the Action Catalog, you have more room to view the macro.

3. Click anywhere in the OpenForm action. Then, click in the **Filter Name** field.

4. Type **qry-Reorder Stock**, as shown in **Figure 11–13**. Next, you will add a comment.

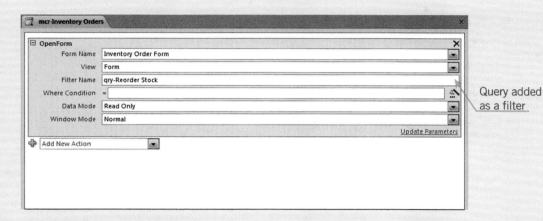

FIGURE 11–13
Macro with filter added

5. Click the **Add New Action** arrow, and then click **Comment**. The Comment box becomes available, as shown in **Figure 11–14**.

FIGURE 11–14
Macro window with Comment box

6. In the Comment box, type **Opens the Inventory Order Form in Read-Only mode when Stock on Hand is equal to or less than 50.** Next, you will move the comment above the action and arguments.

7. Click the **Move Up** button located to the right of the Comment box, and then click outside the Comment box so you can view the comment in the Macro window. Notice that the comment is displayed in green, as shown in **Figure 11–15**.

FIGURE 11–15
Comment shown above action

Comments appear in green

Comment describes action and arguments

8. Save the macro.
9. Click the **Design** tab, and then click **Run** in the Tools group. The Inventory Order Form is displayed, as shown in **Figure 11–16**.

FIGURE 11–16
Form opens when macro runs

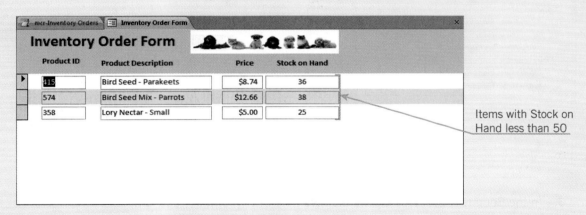

Items with Stock on Hand less than 50

10. Close the Inventory Order Form and the Macro window. Keep this database active for the next Step-by-Step.

Creating a Macro to Open and Print Reports

When you record a macro, you can include multiple actions in it. The actions should be entered in a logical order. For example, if you want to print a form, you will probably want to select an action that first opens the report and then select the action to print the form. And, if you did not want the form to remain open after it is printed, you would include another action to close the form. Then, you could enter these actions again to open, print, and close another form.

Creating a macro for these tasks would be helpful if you needed to review the same forms every month. The macro would perform all of these tasks very quickly to save you time. In this next exercise, you will create a macro that opens, prints, and closes multiple forms.

Step-by-Step 11.5

1. Click the **Create** tab, and then click the **Macro** button in the Macros & Code group. You will first add a comment.

2. Click the **Add New Action** arrow, and then click **Comment**. Type **Open, print, and close the All Customer Purchases form.** Next, you will select an action and arguments for the action.

3. Click the **Add New Action** arrow, and then click **OpenForm**.

4. Click the **Form Name** arrow, and then click **All Customer Purchases**. Next, you will select the action to print the form.

5. Click the **Add New Action** arrow, and then click **PrintObject**. You will now select the action to close the form.

6. Click the **Add New Action** arrow, click **CloseWindow**, click the **Object Type** arrow, and then click **Form**.

7. Click the **Object Name** arrow, and then click **All Customer Purchases Form**. Compare your screen to **Figure 11–17**.

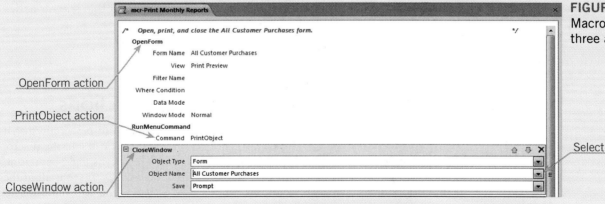

OpenForm action

PrintObject action

CloseWindow action

Select form to close

FIGURE 11–17
Macro window with three actions

8. Click the **Add New Action** arrow, and then click **Comment**.

9. Type **Open, print, and close the Inventory Order Form.** Next, you will select an action and arguments.

10. Click the **Add New Action** arrow, and then click **OpenForm**.

11. Click the **Form Name** arrow, and then click **Inventory Order Form**. Next, you will select the action to print the form.

12. Click the **Add New Action** arrow, and then click **PrintObject**. You will now select the action to close the form.

13. Click the **Add New Action** arrow, click **CloseWindow**, click the **Object Type** arrow, click **Form**, click the **Object Name** arrow, and then click **Inventory Order Form**. Compare your screen to **Figure 11–18**.

FIGURE 11–18
Macro window with six actions

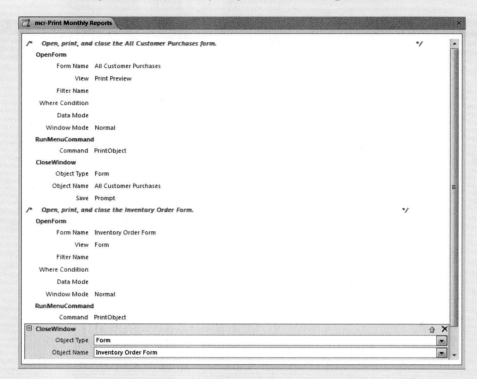

14. Save the macro as **mcr-Print Monthly Reports**. Keep this screen active for the next Step-by-Step.

Running a Macro with Multiple Actions

It is always a good idea to run a macro after you complete it to be certain that it performs the tasks you chose. Then, if there is a problem, you can edit the macro. For example, you may have created a macro with multiple actions that open, print, and close several forms. Running the macro would double-check to see if all of the forms are closed after the macro runs. In this next exercise, you will run a macro with multiple actions.

Step-by-Step 11.6

1. Click the **Design** tab.
2. Click the **Run** button in the Tools group. You may need to click **OK** each time the Print dialog box opens.
3. Close the Macro window.
4. Keep this screen active for the next Step-by-Step.

Creating an Embedded Macro

An *embedded macro* is a macro that performs an action within an object, such as a macro that opens a form when you are already viewing another form. An embedded macro can be part of another object, such as a command button. You can create the macro in the Macro window and then attach it to the object. Or, you can create the object and have the macro embedded as you work through a wizard. For example, you may have a form that contains data for customer purchases. However, this form does not contain any information about the customer other than the customer number. As you look through the form with purchases, you may decide that you need to call a customer to ask a question about a purchase. This information is contained in another form that has the customer's name, address, and telephone number. You decide to create a command button that will open the customer form while you are viewing the purchases form. This type of command button, that performs a macro action, would have an embedded macro. In other words, the macro action that the command button performs by opening another form is embedded in the command button.

Embedded macros have events that run the macro, such as On Click. This event indicates that when you click on the object, the macro will run. **Table 11–2** shows several popular form events.

▶ **VOCABULARY**
embedded macro

TABLE 11–2   Form events

EVENT NAME	ACTION THAT TRIGGERS THE EVENT
On Load	When the form loads
On Unload	When the form is closed
On Click	When the user clicks the left mouse button on any control on the form
On Dbl Click	When the user double-clicks the left mouse button on any control on the form
Before Update	Before changed data is updated
On Delete	When the user begins to delete a record, but before the record is deleted

As you create a command button in an existing form with form operations, Access will add an event that is applicable to the object. For example, you click a command button to open another form. Therefore, the embedded macro is attached to the On Click command. In this next exercise, you will create an embedded macro using the Command Button Wizard.

Step-by-Step 11.7

1. Open the **Customers Form** in Form view. Notice that this form has the company's name, address, and telephone number, as shown in **Figure 11–19**. Close the form.

FIGURE 11–19
Customers Form

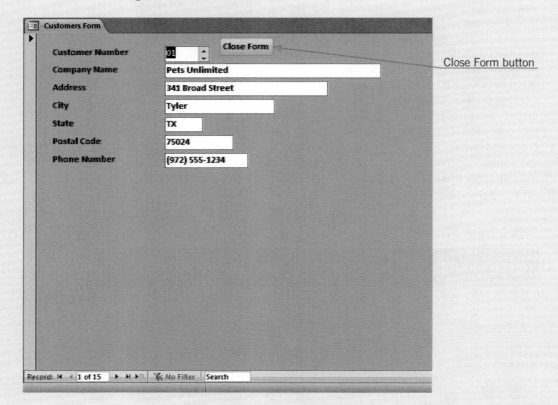

Close Form button

2. Open the **Individual Customer Purchases Form**, type **05** in the Enter Parameter Value dialog box, and then press **Enter**. You will now add the embedded macro to the Individual Customer Purchases Form.

3. Click the **Home** tab, click the **View** button arrow, and then click **Design View** in the Views group.

4. Click the **Design** tab, and then click the **Button** button ⬛ in the Controls group.

5. In the Form Header section, draw a rectangle about 1" wide by ½" tall, as shown in **Figure 11–20**. The Command Button Wizard dialog box opens.

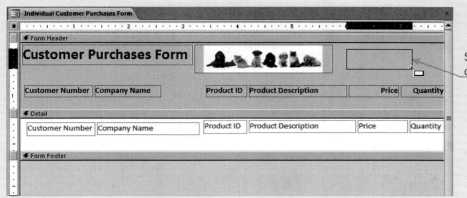

FIGURE 11–20
Button drawn in Form Header

Shape drawn for
command button

6. In the Command Button Wizard dialog box, click **Form Operations** to view the actions associated with form operations.

7. Click **Open Form**, as shown in **Figure 11–21**. Next, you will select the form you want to open.

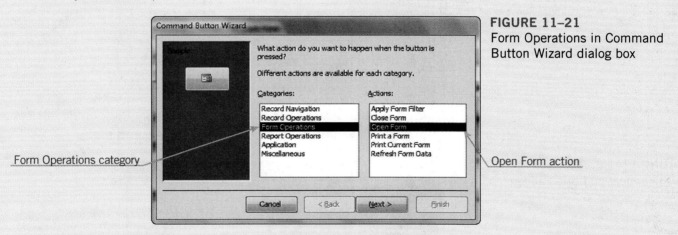

FIGURE 11–21
Form Operations in Command Button Wizard dialog box

Form Operations category

Open Form action

8. Click **Next**, and then click **Customers Form**. You will now select the option to display only specific information from the form selected.

9. Click **Next**, and then click **Open the form and find specific data to display**, as shown in **Figure 11–22**.

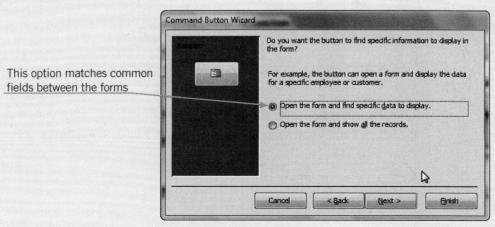

FIGURE 11–22
Choosing what data the button will display in the form

This option matches common fields between the forms

10. Click **Next**. You will now link the field from the Individual Customer Purchases Form with the field in the Customers Form.

11. Click the **Customer Number** field in the Individual Customer area, and then click **Customer Number** in the Customers Form area. Then, click the **double-headed arrow** in the middle of the dialog box. See **Figure 11–23**. You will now enter the text you want to appear on the button.

FIGURE 11–23
Completed link between fields

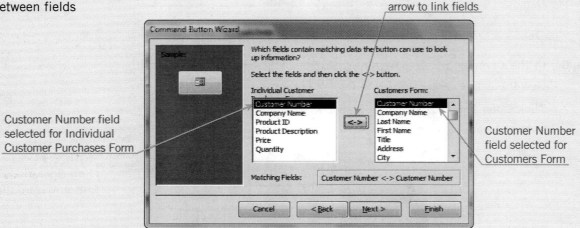

Click double-headed arrow to link fields

Customer Number field selected for Individual Customer Purchases Form

Customer Number field selected for Customers Form

12. Click **Next**, and then click the **Text** option button. Click in the text box and type **Open Customers Form**, as shown in **Figure 11–24**.

FIGURE 11–24
Text to appear on button added

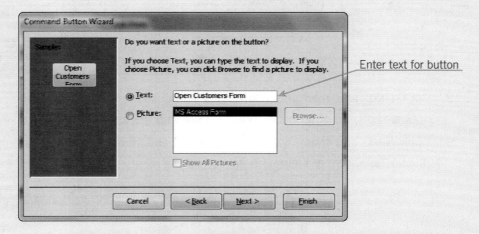

Enter text for button

13. Click **Next**. Type **Open Customers Form** in the text box for a meaningful name, and then click **Finish**.

14. Click the **Home** tab, click the **View** button arrow in the Views group, and then click **Form View**. Compare your completed form to **Figure 11–25**.

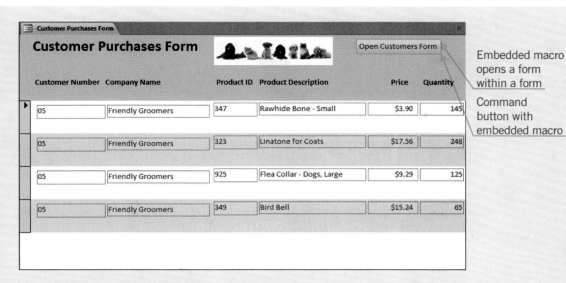

FIGURE 11–25
Completed form

Embedded macro
opens a form
within a form

Command
button with
embedded macro

15. Save the form. Keep this screen active for the next Step-by-Step.

Viewing and Running the Embedded Macro

When you create a command button with an embedded macro, you can view the event and the embedded macro using the Property Sheet. The Event tab in the Property Sheet displays a list of events, and any embedded macros will be listed next to the events that have them.

    To run the macro, you simply click on the command button. In this next exercise, you will view the Property Sheet and the embedded macro. Then, you will run the macro.

Step-by-Step 11.8

1. Click the **Home** tab, click the **View** button arrow in the Views group, and then click **Design View**.

2. Click on the **command button** you created in the Form Header to select it.

3. Click the **Design** tab, and then click the **Property Sheet** button in the Tools group to display the Property Sheet pane.

4. Click the **Event** tab in the Property Sheet pane. The On Click event shows the embedded macro, as shown in **Figure 11–26**. Next, you will display the embedded macro.

FIGURE 11–26
Property Sheet for command button

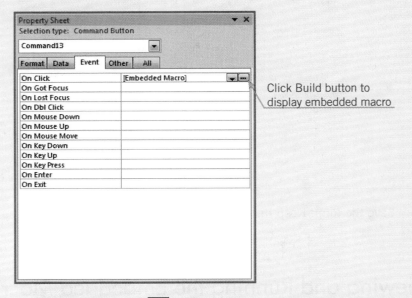

Click Build button to display embedded macro

5. Click the **Build** button ⟨...⟩. The embedded macro displays as shown in **Figure 11–27**.

FIGURE 11–27
Embedded macro

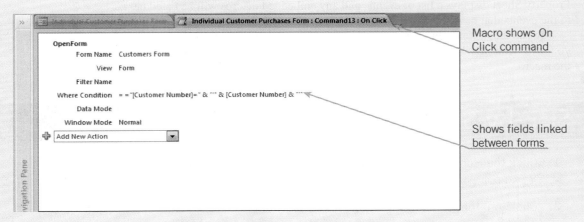

Macro shows On Click command

Shows fields linked between forms

6. Click the **Close** button on the Macro window to close it.

7. Click the **Property Sheet** button to close the Property Sheet pane.

8. Close the **Individual Customer Purchases Form**. Next, you will open the Individual Customer Purchases Form so you can test the command button.

9. Double-click **Individual Customer Purchases Form** in the Navigation pane to open the form. The Enter Parameter Value dialog box opens.

10. Type **05** for the parameter value, and then press **Enter**. The form opens with Customer Number 05 displayed.

11. Click the **Open Customers Form** command button to display this information for Customer Number 05. See **Figure 11–28**.

FIGURE 11–28
Customers Form opened from command button

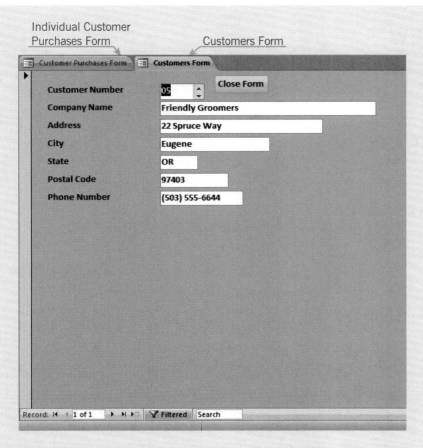

Individual Customer Purchases Form

Customers Form

Customer Number	05
Company Name	Friendly Groomers
Address	22 Spruce Way
City	Eugene
State	OR
Postal Code	97403
Phone Number	(503) 555-6644

Close Form

Record: 1 of 1 Filtered Search

12. Click the **Close Form** command button to close the Customers Form.

13. Close the Individual Customer Purchases Form.

14. Close the database.

SUMMARY

In this lesson, you learned:

- You can view and change macro security settings.
- Recording a macro can save you time for repetitive tasks.
- Running a macro performs the tasks that were recorded.
- Macros can be edited after they are created.
- You can create a macro that opens and prints multiple reports.

- When you run a macro with multiple actions, the actions are performed based on their order in the macro.
- An embedded macro is a macro that can be part of a command button in a form.
- When you view an embedded macro, it appears in the macro window, and you can run the macro by clicking the command button.

■ VOCABULARY REVIEW

argument	embedded macro	run
code	filter	virus
comment	macro	

■ REVIEW QUESTIONS

TRUE / FALSE

Circle T if the statement is true or F if the statement is false.

T   F   1. Macros are not susceptible to virus attacks.

T   F   2. A macro is used to remember and perform repetitive tasks.

T   F   3. There is only one method to run a macro.

T   F   4. After a macro is created, it can be edited.

T   F   5. Macros can have more than one action.

FILL IN THE BLANK

1. A(n) _____ is a macro that performs an action within an object, such as opening a form when you are already viewing a form.

2. The macro security level option that allows all macros to run and does not offer any protection is the _____ option.

3. _____ is (are) the additional information that Access needs to perform a task based on the chosen action.

4. A(n) _____ is explanatory text that you can add to a macro but does not affect the operation of the macro.

5. The On Click event will run a macro when the object is _____.

WRITTEN QUESTIONS

Write a brief answer to the following questions.

1. What does the *Enable all macros* security level option do?

2. Explain the difference between actions and arguments.

3. Write a brief description of the three different ways you can run a macro.

4. Explain how you can add a filter to a macro.

5. Write a brief description on how you would add a comment to a macro.

■ PROJECTS

If you have a SAM 2010 user profile, your instructor may have assigned an autogradable version of the indicated project. If so, log into the SAM 2010 Web site at *www.cengage.com/sam2010* to download the instruction and start files.

PROJECT 11–1

1. Open the **Internet Sales** file from the drive and folder where your Data Files are stored. Save the database as **Internet Sales Database**, followed by your initials.

2. Create a macro that opens the Employees form in Read Only data mode.

3. Save the macro as **mcr-View Employees Form**.

4. Close the macro.

5. Run the macro, and then try to make changes to the Employees form.

6. Close the form.

7. Close the database.

SAM PROJECT 11–2

1. Open the **Regional Sales** file from the drive and folder where your Data Files are stored. Save the database as **Regional Sales Database**, followed by your initials.

2. Create a macro that opens the Sales Information form, prints the form, and then closes the form.

3. Add the comment **Opens, prints, and closes the Sales Information Form** to the macro.

4. Move the comment to the top of the macro window.

5. Save the macro as **mcr-Print Regional Data**.

6. Close the macro window.

7. Run the macro for the **East** region.

8. Close the database.

PROJECT 11–3

1. Open the **Book Sales** file from the drive and folder where your Data Files are stored. Save the database as **Book Sales Database**, followed by your initials.

2. Create an embedded macro in the Book Orders form that opens the Sales Department Form.

3. Use the Employee ID field as the field that links the two forms in the macro.

4. Save the Book Orders form.

5. View the Book Orders form in Form View, and then click on the macro button to test it.

6. Close the Sales Department Form.

7. Close the Book Orders form.

◼ CRITICAL THINKING

ACTIVITY 11–1

You are the new database administrator for the Computer Sales Company. You have viewed the **Computer Sales** database. Since you frequently need to print both the Employees form and the Regional Sales form, you decide to create a macro that opens, prints, and closes both the Employees and the Regional Sales forms. Save the database as **Computer Sales Database** followed by your initials.

ACTIVITY 11–2

Think of a database that you could use for school, work, or around your home. Describe a macro that you would create in the database and what task you would have it perform.

LESSON 12

Automating Database Processes

■ OBJECTIVES

Upon completion of this lesson, you should be able to:

- Create a splash screen.
- Create an AutoExec macro.
- Test an AutoExec macro.
- Create a navigation form.
- Create a second navigation form.
- Design the main navigation form.
- Change startup options.
- Bypass startup options.

■ VOCABULARY

AutoExec macro

hierarchical

navigation form

splash screen

startup options

Introduction

As you add queries, forms, and reports to your database, you will need to manage access to these objects to make the database easy to use without jeopardizing the security of the data. This lesson begins by teaching you how to create a splash screen that appears when the database is opened. The splash screen instantly familiarizes users with how the database will look. An AutoExec macro is used to display the splash screen. In this lesson, you will also use navigation forms to design and implement user-friendly menus so that users can work with only those parts of the database they need. In addition, you will learn how to restrict the Ribbon tabs and the Navigation pane so that users cannot change or modify the design of your database.

Creating a Splash Screen

▶ **VOCABULARY**
splash screen

A *splash screen* is a form that appears when you open a database that welcomes the user to the database. A splash screen can contain information such as a company's name and the same themes used in the database. You can further personalize the splash screen by adding the company logo and a label with text, such as *Welcome to the Database*, at the top of the form. Next, you will create a splash screen using a background color and an image for the Online Sales Database.

Step-by-Step 12.1

1. Open the **Online Sales** file from the drive and folder where your Data Files are stored. Save the database as **Online Sales Database**, followed by your initials.

2. On the Ribbon, click the **Create** tab and then click **Blank Form** in the Forms group.

3. Click the **Design** tab, and then click the **Add Existing Fields** button in the Tools group to close the Field List pane on the right.

4. Click the **Form1 form area**, and then click the **Format** tab on the Ribbon.

5. Click the **Background Color** button arrow [icon], and then click **Dark Purple, Accent 4, Lighter 60%** in the Font group.

6. Click the **Background Image** button arrow, and then click **Browse**.

7. Navigate to the drive and folder where your Data Files are stored, click **Online Sales Logo.tif**, and then click **OK**.

▶ **TIP**

You may need to select All Files from the drop-down menu to the right of File name in the Insert Picture dialog box. Compare your screen to **Figure 12–1**.

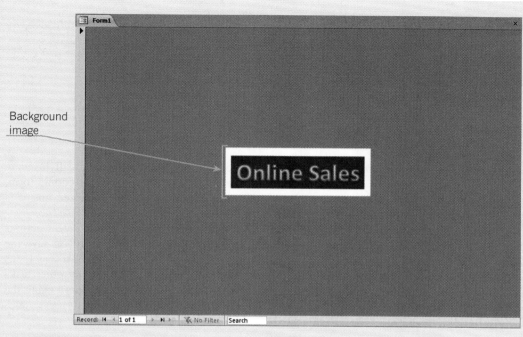

FIGURE 12–1
Splash screen with
background image

Background
image

8. Click the **Design** tab, click the **View** button arrow, and then click **Layout View**.

9. Click the **Label** button in the Controls group, and then click in the upper-left corner of the form.

10. Type **Welcome to the Online Sales Database**, and then press **Enter**.

11. Click the **Format** tab, click the **Font Size** button arrow, and then click **16**.

12. Click the **Bold** button **B** in the Font group, click the **Font Color** button arrow **A ˅**, and then click **Black, Text 1** in the Theme Colors section.

13. Resize the label until it is approximately the same size as shown in **Figure 12–2**. All of the text should be on one line.

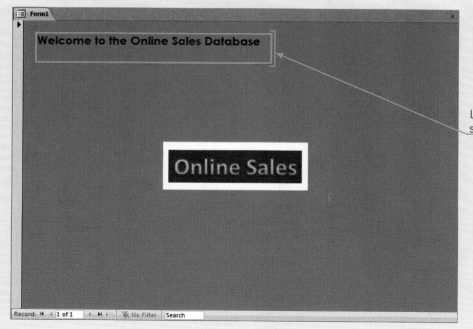

FIGURE 12–2
Splash screen with label

Label added to
splash screen

14. Click the **Save** button 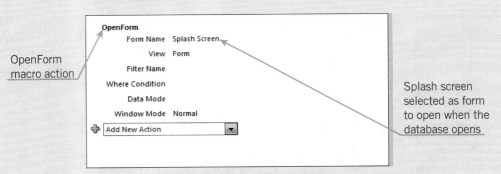 on the Quick Access toolbar, and then save the form as **Splash Screen**. Close the form, but remain in this database for the next Step-by-Step.

Creating an AutoExec Macro

▶ **VOCABULARY**
AutoExec macro

An *AutoExec macro* allows you to have one or more actions automatically execute when the database is opened. For example, you may want to display a certain form, such as a splash screen, when a user opens the database. An AutoExec macro is perfect for that task. You can only have one AutoExec macro per database file.

To create an AutoExec macro, you use the Macro window to select actions you want Access to perform when the database is opened, and then you save the macro using the name AutoExec. Whenever a user opens a database, Access looks for an AutoExec macro; if one is present, the macro runs before any other tasks are performed. In this next exercise, you will create an AutoExec macro using the OpenForm action, with the Splash Screen form as the argument.

Step-by-Step 12.2

1. Click the **Create** tab, and then click the **Macro** button in the Macros & Code group. Next you will add the OpenForm action so you can open a form when the macro runs.

2. In the Macro1 window, click the **Add New Action** drop-down arrow and then click **OpenForm**. Next you will select the form name.

3. Click the **Form Name** drop-down arrow, and then click **Splash Screen**. See **Figure 12–3**.

FIGURE 12–3
AutoExec macro

OpenForm
macro action

OpenForm	
Form Name	Splash Screen
View	Form
Filter Name	
Where Condition	
Data Mode	
Window Mode	Normal

Add New Action

Splash screen selected as form to open when the database opens

4. Click the **Save** button 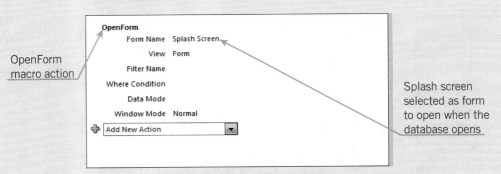 on the Quick Access toolbar.

5. Type **AutoExec** for the macro name, and then click **OK**.

6. Close the Macro window.

Testing an AutoExec Macro

After you create an AutoExec macro, you should test it to be certain that the macro performs the actions that you want. To run an AutoExec macro, you need to close the database and then reopen the database to run the macro. In this next exercise, you will close and reopen the database to see the splash screen appear.

Step-by-Step 12.3

1. Click the **File** tab, and then click **Close Database**.

2. Open the **Online Sales Database**. The splash screen should appear.

3. Click the **Close Form** button on the splash screen.

4. Remain in this database for the next Step-by-Step.

Creating a Navigation Form

A *navigation form* is a special kind of form that has both a main form control and subform controls automatically built in. The use of navigation forms in a database is similar to navigating a Web site. Well-designed Web sites typically have top-level navigation commands and lower-level commands.

▶ **VOCABULARY**
navigation form

▶ **VOCABULARY**
hierarchical

Navigation forms in a database typically appear in a hierarchical format to help users select various database objects easily. *Hierarchical* refers to the different levels of automation. Forms in the lower level of the hierarchy are produced first. For example, a lower-level navigation form lets you select which report you want to view. Then, you create the navigation form that will be used as the main menu. A main menu form has tabs that let you select the lower-level forms. See **Figures 12–4 and 12–5**.

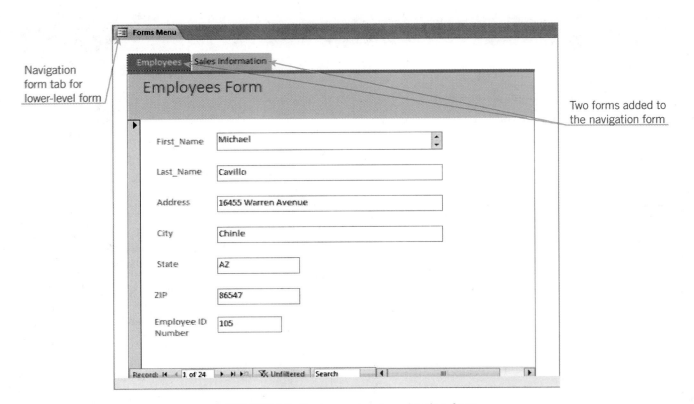

Navigation
form tab for
lower-level form

Two forms added to
the navigation form

FIGURE 12–4   Lower-level navigation form

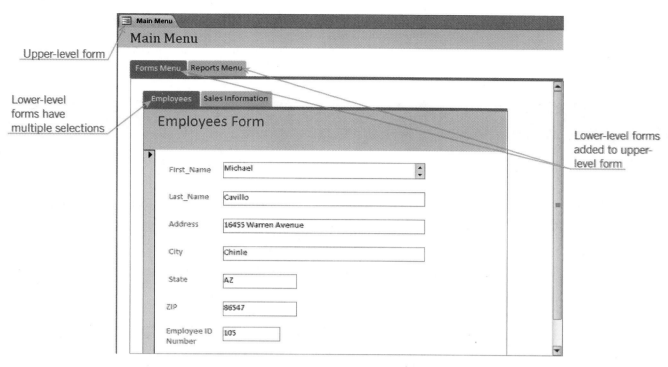

FIGURE 12–5 Upper-level navigation form with lower-level forms added

A navigation form can display tabs for forms, reports, and queries and acts as a main menu for the database. Selecting the tabs on this main menu navigation form lets you instantly view these objects. To add an object, such as a report, to the navigation form, you drag the object directly from the Navigation pane onto the form. A new tab is added to the navigation form; and, selecting this tab lets you view the report in the subform control. The report is still available in the Navigation pane, but you will also have access to it in the navigation form.

Before you begin designing navigation forms, you should decide on the type of layout style you want to use. **Figure 12–6** shows the various types of navigation forms in Access. The icons next to each layout style show you how the tabs will be arranged.

EXTRA FOR EXPERTS

In previous versions of Access, you might have used a Switchboard for the purpose of creating menus in a hierarchical format. With Microsoft Office Access 2010, navigation forms provide this same functionality.

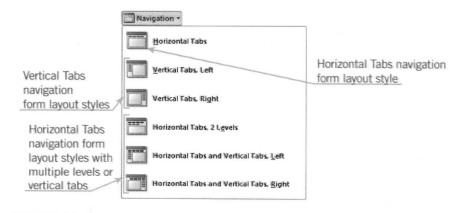

FIGURE 12–6 Types of navigation form layout styles

Once you decide on the navigation form layout style, you should use this same style throughout the database so users do not need to familiarize themselves with a new layout when they select another navigation form. In this next exercise, you will create a Forms Menu, since it is at the lower level of the hierarchy.

Step-by-Step 12.4

1. On the Ribbon, click the **Create** tab, click the **Navigation** button arrow in the Forms group, and then click **Horizontal Tabs**.

2. Close the **Close** button on the Field List pane to close it. The Horizontal Tabs navigation form opens, as shown in **Figure 12–7**. Next, you will add a form to the navigation form.

FIGURE 12–7
Navigation form with horizontal tabs

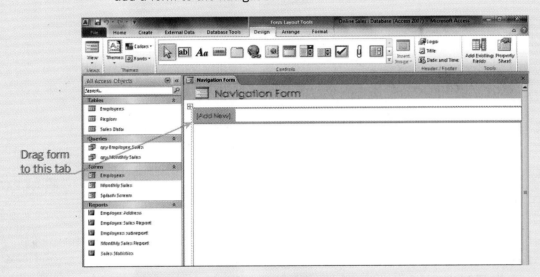

3. In the Navigation pane, drag the **Employees** form in the Forms group on top of the **Add New** tab, as shown in **Figure 12–8**. Release the mouse button. The Employees form appears as a subform in the navigation form but remains available in the Navigation pane. See **Figure 12–9**.

FIGURE 12–8
Form icon appears as you drag object

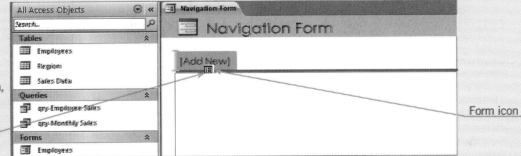

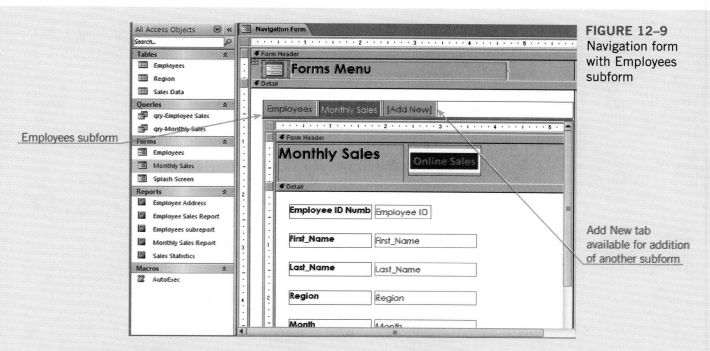

FIGURE 12–9
Navigation form
with Employees
subform

Employees subform

Add New tab
available for addition
of another subform

4. Drag the **Monthly Sales** form in the Navigation pane to the **Add New** tab.
   The Monthly Sales form is added as a subform.

5. On the Design tab, click the **View** button arrow in the Views group and
   then click **Design View**.

6. Click in the title in the Form Header where it says Navigation Form, and
   then type **Forms Menu**.

7. Click outside the label, and then click on the label again to select it.
   Next, you will change the font for the label.

8. Click the **Format** tab, click the **Bold** button **B** in the Font group, click the **Font Color** button arrow, and then click **Black, Text 1**. See **Figure 12–10**.

FIGURE 12–10
Navigation form with subforms and title change

Employees subform and Monthly Sales subform

Title format changed

9. Click the **Design** tab, click the **View** button arrow, and then click **Form View**. Click each form tab to display the subforms. Notice that when a form is selected, such as Monthly Sales, the tab appears in a darker color. Also notice that in Form view, the Add New tab is not available. See **Figure 12–11**.

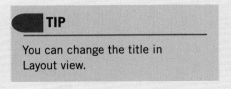

TIP

You can change the title in Layout view.

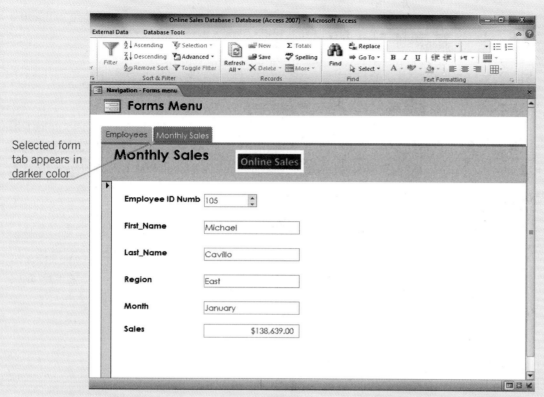

FIGURE 12–11
Forms Menu with
Monthly Sales tab
selected

Selected form
tab appears in
darker color

10. Save the form as **Navigation Form – Forms Menu**, and then close the form.

11. Keep the database open for the next Step-by-Step.

Creating a Second Navigation Form

You will need to create more than one navigation form. At least two lower-level forms will need to be placed on an upper-level navigation form so that you have more than one selection on the upper-level form. The second navigation form will be at the same lower level as the previous navigation form you created. In this exercise, since you have completed the Forms Menu, you will now create a navigation form for the Reports Menu.

Step-by-Step 12.5

1. Click the **Create** tab, click the **Navigation** button arrow, and then click **Horizontal Tabs** in the Forms group. You will now add subreports to the navigation form.

2. Close the Field List pane, and then drag the **Employee Sales Report** in the Reports group in the Navigation pane to the **Add New** tab. Next, you will add the Monthly Sales Report to the navigation form.

3. Drag the **Monthly Sales Report** to the **Add New** tab. Next, you will add a third report to the navigation form.

4. Drag **Sales Statistics** to the **Add New** tab.

5. Click in the **navigation form** title until the insertion point appears, select the text, and then change the title to **Reports Menu**.

6. Click outside the label, and then click on the label again to select it. Click the **Format** tab, and then click the **Bold** button **B**. Click the **Font Color** button arrow **A** ▾, and then click **Black, Text 1**. See **Figure 12–12**.

FIGURE 12–12
Navigation form
for reports

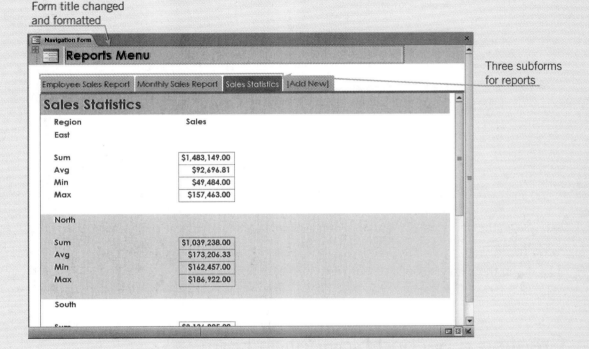

7. Save the form as **Navigation Form – Reports Menu**, and then close the form.

8. Keep the database open for the next Step-by-Step.

Designing the Main Navigation Form

The main navigation form is the upper-level form. It serves as the main menu, letting you select the lower-level navigation forms in the main form. The main navigation form is created last using the other navigation forms that already exist. In this next exercise, you will use the same layout, Horizontal Tabs, and bring the Forms Menu and Reports Menu into this form. Then, you will change their tab names to *Forms Menu* and *Reports Menu*.

Step-by-Step 12.6

1. Click the **Create** tab, click the **Navigation** button arrow in the Forms group, and then click **Horizontal Tabs**. You will now add the Navigation Form – Forms Menu to the navigation form.

2. Drag **Navigation Form – Forms Menu** in the Forms group in the Navigation pane to the **Add New** tab. Next, you will add the Reports menu to the navigation form.

3. Drag the **Navigation Form – Reports Menu** to the **Add New** tab.

4. Click the **Navigation Form** title and change the title to **Main Menu**. Add the Bold format and the Font Color **Black, Text 1** to the title.

5. Save the form as **Navigation Form – Main Menu**. See **Figure 12–13**.

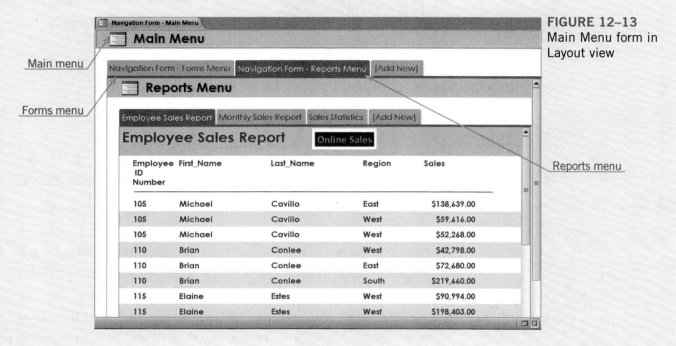

FIGURE 12–13
Main Menu form in
Layout view

6. Switch to Design view, and then click **Navigation Form – Forms Menu** to view it, as shown in **Figure 12–14**. Next, you will change the Navigation Form – Forms Menu tab title.

FIGURE 12–14
Selected label on tab title

Label appears with border when tab is selected

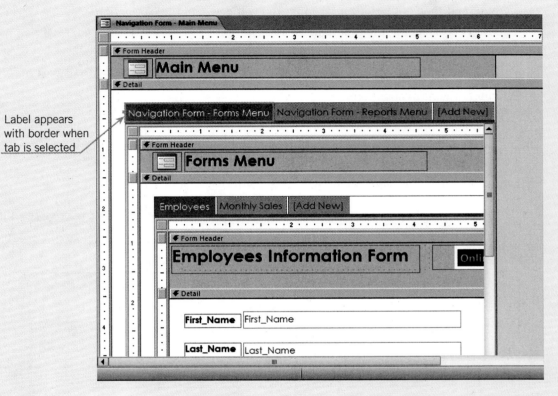

7. Click in the **Navigation Form – Forms Menu** tab title and then change the title to **Forms Menu**.

8. Verify that the text is still selected, and then apply the bold format and the Black, Text 1 color to the text. You no longer need the title Forms Menu in the Form Header because it is repetitive.

9. Click the **Forms Menu** title in the Form Header section of Navigation Form – Forms Menu, press **Delete**, and then delete the form object in the Form Header section.

10. Place your mouse pointer over the top of the Detail section bar and drag it up until the Detail section bar is directly below the Form Header, as shown in **Figure 12–15**.

FIGURE 12–15
Selected Detail header border

Mouse pointer appears as double-headed arrow when dragging header bar

Drag top of Detail header until it is flush with the Form Header

11. Repeat steps 7 through 10 for the Navigation Form – Reports Menu, changing the title to Reports Menu, then compare your screen to **Figure 12–16**.

FIGURE 12–16
Revised Reports Menu tab

Label in Form Header deleted and Form Header area minimized

Reports Menu tab reformatted

12. Place the mouse pointer over the right edge of the form border and drag to the **8"** mark on the horizontal ruler, as shown in **Figure 12–17**, to make additional room for the report.

FIGURE 12–17
Resizing Main
Menu form

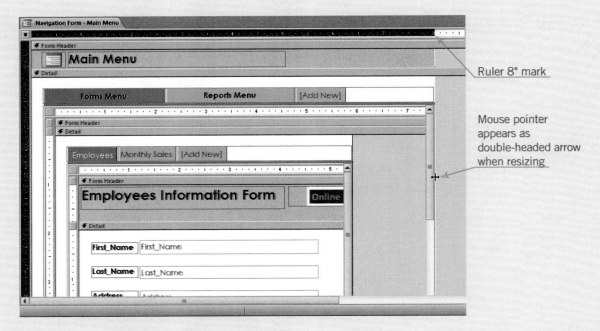

Ruler 8" mark

Mouse pointer
appears as
double-headed arrow
when resizing

13. Save and close the form.
14 Keep the database open for the next Step-by-Step.

Changing Startup Options

▶ **VOCABULARY**
startup options

Startup options are options that Access performs when the database is opened. You can specify which startup options are in place. For example, you can choose startup options that hide the Navigation pane and the Ribbon or open a form. If you choose a startup option that opens a form, such as a main menu, it will appear automatically or after the splash screen is closed. Adding startup options can secure the database by hiding selected tabs on the Ribbon and restricting access to menu commands. These actions allow only authorized users, such as the database manager, to work with tables and other objects in Design view. These startup options are located in the Access Options dialog box.

Step-by-Step 12.7

1. Click the **File** tab, and then click **Options** to open the Access Options dialog box.

2. Click **Current Database** in the left pane and view the options available for the current database, as shown in **Figure 12–18**.

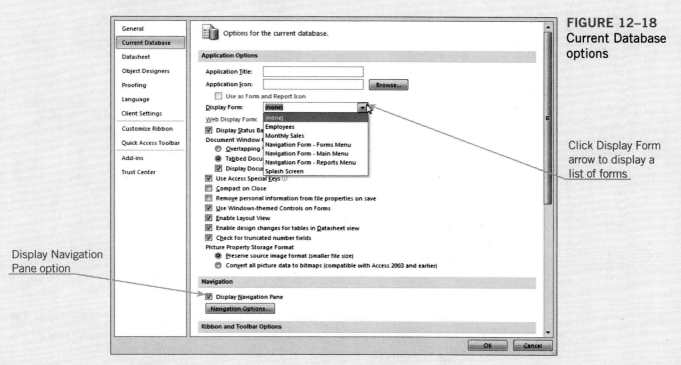

Display Navigation Pane option

FIGURE 12–18
Current Database options

Click Display Form arrow to display a list of forms

3. Click the **Display Form** drop-down arrow to view a list of forms that can be selected to appear first after the splash screen closes.

4. Click **Navigation Form – Main Menu** to select it. This form will be the first one to appear after the splash screen closes. Next, you will opt to remove the Navigation Pane from view when the database opens.

5. Click the **Display Navigation pane** check box to deselect it. Next, you will deselect the Allow Full Menus feature so that most of the Ribbon is not displayed.

6. Scroll down in the Current Database options and click the **Allow Full Menus** check box to deselect it, then compare your screen to **Figure 12–19**.

FIGURE 12–19
Revised Current
Database options

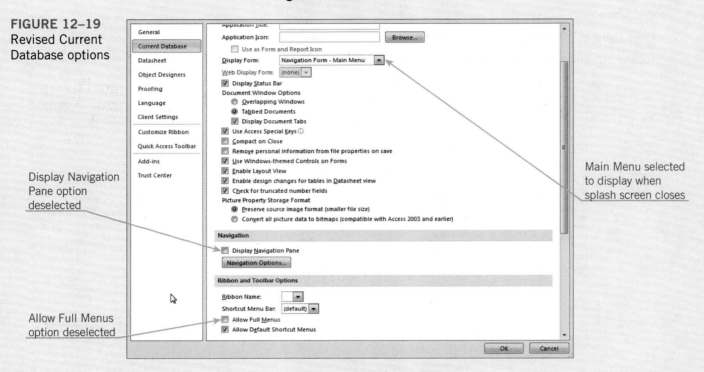

Display Navigation Pane option deselected

Main Menu selected to display when splash screen closes

Allow Full Menus option deselected

7. Click **OK** to save the changes. A message box appears stating that the current database needs to be closed before the options can take effect.

8. Click **OK**.

9. Close the **Online Sales Database** file, and then open it to view the startup options.

As shown in **Figure 12–20**, the Navigation form and only the Home and File tabs appear with limited options.

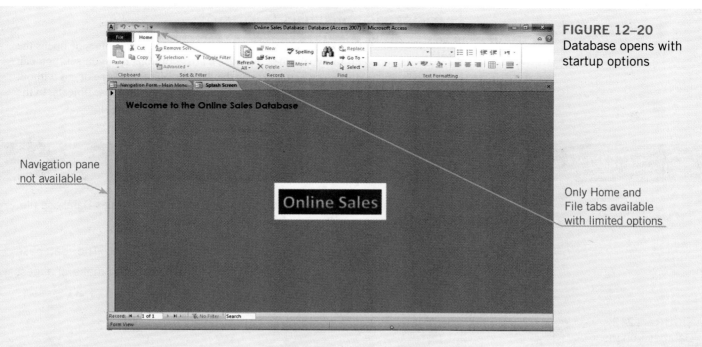

FIGURE 12–20
Database opens with
startup options

Navigation pane
not available

Only Home and
File tabs available
with limited options

10. Click the **Close** button on the splash screen. The Main Menu form appears, as shown in **Figure 12–21**.

FIGURE 12–21
Main Menu appears
as a result of
startup options

Main Menu appears
when splash
screen closes

11. Close the database file.

Bypassing Startup Options

After you set startup options, they are in effect until the next time someone opens the database. If you want to bypass the Current Database options that you set, you can press and hold the Shift key when you open the database. The database opens without the specified startup options, and changes can be made to the database objects. In the next exercise, you will open the database and bypass the startup options.

Step-by-Step 12.8

1. Press and hold the **Shift** key, and then open the **Online Sales Database** file.

2. Release the **Shift** key.

3. Click the **Microsoft Access** button on the taskbar. The database window opens without the startup options, so you can make changes. See **Figure 12–22**.

FIGURE 12–22
Database opens without new startup options

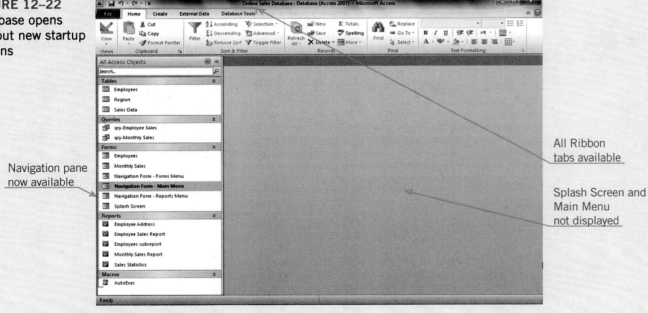

Navigation pane now available

All Ribbon tabs available

Splash Screen and Main Menu not displayed

4. Close the database file.

SUMMARY

In this lesson, you learned:

- You can create a splash screen that welcomes users to the database.

- An AutoExec macro runs when the database opens and before any other macros are run.

- After you create an AutoExec macro, you should test the macro to see if it works correctly.

- Navigation forms have both form and subform features automatically built in.

- The main navigation form acts like a main menu.

- The startup options available with Access can be changed to provide additional database security.

- You can bypass startup options when opening a database.

VOCABULARY REVIEW

Define the following terms:

AutoExec macro

hierarchical

navigation form

splash screen

startup options

REVIEW QUESTIONS

TRUE / FALSE

Circle T if the statement is true or F if the statement is false.

T F **1.** To open a splash screen when the database opens, you can create an AutoExec macro that has the OpenForm option.

T F **2.** The AutoExec macro can only include an action to open a report.

T F **3.** To bypass startup options, you press and hold the Shift key when you open the database.

T F **4.** A navigation form has the subform feature automatically built in.

T F **5.** To add a subform to a navigation form, you drag the form object from the Navigation pane to the Add New tab.

FILL IN THE BLANK

1. To open a database without startup options, you press and hold the _____ key when you open the database.

2. You can only have one _____ macro within a single database.

3. When adding a form object into a navigation form, you drag the form object from the _____ into the navigation form.

4. A macro that runs automatically when you open the database is called the _____ macro.

5. To hide all tabs except for the File tab and the Home tab, you deselect the _____ check box in the Access Options dialog box.

WRITTEN QUESTIONS

Write a brief answer to the following questions.

1. What is an AutoExec macro?

2. How do you change startup options?

3. Why is it important for a splash screen to have the same format as the other forms and reports in a database?

4. Describe how you can bypass startup options.

■ PROJECTS

If you have a SAM 2010 user profile, your instructor may have assigned an autogradable version of the indicated project. If so, log into the SAM 2010 Web site at *www.cengage.com/sam2010* to download the instruction and start files.

PROJECT 12–1

1. Open the **Region Sales** file from the drive and folder where your Data Files are stored. Save the database as **Region Sales Database**, followed by your initials.

2. Create a navigation form that has the Employees and Sales Information forms.

3. Save the navigation form as **Forms Menu** and then close the form.

4. Create a navigation form that has the **Report** for **Employee Numbers and Sales Data by Month** reports.

5. Save the navigation form as **Reports Menu** and then close the form.

6. Create the main navigation form and then bring the Forms Menu and the Reports Menu into this form.

7. Save the form as **Main Menu**.

8. In Design view, delete the label in the Forms Header section of the Forms Menu and then decrease the size of the Form Header.

9. Delete the label in the Reports Menu Form Header section and then decrease the size of the Form Header section.

10. Change the title of the navigation form to **Main Menu**.

11. Save the form.

12. Switch to Form view to view the completed Main Menu.

13. Close the form and close the database.

 PROJECT 12–2

1. Open the **Book Sales** file from the drive and folder where your Data Files are stored. Save the database as **Book Sales Database**, followed by your initials.

2. Create a form with a splash screen and add the Book Sales Logo file, which is located in the drive and folder with your Data Files. Add the logo to the Detail section. (*Hint*: You will need to cut it from the Form Header section and paste it into the Detail section.)

3. Add a label with the text **Welcome to the Book Sales Worldwide Database**. (*Hint*: You will need to click the Design tab and in the Controls group, click Label. Then, type the text.)

4. Change the font size to 18 and change the font color to Black, Text 1.

5. Save the form as **Splash Screen**.

6. Create an AutoExec macro that opens the splash screen in a Read-Only Data Mode when the database is opened. Save the macro as AutoExec. Close the Macro window.

7. Close the database.

8. Reopen the database to test the AutoExec macro.

9. Close the database.

PROJECT 12–3

1. Open the **Pets** file from the drive and folder where your Data Files are stored. Save the database as **Pets Database**, followed by your initials.

2. Change the startup options so that the Navigation Main Menu form opens when the database is opened.

3. Change the startup options so that Full Menus are not allowed and the Navigation pane is not available.

4. Close the database.

5. Reopen the database to test the startup options.

6. Close the database.

■ CRITICAL THINKING

ACTIVITY 12–1

As the new database administrator for the Coastal Sales Corporation, you decide to automate the Coastal Sales database to make it easier to use and to prevent unwanted changes. You first open the **Coastal Sales** file and save it as **Coastal Sales Database**. Then, you create an AutoExec macro that opens the splash screen form. You change the startup options so that the Navigation Main Menu appears after the splash screen form is closed. You also set the startup options to hide the Navigation pane and all but the File and Home tabs on the Ribbon when the database opens.

ACTIVITY 12–2

Think of how you could use the navigation forms in Access to automate a database that contains sports information. For example, the database would probably have the names and contact information of team members, games and practice schedules, and coach information. Write down how you would design the hierarchy of navigation forms to present this information.

LESSON 13

Programming in Access

■ OBJECTIVES

Upon completion of this lesson, you should be able to:

- Create a new function.
- Test a new function.
- Add a control with defined names to a form.
- Create an If procedure.
- View the procedure results.
- Add an Else statement to a procedure.
- Test a revised procedure.

■ VOCABULARY

code
comment
function
procedure
public
syntax

Introduction

Lesson 13 introduces you to Visual Basic for Applications (VBA) and describes how to use VBA to enhance database processing for users. VBA is the programming language for Microsoft Office programs, including Access. VBA has a set of common features for all Microsoft Office programs. In this lesson, you will learn how to define a new function using VBA. After you define the function, you will test the function to be sure that it is working correctly and then add a Text Box control to a form. Finally, you will write a procedure that uses the function you defined and discover that you can change a procedure after it is created to enhance the actions it performs.

Creating a New Function

> **VOCABULARY**
> function
> code
> syntax
> variable name
> comment
> public

A *function* is an action that can be defined in VBA code where you use statements to describe the action you want the function to perform. *Code* refers to the *syntax*, or wording, that is used in VBA. Access already has built-in functions, such as Average, Min, and Max, to calculate an average and to determine minimum and maximum values. If you want to use a function that is not built-in, you will need to define a new function. Defining a new function simply refers to writing VBA code so that the function will perform a certain action.

For example, you might want a function that calculates the number of years between two dates. The function will have two date values referenced using two variables with identifiable variable names. A *variable name* is simply a symbolic name that you assign to a value. Creating variable names that make functions easy to understand can help make your database more user-friendly. For example, the variable names in the date function in the above example could be FirstDate and SecondDate.

You will also need to assign a data type to the variables. In the example calculating years, you would assign a date data type to the variables. To identify these variables as date data types, you would use the syntax (FirstDate As Date, SecondDate As Date). When you actually use the function, you will type in date values for these variables.

You can also add a statement that does not perform an action, but helps the person looking at the code identify the purpose of the code. This statement is called a *comment*. To add a comment, you begin by typing an apostrophe (') before the sentence. Comments appear in green.

If you want the function to be available in various procedures that you may write in the database, you should define the function in a module. Defining a function in a module makes it accessible throughout the database, or *public*. In this next exercise, you will create a function that will be used to determine the number of years between two dates. You will use the function name YearDiff.

Step-by-Step 13.1

1. Open the **New Sales** file from the drive and folder where your Data Files are stored. Save the database as **New Sales Database**, followed by your initials. You may need to click **Enable Content**.

2. Click the **Create** tab, and then click **Module** in the Macros & Code group. The Visual Basic window appears, as shown in **Figure 13–1**.

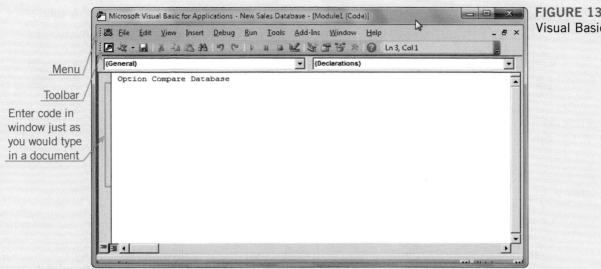

FIGURE 13–1
Visual Basic window

Menu

Toolbar

Enter code in
window just as
you would type
in a document

3. In the Visual Basic window, click the **Insert** menu and then click **Procedure**.

4. In the Name box, type **YearDiff**.

5. In the Type section, click the **Function** option button, then verify that the **Public** option button is selected in the Scope section, as shown in **Figure 13–2**.

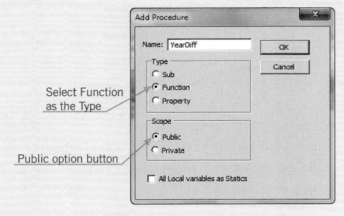

Select Function
as the Type

Public option button

FIGURE 13–2
Add Procedure dialog box

6. Click **OK** to close the Add Procedure dialog box. The new function is added to the VBA window.

7. Click between the parentheses following YearDiff, and then type **FirstDate As Date, SecondDate As Date**, as shown in **Figure 13–3**.

FIGURE 13–3
Variables in YearDiff defined

Data type defined for variables

Indicates Public function

Variable names

8. Click outside the close parenthesis, and then press **Enter**. You will now add another line with a comment.

9. Press **Tab**, type **'Determine the number of years between two dates**, and then press **Enter**. The text becomes a comment indicated by the green font. Next, you will indent the line of code before you type it to make it easier to see in the window.

TIP

You can press Enter to accept the text that automatically appears as you type.

10. Press **Tab** to indent this line, and then type **YearDiff=DateDiff("yyyy", FirstDate,SecondDate)**. Notice that text appears as you type to assist you in creating the function, as shown in **Figure 13–4**.

FIGURE 13–4
Help text appears in VBA window

Text appears to assist you in defining function

11. Click after the End Function, and then compare your completed YearDiff function to the one shown in **Figure 13–5**.

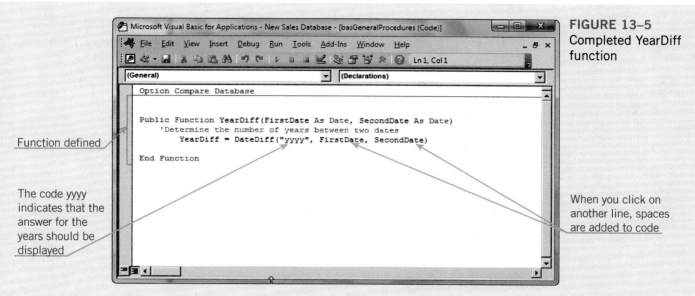

FIGURE 13–5
Completed YearDiff
function

Function defined

The code yyyy
indicates that the
answer for the
years should be
displayed

When you click on
another line, spaces
are added to code

12. Click the **Save** button 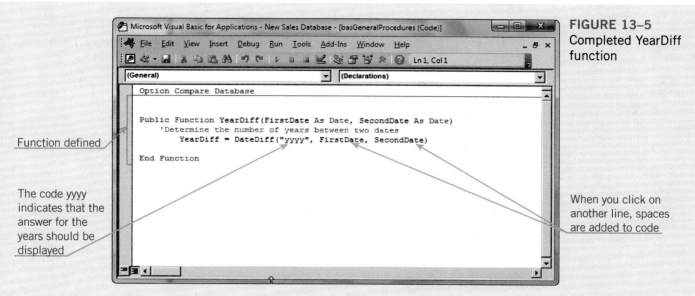 on the toolbar of the Visual Basic window.

13. Type **basGeneralProcedures** in the Module Name text box and then click **OK**.

14. Remain in this database for the next Step-by-Step.

Testing a New Function

After creating a new function, it is smart to check it to make sure the code is correct. The function could contain errors even though the statements have the correct syntax. Even the simplest functions can contain errors, such as spelling errors or logic errors. Logic errors occur when the procedure produces incorrect results. When you enter the dates in the Immediate window, you place a pound sign (#) before and after the date to define when the date starts and ends. To test a function, you use the Immediate window. The Immediate window will return the results of the function based on the values you enter. In order to test the function, you type a question mark (?) before the function name and the variables. In the next exercise, you will test the YearDiff function.

Step-by-Step 13.2

1. In the Visual Basic window, click the **View** menu and then click **Immediate Window**. If you do not see the Immediate window, you may need to increase the size of the window.

2. If necessary, place the mouse pointer over the bottom bar of the window until you see the double-headed arrow, as shown in **Figure 13–6**, then drag the border up until you can see the Immediate window.

FIGURE 13–6
Immediate window
with arrow for resizing

Arrow to resize
Immediate window

Immediate window

3. Click in the Immediate window, and then type **?YearDiff(#3/15/2006#, #11/25/2013#)**. Notice as you start typing that text appears in the window to help you with the syntax.

4. Press **Enter**. As shown in **Figure 13–7**, the answer, 7, appears in the Immediate window.

FIGURE 13–7
Answer appears in
Immediate window

A question mark
indicates that you
want to test this
function

Answer shows
under test

5. Close the Immediate window by clicking the **Close** button in the upper-right corner of the Immediate window.

6. Click the **File** menu, and then click **Close and Return to Microsoft Access**. The Modules group appears in the Navigation pane with the name of the new module, as shown in **Figure 13–8**.

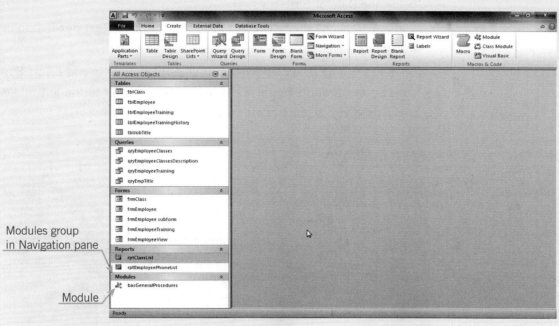

FIGURE 13–8
Module name appears in Modules group

Modules group in Navigation pane

Module

Adding a Control with Defined Names to a Form

You can add controls to a form that display the results of a calculation. If you are going to use a control in a procedure, you first add the control to the form. Then you assign specific names to the parts of the control in the Property Sheet. For example, a Text Box control has two parts: a label part and an unbound part. The label identifies what will appear in the unbound part of the control. The unbound part of the Text Box remains unbound until a field with actual data is assigned to this control. Then, this part of the Text Box is considered bound; in other words, it is bound by the data.

You add names to the parts of the control so that you can use these names in the procedure. It is easier to read and identify the purpose of the function if it has recognizable control names. In the next exercise, you will learn how to assign descriptive names to the label and the unbound part of a Text Box control. The Text Box control that you create will be used in a procedure that you will create later in this lesson.

Step-by-Step 13.3

1. Double-click **frmEmployee** in the Forms section of the Navigation pane.

2. On the Ribbon, click the **Home** tab, click the **View** button arrow in the Views group, and then click **Design View**. You will add a Text Box control below the Date of Birth field.

3. Click the **Design** tab, if necessary, and then click the **Text Box** button in the Controls group.

4. Click in the area below DOB in the Date of Birth field to add a Text Box control, as shown in **Figure 13–9**. If you click too far to the left under this field, the two parts of the control will overlap.

FIGURE 13–9
Text Box control added

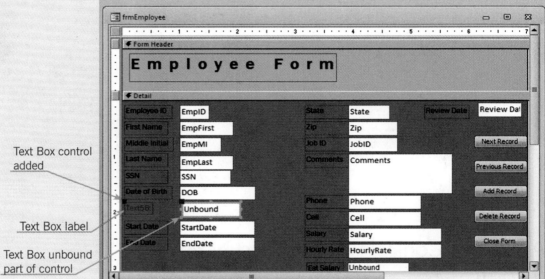

5. Click the **Text Box label** on the left side of the Text Box control, and then click the **Property Sheet** button in the Tools group.

6. In the Property Sheet pane, click the **All** tab, click in the **Name** box, and then type **Age_Label**, replacing the existing text.

7. Click the **Caption** field, and then type **Age**. See **Figure 13–10**. The caption will appear in the title bar in Form view.

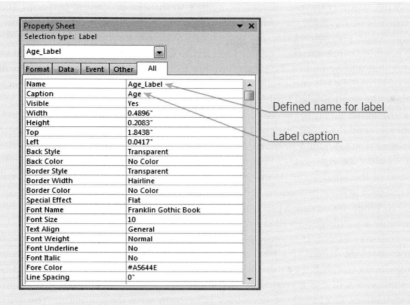

FIGURE 13–10
Property Sheet pane for
Text Box label

Defined name for label

Label caption

8. If necessary, drag the Property Sheet pane out of the way so that you can see the entire form. Click the **Unbound** object on the right side of the Text Box control.

9. On the Property Sheet pane, click in the **Name** box, then type **Age** to replace the existing text. This name will be used when you create the procedure.

10. Close the **Design** tab and then click the **Property Sheet** button.

11. Click the **Text Box label**, and then click the **Format** tab on the Ribbon.

12. Click the **Font Color** button arrow , and then click **Black, Text 1** in the Font group.

13. Save the form and remain in this screen for the next Step-by-Step.

EXTRA FOR EXPERTS

After you create a Text Box control in a form, you can press and hold down the Ctrl key and then use the arrow keys to move the text box to a desired location.

Creating an If Procedure

A *procedure* is a group of statements written in VBA code that can include several functions. Each function can perform one action or multiple actions. Typically, unless a statement is a comment, it performs an action.

Procedures include code that indicates where the procedure begins and additional code that tells where the procedure ends. The *If* procedure begins with the code word **If** and ends with the code words **End If**. Several statements appear between If and End If.

▶ **VOCABULARY**
procedure

VBA requires the use of specific syntax so that the procedure performs actions correctly. For example, to calculate the difference between a date in a form and today's date, you would use the code word *Date* for the current date. You would also need to review the field names used in the form because they will be used in the syntax that will be part of the procedure. For example, if the field name in a form for date of birth is DOB, you would use *DOB* as the syntax in the procedure. If you want to make the control label visible in the procedure, you need to add the syntax *Visible* after the name given to the label. After the syntax Visible, you will need to add an equal sign and the word *True* or *False* so that the label will appear or not appear. For example, if you wanted to make the age label used in the last Step-by-Step visible, you would type *Age_Label.Visible=True*. Notice that you use a period to indicate the end of the label name. If this procedure will be used in only one form, it will be entered as a private procedure versus a public procedure that can be used in several objects. When you create a procedure within a form, Access recognizes it as a private procedure and this code will show when you start creating the procedure.

You may use an If statement to check a form field to see if the field is empty. When checking to see if a field does not have a value, you use the *IsNull* syntax. IsNull looks in the field to see whether the field is null (empty). In the next Step-by-Step, you will use a procedure that looks for employees that are still employed and calculates the length of time they have been with the company. You will use the YearDiff function and the Text Box control names you assigned in the previous Step-by-Step.

Step-by-Step 13.4

1. In the upper-left corner of the Form window, click the **Form Selector** ▢ to select the form. Notice that when the form is selected, the Form Selector box appears with a dark square. See **Figure 13–11**. You select the Form Selector so that Access knows you will be working within this form. Also notice the right side of the Date of Birth field is identified as DOB.

FIGURE 13–11
Form Selector selected

Form Selector

2. Click the **Property Sheet** button, and then click the **Event** tab in the Property Sheet pane.

3. Click the **Build** button ▣ next to the **On Current** event. The Choose Builder dialog box opens, as shown in **Figure 13–12**.

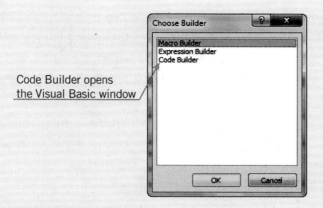

FIGURE 13–12
Choose Builder dialog box

Code Builder opens
the Visual Basic window

4. Click **Code Builder** and then click **OK**. The Visual Basic window opens, as shown in **Figure 13–13**. Next you will type a comment that explains the procedure. The insertion point should be between the Private Sub and End Sub commands.

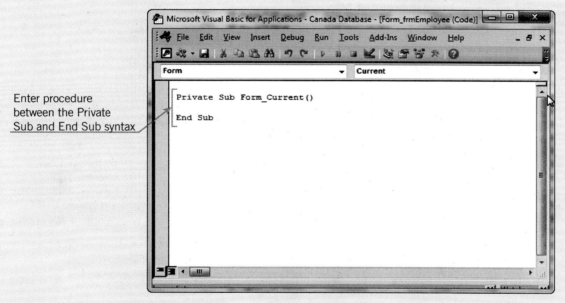

FIGURE 13–13
Visual Basic window

Enter procedure
between the Private
Sub and End Sub syntax

5. Type **'For current employees, display the age of the employee.**

6. Press **Enter** to move to the next line. The comment appears in green. Next, you will type code that looks at the EndDate field; if it is not empty, then the person is still employed with the company. Then, you will review the DOB field and if it is not null, the procedure can continue and calculate the employee's age.

7. Press **Tab** to indent the next statement and then type the following:
   If IsNull (EndDate) And Not IsNull (DOB) Then.

   In the next step, you will add code that calculates the difference between today's date and the employee's date of birth to determine their age.

8. Press **Enter** to start a new line, press **Tab** to indent the line, and then type **Age = YearDiff (DOB, Date)**. Note that each time you move to a new line, spaces are automatically added within the syntax. Indenting each line helps make it clear that the next line is a subset of what occurred in the previous line of code.

9. Press **Enter** and then type **Age_Label.Visible = True**. This line of code will make the Age label visible if the person is still employed with the company and if their DOB field contains data.

10. Press **Enter** and then type **Age.Visible = True**.

11. Press **Enter**, and then press the **Backspace** key to move the next line so that it is even with the If statement.

12. Type **End If**. Compare your screen to **Figure 13–14**.

FIGURE 13–14
Visual Basic window with procedure

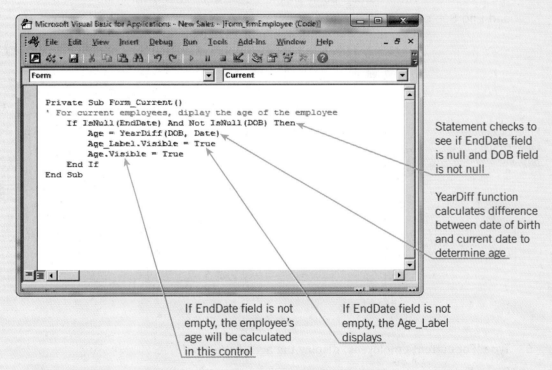

Statement checks to see if EndDate field is null and DOB field is not null

YearDiff function calculates difference between date of birth and current date to determine age

If EndDate field is not empty, the employee's age will be calculated in this control

If EndDate field is not empty, the Age_Label displays

13. Click the **Save** button 🖫 on the Visual Basic toolbar. You are saving the function as a part of this form.

14. Close the Visual Basic window. Remain in this screen for the next Step-by-Step.

Viewing the Procedure Results

After creating a procedure, you will need to view the results to be certain that the procedure is doing what you expect. If the procedure is working correctly, the results of the procedure will show accurate results. If the procedure returns incorrect results, the syntax may not be entered correctly or may include a misspelled word. In this next exercise, you will view the Age text box to see if the function is calculating the correct results.

Step-by-Step 13.5

1. Close the Property Sheet pane.

2. Click the **Design** tab, click the **View** button arrow, and then click **Form View**. Notice that the age field appears but an age is not displayed because the employee is no longer employed. You can determine if an employee is no longer employed based on the End Date.

3. Click the **Next Record** button on the right side of the form. The second record appears for a current employee and displays their age, as shown in **Figure 13–15**. Note, the age shown on your screen may differ depending on the current date that you are viewing the form.

Age control is visible and age is calculated

EndDate field is empty so employee is still active

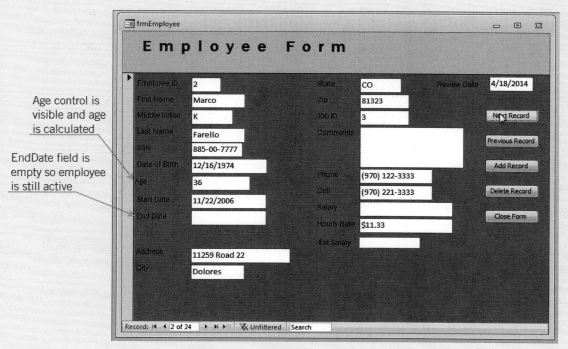

FIGURE 13–15
Record shows age of employee

4. Remain in this screen for the next Step-by-Step.

Adding an Else Statement to the Procedure

In an *If* procedure, you may have the procedure look at a field and check to see if it contains a value. If it does contain a value, the procedure continues; if it doesn't, the procedure ends. However, you may want the procedure to perform a specific action if the field does contain a value and another action if it doesn't contain a value. By placing an *Else* statement in the code, the procedure will perform one action or else it will perform another action. In this next exercise, you will add an *Else* statement to the *If* procedure you created previously. The procedure will determine if the End Date field is empty and, if so, calculate the person's age. Or, if a value is found in the End Date field, the statements after *Else* will run and the Age field will not display.

Step-by-Step 13.6

1. Click the **View** button arrow, and then click **Design View**.

2. Verify that the Form Selector is still selected and then, in the Tools group, click the **Property Sheet** button. If necessary, click the **Event** tab to view this tab. See **Figure 13–16**.

FIGURE 13–16
Event tab indicates procedure in the On Current event

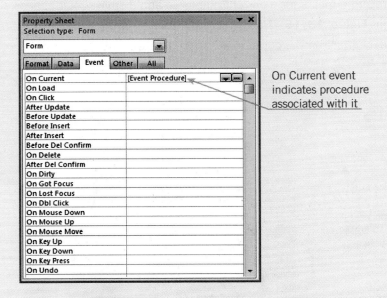

On Current event indicates procedure associated with it

3. Click the **Build** button next to the On Current box to display the Visual Basic for Applications window.

4. Click at the end of the Age.Visible = True line, and then press **Enter** to add another line to the function.

5. Press **Backspace** to line up the row with the If and End If functions.

6 Type **Else** and then press **Enter**.

7. Press **Tab** to indent this line, and then type **Age_Label.Visible=False**.

8. Press **Enter** to move to the next line.

9. Type **Age.Visible=False**. Compare your screen to **Figure 13–17**.

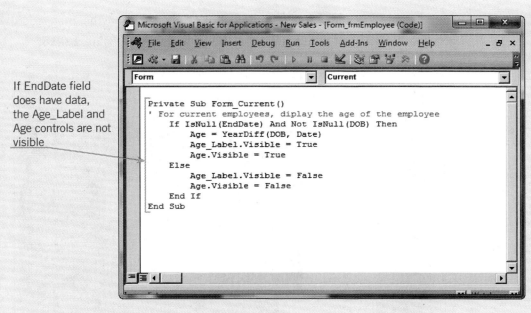

If EndDate field does have data, the Age_Label and Age controls are not visible

FIGURE 13–17
Revised procedure with Else statement

10. Click the **Save** button on the toolbar in the Visual Basic window.

11. Click the **File** menu, and then click **Close and Return to Microsoft Access**. Close the Property Sheet pane, if necessary.

12. Remain in this screen for the next Step-by-Step.

Testing a Revised Procedure

Even though you tested the function previously, since the procedure has changed, you will need to check it again. You will review the results for several records to be sure that the procedure is working correctly as you move through the records.

Step-by-Step 13.7

1. Click the **View** button arrow, and then click **Form View**.

2. Check to see that the Age field is not displayed on the first record because an end date appears for the employee. See **Figure 13–18**.

FIGURE EX 13–18
Record does not display
Text Box for age

Text Box not
displayed

End Date field
has data entered
indicating employee
is no longer with
the company

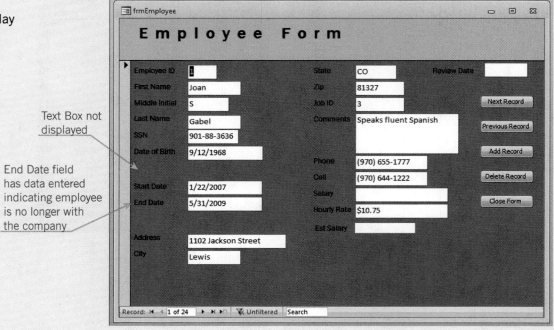

3. Click the **Next Record** button. The age for this current employee is displayed.

4. Save the form by clicking the **Save** button on the Quick Access toolbar.

5. Close the form.

6. Close the database.

SUMMARY

In this lesson, you learned:

■ If the function you want to use is not a built-in function, you will need to create a new function.

■ After creating a new function, you will need to test the function to see if it produces the correct results.

■ You can add a control with defined names to a form.

■ An If procedure starts with the *If* syntax and ends with the *End If* syntax.

■ You should review the results of an If procedure to be certain that it is working correctly.

■ You can add an Else statement to an If procedure.

■ A revised procedure will need to be tested.

■ VOCABULARY REVIEW

Define the following terms:

code	function	public
comment	procedure	syntax

■ REVIEW QUESTIONS

TRUE / FALSE

Circle T if the statement is true or F if the statement is false.

T   F   **1.**   After a procedure is created and tested, it cannot be changed.

T   F   **2.**   VBA is an abbreviation for Visual Basic for Applications.

T   F   **3.**   A function is an action that can be defined in VBA code where you use statements to describe the action you want the function to perform.

T   F   **4.**   Code refers to the syntax, or wording, that is used in VBA.

T   F   **5.**   An If procedure begins with an *If* code word and ends with the code words *End If*.

FILL IN THE BLANK

1. If you want a function to be available in more than one procedure, you should define it as a(n) _____ function.

2. In order to test the function, you need to type a(n) _____ before the function name and the variables.

3. A(n) _____ is a symbolic name that you assign to a value.

4. To add a comment, you begin by typing a(n) _____ before the sentence.

5. Defining a function in a module makes the function accessible throughout the database, also referred to as making the function _____.

WRITTEN QUESTIONS

Write a brief answer to the following questions.

1. Explain how you would add a comment to a procedure.

2. Describe how a function can be tested.

3. If you want to make a label with the defined name *age* not visible, what code could you use for this action?

4. Explain why a procedure may return incorrect results.

5. Describe what occurs in a procedure if you add the Else statement.

■ PROJECTS

If you have a SAM 2010 user profile, your instructor may have assigned an autogradable version of the indicated project. If so, log into the SAM 2010 Web site at *www.cengage.com/sam2010* to download the instruction and start files.

PROJECT 13–1

1. Open the **Epic Internet Sales** file from the drive and folder where your Data Files are stored. Save the database as **Epic Internet Sales Database**, followed by your initials.

2. Define a function named **YearDiff** that calculates the difference between two dates. Define the function as public.

3. Add the comment **Determine the number of years between two dates** to the function.

4. For the date variables, use the variable names **FirstDate** and **SecondDate**.

5. Assign the Date data type to both variables.

6. Save the module as **basGeneralProcedures**.

7. Test the function in the Immediate window to see if it is working correctly.

8. Close the database.

SAM PROJECT 13–2

1. Open the **End of Year Sales** file from the drive and folder where your Data Files are stored. Save the database as **End of Year Sales Database**, followed by your initials.

2. Open **basGeneralProcedures** and view the defined function. Notice the YearDiff function is already defined.

3. Close basGeneralProcedures.

4. Open **frmEmployee** in Design view.

5. View the Property Sheet for the Age: field label and Text Box control.

6. Click the Form Selector button.

7. Add an If procedure to the On Current event that uses the YearDiff function to calculate the employee's age by using their date of birth and the current date. (*Hint*: Use the Date variable for the current date.)

8. In the If procedure, make the label and the Text Box control visible when the age is calculated.

9. View the results. (Remember to view several records to be sure the age is calculating correctly.)

10. Save and close the form.

11. Close the database.

PROJECT 13-3

1. Open the **National Events** file from the drive and folder where your Data Files are stored. Save the database as **National Events**, followed by your initials.

2. Open **frmEmployee** in Design view, select the Form Selector, and then click the Property Sheet button.

3. If necessary, click the Event tab to view this tab.

4. Click the Build button next to the On Current box to display the Visual Basic for Applications window.

5. Click at the end of the Age.Visible = True line, and then press Enter to add another line to the function.

6. Add an Else statement, and then add statements to make the Age_Label and Age control not visible if there is data in the EndDate field.

7. Click the Save button on the toolbar in the Visual Basic window, click the File menu, and then click Close and Return to Microsoft Access.

8. Test the new procedure to see if it is working correctly.

9. Close the database

■ CRITICAL THINKING

ACTIVITY 13-1

Open the **Wholesale International Sales** file and then save it as **Wholesale International Sales Database**. Imagine you are the new database administrator for the Wholesale International Sales Corporation. You decide to automate the Wholesale International Sales database to calculate the difference between dates in the frmEmployee form. You view the basGeneralProcedures procedure and notice that the YearDiff function is defined, but it is not used in the database. You decide to add a Text Box control to frmEmployee that will show the difference in dates between the employee's Start Date and End Date. This control would only need to be displayed for former employees, so you create a procedure that only has the field display when then EndDate field includes data. You use LOE as the code for length of employment when you define the label name and the control name. You decide to review several records to be sure the procedure is working correctly.

ACTIVITY 13-2

Imagine a database that has a form that shows the start date and end date for three sports seasons. Think of how you could add a function and a procedure to calculate the length of a sports season for football, basketball, and baseball. Write down your thoughts and how you would present this report to a coach.

LESSON 14

Creating Database Security and Documentation

■ OBJECTIVES

Upon completion of this lesson, you should be able to:

■ Open a database in the Open Exclusive mode.

■ Encrypt a database with a password.

■ Open an encrypted database.

■ Remove encryption from a database.

■ Make a backup copy of a database.

■ Create database documentation.

■ VOCABULARY

backup

Database Documenter

encryption

Open Exclusive mode

password

Introduction

Microsoft Access offers several security and documentation features to protect a database from losing important information that can be caused by power failures or individuals who maliciously or accidentally delete database objects. To avoid losing database information, you can open a database in the Open Exclusive mode. In this mode, you are the only person who can access the database. You can also add a password to a database in Open Exclusive mode, which encrypts, or scrambles, the data. Encrypting a database places the data in an unintelligible format so it cannot be viewed or understood unless it is opened with the correct password. If necessary, you can also remove the password and encryption to allow easier access to the data. Creating a backup copy of a database is another method for protecting important data. In this lesson, you will also learn about the Database Documenter feature, which is used to create a report that documents each selected object in the database.

Opening a Database in the Open Exclusive Mode

You can open an Access database using several methods, including Open mode, Open Read-Only mode, Open Exclusive Read-Only mode, and Open Exclusive mode. Typically when you open a database, you use the Open mode, which allows several users to open and use the database at the same time. Using the Open Read-Only mode allows multiple users to open a database, but they cannot add or change records and they cannot create new objects. The Open Exclusive Read-Only mode opens the database so that all users except for the current user are locked out; however, the current user can only view the data in the database.

In the *Open Exclusive mode*, only the person who opened the database can use and make changes to it; all other users are locked out from opening and using the database. This option is typically used when you want to encrypt a database with a password. In this next exercise, you will first open the data file and save it with a new name, then you will close Access. When you start Access again, you will open a database in Open Exclusive mode.

▶ **VOCABULARY**
Open Exclusive mode

Step-by-Step 14.1

1. Open the **Employee Sales** file from the drive and folder where your Data Files are stored. Save the database as **Employee Sales Database**, followed by your initials.

2. Exit Access.

3. Start Access. The File tab is displayed in the window.

4. Click **Open**.

5. Locate the folder where your Data Files are stored.

6. In the Open dialog box, click **Employee Sales Database** once and then click the **drop-down arrow** next to the Open button. See **Figure 14–1**.

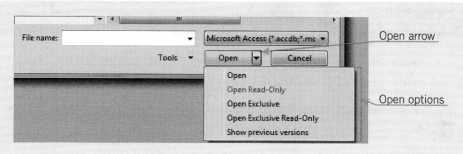

FIGURE 14–1
Open options in the
Open dialog box

7. Click the **Open Exclusive** option. The database opens in the Exclusive mode.

8. Remain in this database for the next Step-by-Step.

Encrypting with a Password

If your database has sensitive information, such as Social Security numbers or salary information, you might decide to protect it from unauthorized use. Access 2010 combines two tools for database security: database passwords and encryption. A *password* is a collection of characters that a user types to gain access to a file. When a database is password protected, users cannot open the database unless they provide the correct password. When you *encrypt* a database with a password, data within the database is made unreadable. This combined safety feature provides stronger protection than previous versions of Access. You can only encrypt a database with a password if the database is opened in the Open Exclusive mode.

In Access, row level locking is turned on by default. Row level locking means that when you change values in a record in an encrypted database, only the changed record will be encrypted, not the entire database. Therefore, when you encrypt a database with row level locking turned off, you will see a message that states a *block cipher is incompatible with row level locking and so row level locking will be ignored*. This message ensures that the entire database will be encrypted. In this next exercise, you will encrypt the database with a password.

▶ **VOCABULARY**
password

encrypt

Step-by-Step 14.2

1. Click the **File** tab and, if necessary, click the **Info** tab. Notice the Encrypt with Password option is available, as shown in **Figure 14–2**.

FIGURE 14–2
Encrypt with Password option

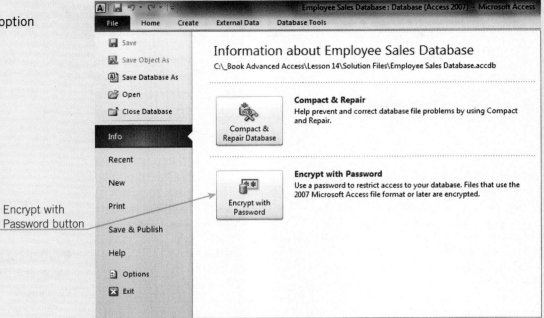

Encrypt with
Password button

2. Click the **Encrypt with Password** button. The Set Database Password dialog box opens, as shown in **Figure 14–3**. Note, if the database is not opened in the Exclusive mode, you would receive an error message at this time.

FIGURE 14–3
Set Database Password dialog box

Enter password in
both text boxes

3. In the **Password** text box, type **CatCat**.

4. Press **Tab** to move to the **Verify** text box, and then type **CatCat** again.

5. Click **OK**. A message appears showing that row level locking will be ignored, as shown in **Figure 14–4**.

FIGURE 14–4
Message about row level locking

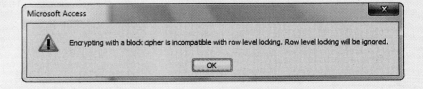

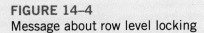

6. Click **OK** to close the message box. Next, you will save the database with another name so you can still have a copy of the encrypted database.

7. Save the database as **Employee Sales Database 2**.

8. In the Password Required text box, type **CatCat** and then press **Enter**.

9. Click **Enable Content** in the Message bar.

10. Close the database.

Opening an Encrypted Database

When opening an encrypted database, you will be asked for a password. After you enter the password, the database should open so that you can view and make changes to the database objects. Until the correct password is entered, no objects in the database can be viewed. In this next exercise, you will open an encrypted database.

Step-by-Step 14.3

1. Open the **Employee Sales Database 2**. The Password Required dialog box opens, as shown in **Figure 14–5**.

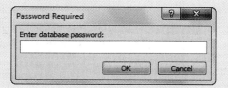

FIGURE 14–5
Password Required dialog box

2. Type **CatCat**.

3. Click **OK**.

4. Open the **Employees** table and view the data.

5. Close the table.

6. Close the database and remain in this screen for the next Step-by-Step.

Removing Encryption from a Database

To remove the password and encryption from a database, you first need to open the database in the Open Exclusive mode. After you enter the password to open the database, you can then remove the encryption using the Remove Encryption button. In this next exercise, you will save the database with a new name so you still have a password-protected and encrypted version of the database.

Step-by-Step 14.4

1. If necessary, click the **File** tab and click **Open**.

2. Navigate to the **Employee Sales Database 2** file.

3. Click the **Open** button arrow, and then click **Open Exclusive**.

4. Type **CatCat** in the Password Required dialog box.

5. Click **OK**.

6. Click the **File** tab. The Decrypt Database option is displayed. See **Figure 14–6**.

FIGURE 14–6
File tab with Decrypt Database option

Decrypt Database button

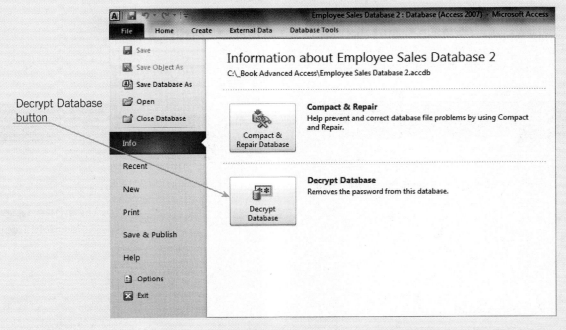

7. Click the **Decrypt Database** button. The Unset Database Password dialog box opens, as shown in **Figure 14–7**.

FIGURE 14–7
Unset Database Password dialog box

8. Type **CatCat** and then click **OK**.

9. Click the **File** tab. Notice that the Encrypt with Password option is displayed, indicating that the password and encryption are removed.

10. Leave the database open for the next Step-by-Step.

Making a Backup Copy of a Database

It is a good idea to regularly make a backup copy of your database. A *backup* is a duplicate copy of your database created by using the Back Up Database option when you save the file. By creating a backup, the database can be restored in the event of a loss resulting from a power failure, a hard disk crash, or malicious or accidental deletion of database objects. A good rule of thumb is to schedule a database backup on a regular basis. For example, you could schedule a backup at the end of each day or at the end of each week. The Back Up Database command uses the same filename and the date that the file was backed up. In this next exercise, you will make a backup copy of a database.

▶ **VOCABULARY**
backup

Step-by-Step 14.5

1. In the Employee Sales Database, click the **File** tab.

2. Click the **Save & Publish** option. Notice the Back Up Database option, as shown in **Figure 14–8**.

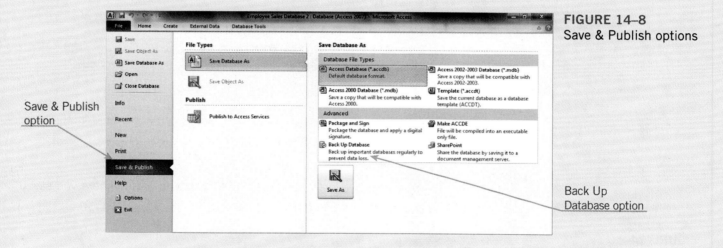

Save & Publish option

Back Up Database option

FIGURE 14–8
Save & Publish options

3. Click the **Back Up Database** option. Selecting this option alerts Access that when you click Save As, you want to create a backup of the database.

4. Click the **Save As** button. The Save As dialog box opens, as shown in **Figure 14–9**.

FIGURE 14–9
Save As dialog box

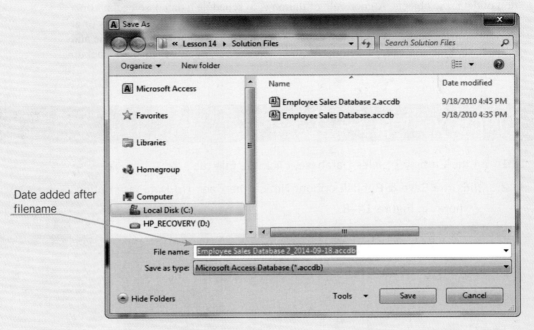

Date added after filename

5. Click the **Save** button. Review the Access title bar and notice that Employee Sales Database 2 still appears as the filename.

6. Close the database.

7. In Windows Explorer, navigate to the drive and folder where you saved the backup file, and then view the results. See **Figure 14–10**.

FIGURE 14–10
File list with backup file

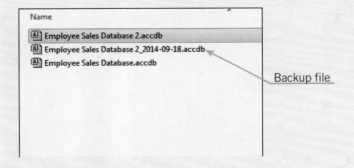

Backup file

8. Close Windows Explorer and return to the Access window.

Documenting the Database Design

Another safety feature for your database is to document the database design in case the file gets damaged or corrupted. The database design refers to the objects in the database, such as tables, queries, forms, reports, macros, and the relationship between these objects. Documenting this design is a good idea so you have it for future reference. In Access, the ***Database Documenter*** produces a report of selected objects or every object in a database. You can document the properties of these objects and the relationships of objects that you select. Then, if a database file gets damaged or corrupted, you should be able to look at the documentation and fix the database or re-create it. In this next exercise, you will create a report that shows information for all the objects in a database.

▶ **VOCABULARY**
Database Documenter

Step-by-Step 14.6

1. Open the **Happy Pets** file from the drive and folder where your Data Files are stored. Save the database as **Happy Pets Database**, followed by your initials.

2. Click the **Enable Content** button.

3. Click the **Database Tools** tab.

4. In the Analyze group, click the **Database Documenter** button to open the Documenter dialog box, as shown in **Figure 14–11**.

Tabs show various parts of the database

FIGURE 14–11
Documenter dialog box

5. Click the **All Object Types** tab to see all of the objects in the database. To select all of these objects, you can click each check box or click the Select All button.

6. Click the **Select All** button. Compare your screen to **Figure 14–12**.

FIGURE 14–12
All Object Types selected

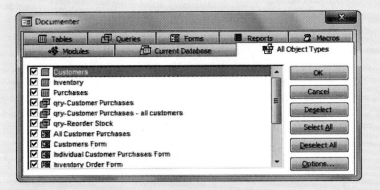

7. Click **OK**. The Object Definition report is displayed. See **Figure 14–13**. To keep a copy of this report, you will save it as a PDF file.

FIGURE 14–13
Object Definition report

Information for
the Customer
Number field
in the Customers
table

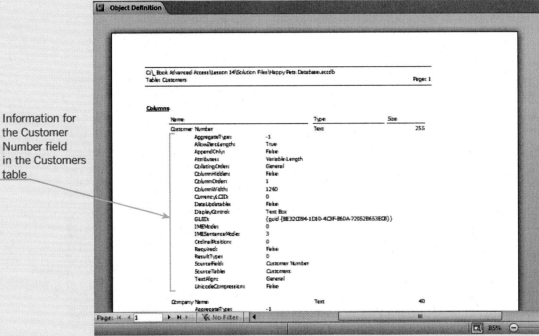

8. In the Data group, click the **PDF or XPS** button.

9. Leave the filename as doc_rptObjects.pdf, and then navigate to the drive and folder where your Data Files are stored. Click **Publish**. It will take a minute while the report is converted to a PDF file since there are over 100 pages in this document. The Publish dialog box shows the progress as you wait.

10. Click the **Close** button in the Export – PDF dialog box.

11. In Access, click the **Close Print Preview** button.

12. Close the database.

SUMMARY

In this lesson, you learned:

- When you open a database in the Open Exclusive mode, you are the only individual who can view or make changes to the file.

- Encrypting a database with a password allows only individuals who know the password to open the file.

- Opening an encrypted database requires entering a password.

- The database password and encryption can be removed.

- A backup is a duplicate copy of your database created by using the Back Up Database option when you save the file.

- Documenting the design of a database provides information that can be reviewed if an unwanted change occurs.

VOCABULARY REVIEW

Define the following terms:

backup   encryption   password
Database Documenter   Open Exclusive mode

REVIEW QUESTIONS

TRUE / FALSE

Circle T if the statement is true or F if the statement is false.

T   F   **1.**   You can open an encrypted database without a password, but you cannot read the data.

T   F   **2.**   The password and database encryption can be removed.

T   F   **3.**   A good rule of thumb is to schedule a database backup on a regular basis.

T   F   **4.**   Power failures or individuals who maliciously or accidentally delete database objects can cause losses of data in a database.

T   F   **5.**   The Open Exclusive Read-Only mode opens the database so that all users except for the current user are locked out and the current user can only view the data in the database.

FILL IN THE BLANK

1. In Access, the _____ produces a report of selected objects or every object in a database.

2. To add a password and encrypt a database, you need to open the database in _____ mode.

3. Until a(n) _____ is entered correctly, no objects in the database can be viewed.

4. To make a copy of a database, you would create a(n) _____ of the database.

5. A(n) _____ is a collection of characters that a user types to gain access to a file.

WRITTEN QUESTIONS

Write a brief answer to the following questions.

1. Explain the difference between Open Exclusive Read-Only mode and Open Exclusive mode.

2. Describe what you would do if you only wanted to document the queries in a database.

3. Describe how data loss in a database could occur.

4. Explain the purpose of a backup.

5. Explain the difference between a password and encryption.

■ PROJECTS

If you have a SAM 2010 user profile, your instructor may have assigned an autogradable version of the indicated project. If so, log into the SAM 2010 Web site at *www.cengage.com/sam2010* to download the instruction and start files.

PROJECT 14–1

1. Open the **Book Sales** file from the drive and folder where your Data Files are stored. Save the database as **Book Sales Database**, followed by your initials.

2. Create a backup of the database.

3. Make sure the date on which you created the backup is in the filename.

4. Close the database.

SAM PROJECT 14–2

1. Open the **Coach Files** file from the drive and folder where your Data Files are stored. Save the database as **Coach Files Database**, followed by your initials.

2. Close the **Coach Files Database** file.

3. Open the **Coach Files Database** in Open Exclusive mode.

4. Encrypt the database with the password **DogDog**.

5. Close the Coach Files Database.

6. Reopen the **Coach Files Database** to test the encryption.

7. Close the database.

PROJECT 14–3

1. Open the **Student Teams** file from the drive and folder where your Data Files are stored. Save the database as **Student Teams Database**, followed by your initials.

2. Use the Database Documenter to document the database.

3. Document all object types.

4. Create a PDF file of the documentation.

5. Name the PDF file **doc_rptObjects – Student Teams.pdf**.

6. Close the database.

■ CRITICAL THINKING

ACTIVITY 14–1

Open the **Coastal Sales** file from the drive and folder where your Data Files are stored, and then save it as **Coastal Sales Database**. As the new manager for the Coastal Sales Corporation, you decide that the database could use some additional security since it contains customer names, addresses, and sales information. Encrypt the database with the password **CSD2014**. After closing the database, open it to test if you are required to enter a password, then close the database.

ACTIVITY 14–2

Outline the positive aspects and negative aspects of password protecting a database file.

Advanced Microsoft Access

REVIEW QUESTIONS

TRUE / FALSE

Circle T if the statement is true or F if the statement is false.

T   F   **1.** An input mask is a pattern for common types of data entered in a field.

T   F   **2.** A parameter query allows you to enter a new criterion each time you run the query.

T   F   **3.** It is safe to run an action query without first creating a copy of the table where the actions will be applied.

T   F   **4.** The tab order in a form cannot be changed.

T   F   **5.** Conditional formatting will apply different formats to the control data if certain criteria are met.

T   F   **6.** Macros are susceptible to virus attacks.

T   F   **7.** The AutoExec macro can include an action that opens a form, such as a splash screen.

T   F   **8.** VBA is an abbreviation for Virtual Basic for Applications.

T   F   **9.** A database password and encryption cannot be removed.

T   F **10.** A wildcard, such as an asterisk, can be used in a query to search for data if you do not know the exact spelling of a person's last name.

FILL IN THE BLANK

Complete the following sentences by writing the correct word or words in the blanks provided.

1. A(n) _____ query can instantly update several records in a query at one time.

2. To simplify the process of moving from one record to another in a form or adding a new record to a form, you can add _____.

3. A report that is added to another report is called a(n) _____.

4. A(n) _____ is explanatory text that you can add to a macro, but it does not affect the operation of the macro.

5. To open a database without the startup options, you simply press and hold the _____ key when you open the database.

6. If you want a function to be available in more than one procedure, you would define the function as a(n) _____ function.

7. To add a password and encrypt a database, you need to open the database in _____ mode.

8. A(n) _____ improves the accuracy of the data entered by automatically adding symbols, such as dashes in a social security number.

9. For format and design consistency, you can add a(n) _____ to a form.

10. If you want sales data over $150,000 to appear in a unique format, you can add _____ to the control.

MULTIPLE CHOICE

Select the best response for each of the following statements.

1. The specific information you are searching for in a query is called a _____.

   A.   parameter

   B.   criterion

   C.   prompt

   D.   text

2. If you want to change the way a user moves from field to field in a form record, you change the _____.

   A.   tab order

   B.   combo box

   C.   query control

   D.   format

3. To include a graphical display in a report, you can add a(n) _____.

   A.   calculated control

   B.   subform

   C.   graph

   D.   comment

4. Additional information required to perform a task based on the chosen action in a macro are referred to as _____.

   A.   AutoExec

   B.   comment

   C.   security level

   D.   arguments

5. After you set the lookup properties for a field, a(n) _____ will appear in the field when it is selected.

   A.   arrow

   B.   expression

   C.   parameter

   D.   text control

6. A(n) _____ can be added to a report to perform calculations using data in the report.

   A.   subreport

   B.   password

   C.   calculated control

   D.   input mask

7. You can only have one _____ within a dabase.

   A. AutoExec macro

   B. function

   C. navigation form

   D. startup

8. An *If* procedure begins with an *If* code word and ends with the code words _____.

   A. *End*

   B. *End If*

   C. *Sum*

   D. *If Then*

9. The _____ mode opens the database so that all users except the current user are locked out and a password and encryption can be added to the database.

   A. Open Exclusive

   B. Open Only

   C. Open Exclusive Read-Only

   D. Open

10. The default placeholder for an input mask is the _____.

   A. asterisk

   B. comma

   C. question mark

   D. underscore

■ PROJECTS

PROJECT 1

To identify the number of employees at the New Book Sales Corporation, you view the records in the Sales Department table. You decide to add a parameter query where you can enter a title for a group of employees and have all employees in that group displayed in the query results.

1. Open the **New Book Sales** file from the drive and folder where your Data Files are stored. Save the database as **New Book Sales Database,** followed by your initials.

2. Create a parameter query for the Sales Department table. In the Design window, add the Employee ID, Last Name, First Name, and Title fields to the query grid. Since each field in the table will be included in the query, think of a quick way to put each field in the query grid.

3. Enter a prompt in the **Title** field that will prompt the user to enter a title for a group of employees.

4. Sort the query in ascending order by the Last Name field, and then add another sort in ascending order to the First Name field.

5. Save the query as **Qry-Employees by Title**.

6. Run the parameter query using Sales Rep as the criterion. Adjust the column widths if necessary. Print the query results.

7. Run the query using the Sales Assistant and the Sales Manager parameters. Print the results of each query.

8. Close the query and the database file.

PROJECT 2

You have a form that displays purchases made for individual customers. You want to add an embedded macro in the form that will open a second form to display the customer information.

1. Open the **Pet Supplies** file from the drive and folder where your Data Files are stored. Save the database as **Pet Supplies Database**, followed by your initials.

2. Create an embedded macro in the Individual Customer Purchases Form that opens the Customers Form.

3. Use the Customer number field as the field that links the two forms in the macro.

4. Save the Individual Customer Purchases Form.

5. View the Individual Customer Purchases Form in Form View for customer number 10, and then click on the macro button to test it.

6. Close the Customers Form.

7. Close the Individual Customer Purchases Form.

8. Close the database.

PROJECT 3

The Winter Sales file contains information about employee sales. You will create conditional formatting in the Employee Sales Data Report so that employees with sales greater than $125,000 are easy to locate.

1. Open the **Winter Sales** file from the drive and folder where your Data Files are stored.

2. Save the database as **Winter Sales Database** followed by your initials.

3. Open the Employee Sales Data Report to view the data.

4. Switch to Design View.

5. Add a conditional formatting rule to the Sales control that displays sales amounts greater than or equal to $125,000 in a red, bold font.

6. View the report in Report View to be certain the conditional formatting is working correctly.

7. Save the report.

8. Print the report.

9. Close the database.

PROJECT 4

The West Coast Sales file is password protected with the password UnitR. You will open the database and remove the password and encryption. Then, you will use the Database Documenter feature to document the database.

1. Open the **West Coast Sales** file in the appropriate mode so that you can remove the password and encryption.

2. Decrypt the database.

3. Save the database as **West Coast Sales Database**, followed by your initials.

4. Use the Database Documenter to document the database.

5. Document all object types.

6. Document the Properties and Relationships.

7. Create a PDF file of the documentation.

8. Name the PDF file **doc_rptObjects – West Coast Sales.pdf**.

9. Close the database.

10. Open the West Coast Sales Database and check to see that the password is removed.

11. Close the database.

■ CRITICAL THINKING

JOB 1

As the database administrator for the New Generation Internet Corporation, you want to add automation features to the database. You first decide to create a function that will calculate the difference between two dates. Since you will use the function in several objects throughout the database, you will save it as a public function in a module named basNewProcedures.

1. Open the **New Generation** file from the drive and folder where your Data Files are stored. Save the database as **New Generation Database**, followed by your initials.

2. Define a function named **YearDiff** that calculates the difference between two dates. This function will need to be defined as a public function.

3. Add a comment to the function that explains the purpose of the function.

4. For the date variables, use the variable names **FirstDate** and **SecondDate**.

5. Assign the **Date** data type to both variables.

6. Save the module.

7. Test the function in the Immediate window using the dates 3/15/2006 and 1/15/2014 to see if it is working correctly.

8. Close the module and the database.

JOB 2

As the new database administrator for the Revelation Sales Corporation, you decide to automate the Coastal Sales database to make it easier to use and to prevent unwanted changes. You first open the **Revelation Sales** file and save it as **Revelation Sales Database**. You then create a navigation form for the Main Menu that will include the Navigation – Forms Menu and the Navigation – Reports Menu. Change the tab titles to read Forms Menu and Reports Menu. Change the title of the Main Menu navigation form to read Main Menu, and save the form as Navigation – Main Menu. Then, you change the startup options so that the Navigation – Main Menu form appears when the database is opened. You also set the startup options to hide the Navigation pane and all but the File and Home tabs on the Ribbon when the database opens. Close the database, and then reopen it to be certain that all the features are working correctly. Close the database.

APPENDIX A

Computer Concepts

The Computer: An Overview

A computer is a machine that is used to store, retrieve, and manipulate data. A computer takes *input*, uses instructions to *process* and *store* that data, and then produces *output*. You enter the data into the computer through a variety of input devices, such as a keyboard or mouse. The processor processes the data to produce information. Information is output presented in many ways such as an image on a monitor, printed pages from a printer, or sound through speakers. Computer *software* is stored instructions or programming that runs the computer. *Memory* inside the computer stores the programs or instructions that run the computer as well as the data and information. Various *storage devices* are used to transfer or safely store the data and information on *storage media*.

A *computer system* is made up of components that include the computer, input, and output devices. Computer systems come in many shapes, sizes, and configurations. The computer you use at home or in school is often called a *personal computer*. *Desktop computers* often have a 'computer case' or a *system unit*, which contains

APPENDIX A

processing devices, memory, and some storage devices. **Figure A–1** shows a typical desktop computer. Input devices such as the mouse or pointing device, and keyboard are attached to the system unit by cables or wires. Output devices, such as the monitor (display device), speakers, and printer are also attached to the system unit by cables or wires. *Wireless technology* makes it possible to eliminate wires and use the airwaves to connect devices. *Laptop* or *notebook* computers have all the essential parts: the keyboard, pointing device, and display device all in one unit. See **Figure A–2** for a typical notebook computer.

FIGURE A–1   A desktop computer system

FIGURE A–2   A laptop computer

When learning about computers, it is helpful to organize the topics into a discussion about the hardware and the software, and then how the computer processes the data.

Computer Hardware

The physical components, devices, or parts of the computer are called *hardware*. Computer hardware includes the essential components found on all computers such as the central processing unit (CPU), the monitor, the keyboard, and the mouse. Hardware can be divided into categories: Input devices, processors, storage devices, and output devices. ***Peripheral devices*** are additional components, such as printers, speakers, and scanners that enhance the computing experience. Peripherals are not essential to the computer, but provide additional functions for the computer.

Input Devices

There are many different types of input devices. You enter information into a computer by typing on a keyboard or by pointing, clicking, or dragging a mouse. A ***mouse*** is a handheld device used to move a pointer on the computer screen. Similar to a mouse, a ***trackball*** has a roller ball that turns to control a pointer on the screen. Tracking devices, such as a ***touchpad***, are an alternative to the trackball or mouse. Situated on the keyboard of a laptop computer, they allow you to simply move and tap your finger on a small electronic pad to control the pointer on the screen.

    Tablet PCs allow you to input data by writing directly on the computer screen. Handwriting recognition technology converts handwritten writing to text. Many computers have a microphone or other ***sound input device*** which accepts speech or sounds as input and converts the speech to text or data. For example, when you telephone a company or bank for customer service, you often have the option to say your requests or account number. That is ***speech recognition technology*** at work!

    Other input devices include scanners and bar code readers. You can use a ***scanner*** to convert text or graphics from a printed page into code that a computer can process. You have probably seen ***bar code readers*** being used in stores. These are used to read bar codes, such as the UPC (Universal Product Code), to track merchandise or other inventory in a store. See **Figure A–3**.

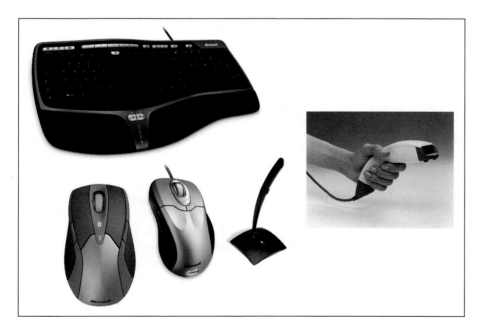

FIGURE A–3   Examples of input devices

APPENDIX A

Processing Devices

Processing devices are mounted inside the system unit of the computer. The *motherboard* is where the computer memory and other vital electronic parts are stored. See **Figure A–4**. The *central processing unit* (**CPU**) is a silicon chip that processes data and carries out instructions given to the computer. The CPU is stored on the motherboard of the computer. The *data bus* includes the wiring and pathways by which the CPU communicates with the peripherals and components of the computer.

FIGURE A–4   A motherboard

Storage Devices

Computers have to store and retrieve data for them to be of any use at all. Storage devices are both input and output devices. A *storage medium* holds data. Storage media include hard drives, tape, memory cards, solid state flash drives, CDs, and DVDs. A *storage device* is the hardware that stores and retrieves data from a storage medium. Storage devices include hard drives, card readers, tape drives, and CD and DVD drives.

Storage devices use magnetic, optical, or solid state technologies. Magnetic storage uses magnetic fields to store data and can be erased and used over and over again. Optical technology uses light to store data. Optical storage media use one of three technologies: read-only (ROM), recordable (R), or rewritable (RW). Solid state storage uses no moving parts and can be used over and over again. There are advantages and disadvantages to each technology.

Most computers have more than one type of storage device. The main storage device for a computer is the *hard drive* that is usually inside the system unit. Hard drives use magnetic storage. The hard drive reads and writes data to and from a round magnetic platter, or disk. **Figure A–5** shows a fixed storage unit. It is not removable from the computer.

EXTRA FOR EXPERTS

What does it mean when a computer advertisement refers to megabytes or gigabytes? Data is digitally encoded on a disk as a series of 1s and 0s. A **byte** stands for a single character of data. The prefix "mega" means a million. A megabyte is a million bytes. The prefix "giga" means a billion. A gigabyte (GB or Gbyte) is approximately one billion bytes. The term 'tera' means a trillion. A terabyte (TB or Tbyte) is one thousand gigabytes.

FIGURE A–5   An internal hard drive

External and removable hard drives that can plug into the USB port on the system unit are also available. External drives offer flexibility; allowing you to transfer data between computers easily. See **Figure A–6**. At the time this book was written, typical hard drives for a computer system that you might buy for your personal home use range from 500 gigabytes (GB) to 2 terabytes.

FIGURE A–6   An external hard drive

APPENDIX A

The *floppy disk drive* is older technology that is no longer available on new computers. Some older computers still have a floppy disk drive which is mounted in the system unit with access to the outside. A floppy disk is the medium that stores the data. You put the floppy disk into the floppy disk drive so the computer can read and write the data. The floppy disk's main advantage was portability. You can store data on a floppy disk and transport it for use on another computer. A floppy disk can hold up to 1.4MB (megabytes) of information. A Zip disk is similar to a floppy disk. A *Zip disk* is also an older portable disk technology that was contained in a plastic sleeve. Each disk held 100MB or 250MB of information. A special disk drive called a *Zip drive* is required to read and write data to a Zip disk.

Optical storage devices include the *CD drive* or *DVD drive* or *Blu-ray drive*. CDs, DVDs, and *Blu-ray drive (BD)* use optical storage technology. See **Figure A–7**.

FIGURE A–7   A CD/DVD/Blu-ray drive

These drives are typically mounted inside the system unit, although external versions of these devices are also available. Most new computers are equipped with CD/DVD burners. That means they have read and write capabilities. You use a CD/DVD drive to read and write CDs and DVDs. A *CD* is a compact disc, which is a form of optical storage. Compact discs can store 700 MB of data. These discs have a great advantage over other forms of removable storage as they can hold vast quantities of information—the entire contents of a small library, for instance. They are also fairly durable. Another advantage of CDs is their ability to hold graphic information, including moving pictures, with the highest quality stereo sound. A *DVD* is also an optical disc that looks like a CD. It is a high-capacity storage device that can contain up to 4.7GB of data, which is a seven-fold increase over a CD. There are two variations of DVDs that offer even more storage—a 2-layer version with 9.4GB capacity and double-sided discs with 17GB capacity. A DVD holds 133 minutes of data on each side, which means that two two-hour full-length feature movies can be stored on one disc. Information is encoded on the disk by a laser and read by a CD/DVD drive in the computer. *Blu-ray discs (BD)* offer even more storage capacity. These highest-capacity discs are designed to record full-length high-definition feature films. As of this writing, a BD can store upwards of 35GB of data. Special Blu-ray hardware, including disc players available in gaming systems and Blu-ray burners, are needed to read Blu-ray discs.

A CD drive only reads CDs, a DVD drive can read CDs and DVDs, a Blu-ray drive reads BDs, CDs, and DVDs. CD/DVD/BD drives look quite similar, as do the discs. See **Figure A–8**.

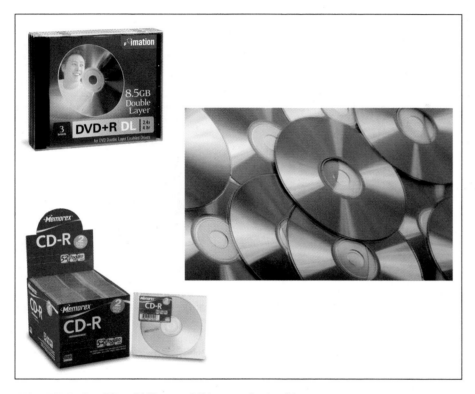

FIGURE A–8   CDs, DVDs, and Blu-rays look alike

APPENDIX A

Solid state storage is another popular storage technology. A *USB flash drive* is a very portable small store device that works both as a drive and medium. It plugs directly into a USB port on the computer system unit. You read and write data to the flash drive. See **Figure A–9**.

FIGURE A–9   A flash drive

Solid state card readers are devices that can read solid state cards. Solid state storage is often used in cameras. See **Figure A–10**.

FIGURE A–10   Solid state card and card reader

Magnetic tape is a medium most commonly used for backing up a computer system, which means making a copy of files from a hard drive. Although it is relatively rare for data on a hard drive to be completely lost in a crash (that is, for the data or pointers to the data to be partially or totally destroyed), it can and does happen. Therefore, most businesses and some individuals routinely back up files on tape. If you have a small hard drive, you can use DVDs or CD-ROMs or solid state storage such as a flash drive or memory card to back up your system. **Figure A–11** shows a tape storage system.

FIGURE A–11   Tape storage system

Output Devices

The ***monitor*** on which you view your computer work is an output device. It provides a visual representation of the information stored in or produced by your computer. The typical monitor for today's system is a flat-screen monitor similar to a television. Computer monitors typically use ***LCD technology***. LCD stands for Liquid Crystal Display. See **Figure A–12**. LCD monitors provide a very sharp picture because of the large number of tiny dots, called ***pixels***, which make up the display as well as its ability to present the full spectrum of colors. ***Resolution*** is the term that tells you how clear an image will be on the screen. Resolution is measured in pixels. A typical resolution is 1024 × 768. A high-quality monitor may have a resolution of 1920 × 1080, or 2560 × 1440 or higher. Monitors come in different sizes. The size of a monitor is determined by measuring the diagonal of the screen. Laptops have smaller monitors than desktop computers. A laptop monitor may be 13", 15", or 17". Desktop monitors can be as large as 19"–27" or even larger.

FIGURE A–12   An LCD monitor

Printers are a type of output device. They let you produce a paper printout of information contained in the computer. Today, most printers use either inkjet or laser technology to produce high-quality print. Like a copy machine, a *laser printer* uses heat to fuse a powdery substance called *toner* to the page. *Ink-jet printers* use a spray of ink to print. Laser printers give the sharpest image and often print more pages per minute (ppm) than ink-jet printers. Ink-jet printers provide nearly as sharp an image, but the wet printouts can smear when they first are printed. Most color printers, or photo printers for printing photographs, are ink-jet printers. Color laser printers are more costly. These printers allow you to print information in a full array of colors, just as you see it on your monitor. See **Figure A–13**.

FIGURE A–13   Printers

Laptop or Notebook Computer

A *laptop computer*, also called a *notebook computer*, is a small folding computer that can literally fit in a person's lap or in a backpack. Within the fold-up case of a laptop is the CPU, data bus, monitor (built into the lid), hard drive (sometimes removable), USB ports, CD/DVD drive, and trackball or digital tracking device. The advantage of the laptop is its portability—you can work anywhere because you can use power either from an outlet or from the computer's internal, rechargeable batteries. Almost all laptops have wireless Internet access built into the system. The drawbacks are the smaller keyboard, smaller monitor, smaller capacity, and higher price, though some laptops offer full-sized keyboards and higher quality monitors. As technology allows, storage capacity on smaller devices is making it possible to offer laptops with as much power and storage as a full-sized computer. See **Figure A–14**.

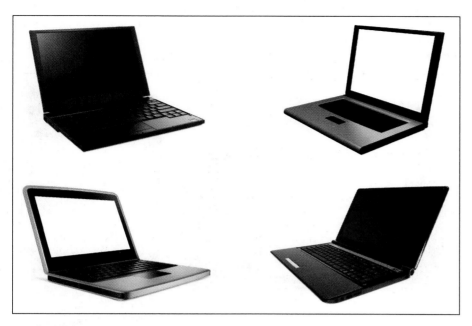

FIGURE A–14   Laptop computers

Personal Digital Assistants (PDA) and Smartphones

A ***Personal Digital Assistant (PDA)*** is a pocket-sized electronic organizer that helps you to manage addresses, appointments, expenses, tasks, and memos. If you own a cell phone, chances are it is a ***Smartphone*** and it can do more than just make and receive phone calls. Today, many handheld devices, such as cell phones and Personal Digital Assistants include features such as a full keypad for text messaging and writing notes, e-mail, a browser for Web access, a calendar and address book to manage

APPENDIX A

contacts and appointments, a digital camera, radio, and digital music player. Most handheld devices also include software for games, financial management, personal organizer, GPS, and maps. See **Figure A–15**.

FIGURE A–15   Smartphones

The common input devices for PDAs and some Smartphones include touch-sensitive screens that accept input through a stylus pen or small keyboards that are either built in to the device or available as software on the screen. Data and information can be shared with a Windows-based or Macintosh computer through a process called synchronization. By placing your handheld in a cradle or through a USB port attached to your computer, you can transfer data from your PDA's calendar, address book, or memo program into your computer's information manager program and vice versa. The information is updated on both sides, making your handheld device a portable extension of your computer.

How Computers Work

All input, processing, storage, and output devices function together to make the manipulation, storage, and distribution of data and information possible. Data is information entered into and manipulated or processed within a computer. Processing includes computation, such as adding, subtracting, multiplying, and dividing; analysis planning, such as sorting data; and reporting, such as presenting data for others in a chart or graph. This next section explains how computers work.

Memory

Computers have two types of memory—RAM and ROM. **RAM**, or **random access memory**, is the silicon chips in the system unit that temporarily store information when the computer is turned on. RAM is what keeps the software programs up and running and provides visuals that appear on your screen. You work with data in RAM up until you save it to a storage media such as a hard disk, CD, DVD, or solid state storage such as flash drive.

Computers have sophisticated application programs that include a lot of graphics, video, and data. In order to run these programs, computers require a lot of memory. Therefore, computers have a minimum of 512MB of RAM. Typical computers include between 2GB and 4GB of RAM to be able to run most programs. Most computer systems are expandable and you can add on RAM after you buy the computer. The more RAM available for the programs, the faster and more efficiently the machine will be able to operate. RAM chips are shown in **Figure A–16**.

FIGURE A–16   RAM chips

ROM, or **read-only memory**, is the memory that stays in the computer when it is turned off. It is ROM that stores the programs that run the computer as it starts or "boots up." ROM holds the instructions that tell the computer how to begin to load its operating system software programs.

Speed

The speed of a computer is measured by how fast the computer processes each instruction. There are several factors that affect the performance of a computer: the speed of the processor, or the **clock speed**, the **front side bus speed**—the speed of the bus that connects the processor to main memory—the speed in which data is written and retrieved from the hard drive or other storage media, and the speed of the graphics card if you are working on programs that use a lot of graphic images. These all factor into a computer's performance.

The speed of a computer is measured in **megahertz (MHz)** and **gigahertz (GHz)**. Processor speed is part of the specifications when you buy a computer. For example, to run Windows 7 on a computer, you need a processor that has 1 gigahertz (GHz) or faster 32-bit (x86) or 64-bit (x64) processor. Processors are sold by name and each brand or series has its own specifications. Processor manufacturers include AMD, Intel, and Motorola.

Networks

Computers have expanded the world of communications. A *network* is defined as two or more computers connected to share data. *LANs (local area networks)* connect computers within a small area such as a home, office, school, or building. Networks can be wired or wireless. The *Internet* is the largest network in the world connecting millions of computers across the globe. Using the Internet, people can communicate across the world instantly.

Networks require various communication devices and software. *Modems* allow computers to communicate with each other by telephone lines. Modem is an acronym that stands for "MOdulator/DEModulator." Modems convert data in bytes to sound media in order to send data over the phone lines and then convert it back to bytes after receiving data. Modems operate at various rates or speeds. *Network cards* in the system unit allow computers to access networks. A *router* is an electronic device that joins two or more networks. For example, a home network can use a router and a modem to connect the home's LAN to the Internet. A *server* is the computer hardware and software that "serves" the computers on a network. Network technology is sometimes called "client-server." A personal computer that requests data from a server is referred to as a *client*. The computer that stores the data is the *server*. On the Internet, the computer that stores Web pages is the *Web server*. **Figure A–17** shows a network diagram.

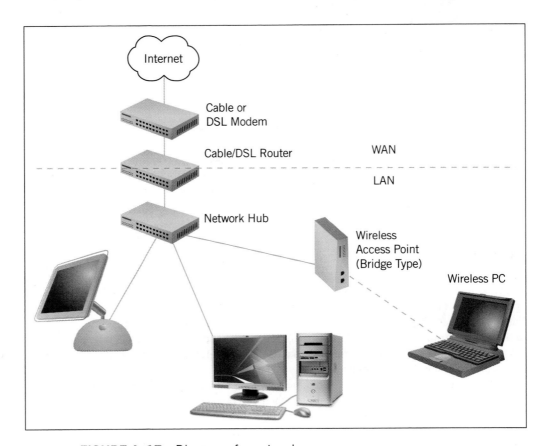

FIGURE A–17   Diagram of a network

Networks have certain advantages over stand-alone computers: they allow communication among the computers; they allow smaller capacity computers to access the larger capacity of the server computers on the network; they allow several computers to share peripherals, such as one printer; and they can make it possible for all computers on the network to have access to the Internet.

Connect to the Internet

To connect to the Internet you need to subscribe to an ***Internet Service Provider (ISP)***. There are several technologies available. Connection speeds are measured in bits per second. Upload speeds are slower than download speeds. ***Dial-up*** is the oldest, and the slowest Internet access technology that is offered by local telephone companies. To get access to the Internet, your computer has to dial out through a phone line. Many people have moved to ***always-on connection technologies***. The computer is always connected to the Internet if you turn the computer on, so you don't have to dial out. These always-on faster technologies, known as a ***Digital Subscriber Line (DSL)***, include cable connections, satellites, and fiber optic. They are offered by telephone and cable television companies, as well as satellite service providers. It can be noted that satellite Internet access is the most expensive and dialup is the cheapest. DSL is through phone lines. **Table A–1** shows a brief comparison of these technologies based on the time this book was written and average speed assessments.

TABLE A–1   Comparing average Internet access options

FEATURE	SATELLITE	DSL	CABLE	FIBER OPTIC
Max. High Speed	Download speeds ranging anywhere from 768 Kbps up to 5.0 Mbps	Download speed 10 Mbps/ upload speed 5 Mbps	Download speed 30 Mbps/ upload speed 10 Mbps	Download speed 50 Mbps/ upload speed 20 Mbps
Access is through	Satellite dish	Existing phone line	Existing TV cable	Fiber-optic phone lines
Availability	Available in all areas; note that satellite service is sensitive to weather conditions	Generally available in populated areas	Might not be available in rural areas	Might not be available in all areas as fiber-optic lines are still being installed in many areas

Software

A ***program*** is a set of instructions that the computer uses to operate. ***Software*** is the collection of programs and other data input that tells the computer how to run its devices, how to manipulate, store, and output information, and how to accept the input you give it. Software fits into two basic categories: systems software and applications software. A third category, network software, is really a type of application.

Systems Software

The ***operating system*** is the main software or ***system software*** that runs a computer and often defines the type of computer. There are two main types or platforms for personal computers. The Macintosh computer, or Mac, is produced by Apple Computer, Inc. and runs the Mac operating system. The PC is a Windows-based

APPENDIX A

computer produced by many different companies, but which runs the Microsoft Windows operating system.

Systems software refers to the operating system of the computer. The operating system is a group of programs that is automatically copied in from the time the computer is turned on until the computer is turned off. Operating systems serve two functions: they control data flow among computer parts, and they provide the platform on which application and network software work—in effect, they allow the "space" for software and translate its commands to the computer. The most popular operating systems in use today are the Macintosh operating system, MAC OS X and several different versions of Microsoft Windows, such as Windows XP, Windows Vista, or Windows 7. See **Figure A–18** and **Figure A–19**.

FIGURE A–18   Windows 7 operating system

FIGURE A–19   Mac OS

Since its introduction in the mid-1970s, Macintosh has used its own operating system, a graphical user interface (GUI) system that has evolved over the years. The OS is designed so users "click" with a mouse on pictures, called icons, or on text to give commands to the system. Data is available to you in the WYSIWYG (what-you-see-is-what-you-get) format; that is, you can see on-screen what a document will look like when it is printed. Graphics and other kinds of data, such as spreadsheets, can be placed into text documents. However, GUIs take a great deal of RAM to keep all of the graphics and programs operating.

The original OS for IBM and IBM-compatible computers (machines made by other companies that operate similarly) was DOS (disk operating system). It did not have a graphical interface. The GUI system, Windows™, was developed to make using the IBM/IBM-compatible computer more "friendly." Today's Windows applications are the logical evolution of GUI for IBM and IBM-compatible machines. Windows is a point-and-click system that automatically configures hardware to work together. You should note, however, that with all of its abilities comes the need for more RAM, or a system running Windows will operate slowly.

Applications Software

When you use a computer program to perform a data manipulation or processing task, you are using applications software. Word processors, databases, spreadsheets, graphics programs, desktop publishers, fax systems, and Internet browsers are all applications software.

Network Software

A traditional network is a group of computers that are hardwired (connected together with cables) to communicate and operate together. Today, some computer networks use RF (radio frequency) wireless technology to communicate with each other. This is called a *wireless network*, because you do not need to physically hook the network together with cables. In a typical network, one computer acts as the server, controlling the flow of data among the other computers, called nodes, or clients on the network. Network software manages this flow of information.

History of the Computer

Though various types of calculating machines were developed in the nineteenth century, the history of the modern computer begins about the middle of the last century. The strides made in developing today's personal computer have been truly astounding.

Early Development

The ENIAC, or Electronic Numerical Integrator and Computer, (see **Figure A–20**) was designed for military use in calculating ballistic trajectories and was the first electronic, digital computer to be developed in the United States. For its day, 1946, it was quite a marvel because it was able to accomplish a task in 20 seconds that normally would take a human three days to complete. However, it was an enormous machine that weighed more than 20 tons and contained thousands of vacuum tubes, which often failed. The tasks that it could accomplish were limited, as well.

FIGURE A–20 The ENIAC

From this awkward beginning, however, the seeds of an information revolution grew. The invention of the silicon chip in 1971, and the release of the first personal computer in 1974, launched the fast-paced information revolution in which we now all live and participate.

Significant dates in the history of computer development are listed in **Table A–2**.

TABLE A–2   Milestones in the development of computers

YEAR	DEVELOPMENT
1948	First electronically stored program
1951	First junction transistor
1953	Replacement of tubes with magnetic cores
1957	First high-level computer language
1961	First integrated circuit
1965	First minicomputer
1971	Invention of the microprocessor (the silicon chip) and floppy disk
1974	First personal computer (made possible by the microprocessor)

The Personal Computer

The PC, or personal computer, was mass marketed by Apple beginning in 1977, and by IBM in 1981. It is this desktop device with which people are so familiar and which, today, contains much more power and ability than did the original computer that took up an entire room. The PC is a small computer (desktop size or less) that uses a microprocessor to manipulate data. PCs may stand alone, be linked together in a network, or be attached to a large mainframe computer. See **Figure A–21**.

FIGURE A–21   An early IBM PC

APPENDIX A

Computer Utilities and System Maintenance

Computer operating systems let you run certain utilities and perform system maintenance to keep your computer running well. When you add hardware or software, you make changes in the way the system operates. With Plug and Play, most configuration changes are done automatically. The *drivers*, software that runs the peripherals, are installed automatically when your computer identifies the new hardware. When you install new software, many changes are made to the system automatically that determine how the software starts and runs.

In addition, you might want to customize the way the new software or hardware works with your system. You use *utility software* to make changes to the way hardware and software works. For example, you can change the speed at which your mouse clicks, how quickly or slowly keys repeat on the keyboard, and the resolution of the screen display. Utilities are included with your operating system. If you are running Windows XP, Windows Vista, or Windows 7, the Windows Control Panel provides access to the many Windows operating system utilities. **Figure A–22** shows the System and Security utilities in the Control Panel for Windows 7.

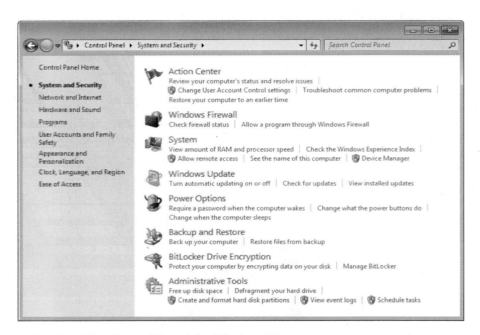

FIGURE A–22 Control Panel for Windows 7

Virus and Spyware Protection

Certain maintenance should be performed regularly on computers. *Viruses* are malicious software programs that can damage the programs on your computer causing the computer to either stop working or run slowly. These programs are created by people, called *hackers*, who send the programs out solely to do harm to computers. Viruses are loaded onto your computer without your knowledge and run against your wishes. *Spyware* is also a form of a program that can harm your computer. There are utilities and programs called *antispyware* and *antivirus* programs that protect your computer from spyware and viruses.

You should install and update your antivirus and spyware protection software regularly, and scan all new disks and any incoming information from online sources for viruses. Some systems do this automatically; others require you to install software to do it.

Disk Maintenance

From time to time, you should run a program that scans or checks the hard drive to see that there are not bad sectors (areas) and look for corrupted files. Optimizing or defragmenting the hard disk is another way to keep your computer running at its best. Scanning and checking programs often offers the option of "fixing" the bad areas or problems, although you should be aware that this could result in data loss.

Society and Computers

The electronic information era has had global effects and influenced global change in all areas of people's lives including education, government, society, and commerce. With the changes of this era have come many new questions and responsibilities. There are issues of ethics, security, and privacy.

Ethics

When you access information—whether online, in the workplace, or via purchased software—you have a responsibility to respect the rights of the person or people who created that information. Digital information, text, images, and sound are very easy to copy and share, however, that does not make it right to do so. You have to treat electronic information with respect. Often images, text, and sound are copyrighted. *Copyright* is the legal method for protecting the intellectual property of the author— the same way as you would a book, article, or painting. For instance, you must give credit when you copy information from the Web or another person's document.

If you come across another person's personal information, you must treat it with respect. Do not share personal information unless you have that person's permission. For example, if you happen to pass a computer where a person left personal banking information software open on the computer or a personal calendar available, you should not share that information. If e-mail comes to you erroneously, you should delete it before reading it.

When you use equipment that belongs to your school, a company for which you work, or others, here are some rules you should follow:

1. Do not damage computer hardware.

2. Do not add or remove equipment without permission.

3. Do not use an access code or equipment without permission.

4. Do not read others' e-mail.

5. Do not alter data belonging to someone else without permission.

6. Do not use the computer for play during work hours or use it for personal profit.

7. Do not access the Internet for nonbusiness related activities during work hours.

8. Do not install or uninstall software without permission.

9. Do not make unauthorized copies of data or software or copy company files or procedures for personal use.

10. Do not copy software programs to use at home or at another site in the company without permission.

APPENDIX A

Security and Privacy

The Internet provides access to business and life-enhancing resources, such as distance learning, remote medical diagnostics, and the ability to work from home more effectively. Businesses, colleges and universities, and governments throughout the world depend on the Internet every day to get work done. Disruptions in the Internet can create havoc and dramatically decrease productivity.

With more and more financial transactions taking place online, ***identity theft*** is a growing problem, proving a person's online identity relies heavily upon their usernames and passwords. If you do online banking, there are several levels of security that you must pass through, verifying that you are who you claim to be, before gaining access to your accounts. If you divulge your usernames and passwords, someone can easily access your accounts online with devastating effects to your credit rating and to your accounts.

Phishing is a criminal activity that is used by people to fraudulently obtain your personal information, such as usernames, passwords, credit card details, and your Social Security information. Your Social Security number should never be given out online. Phishers send e-mails that look legitimate, but in fact are not. Phishing e-mails will often include fake information saying that your account needs your immediate attention because of unusual or suspected fraudulent activity. You are asked to click a link in the e-mail to access a Web site where you are then instructed to enter personal information. See **Figure A–23** and **Figure A–24**. Phishing e-mail might also come with a promise of winning some money or gifts. When you get mail from people you don't know, the rules to remember are "you never get something for nothing," and "if it looks too good to be true, it's most likely not true."

PayPal would not use a yahoo.com Domain for e-mail

No recipient

Fake URL as you can see from ScreenTip

FIGURE A–23   Fake PayPal e-mail for phishing

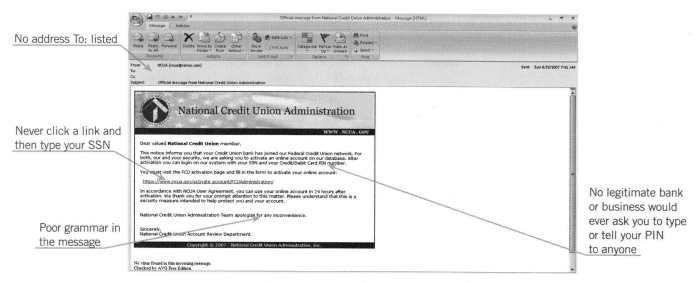

Callout labels:
No address To: listed

Never click a link and then type your SSN

Poor grammar in the message

No legitimate bank or business would ever ask you to type or tell your PIN to anyone

FIGURE A–24 Fake Credit Union e-mail for phishing

Whatever the ruse, when you click the link provided in the phishing e-mail, your browser will open a Web site that looks real, perhaps like your bank's site, eBay, or PayPal. But, in fact, this is a fake site set up to get you to give up your personal information. Phishing sites are growing. You should never click a link provided in an e-mail to get to sites such as your bank, eBay, or PayPal. Your bank or any other legitimate Web site will never ask you to type personal information on a page linked from an e-mail message. Always type the Web page address directly in the browser. Banks and Web sites have been trying to stop phishing sites through technology. Other attempts to reduce the growing number of reported phishing incidents include legislation and simply educating users about the practice.

Just as you would not open someone else's mail, you must respect the privacy of e-mail sent to others. When interacting with others online, you must keep confidential information confidential. Do not endanger your privacy, safety, or financial security by giving out personal information to someone you do not know.

> **EXTRA FOR EXPERTS**
>
> Ebay is an online auction Web site that provides people a way to buy and sell merchandise through the Internet. PayPal is a financial services Web site that provides a way to transfer funds between people who perform financial transactions on the Internet.

Career Opportunities

In one way or another, all careers involve the computer. Whether you are a grocery store clerk using a scanner to read the prices, a busy executive writing a report that includes charts, graphics, and detailed analysis on a laptop on an airplane, or a programmer writing new software—almost everyone uses computers in their jobs. Farmers use computers to optimize crops and order seeds and feed. Most scientific research is done using computers.

There are specific careers available if you want to work with computers in the computer industry. Schools offer degrees in computer programming, computer repair, computer engineering, and software design. The most popular jobs are systems analysts, computer operators, database managers, database specialists, and programmers. Analysts figure out ways to make computers work (or work better) for a particular business or type of business. Computer operators use the programs and devices to conduct business with computers. Programmers write the software for applications or new systems. There are degrees and jobs for people who want to create and maintain Web sites. Working for a company maintaining their Web site can be a very exciting career.

APPENDIX A

There are courses of study in using CAD (computer-aided design) and CAM (computer-aided manufacturing). There are positions available to instruct others in computer software use within companies and schools. Technical writers and editors must be available to write manuals about using computers and software. Computer-assisted instruction (CAI) is a system of teaching any given subject using the computer. Designing video games is another exciting and ever-growing field of computer work. And these are just a few of the possible career opportunities in an ever-changing work environment. See **Figure A–25**.

FIGURE A–25 Working in the computer field

What Does the Future Hold?

The possibilities for computer development and application are endless. Things that were dreams or science fiction only 10 or 20 years ago are now reality. New technologies are emerging constantly. Some new technologies are replacing old ways of doing things; others are merging with those older methods and devices. Some new technologies are creating new markets. The Internet (more specifically, the Web), cell phones, and DVD videos are just a few inventions of the past decades that did not have counterparts prior to their inventions. We are learning new ways to work and play because of the computer. It is definitely a device that has become part of our offices, our homes, and our lives.

Social networking has moved from the streets and onto the Web. People meet and greet through the Internet using sites such as MySpace, Facebook, and Twitter.

Emerging Technologies

Today the various technologies and systems are coming together to operate more efficiently. Convergence is the merging of these technologies. Telephone communication is being combined with computer e-mail and Web browsing so users can set a time to meet online and, with the addition of voice technology, actually speak to each other using one small portable device.

The Web, now an important part of commerce and education, began as a one-way vehicle where users visited to view Web pages and get information. It has evolved into sites where shopping and commerce takes place and is now evolving into a technology where users create the content. Web 2.0 and sites such as Facebook.com, flickr.com, LinkedIn.com, twitter.com, wikipedia.com, and youtube.com have content generated by the people that visit the Web sites. See **Figure A–26**.

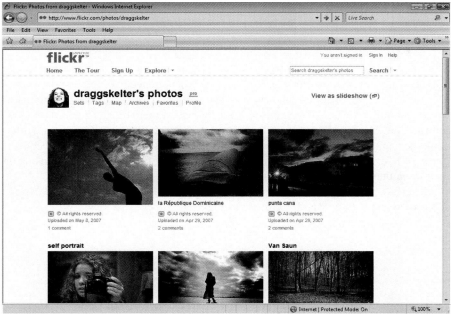

FIGURE A–26   User generated content

Computers have radically changed the way the medical profession delivers health care. Through the medical community, computers have enhanced medicine and healthcare throughout the world.

Trends

There are many trends that drive the computer industry. One trend is for larger and faster storage. From megabytes, to gigabytes, to terabytes, storage is becoming less an issue as the cost of storage is also dropping. RAM today is increasing exponentially. The trend is to sell larger blocks of RAM with every new personal computer. Newer processors also operate at speeds that are faster than the previous generation processors.

The actual size of computers is decreasing. Technology is allowing more powerful components to fit into smaller devices—laptops are lighter, monitors take up less space on the desktop, and flash drives can fit in your pocket and store gigabytes of data.

Home Offices

More and more frequently, people are working out of their homes—whether they are employees who are linked to their office in another location or individuals running their own businesses. *Telecommuting* meets the needs of many industries. Many companies allow workers to have a computer at home that is linked to their office and employees can use laptop computers to work both from home and on the road as they travel. A laptop computer, in combination with a wireless network, allows an employee to work from virtually anywhere and still keep in constant contact with her or his employer and customers.

Business communication is primarily by e-mail and telephone. It is very common for serious business transactions and communications to occur via e-mail rather than through the regular mail. Such an arrangement saves companies time and workspace and, thus, money.

Home Use

More and more households have personal computers. The statistics are constantly proving that a computer is an essential household appliance. Computers are used to access the Internet for shopping, education, and leisure. Computers are used to maintain financial records, manage household accounts, and record and manage personal information. More and more people are using electronic banking. Games and other computer applications offer another way to spend leisure dollars, and the convergence of television, the Internet, and the computer will find more households using their computers for media such as movies and music.

The future is computing. It's clear that this technology will continue to expand and provide us with new and exciting trends.

APPENDIX B

Keyboarding Touch System Improvement

Introduction

■ *Your Goal—Improve your keyboarding skills using the touch system so you are able to type without looking at the keyboard.*

Why Improve Your Keyboarding Skills?

■ To type faster and more accurately every time you use the computer
■ To increase your enjoyment while using the computer

Instead of looking back and forth from the page to see the text you have to type and then turning back to the keyboard and pressing keys with one or two fingers, using the touch system you will type faster and more accurately.

Getting Ready to Build Skills

In order to get ready you should:

1. **Prepare your desk and computer area.**
   a. Clear your desk of all clutter, except your book, a pencil or pen, the keyboard, the mouse, and the monitor.
   b. Position your keyboard and book so that you are comfortable and able to move your hands and fingers freely on the keyboard and read the book at the same time.
   c. Keep your feet flat on the floor, sit with your back straight, and rest your arms slightly bent with your finger tips on the keyboard.
   d. Start a word-processing program, such as Microsoft Word, or any other text editor. You can also use any simple program such as the Microsoft Works word processor or WordPad that is part of the Windows operating system. Ask your teacher for assistance.

WARNING

Using two fingers to type while looking at the keyboard is called the "hunt and peck" system and is not efficient when typing large documents.

2. Take a two-minute timed typing test according to your teacher's directions.

3. Calculate your words a minute (WAM) and errors a minute (EAM) using the instructions on the timed typing progress chart. This will be the base score you will compare to future timed typing.

4. Record today's Date, WAM, and EAM on the Base Score line of the writing progress chart.

5. Repeat the timed typing test many times to see improvements in your score.

6. Record each attempt on the Introduction line of the chart.

Getting Started

Keyboarding is an essential skill in today's workplace. No matter what your job, most likely you have to learn to be an effective typist. Follow the hints below to help you achieve this goal:

- Ignore errors.
- To complete the following exercises, you will type text that is bold and is not italicized and looks **like this**.
- If you have difficulty reaching for any key, for example the y key, practice by looking at the reach your fingertips make from the j key to the y key until the reach is visualized in your mind. The reach will become natural with very little practice.
- To start on a new line, press Enter.

Skill Builder 1

Your Goal—Use the touch system to type the letters j u y h n m and to learn to press the spacebar.

Keys

What to Do

1. Place your fingertips on the home row keys as shown in **Figure B–1**.

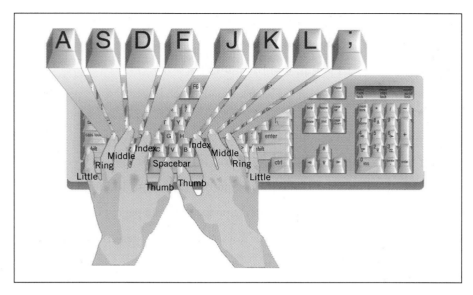

FIGURE B–1   Place your fingertips on the Home Row keys

2.   Look at **Figure B–2**. In step 3, you will press the letter keys j u y h n m. To press these keys, you use your right index finger. You will press the spacebar after typing each letter three times. The spacebar is the long bar beneath the bottom row of letter keys. You will press the spacebar with your right thumb.

> **TIP**
>
> The home row keys are where you rest your fingertips when they are not typing. The index finger of your right hand rests on the J key. The index finger of your left hand rests on the F key. Feel the slight bump on these keys to help find the home row keys without looking at the keyboard.

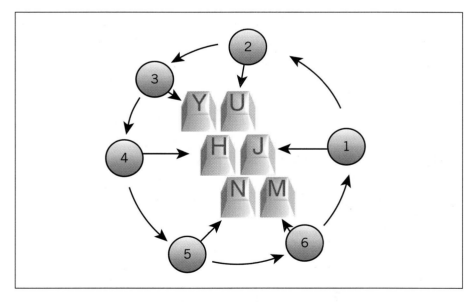

FIGURE B–2   Pressing the J U Y H N M keys

3.   Look at your keyboard. Repeat the letters silently to yourself as you move your right index finger from the j key to press each key three times, and then press the spacebar. Start typing:

jjj uuu jjj yyy jjj hhh jjj nnn jjj mmm

jjj uuu jjj yyy jjj hhh jjj nnn jjj mmm jjj

4. Repeat the same drill as many times as it takes for you to reach your comfort level.

   jjj uuu jjj yyy jjj hhh jjj nnn jjj mmm

   jjj uuu jjj yyy jjj hhh jjj nnn jjj mmm jjj

5. Close your eyes and visualize each key under each finger as you repeat the drill in step 4.

6. Look at the following two lines and type:

   jjj jjj jjj juj juj juj jyj jyj jyj jhj jhj jhj jnj jnj jnj jmj jmj jmj

   jjj jjj jjj juj juj juj jyj jyj jyj jhj jhj jhj jnj jnj jnj jmj jmj jmj

7. Repeat step 6, this time concentrating on the rhythmic pattern of the keys.

8. Close your eyes and visualize the keys under your fingertips as you type the drill in step 4 from memory.

9. Look at the following two lines and type these groups of letters:

   j ju juj j jy jyj j jh jhj j jn jnj j jm jmj j ju juj j jy jyj j jh jhj j jn jnj j jm jmj

   jjj ju jhj jn jm ju jm jh jnj jm ju jmj jy ju jh j u ju juj jy jh jnj ju jm jmj jy

10. You may want to repeat Skill Builder 1, striving to improve typing letters that are most difficult for you.

Skill Builder 2

The left index finger is used to type the letters f r t g b v. Always return your left index finger to the f key on the home row after pressing the other keys.

Your Goal—Use the touch system to type f r t g b v .

Keys

What to Do

1. Place your fingertips on the home row keys as you did in Skill Builder 1, Figure B–1.

2. Look at **Figure B–3**. Notice how you will type the letters f r t g b v and then press the spacebar with your right thumb.

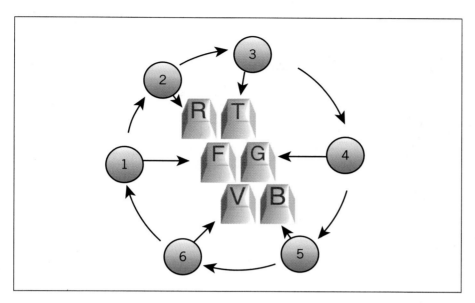

FIGURE B–3   Pressing the F R T G B V keys

3. Look at your keyboard. To press these keys, you use your left index finger. You will press the spacebar after typing each letter three times. The spacebar is the long bar beneath the bottom row of letter keys. You will press the spacebar with your right thumb.

    After pressing each letter in the circle, press the home key f three times as shown. Don't worry about errors. Ignore them.

    fff rrr fff ttt fff ggg fff bbb fff vvv

    fff rrr fff ttt fff ggg fff bbb fff vvv fff

4. Repeat the same drill two more times using a quicker, sharper stroke.

    fff rrr fff ttt fff ggg fff bbb fff vvv

    fff rrr fff ttt fff ggg fff bbb fff vvv fff

5. Close your eyes and visualize each key under each finger as you repeat the drill in step 4.

6. Look at the following two lines and key these groups of letters:

    fff fff fff frf frf frf ftf ftf ftf fgf fgf fgf fbf fbf fbf fvf fvf fvf

    fff fff fff frf frf frf ftf ftf ftf fgf fgf fgf fbf fbf fbf fvf fvf fvf

7. Repeat step 6, this time concentrating on a rhythmic pattern of the keys.

8. Close your eyes and visualize the keys under your fingertips as you type the drill in step 4 from memory.

9. Look at the following two lines and type these groups of letters:

    fr frf ft ftf fg fgf fb fbf fv fvf

    ft fgf fv frf ft fbf fv frf ft fgf

10. You are about ready to type your first words. Look at the following lines and type these groups of letters (remember to press the spacebar after each group):

jjj juj jug jug jug rrr rur rug rug rug

ttt tut tug tug tug rrr rur rub rub rub

ggg gug gum gum gum mmm mum

mug mug mug hhh huh hum hum hum

11. Complete the Keyboarding Technique Checklist.

Skill Builder 3

Your Goal—Use the touch system to type k i , d e c.

Keys ⬚K⬚ ⬚I⬚ ⬚,⬚ (comma)

What to Do

1. Place your fingertips on the home row keys. The home row key for the left middle finger is d. The home row key for the right middle finger is k. You use your left middle finger to type d, e, c. You use your right middle finger to type k, i, , as shown in **Figure B–4**.

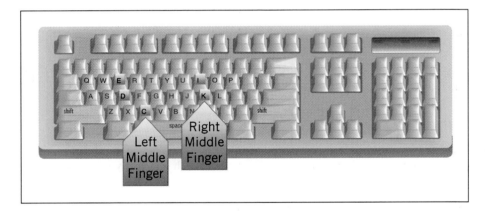

FIGURE B–4   Pressing the K I , D E C keys

2. Look at your keyboard and locate these keys: k i , (the letter k key, the letter i key, and the comma key).

3. Look at your keyboard. Repeat the letters silently to yourself as you press each key three times and put a space between each set of letters and the comma to type:

kkk iii kkk ,,, kkk iii kkk ,,, kkk iii kkk ,,, kkk iii kkk ,,, kkk iii kkk ,,, kkk

4. Look at the characters in step 3 and repeat the drill two more times using a quicker, sharper stroke.

5. Close your eyes and repeat the drill in step 3 as you visualize each key under each finger.

6. Repeat step 3, do not look at the keyboard, and concentrate on the rhythmic pattern of the keys.

Keys (D) (E) (C)

What to Do

1. Place your fingertips on the home row keys.

2. Look at your keyboard and locate these keys: d e c (the letter d key, the letter e key, and the letter c key).

3. Look at your keyboard. Repeat the letters silently to yourself as you press each key three times and put a space between each set of letters to type:

   ddd eee ddd ccc ddd eee ddd ccc ddd eee ddd ccc ddd eee ddd ccc ddd

4. Look at the letters in step 3 and repeat the drill two more times using a quicker, sharper stroke.

5. Close your eyes and repeat the drill in step 3 as you visualize each key under each finger.

6. Repeat step 3, do not look at the keyboard, and concentrate on the rhythmic pattern of the keys.

7. Look at the following lines of letters and type these groups of letters and words:

   fff fuf fun fun fun ddd ded den den den

   ccc cuc cub cub cub vvv vev vet

   fff fuf fun fun fun ddd ded den den den

   ccc cuc cub cub cub vvv vev vet

8. Complete the Keyboarding Technique Checklist.

Skill Builder 4

Your Goal—Use the touch system to type l o . s w x and to press the left Shift key.

Keys (L) (O) (.) (period)

APPENDIX B

What to Do

1. Place your fingertips on the home row keys. The home row key for the left ring finger is s. The home row key for the right ring finger is l. You use your left ring finger to type s w x. You use your right ring finger to type l o . as shown in **Figure B–5**.

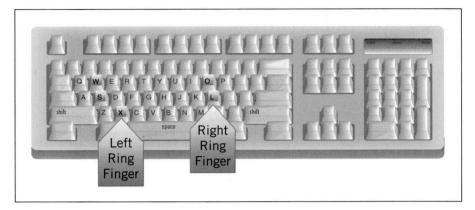

FIGURE B–5   Pressing the L O . S W X keys

2. Look at your keyboard and locate the following keys: l o . (the letter l key, the letter o key, and the period key).

3. Look at your keyboard. Repeat the letters silently to yourself as you press each key three times and put a space between each set of letters and the periods to type:

   lll ooo lll ... lll ooo lll ... lll ooo lll ... lll ooo lll ... lll ooo lll ... lll ooo lll ... lll

4. Look at the line in step 3 and repeat the drill two more times using a quicker, sharper stroke.

5. Close your eyes and repeat the drill in step 3 as you visualize each key under each finger.

6. Repeat step 3, do not look at the keyboard, and concentrate on the rhythmic pattern of the keys.

Keys

1. Place your fingertips on the home row keys.

2. Look at your keyboard and locate the following letter keys: s w x

3. Look at your keyboard. Repeat the letters silently to yourself as you press each key three times and put a space between each set of letters to type:

   sss www sss xxx sss www sss xxx sss www sss xxx sss www sss xxx sss

4. Look at the line in step 3 and repeat the same drill two more times using a quicker, sharper stroke.

5. Close your eyes and repeat the drill in step 3 as you visualize each key under each finger.

6. Repeat step 3, do not look at the keyboard, and concentrate on the rhythmic pattern of the keys.

Key Shift ⬚SHIFT⬚ (Left Shift Key)

You press and hold the Shift key as you press a letter key to type a capital letter. You press and hold the Shift key to type the character that appears above the numbers in the top row of the keyboard and on a few other keys that show two characters.

Press and hold down the left Shift key with the little finger on your left hand while you press each letter to type capital letters for keys that are typed with the fingertips on your right hand. See **Figure B–6**.

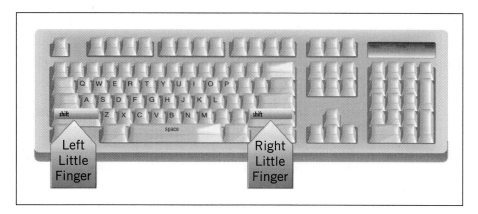

FIGURE B–6   Using the Shift keys

1. Type the following groups of letters and the sentence that follows.

   jjj JJJ jjj JJJ yyy YYY yyy YYY nnn NNN nnn NNN mmm MMM

   Just look in the book. You can see well.

2. Complete a column in the Keyboarding Technique Checklist.

Skill Builder 5

Your Goal—Use the touch system to type a q z ; p / and to press the right Shift key.

Keys ⬚;⬚ (Semi-Colon) ⬚P⬚ ⬚/⬚

APPENDIX B

What to Do

1. Place your fingertips on the home row keys. The home row key for the left little finger is a. The home row key for the right little finger is ;. You use your left little finger to type a q z. You use your right little finger to type ; p / as shown in **Figure B–7**.

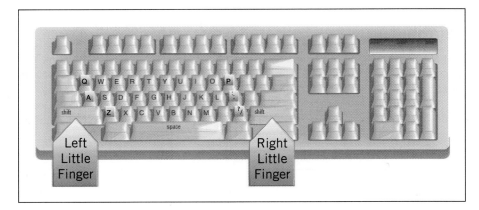

FIGURE B–7   Pressing the A Q Z ; P / and the right Shift key

2. Look at your keyboard and locate the following keys: ; p / (the semi-colon, the letter p, and the forward slash).

3. Repeat the letters silently to yourself as you press each key three times and put a space between each set of characters to type:

    ;;; ppp ;;; /// ;;; ppp ;;; /// ;;; ppp ;;; ///

    ;;; ppp ;;; /// ;;; ppp ;;; /// ;;; ppp ;;; /// ;;;

4. Look at the lines in step 3 and repeat the drill two more times using a quicker, sharper stroke.

5. Close your eyes and repeat the drill in step 3 as you visualize each key under each finger.

6. Repeat step 3, do not look at the keyboard, and concentrate on a rhythmic pattern of the keys.

Keys Ⓐ Ⓠ Ⓩ

1. Place your fingertips on the home row keys.

2. Look at your keyboard and locate the following keys: a q z (the letter a, the letter q, and the letter z).

3. Look at your keyboard. Repeat the letters silently to yourself as you press each key three times and put a space between each set of letters and type:

    aaa qqq aaa zzz aaa qqq aaa zzz aaa qqq aaa zzz aaa qqq aaa zzz aaa

4. Look at the line in step 3 and repeat the same drill two more times using a quicker, sharper stroke.

5. Close your eyes and repeat the drill in step 3 as you visualize each key under each finger.

6. Repeat step 3, do not look at the keyboard, and concentrate on the rhythmic pattern of the keys.

Key Shift ⟨SHIFT⟩ (Right Shift Key)

Press and hold down the right Shift key with the little finger on your right hand while you press each letter to type capital letters for keys that are typed with the fingertips on your left hand.

1. Type the following lines. Press and hold down the right Shift key with the little finger of your right hand to make capitals of letters you type with the fingertips on your left hand.

   sss SSS rrr RRR

   Press each key quickly. Relax when you type.

2. Complete another column in the Keyboarding Technique Checklist.

Skill Builder 6

You will probably have to type slowly at first, but with practice you will learn to type faster and accurately.

Your Goal—Use the touch system to type all letters of the alphabet.

What to Do

1. Close your eyes. Do not look at the keyboard and type all letters of the alphabet in groups of three with a space between each set as shown:

   aaa bbb ccc ddd eee fff ggg hhh iii jjj

   kkk lll mmm nnn ooo ppp qqq rrr sss

   ttt uuu vvv www xxx yyy zzz

2. Repeat step 1, concentrating on a rhythmic pattern of the keys.

3. Repeat step 1, but faster than you did for step 2.

4. Type the following sets of letters, all letters of the alphabet in groups of two with a space between each set as shown:

   aa bb cc dd ee ff gg hh ii jj kk ll mm nn oo pp qq rr ss tt uu vv ww xx yy zz

5. Type the following letters, all letters of the alphabet with a space between each letter as shown:

   a b c d e f g h i j k l m n o p q r s t u v w x y z

6. Continue to look at this book. Do not look at the keyboard, and type all letters of the alphabet backwards in groups of three with a space between each set as shown:

   zzz yyy xxx www vvv uuu ttt sss rrr

   qqq ppp ooo nnn mmm lll kkk jjj iii

   hhh ggg fff eee ddd ccc bbb aaa

7. Repeat step 6, but faster than the last time.

8. Type each letter of the alphabet once backwards:

   z y x w v u t s r q p o n m l k j i h g f e d c b a

9. Think about the letters that took you the most amount of time to find the key on the keyboard. Go back to the Skill Builder for those letters, and repeat the drills until you are confident about their locations.

Timed Typing

Prepare to take the timed typing test, according to your teacher's directions.

1. **Prepare your desk and computer area.**
   a. Clear your desk of all clutter except your book, a pencil or pen, the keyboard, the mouse, the monitor, and the computer if it is located on the desk.
   b. Position your keyboard and book so that you are comfortable and able to move your hands and fingertips freely.
   c. Keep your feet flat on the floor, sitting with your back straight, resting your arms slightly bent with your fingertips on the keyboard.

2. Take a two-minute timed typing test according to your teacher's directions.

3. Calculate your words a minute (WAM) and errors a minute (EAM) scores using the instructions on the Timed Typing Progress Chart in this book.

4. Record the date, WAM, and EAM on the Skill Builder 6 line in the Timed Typing Progress Chart printed at the end of this appendix.

5. Repeat the timed typing test as many times as you can and record each attempt in the Timed Typing Progress Chart.

Skill Builder 7

Your Goal—Improve your typing techniques—which is the secret for improving your speed and accuracy.

What to Do

1. Rate yourself for each item on the Keyboarding Technique Checklist printed at the end of this appendix.

2. Do not time yourself as you concentrate on a single technique you marked with a "0." Type only the first paragraph of the timed typing.

3. Repeat step 2 as many times as possible for each of the items marked with an "0" that need improvement.

4. Take a two-minute timed typing test. Record your WAM and EAM on the Timed Typing Progress Chart as 1st Attempt on the Skill Builder 7 line. Compare this score with your base score.

5. Looking only at the book and using your best techniques, type the following technique sentence for one minute:

    . 2 . 4 . 6 . 8 . 10 . 12 . 14 . 16

Now is the time for all good men and women to come to the aid of their country.

6. Record your WAM and EAM in the Timed Typing Progress Chart on the 7 Technique Sentence line.

7. Repeat steps 5 and 6 as many times as you can and record your scores in the Timed Typing Progress Chart.

Skill Builder 8

Your Goal—Increase your words a minute (WAM) score.

What to Do

You can now type letters in the speed line very well and with confidence. Practicing all of the other letters of the alphabet will further increase your skill and confidence in keyboarding.

1. Take a two-minute timed typing test.

2. Record your WAM and EAM scores as the 1st Attempt in the Timed Typing Progress Chart.

3. Type only the first paragraph only one time as fast as you can. Ignore errors.

4. Type only the first and second paragraphs only one time as fast as you can. Ignore errors.

5. Take a two-minute timed typing test again. Ignore errors.

6. Record only your WAM score as the 2nd Attempt in the Timed Typing Progress Chart. Compare only this WAM with your 1st Attempt WAM and your base score WAM.

Get Your Best WAM

1. To get your best WAM on easy text for 15 seconds, type the following speed line as fast as you can, as many times as you can. Ignore errors.

    . 2 . 4 . 6 . 8 . 10

Now is the time, now is the time, now is the time,

2. Multiply the number of words typed by four to get your WAM (15 seconds × 4 = 1 minute). For example, if you type 12 words for 15 seconds, 12 × 4 = 48 WAM.

3. Record only your WAM in the 8 Speed Line box in the Timed Typing Progress Chart.

4. Repeat steps 1–3 as many times as you can to get your very best WAM. Ignore errors.

5. Record only your WAM for each attempt in the Timed Typing Progress Chart.

Skill Builder 9

Your Goal—Decrease errors a minute (EAM) score.

What to Do

1. Take a two-minute timed typing test.

2. Record your WAM and EAM as the 1st Attempt in the Timed Typing Progress Chart.

3. Type only the first paragraph only one time at a controlled rate of speed so you reduce errors. Ignore speed.

4. Type only the first and second paragraphs only one time at a controlled rate of speed so you reduce errors. Ignore speed.

5. Take a two-minute timed typing test again. Ignore speed.

6. Record only your EAM score as the 2nd Attempt in the Timed Typing Progress Chart. Compare only the EAM with your 1st Attempt EAM and your base score EAM.

Get Your Best EAM

1. To get your best EAM, type the following accuracy sentence (same as the technique sentence) for one minute. Ignore speed.

   Now is the time for all good men and women to come to the aid of their country.

2. Record only your EAM score on the Accuracy Sentence 9 line in the Timed Typing Progress Chart.

3. Repeat step 1 as many times as you can to get your best EAM. Ignore speed.

4. Record only your EAM score for each attempt in the Timed Typing Progress Chart.

> **TIP**
>
> How much you improve depends upon how much you want to improve.

Skill Builder 10

Your Goal—Use the touch system and your best techniques to type faster and more accurately than you have ever typed before.

What to Do

1. Take a one-minute timed typing test.

2. Record your WAM and EAM as the 1st Attempt on the Skill Builder 10 line in the Timed Typing Progress Chart.

3. Repeat the timed typing test for two minutes as many times as necessary to get your best ever WAM with no more than one EAM. Record your scores as 2nd, 3rd, and 4th Attempts.

> **TIP**
>
> You may want to get advice regarding which techniques you need to improve from a classmate or your instructor.

Assessing Your Improvement

1. Circle your best timed typing test for Skill Builders 6-10 in the Timed Typing Progress Chart.

2. Record your best score and your base score. Compare the two scores. Did you improve?

	WAM	EAM
Best Score	_____	_____
Base Score	_____	_____

3. Use the Keyboarding Technique Checklist to identify techniques you still need to improve. You may want to practice these techniques now to increase your WAM or decrease your EAM.

Timed Typing

Every five strokes in a timed typing test is a word, including punctuation marks and spaces. Use the scale above each line to tell you how many words you typed.

```
        .        2        .        4        .        6        .
If you learn how to key well now, it
    8        .        10        .        12        .        14        .        16
is a skill that will help you for the rest
        .        18        .        20        .        22        .        24
of your life. How you sit will help you key
        .        26        .        28        .        30        .        32        .        34
with more speed and less errors.  Sit with your
        .        36        .        38        .        40        .        42        .
feet flat on the floor and your back erect.
        44        .        46        .        48        .        50
To key fast by touch, try to keep your
    .        52        .        54        .        56        .        58        .
eyes on the copy and not on your hands or
    60        .        62        .        64        .        66        .        68
the screen.  Curve your fingers and make sharp,
        .        70        .
quick strokes.
    72        .        74        .        76        .        78        .
Work for speed first.  If you make more
    80        .        82        .        84        .        86        .        88
than two errors a minute, you are keying too
        .        90        .        92        .        94        .        96        .
fast. Slow down to get fewer errors. If you
    98        .        100        .        102        .        104        .
get fewer than two errors a minute, go for
    106        .
speed.
```

Timed Typing Progress Chart

Timed Writing Progress Chart

Last Name: _____   *First Name:* _____

Instructions

Calculate your scores as shown in the following sample. Repeat timed writings as many times as you can and record your scores for each attempt.

Base Score	Date	WAM	EAM	Time

To calculate WAM: Divide words keyed by number of minutes to get WAM. For example: 44 words keyed in 2 minutes = 22 WAM [44/2=22]

To calculate EAM: Divide errors made by minutes of typing to get EAM

For example: 7 errors made in 2 minutes of typing = 3.5 EAM [7/2=3.5]

Skill Builder	Date	1st Attempt (a) WAM	1st Attempt (b) EAM	2nd Attempt WAM	2nd Attempt EAM	3rd Attempt WAM	3rd Attempt EAM	4th Attempt WAM	4th Attempt EAM
Sample	9/2	22	3.5	23	2.0	25	1.0	29	2.0
Introduction									
6									
7									
8					-----				
9				-----					
10									
7 Technique Sentence									
8 Speed Line			-----		-----		-----		-----
9 Accuracy Sentence		-----		-----		-----		-----	

APPENDIX B

Keyboarding Technique Checklist

Last Name: _____   *First Name:* _____

Instructions

1. Write the Skill Builder number, the date, and the initials of the evaluator in the proper spaces.

2. Place a check mark (✓) after a technique that is performed satisfactorily.

3. Place a large zero (0) after a technique that needs improvement.

Technique	Sample										
Skill Builder Number:	Sample										
Date:	9/1										
Evaluator:	SL										
Attitude											
1. Enthusiastic about learning	✓										
2. Optimistic about improving	✓										
3. Alert but relaxed	✓										
4. Sticks to the task; not distracted	✓										
Getting Ready	✓										
1. Desk uncluttered											
2. Properly positions keyboard and book	✓										
3. Feet flat on the floor	✓										
4. Body erect, but relaxed	0										
Keyboarding											
1. Curves fingers	0										
2. Keeps eyes on the book	✓										
3. Taps the keys lightly; does not "pound" them	0										
4. Makes quick, "bouncy," strokes	0										
5. Smooth rhythm	0										
6. Minimum pauses between strokes	✓										

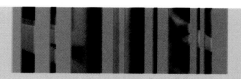

APPENDIX C

Differences between Windows 7, Windows Vista, and Windows XP

The Windows Experience

- Microsoft offers many new features in Windows 7 that are not available in Windows XP and Windows Vista.

- The overall Windows experience has been vastly improved from Windows XP to Windows 7. If you make the jump from XP to Windows 7, you will discover a great number of changes that are for the better. In addition, many of the new features introduced in Windows Vista were retained in this latest version of the popular operating system. Upgrading to Windows 7 is also an easier, more streamlined transition.

APPENDIX C

- With Windows 7, Microsoft has simplified everyday tasks and works more efficiently. This is all in response to issues users had with the Windows XP and Windows Vista experience. The major differences between Windows XP, Windows Vista, and Windows 7 are in the Start menu, dynamic navigation, desktop gadgets, improved security, search options, parental controls, and firewall, as well as improvements to the Windows Aero feature, see **Figure C–1**.

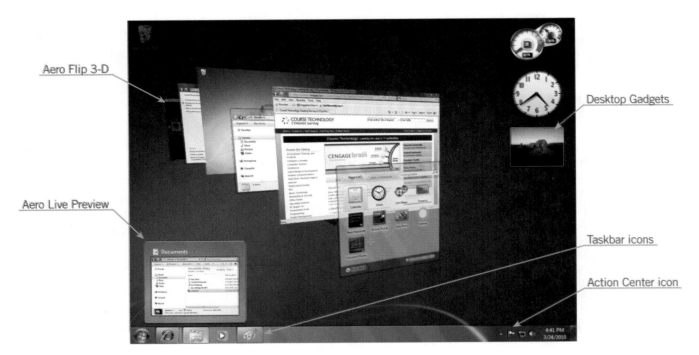

Aero Flip 3-D

Aero Live Preview

Desktop Gadgets

Taskbar icons

Action Center icon

FIGURE C–1   Windows 7 Features

Windows Aero

- Windows Aero is a new graphic interface feature which gives a "transparent" quality to windows, dialog boxes, and other items in the Windows Vista and Windows 7 environment.

- Flip 3-D, or simply Flip, shows mini versions of windows and thumbnails in the Windows 7 environment when turned on.

Windows XP users had to download Windows Desktop Enhancements and PowerTools from the Microsoft Web site to change their Windows experience. Windows Vista and Windows 7 now have many different themes and options built into the operating system, making it easy to modify the Windows experience. One theme, introduced in Windows Vista is Aero.

Windows Aero is a feature which was first introduced in Windows Vista and is not available in the Windows XP operating system. Windows Aero, enabled by default in Windows 7, is a more aesthetically pleasing user interface to Windows Vista and Windows 7 systems. For example, Windows XP utilizes ScreenTips only when pointing to items on the Taskbar, Desktop, and Menus. The basic ScreenTips found in Windows XP have been enhanced to show live "sneak-previews" of windows with a simple point to the icon on the taskbar , as shown in **Figure C–2**.

Windows 7 made major improvements to the function of Aero. These new features include Aero Peek, Aero Shake, Aero Snap, Touch UI, and many other visual effects covered in this section. Compare the evolution of the Taskbar ScreenTip in Windows XP to Windows Vista and finally in Windows 7 in the figures below.

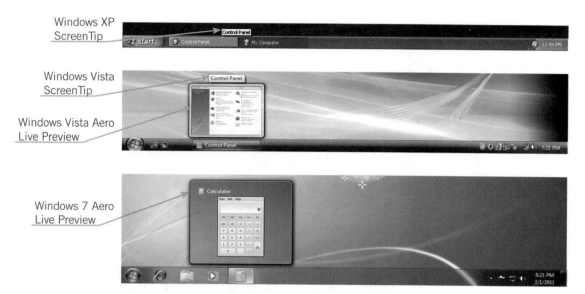

FIGURE C–2   Comparing Windows XP taskbar with Windows Vista and Windows 7

Understanding the Desktop

- Gadgets, introduced in Windows Vista, and Jump Lists, introduced in Windows 7, are two new desktop features.
- Windows 7 also includes multiple Aero themes to customize your desktop including the Desktop Background Slideshow.

APPENDIX C

At first glance, the Windows XP desktop only appears to differ slightly from that of Windows Vista, but the new features available with Windows 7 are substantial. The icons, shortcuts, folders, and files are generally the same; however, there are major aesthetic visual differences in this version. The most obvious addition from XP to Vista is the desktop gadget. Gadgets were not available in Windows XP. In **Figure C–4**, notice the appearance of three gadgets on the sidebar. Desktop gadgets are also available in Windows 7; however the sidebar function has been abandoned. Users simply add the gadget to the desktop.

The Taskbar in Windows XP includes the notification area, quick launch (when enabled), Start button, and icon(s) representing open programs. Beginning with Windows 7, you can now easily pin items to the Taskbar instead of using a quick launch feature. Jump lists, Aero themes and the Desktop Background Slideshow, explained in this chapter, are also new features to Windows 7.

FIGURE C–3 Windows XP Start menu and Desktop

The Start menu has been slightly enhanced from Windows XP to Windows 7. All Programs no longer appears on an additional menu, it has been merged with the Start menu. Windows Vista introduced a search function built into the Start menu, which allows users to search the computer easily for documents, applications, and help. Compare the evolution in desktops from Windows XP to Windows 7 in **Figures C–3, C–4,** and **C–5.**

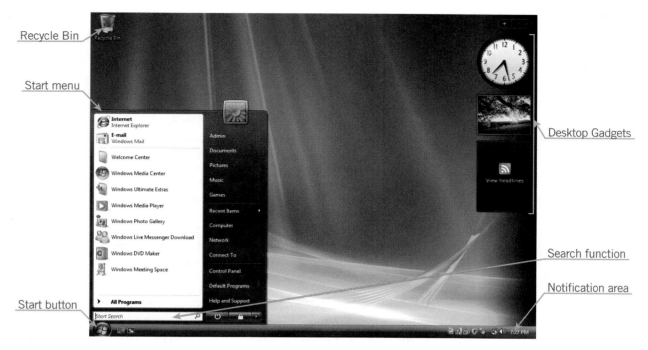

FIGURE C–4   Windows Vista Start menu and Desktop

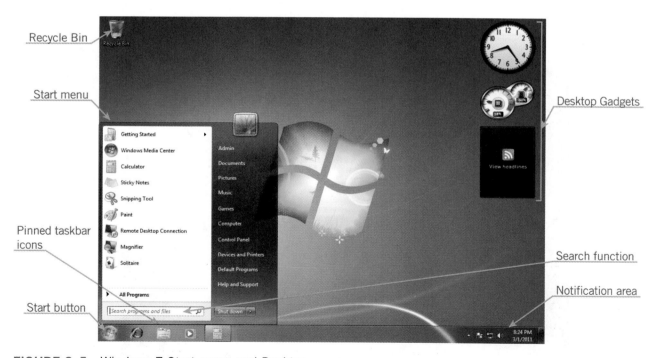

FIGURE C–5   Windows 7 Start menu and Desktop

Navigating in Windows

- The Address bar in Windows 7 now functions differently, with more direct navigation functions.
- Windows 7 now includes a comprehensive Navigation pane in Windows Explorer.

Windows Explorer provides the tools to navigate and locate items on your computer. The Address bar has been upgraded from Windows XP to allow for easier movement between folders. In Windows XP, the only available methods were the Back button and drop-down arrow. See **Figure C–6**. A big difference is in the function of the path. You may now click the folder in your path to move back. You may also begin a search directly from the Address bar, which is a new Windows 7 feature. Windows XP users' only option to search was to utilize the Search Companion.

The Navigation pane, which provides links to common or recently used folders, is dramatically different in Windows 7, compared to Windows XP, which only featured Favorites. "My Documents", the default user folder in Windows XP, is now a collection of folders grouped in Libraries in Windows 7. These folders, as well as Favorites, are easily found on the new Navigation pane and are easily customizable.

To switch between open programs easily, Windows XP's only option aside from clicking the icon on the Taskbar, was to tab through available programs, in a basic method with no preview of the program state. Windows Flip, introduced in Windows Vista, allows you to move to an open file, window or program by pressing the Alt+Tab keys, while showing a preview of the program's current state in Aero. The Windows Vista version of Flip was enhanced for Windows 7 users, although the function remains the same. See **Figures C–8** and **C-9** on the following pages.

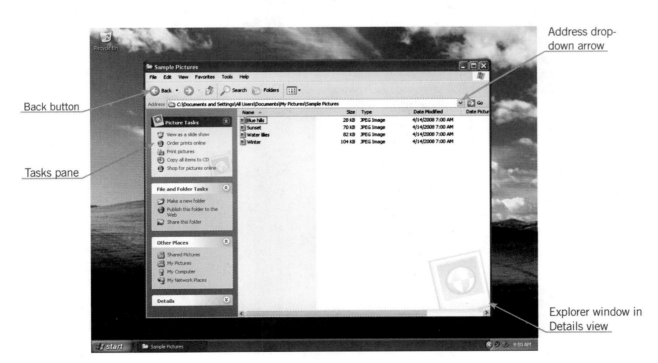

FIGURE C–6   Windows Explorer as seen in Windows XP

Dynamic
Address bar

Back button

Favorite
Links pane

Search text box

Explorer window in
Tiles view

FIGURE C–7   Windows Explorer as seen in Windows Vista

Aero Flip tabs
through open
programs

Taskbar buttons for
open programs

FIGURE C–8   Flip in Windows Vista

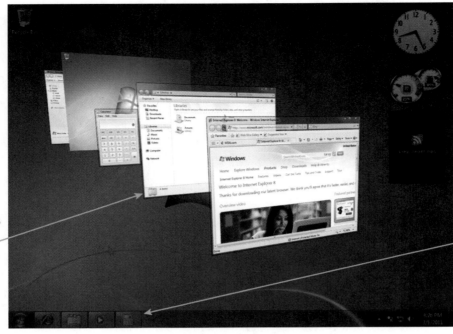

Aero Flip 3-D tabs
through open
programs

Taskbar buttons for
open programs

FIGURE C–9   Flip 3-D in Windows 7

Using Windows

- The new Aero Shake and Aero Snap allow you to easily move, resize, minimize and maximize open windows.
- The Control Panel now includes additional descriptive links, making it easy to find the item you are looking to modify.

Moving and resizing windows in Windows 7 provides the same essential functions as it did in previous Windows versions, with a few additions. In Windows XP and Vista, you had to manipulate each window individually, by clicking and dragging. You can still click and drag to resize and move windows; however this function has been upgraded and revamped in Windows 7. Aero Shake allows you to "shake" all open windows except that particular window to a minimized state. Aero Snap is a new way to easily resize open windows to expand vertically, or side-by-side.

The Control Panel, revamped in Windows Vista, has a new look in Windows 7, compared to that in Windows XP. The Search text box allows you to search for the Control Panel task you wish to perform. There are also descriptive linked items now replacing the "classic" icon format. **Figures C–10, C–11**, and **C–12**, which are shown on the following pages, illustrate the differences in the Control Panel from Windows XP to Windows 7.

Switch to Classic View for basic icon arrangement

Control Panel

Grouped categories

FIGURE C–10   Windows XP Control Panel

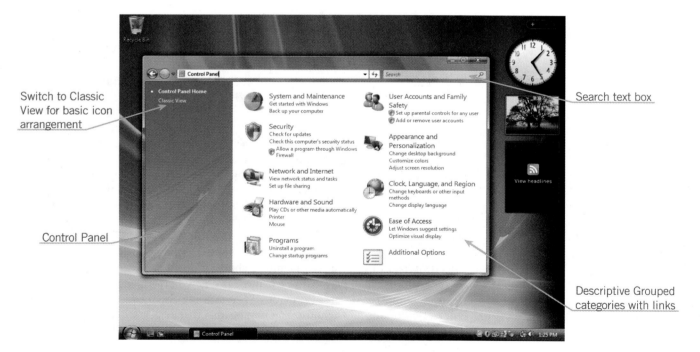

Switch to Classic View for basic icon arrangement

Control Panel

Search text box

Descriptive Grouped categories with links

FIGURE C–11   Windows Vista Control Panel

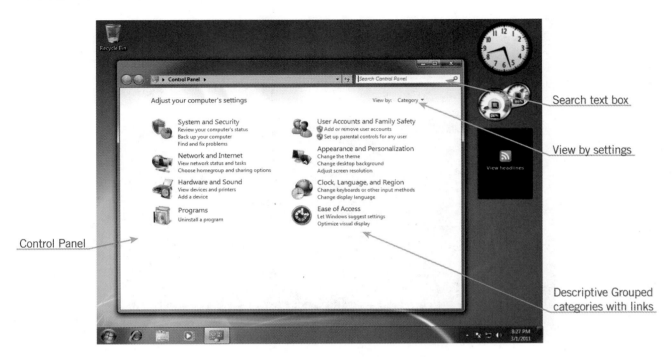

FIGURE C–12   Windows 7 Control Panel

Managing Your Computer

- The Action Center is a new feature in Windows 7 which consolidates message traffic from Windows maintenance and security features.

- Basic system utilities, such as Disk Cleanup and Disk Defragmenter, remain essentially the same from Windows XP to Windows 7.

Windows XP and Windows Vista's only method of receiving information on security and maintenance was the Security Center, available from the Control Panel. Windows 7 has improved this function, by creating a new Action Center, which communicates with the firewall, spyware protection, and antivirus software. Windows 7 users can now navigate to the Action Center by visiting the System and Security section of the Control Panel to view computer status and resolve issues. The Action Center is also pre-configured in Windows 7 to send important alerts to the Notification area of the taskbar.

One of the major upgrades in Windows 7 is in performance. Windows 7 was designed to run on less memory, shutting down services when not in use. In the Control Panel of Windows 7, there is a new Performance and Information Tools section. If you are a previous Windows XP user, you should familiarize yourself with this new feature. You will be able to assess your computer's performance, adjust settings, run disk cleanup, and launch advanced tools to manage your computer.

Windows Defender, introduced in Windows Vista is Microsoft's answer to spyware protection. This was not available for Windows XP users, pre Windows XP Service Pack 2. Windows XP Service Pack 2 users could download it from the Microsoft Web site and install it manually. Windows 7 also includes Windows Defender by default.

Windows Update, introduced in Windows XP has remained the same throughout the transitions through Windows Vista and Windows 7. Windows Update, which automatically downloads and installs important updates, was one of the only ways

Microsoft offered to maintain a secure PC with Windows XP. Now, in Windows 7, the Action Center, Performance Information and Tools, Windows Defender, and Windows Update work together to keep your computer secure. **Figures C–13**, **C–14**, and **C–15**, which are shown on the next few pages, compare Windows XP and Vista's Security Centers with Windows 7 Security Center and Action Center.

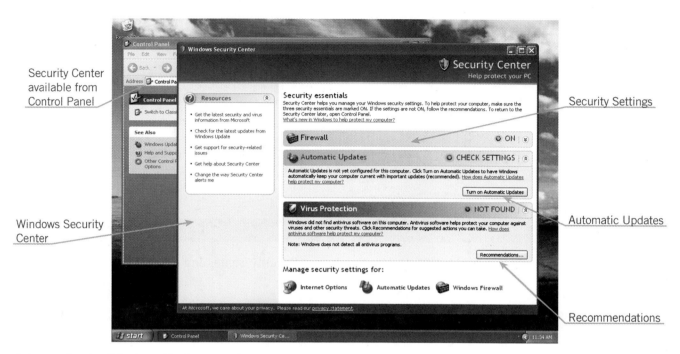

FIGURE C–13   Windows XP Security Center

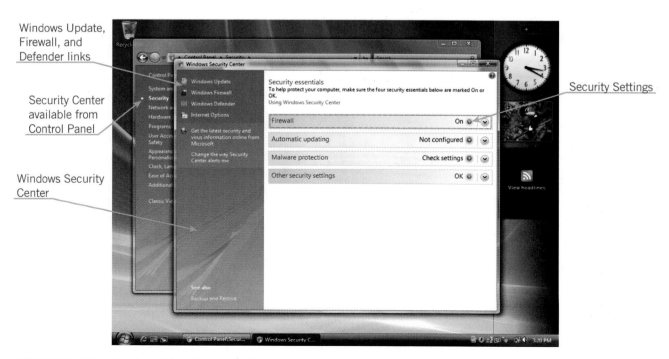

FIGURE C–14   Windows Vista Security Center

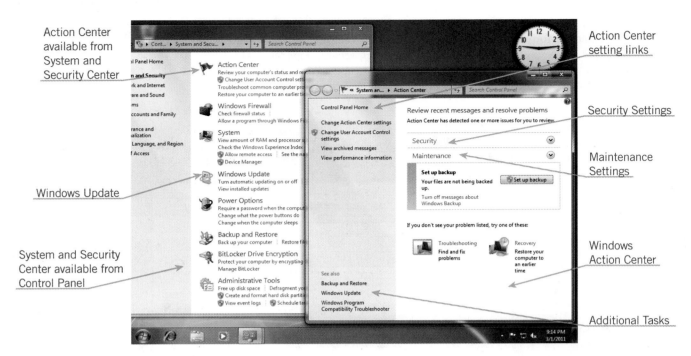

FIGURE C–15   Windows 7 Security Center and Action Center

APPENDIX D

Using SkyDrive and Office Web Apps

■ OBJECTIVES

Upon completion of this lesson, you should be able to:

- Explore cloud computing and Windows Live.
- Obtain a Windows Live ID and sign in to Windows Live.
- Upload files to SkyDrive.
- Use Office Web Apps View and Edit modes.
- Create folders on SkyDrive.
- Organize files on SkyDrive.
- Give permission for access to a folder on your SkyDrive.
- Co-author using the Excel Web App.

■ VOCABULARY

cloud computing

co-author

Office Web Apps

OneNote

SkyDrive

Windows Live

If the computer you are using has an active Internet connection, you can go to the Microsoft Windows Live Web site and use SkyDrive to store and share files. From SkyDrive, you can also use Office Web Apps to create and edit Word, PowerPoint, Excel, and OneNote files, even when you are using a computer that does not have Office 2010 installed. In this Appendix, you will learn how to obtain a Windows Live ID, how to share files with others on SkyDrive, and how to use the Word, Excel, and PowerPoint Web Apps, including co-authoring in the Excel Web App.

Understanding Cloud Computing and Windows Live

▶ **VOCABULARY**
cloud computing
Windows Live

Cloud computing refers to data, applications, and even resources that are stored on servers that you access over the Internet rather than on your own computer. With cloud computing, you access only what you need when you need it. Many individuals and companies are moving towards "the cloud" for at least some of their needs. For example, some companies provide space and computing power to developers for a fee. Individuals might subscribe to an online backup service so that data is automatically backed up on a computer at the physical location of the companies that provide that service.

Windows Live is a collection of services and Web applications that you can use to help you be more productive both personally and professionally. For example, you can use Windows Live to send and receive email, chat with friends via instant messaging, share photos, create a blog, and store and edit files. Windows Live is a free service that you sign up for. When you sign up, you receive a Windows Live ID, which you use to sign into your Windows Live account. **Table D–1** describes the services available on Windows Live.

TABLE D–1 Services available via Windows Live

SERVICE	DESCRIPTION
Email	Send and receive e-mail using a Hotmail account
Instant Messaging	Use Messenger to chat with friends, share photos, and play games
SkyDrive	Store files, work on files using Web Apps, and share files with people in your network
Photos	Upload and share photos with friends
People	Develop a network of friends and coworkers and use it to distribute information and stay in touch
Downloads	Access a variety of free programs available for download to a PC
Mobile Device	Access applications for a mobile device: text messaging, using Hotmail, networking, and sharing photos

SkyDrive is an online storage and file sharing service. With a Windows Live account, you receive access to your own SkyDrive, which is your personal storage area on the Internet. You upload files to your SkyDrive so you can share the files with other people, access the files from another computer, or use SkyDrive's additional storage. On your SkyDrive, you are given space to store up to 25 GB of data online. Each file can be a maximum size of 50 MB. You can also use your SkyDrive to share files with friends and coworkers. After you upload a file to your SkyDrive, you can choose to make the file visible to the public, to anyone you invite to share your files, or only to yourself. You can also use SkyDrive to access Office Web Apps. When you save files to SkyDrive on Windows Live, you are saving your files to an online location. SkyDrive is like having a personal hard drive "in the cloud."

Office Web Apps are versions of Microsoft Word, Excel, PowerPoint, and *OneNote*, an electronic notebook program included with Microsoft Office, that you can access online from your SkyDrive. Office Web Apps offer basic functionality, allowing you to create and edit files created in Word, PowerPoint, and Excel online in your Web browser. An Office Web App does not include all of the features and functions included with the full Office version of its associated application. However, you can use the Office Web Apps from any computer that is connected to the Internet, even if Microsoft Office 2010 is not installed on that computer.

Obtaining a Windows Live ID

To save files to SkyDrive or to use Office Web Apps, you need a Windows Live ID. You obtain a Windows Live ID by going to the Windows Live Web site and creating a new account.

Note: If you already have a Windows Live ID, you can skip Step-by-Step D.1.

▶ **VOCABULARY**
SkyDrive
Office Web Apps
OneNote

Step-by-Step D.1

1. Start Internet Explorer. Click in the Address bar, type **www.windowslive.com**, and then press **Enter**. The page where you can sign into Windows Live opens.

2. Click the **Sign up** button. The Create your Windows Live ID page opens.

3. Follow the instructions on the screen to create an ID with a new, live.com email address or create an ID using an existing email address.

4. After completing the process, if you signed up with an existing email address, open your email program or go to your Web-based email home page, and open the email message automatically sent to you from the Windows Live site. Click the link to open the Sign In page again, sign in with your user name and password if necessary, and then click the **OK** button in the page that appears telling you that your email address is verified.

5. Exit Internet Explorer.

WARNING

If the URL doesn't bring you to the page where you can sign into Windows Live, use a search engine to search for *Windows Live*.

Uploading Files to SkyDrive

You can access your SkyDrive from the Windows Live page in your browser after you signed in with your Windows Live ID, or from Word, Excel, PowerPoint, or OneNote. Then you can upload a file to a private or public folder on your SkyDrive.

Uploading a File to SkyDrive from Backstage View

If you are working in a file in Word, Excel, or PowerPoint, you can save the file to your SkyDrive from Backstage view. To do this, you click the File tab, click Save & Send in the navigation bar, and then click Save to Web. After you do this, the right pane changes to display a Sign In button that you can use to sign in to your Windows Live account. See **Figure D–1**.

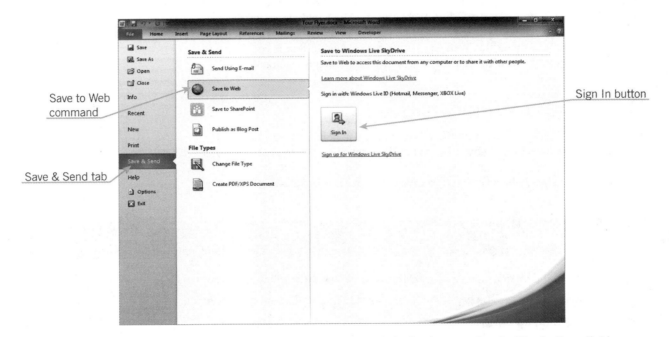

FIGURE D–1   Save & Send tab in Backstage view in Word after clicking Save to Web

Click the Sign In button to sign into Windows Live. After you enter your user name and password, the right pane in Backstage view changes to list the folders on your SkyDrive and a Save As button now appears in the right pane. See **Figure D–2**.

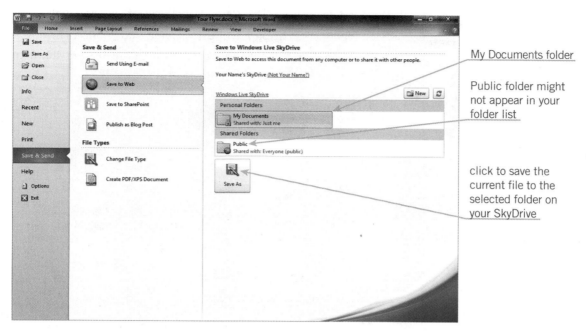

FIGURE D–2 Save & Send tab after connecting to Windows Live

To save the file, click the correct folder, and then click the Save As button.

Step-by-Step D.2

1. Start Word. Open the file named **Tour Flyer.docx** document from the drive and folder where your Data Files are stored.

2. Click the **File** tab, and then click **Save & Send** on the navigation bar. The Save & Send options appear in Backstage view as shown in Figure D–1.

3. Under Save & Send, click **Save to Web**.

4. Click the **Sign In** button. The Connecting to docs.live.net dialog box opens. See **Figure D–3**. If you are already signed into Windows Live, you will see the folders in your SkyDrive account listed instead of the Sign In button. Skip this step (Step 4) and Step 5.

FIGURE D–3
Connecting to docs.live.net
dialog box

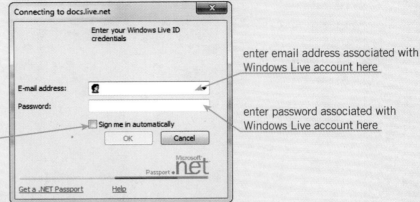

enter email address associated with Windows Live account here

enter password associated with Windows Live account here

do not select if you are working on a lab or other public computer

5. In the E-mail address box, type the email address associated with your Windows Live ID account. Press **Tab**, and then type the password associated with your Windows Live account in the Password box. Click the **OK** button. The dialog box closes, and another dialog box appears briefly while you connect to the Windows Live server. After you are connected, the folders on your SkyDrive appear in the right pane in Backstage view, as shown in Figure D–2.

6. In the right pane, click the **My Documents** folder, and then click the **Save As** button. Backstage view closes, and then after a few moments, the Save As dialog box opens. The path in the Address bar identifies the Public folder location on your SkyDrive.

7. Click the **Save** button. The dialog box closes and the Tour Flyer file is saved to the My Documents folder on your SkyDrive.

8. Exit Word.

Uploading a File to SkyDrive in a Browser

You can also add files to SkyDrive by starting from an Internet Explorer window. To do this, go to www.windowslive.com, and then log in to your Windows Live account. See **Figure D–4**.

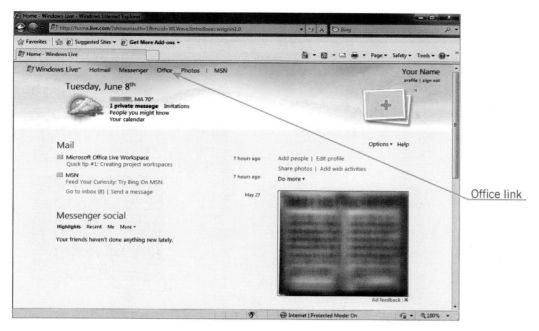

FIGURE D–4 Windows Live home page

To get to your SkyDrive, you click the Office link in the list of navigation links at the top of the window. To see all the folders on your SkyDrive, click View all in the Folders list on the left. See **Figure D–5**.

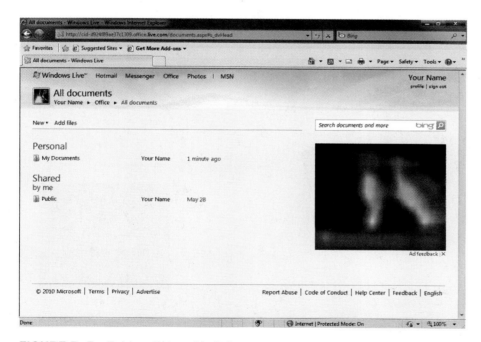

FIGURE D–5 Folders list on SkyDrive

Click the folder to which you want to add the file to open it. See **Figure D–6**.

click to add files
to this folder

contents of folder
are listed here

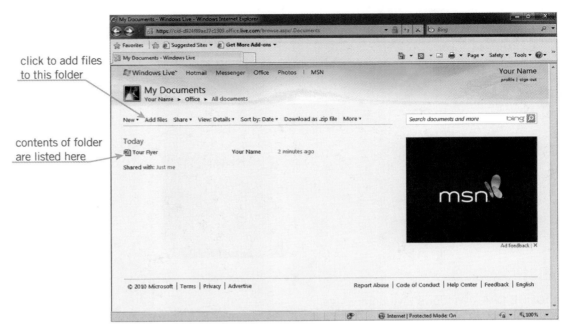

FIGURE D–6   My Documents folder page on SkyDrive

Click the Add files link to open the Add documents to *Folder Name* page; for
example, if you click the Add files link in the My Documents folder, the Add documents to My Documents page appears. See **Figure D–7**.

page name

click this link to
display the Open
dialog box

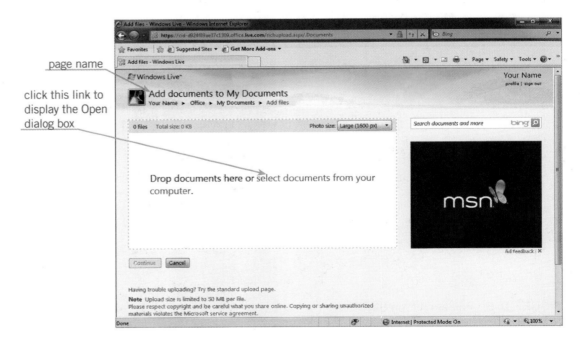

FIGURE D–7   Add documents to My Documents page on SkyDrive

Click the "select documents from your computer" link to display the Open dialog box. Locate the drive and folder where the file is stored, click it, and then click Open. The file uploads and is listed in the box. Click Continue to display the folder containing the files you uploaded to your SkyDrive.

Step-by-Step D.3

1. Start Internet Explorer. Click in the Address bar, type **www.windowslive. com**, and then press **Enter**.

2. If the Sign In page appears, type your Windows Live ID user name and password in the appropriate boxes, and then click **Sign in**. Your Windows Live home page appears similar to the one shown in Figure D–4.

3. In the list of command links at the top of the window, click **Office**. Your SkyDrive page appears.

4. In the list under Folders on the left, click **View all**. All the folders on your SkyDrive appear, similar to Figure D–5.

5. Click the **My Documents** folder. The My Documents page appears, similar to Figure D–6.

6. In the list of command links, click the **Add files** link. The Add documents to My Documents page appears, as shown in Figure D–7.

7. Click the **select documents from your computer** link, navigate to the drive and folder where your Data Files are stored, click **Tour Sales.pptx**, and then click the **Open** button. The file uploads and appears in the box on the Add documents to My Documents page.

8. At the bottom of the box, click the **select more documents from your computer** link. In the Open dialog box, click **Tour Data.xlsx**, and then click **Open**. The Excel file is listed in the box along with the PowerPoint file.

9. Below the box, click **Continue**. The My Documents folder page appears listing the files in that folder.

10. Keep the My Documents folder page displayed in Internet Explorer for the next Step-by-Step.

Using Office Web Apps

There are two ways to work with files using the Office Web Apps. You can view a file or you can edit it using its corresponding Office Web App. From your SkyDrive, you can also open the document directly in the full Office 2010 application if the application is installed on the computer you are using. You do not need to have Microsoft Office 2010 programs installed on the computer you use to access Office Web Apps.

Using a Web App in View Mode

To use a Web App in View mode, simply click its filename in the folder. This opens the file in View mode in the Web App. **Figure D–8** shows the Tour Flyer Word file open in the Word Web App in View mode.

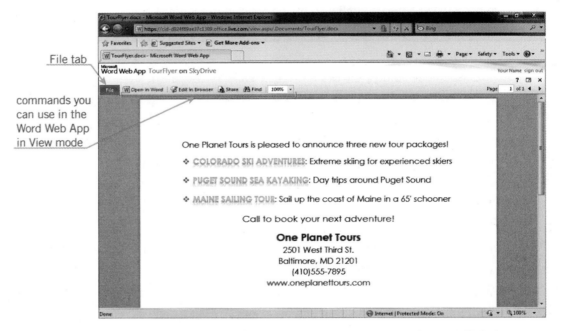

FIGURE D–8   Tour Flyer document open in View mode in Word Web App

Step-by-Step D.4

1. Click **Tour Flyer**. The Tour Flyer document opens in the Word Web App in View mode, as shown in Figure D–8.

2. Click anywhere in the document window, and then type any character. Nothing happens because you are allowed only to view the document in View mode.

3. Click the **File** tab. A list of commands opens. Note that you can print the document using the Print command on this menu.

4. Click **Close**. The document closes and the My Documents folder page appears again.

5. Leave the My Documents folder page open for the next Step-by-Step.

> **TIP**
>
> Position the mouse over a file icon to see the full filename and other details about the file.

Using a Web App in Edit Mode

You can also edit documents in the Office Web Apps. Although the interface for each Office Web App is similar to the interface of the full-featured program on your computer, a limited number of commands are available for editing documents using the Office Web App for each program. To edit a file in a Web App, point to the file in the folder page, and then click the Edit in browser link. You will see a Ribbon with a limited number of tabs and commands on the tabs. **Figure D–9** shows the file Tour Sales open in the PowerPoint Web App in Edit mode.

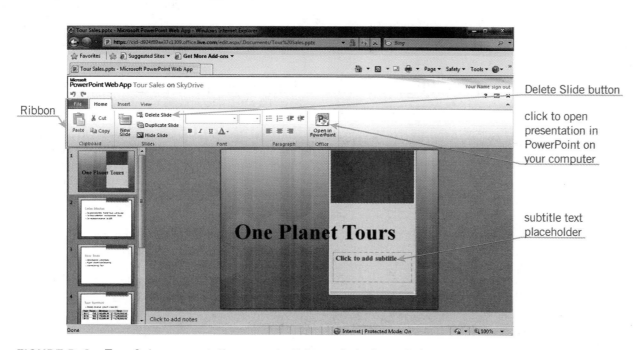

FIGURE D–9   Tour Sales presentation open in Edit mode in PowerPoint Web App

Step-by-Step D.5

TIP

To create a new file on SkyDrive using an Office Web App, open a folder, click the New link, and then select the appropriate Office Web App.

TIP

When you make changes to a file using a Web App, you do not need to save your changes before you close it because changes are saved automatically.

1. In the list of files in the My Documents folder, point to **Tour Sales**. A list of commands for working with the file appears.

2. In the list of commands, click the **Edit in browser** link. The Tour Sales presentation appears in the PowerPoint Web App in Edit mode, as shown in Figure D–9. In Edit mode, you see a version of the familiar Ribbon.

3. In the Slide pane, click in the subtitle text placeholder, and then type your name.

4. In the Slides tab, click **Slide 3** to display it in the Slide pane. The slide title is _New Tours_.

5. On the Home tab, in the Slides group, click the **Delete Slide** button. The _New Tours_ slide is deleted from the presentation and the new Slide 3 (_Tour Revenue_) appears in the Slide pane. Now you will examine the other two tabs available to you in the PowerPoint Web App.

6. Click the **Insert** tab on the Ribbon. The only objects you can insert in a slide using the PowerPoint Web App in Edit mode are pictures and SmartArt. You can also create a hyperlink.

7. Click the View tab. Note that you cannot switch to Slide Master view in the PowerPoint Web App.

8. Leave the Tour Sales file open in the PowerPoint Web App for the next Step-by-Step.

Editing a File Stored on SkyDrive in the Program on Your Computer

If you are working with a file stored on your SkyDrive and you want to use a command that is available in the full-featured program on your computer but is not available in the Web App, you need to open the file in the full-featured program on your computer. You can do this from the corresponding Office Web App by clicking the Open in _Program Name_ button on the Home tab on the Web App Ribbon.

Step-by-Step D.6

1. Click the **Home** tab. In the Office group, click the **Open in PowerPoint** button. The Open Document dialog box appears warning you that some files can harm your computer. This dialog box opens when you try to open a document stored on a Web site.

2. Click the **OK** button. PowerPoint starts on your computer and the revised version of the Tour Sales presentation opens on your computer. The presentation is in Protected view because it is not stored on the local computer you are using.

3. In the yellow Protected View bar, click the **Enable Editing** button. Now you can insert a footer on the slides.

4. Click the **Insert** tab, and then click the **Header & Footer** button in the Text group.

5. Click the **Footer** check box, type **2013 Sales Projections** in the Footer box, and then click the **Apply to All** button. When you use the full-featured version of a program, you do need to save the changes you made, even when it is stored in a folder on your SkyDrive.

6. On the Quick Access Toolbar, click the **Save** button 🖫. The modified file is saved to your SkyDrive.

7. In the PowerPoint window title bar, click the **Close** button 🞩. The PowerPoint program closes and you see your browser window listing the contents of the My Documents folder.

8. Click the **Tour Sales** file. Slide 1 of the Tour Sales file appears in the PowerPoint Web app in View mode.

9. At the bottom of the window, click the **Next Slide** button ▶ twice. Slide 3 (*Tour Revenue*) appears in the window. Remember that you deleted the original Slide 3, *New Tours*. Also note that the footer you added is on the slide.

10. Click the **File** tab, and then click **Close**. The PowerPoint Web App closes and the My Documents page appears.

11. Leave the My Documents page open for the next Step-by-Step.

WARNING

You can also open a document stored on your SkyDrive in the program stored on your computer from View mode in the corresponding Office Web App.

WARNING

If the Connecting to dialog box opens asking for your Windows Live ID credentials, type the email address associated with your Windows Live ID in the E-mail address box, type your password in the Password box, and then click the OK button.

Creating Folders on Your SkyDrive

You can keep your SkyDrive organized by using file management techniques, similar to the way you organize files on your computer's hard drive. You can create a folder in your SkyDrive in the Internet Explorer window or from Backstage view in the program on your computer.

To create a folder on your SkyDrive in Internet Explorer, click the New link in the list of commands, and then click Folder to open the Create a new folder page on your SkyDrive. See **Figure D–10**.

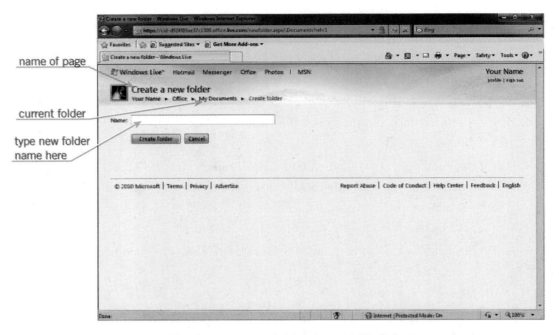

name of page

current folder

type new folder name here

FIGURE D–10 Create a new folder page on SkyDrive

To create a new folder on your SkyDrive from the Save & Send tab in Backstage view in an application, click the New button in the upper-right. This opens the same Create a new folder page shown in Figure D–10.

Type the name for the new folder in the Name box, and then click Next. The Add files to *Folder Name* page that you saw earlier appears. If you want to upload a file to the new folder, you can do so at this point. If you don't, you can click the link for the new folder or click the SkyDrive link to return to your SkyDrive home page.

Step-by-Step D.7

1. In the list of command links, click the **New** link, and then click **Folder**. The Create a new folder page appears with the insertion point in the Name box.

2. In the Name box, type **Sales**, and then click **Create folder**. The new empty folder is displayed in the browser window. You can see that you are looking at the contents of the new folder by looking at the navigation links. See **Figure D–11**.

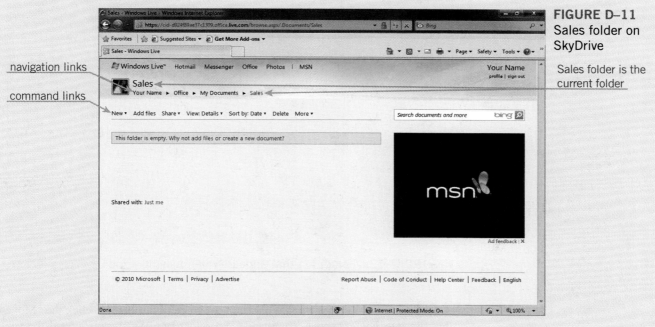

FIGURE D–11
Sales folder on SkyDrive

Sales folder is the current folder

3. Leave the Sales folder page open for the next Step-by-Step.

Organizing Files on Your SkyDrive

As on your hard drive, you can move and delete files on your SkyDrive. To move or delete a file, first display the commands for working with the file by pointing to its name in the file list in the folder. To move a file, click the More link, and then click Move to open the "Where would you like to move *File Name*?" page. See **Figure D–12**.

click to select
this folder

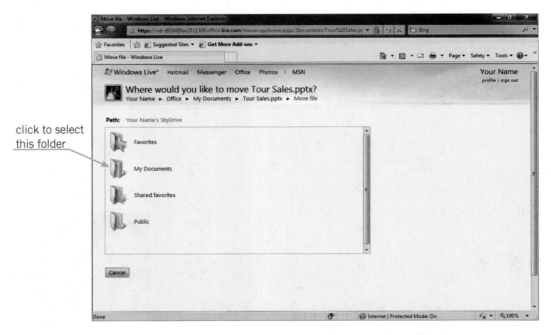

FIGURE D–12 Folder list that appears when moving a file

In the list of folders, click a folder. Then, at the top of the list, click the "Move this file into *Folder Name*" command. The folder into which you moved the file appears, along with a message telling you that the file was moved.

To delete a file, point to it to display the commands for working with the file, and then click the Delete button in the list of command links.

Step-by-Step D.8

1. In the list of navigation links, click the **My Documents** link. Point to **Tour Sales**. The commands for working with this file appear.

2. In the list of command links, click the **More** link, and then click **Move**. The "Where would you like to move Tour Sales.pptx?" page appears, and a list of folders on your SkyDrive appears.

3. In the list of folders, click the **My Documents** folder to display the list of folders located inside that folder. Click the **Sales** folder. The contents of the Sales folder appear in the list of folders. Because this folder does not contain any additional folders, you see only a command to create a New folder and the command to move the file.

4. In the list of folders, click **Move this file into Sales**. After a moment, the contents of the Sales folder appear, along with a message telling you that you have moved the Tour Sales file from the My Documents folder.

5. In the list of navigation links, click the **My Documents** link. The contents of the My Documents folder appear.

6. Point to **Tour Flyer**. In the list of command links, click the **Delete** button . A dialog box opens warning you that you are about to permanently delete the file.

7. Click **OK**. The dialog box closes, the file is deleted from the My Documents folder on your SkyDrive.

8. Leave the My Documents folder page open for the next Step-by-Step.

> **WARNING**
>
> Depending on the resolution of your computer, you might not need to click the More link to access the Move command.

Giving Permission for Access to a Folder on Your SkyDrive

If you upload a file to a private folder, you can grant permission to access the file to anyone else with a Windows Live ID. You can grant permission to folders located at the same level as the My Documents folder. You cannot grant permission to individual files or to folders located inside a locked folder. If you grant permission to someone to access a folder, that person will have access to all the files in that folder.

To grant permission to someone, click the folder to display its contents, click the Share link in the list of navigation links, and then click Edit permissions. The Edit permissions for *Folder Name* page appears. You can use the slider bar to make the contents of the new folder public by sharing it with everyone, your friends as listed on your Windows Live ID account and their friends, just your friends, or only some friends. You can also share it only with specific people that you list in the box in the Add Specific People section. When you type someone's name or email address associated with the person's Windows Live ID account in the box in the Add specific people section, and then press Enter, the person's name appears in a box below with a check box next to the name or email address. The box to the right of the person's name or email address indicates that the person can view files in the shared folder. You can then click the arrow to change this so that the person can view, edit, or delete files. See **Figure D–13**. Click Save at the bottom of the window to save the permissions you set.

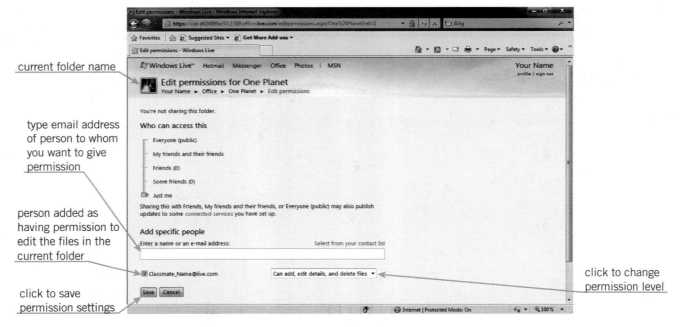

FIGURE D–13 Edit permissions for One Planet page on SkyDrive

To complete the next Step-by-Step, you need to work with a partner who also has a Windows Live ID account.

Step-by-Step D.9

1. In the list of navigation links, click the **Office** link, and then in the list of links on the left, click **View all**. The All documents page appears.

2. In the list of command links, click the **New** link, and the click **Folder**. The Create a folder page appears with a temporary folder name in the Name box. The temporary name is selected, so you can just type the new name.

3. In the Name box, type **One Planet**. Click **Next**. The One Planet folder page appears.

4. In the list of navigation links, click the **Office** link. In the list of folders on the left, click the **My Documents** link. The My Documents folder page appears.

5. In the file list, point to **Tour Data**, click the **More** link, and then click **Move**. The Where would you like to move Tour Data.xlsx? page appears.

6. In the list of folders, click **One Planet**. In the new list that appears, click the **Move this file into One Planet**. The One Planet page appears with the Tour Data file listed.

7. In the list of command links, click the **Share** link. Click **Edit permissions**. The Edit permissions for One Planet page appears.

8. Under Add specific people, click in the **Enter a name or an e-mail address** box, type the email address of your partner, and then press **Enter**. The email address you typed appears below the box. A check box next to the email address is selected, and a list box to the right identifies the level of access for this person. The default is Can add, edit details, and delete files, similar to Figure D–13. You want your partner to be able to edit the file, so you don't need to change this.

9. At the bottom of the window, click **Save**. The Send a notification for One Planet page appears. You can send a notification to each individual when you grant permission to access your files. This is a good idea so that each person will have the URL of your folder. Your partner's email address appears in the To box.

TIP

Because you are creating a folder at the same level as the My Documents folder, there is a Share with box below the Name box. You can set the permissions when you create the folder if you want.

TIP

To make the contents of the folder available to anyone, drag the slider up to the top so it is next to the Everyone (public).

10. Click in the Include your own message box, type **You can now access the contents of the One Planet folder on my SkyDrive.**, and then click **Send**. Your partner will receive an email message from you advising him or her that you have shared your One Planet folder. If your partner is completing the steps at the same time, you will receive an email message from your partner.

11. Check your email for a message from your partner advising you that your partner has shared his or her Sales folder with you. The subject of the email message will be "*Your Partner's Name* has shared documents with you."

12. If you have received the email, click the **View folder** button in the email message, and then sign in to Windows Live if you are requested to do so. You are now able to access your partner's One Planet folder on his or her SkyDrive. See **Figure D–14**.

FIGURE D–14
One Planet folder on someone else's SkyDrive

name of person who gave you permission to access the One Planet folder on his or her SkyDrive

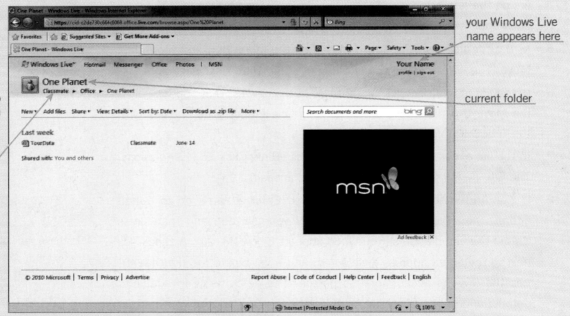

your Windows Live name appears here

current folder

13. Leave Internet Explorer open for the next Step-by-Step.

Co-Authoring with the Excel Web App

When you work with the Excel Web App, you can use its *co-authoring* feature to simultaneously edit an Excel workbook at the same time as a colleague. When you co-author a workbook, a list of the people currently co-authoring the workbook appears at the bottom of the window. Co-authoring is not available in the Word or PowerPoint Web Apps. When you open a file in the Excel Web App, a notification appears at the right end of the status bar notifying you that two people are editing the document. See **Figure D–15**. You can click this to see the email addresses of the people currently editing the workbook.

▶ **VOCABULARY**
co-author

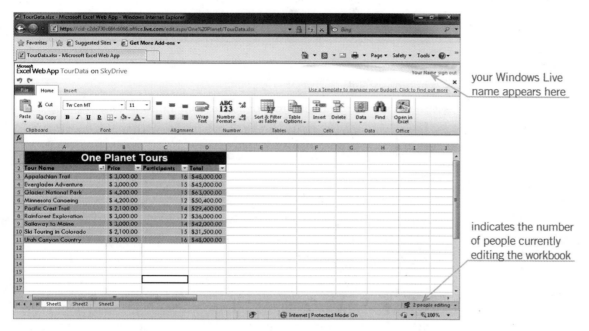

your Windows Live name appears here

indicates the number of people currently editing the workbook

FIGURE D–15 Tour Data file open in Edit mode in Excel Web App with two people editing

To complete this next Step-by-Step, you need to continue working with the partner who has permission to access the One Planet folder on your SkyDrive and who gave you permission to access his or her One Planet folder.

Step-by-Step D.10

1. Decide with your partner whether you will modify the Tour Data file stored on your SkyDrive or on his or her SkyDrive. After you decide the SkyDrive account with which you are going to work, both of you display the contents of that One Planet folder.

2. Point to **Tour Data**, and then in the list of command links, click the **Edit in browser** link.

3. In the status bar, click the **2 people editing** button. A list pops up identifying you and your partner as the two people editing the document.

    Decide with your partner which one of you will execute Step 4. The other person will then execute Step 5.

4. Either you or your partner click cell **A12**, type **Gulf Islands Sailing**, press **Tab**, type **3000**, press **Tab**, type **10**, and then press **Tab**. The formula in the other cells in column D is copied automatically to cell D12 because the data in the original Excel file was created and formatted as an Excel table. Both you and your partner see the data entered in row 12.

    If you entered the data in row 12, you partner should execute Step 5; if your partner entered the data in row 12, you should execute Step 5.

5. Either you or your partner—the person who did not execute Step 4—click cell **B12**, type **3700**, and then press **Tab**. The data entered is reformatted in the Accounting number format, and the total in cell D12 is recalculated. Again, both you and your partner see the change executed.

    Both you and your partner should execute the rest of the steps in this section.

6. Click the **File** tab, and then click **Close**. The changes you made to the Excel workbook are saved automatically on the current SkyDrive account. You are finished working with the Office Web Apps, so you can sign out of Windows Live.

7. In the upper-right of the SkyDrive window, click the **sign out** link. You are signed out of Windows Live.

8. In the title bar of your Web browser window, click the **Close** button ☒ to exit your Web browser.

OneNote Web App

The other Office Web App is OneNote. As with Word, Excel, and PowerPoint files, you can share OneNote files on SkyDrive directly from OneNote. Note that you need to click the Share tab in the navigation bar in Backstage view, and then click Web and specify Windows Live as the Web location. After you upload a OneNote file to SkyDrive, you can work with it in its corresponding Web App.

GLOSSARY

A

action query An action query makes changes to the records in a table.

alphanumeric data Data that contains numbers, text, or a combination of numbers and text.

and operator An operator used in a query that selects records that match all of two or more conditions in a query.

append Append means to add.

argument Arguments are the additional information that Access needs based on the chosen action.

ascending A sort order that arranges records using the values in a specific field or column from A to Z or from smallest to largest.

AutoExec macro An AutoExec macro allows you to have one or more actions automatically execute when the database is opened.

AutoFilter A menu that opens when you click the arrow on the right side of a field selector in a datasheet. The menu contains options for sorting data and for applying and clearing filters.

AutoNumber A data type that automatically adds a unique field value to each record in a table.

B

backup A backup is a duplicate copy of your database created by using the Back Up Database option when you save the file.

best fit The term used when a column in a datasheet is resized to the best width for the data contained in the column.

Blank Database template A template that creates a database that contains only an empty table.

bound control A control in a form or report that is connected to a field in the record source and is used to display, enter, and update data.

C

calculated control A calculated control can be used to perform calculations on the values in other fields.

calculated field A field in a query, form, or report that displays a value that is calculated using a combination of operators, constants, and the values in other fields.

chart A chart is a graphical display of data.

code Code is simply the macro actions formatted in easy-to-read sentences, just like text in a book.

combo box A combo box displays a list of values and lets you select one from a list.

comma-separated values (CSV) A file format in which commas separate the field values of each record in the data source and paragraph marks separate individual records.

command button A command button is a button that users can click to perform common tasks, such as moving to the next record in a form or adding a record.

comment A comment is explanatory text that you can add to a macro that does not affect the way the macro is executed.

common field A field that appears in two or more tables in a database and that has the same data type and field values. A common field (also called a matching field) is used to relate tables and usually has the same field name in the related tables.

compacting A process that rearranges the way a database is stored on disk and optimizes the performance of the database.

condition In a query, a condition (also called a criterion) specifies which data to display in the query results.

conditional formatting Conditional formatting allows you to add formatting features to the data based on criteria you specify.

control An object in a form or report, such as a label or text box, that displays data from the record source on which the form or report is based.

control layout   A "container" that groups together the controls in a form or report so that you can change the formatting of and move these controls as a group.

criteria   A term indicating that a query contains two or more conditions.

criterion   Criterion refers to the specific information you are searching for.

D

data source   When used with a form letter, the term given to the file that contains the records to insert in the form letter. The data source might be a Word document, an Excel workbook, or an Access database.

data type   The property of a field that determines the type of data that you can enter into the field, such as numbers or text.

database   A collection of objects that work together to store, retrieve, display, and summarize data and also to automate tasks.

Database Documenter   A procedure is a group of statements written in VBA code that can include several functions.

database management system (DBMS)   A program that you use to store, retrieve, analyze, and print information.

datasheet   Displays the data for a table or query in rows and columns, with records in rows and fields in columns.

datasheet selector   The box in the upper-left corner of a datasheet that, when clicked, selects all fields and records in the datasheet.

datasheet tool   An Access tool that creates a form that looks like a datasheet.

datasheet view   The view of a database table that displays data in rows and columns.

Default Value property   A field property that lets you specify the value to enter into that field for each record in a table.

delimited data   Data that is stored in text format and separated by delimiters, such as commas.

delimiter   A punctuation mark or other character in a text file that separates data into fields and records.

descending   A sort order that arranges records using the values in a specific field or column from Z to A or from largest to smallest.

description property   An optional field property that you can use to describe the data to store in the field.

design grid   The top half of the Table window in Design view that displays the name, data type, and optional Description property for each field in a table.

Design view (table)   The view of a table that lets you add, delete, and rearrange fields. You can also use Design view to make changes to the way that fields store data.

detail query   A query that shows every field in each record in the query results.

detail section   The section in Design view for a form or report that contains the detail records from the record source.

E

embedded macro   An embedded macro is a macro that performs an action within an object, such as a macro that opens a form when you are already viewing another form.

encryption   Encryption refers to a database with a password in which the data within the database is made unreadable.

exact match condition   A condition in a query that specifies the exact condition that a record must satisfy to be displayed in the query results.

export   A term used when data is saved into a different file format.

expression   An arithmetic formula that performs a calculation.

Expression Builder   The Expression Builder is where you type, or build, an expression.

F

field   A single characteristic in a table's design that appears in a datasheet as a column.

Field List pane   A pane in Design view for a form or report that displays the tables and other objects in the database and the fields they contain.

field name   The name of a column in a database table.

Field Properties pane   The bottom half of the Table window in Design view that displays properties for the selected field in a table.

field property   An additional description of a field beyond the field's data type that specifies how to store data in the field, such as the number of characters the field can store.

field selector   The top of a column in a datasheet that contains the field name. Clicking a field selector selects the column.

Field Size property   The property that identifies the number of characters that a Text, a Number, or an AutoNumber field can store.

field value   The specific data stored in a field for a record.

filter A temporary rearrangement of the records in a table, query, form, or report based on one or more specified conditions.

Filter By Form A filter that you can apply to a datasheet or form that rearranges the records based on one or more field values that you select from a list.

Filter By Selection A filter that you can apply to a datasheet or form that rearranges the records based on a selected field value or part of a field value.

find An Access command that lets you specify how to locate data in an object.

foreign key When two tables in a database are related, the common field in the related table is called a foreign key.

form A database object that displays data from one or more tables or queries in a format that has a similar appearance to a paper form.

Form Footer section The section in Design view for a form that contains the information that is displayed at the bottom of the form.

Form Header section The section in Design view for a form that contains the information that is displayed at the top of the form.

form letter A document that contains merge fields that indicate where to insert data from a data source, such as an Access database or an Excel workbook.

form tool An Access tool that creates a simple form that includes all the fields in the selected table or query.

form view A view of a form that displays the data in the record source in a form.

Form Wizard An Access wizard that creates a form based on a record source and using options that the user specifies to select the form's record source and layout.

format property A property for a field that specifies how to display numbers, dates, times, and text.

function A function is an action that can be defined in VBA code where you use statements to describe the action you want the function to perform.

G

grouping level An option for reports that organizes data based on one or more fields into groups.

H

hierarchical Hierarchical refers to the different levels of automation in a form.

I

import A term used when data is copied from a file into a different location.

input mask A pattern for common types of data entered in a field. Access includes several input mask formats, such as phone numbers, social security numbers, and ZIP codes.

J

join line The line that connects tables that have a relationship; the join line connects the common fields and indicates the relationship type.

L

Label Wizard An Access wizard that creates a report of standard or custom labels.

layout view A view of a form or report that displays data from the record source and that lets you make certain types of changes to the form or report, such as increasing the size of a text box control.

line tool An Access tool that you can use to draw a line in a form or report.

list box A list box lets you select more than one value, and a combo box lets you enter a value or select a value from a list.

live preview A live preview occurs when you move your mouse pointer over a theme in the Themes gallery and it is temporarily applied to the form so that you can see how your form would look with that theme applied.

logo A logo is a graphic or picture that can be placed in a form.

M

macro A macro is a series of actions that you want Access to perform. Macros automate repetitive tasks, such as opening forms, printing reports, and running queries.

main document The term given to a form letter when it is used in a mail merge operation in Word.

merge field The term given to a field in a data source when it is inserted in a Word document that is being used in a mail merge operation.

Multiple Items tool An Access tool that creates a form that lists all the fields in the record source in a datasheet format.

multitable query A query that is based on the data in two or more tables.

N

navigation form   A navigation form is a special kind of form that has both a main form control and subform controls automatically built in.

Navigation Pane   The pane in Access that displays the objects in a database.

O

one-to-many relationship   A relationship between two tables in a database in which one record in the primary table can match many (zero, one, or many) records in the related table.

Open Exclusive mode   In the Open Exclusive mode, only the person who opened the database can use and make changes to it; all other users are locked out from opening and using the database.

operator   Operators are the mathematical characters—such as plus (+), minus (–), multiplication (*), and division (/)—that determine the type of calculation in the expression.

or operator   An operator used in a query that selects records that match at least one of two or more conditions in a query.

P

parameter   Parameter means to vary. In Access, a parameter query will produce data that varies.

password   A password is a collection of characters that a user types to gain access to a file.

placeholder   A placeholder appears in a field before the value is entered.

primary key   The field in a database table that contains a unique field value for each record in the table.

primary table   In a one-to-many relationship, the table that contains the records on the "one" side of the relationship.

Print Preview   The view of a table, query, form, or report in Access that shows how the object will appear when printed and that lets you make adjustments to the printer and print settings.

procedure   A procedure is a group of statements written in VBA code that can include several functions.

public   A function in a module that is accessible throughout the database.

Q

query   A database object that lets you ask the database about the data it contains.

R

range-of-values condition   A condition in a query that specifies a range of values that a record must satisfy to be displayed in the query results.

read-only   A term used to describe data that can be viewed but not changed.

record   The collection of field values for a complete set of data.

record selector   The box to the left of a record in a datasheet that, when clicked, selects the entire record.

record source   The tables or queries that contain the data used in a form or report.

referential integrity   A set of rules that a DBMS follows to ensure that there are matching values in the common field used to create the relationship between related tables and that protects the data in related tables to make sure that data is not accidentally deleted or changed.

related table   In a one-to-many relationship, the table that contains the records on the "many" side of the relationship.

relationship   The feature of a DBMS that lets you connect the data in the tables in the database so you can create queries and other objects using the data from two or more tables.

report   A database object that displays data from one or more tables or queries in a format that has an appearance similar to a printed report.

report selector   The box in the upper-left corner of a report where the horizontal and vertical rulers intersect that you can click to select the entire report.

report tool   An Access tool that creates a simple report that includes all the fields in the selected table or query on which it is based, uses a columnar format, formats the report using a theme, and includes a title with the same name as the record source.

report Wizard   An Access wizard that you can use to create a report by specifying a record source, layout, sort order, and grouping level.

required property   A field property that specifies whether a value must be entered into the field.

Run   The term given to the act of opening a query and displaying the query results.

S

Simple Query Wizard   The wizard in Access that lets you create a query and indicate what you'd like to see in the query results by selecting options in dialog boxes.

sort   A method of arranging the records in a table, query, form, or report using the values in one or more fields.

splash screen   A splash screen is a form that appears when you open a database that welcomes the user to the database. A splash screen can contain information such as a company's name and the same themes used in the database.

Split Form tool   An Access tool that creates a form using all the fields in the selected record source and splits the window into two panes, with one displaying the form in Form view and the other displaying the form in Datasheet view.

startup options   Startup options are options that Access performs when the database is opened.

subdatasheet   When two tables are related, the datasheet for the primary table contains expand indicators for each record. Clicking an expand indicator in the primary table displays the records in the related table in a subdatasheet.

subreport   Subreports are reports you create and then embed in another report.

summary query   A query that summarizes relevant data, such as adding the field values in a column that displays price data, in the query results.

syntax   Syntax is a name for the wording that is used in VBA (Visual Basic for Applications).

T

tab order   Tab order is the order of movement in a record when you press the Tab key.

template   An object that you can use to create a database, table, or field in a database.

theme   A predesigned set of fonts, colors, and design elements that you can apply to a form or report to format it.

total row   The optional row in a datasheet that counts of the number of values in a column. When a field contains numeric data, you can use the Total row to calculate the total, average, minimum, or maximum value in a column.

U

unbound control   A control in a form or report, such as a line, rectangle, or picture, that is not connected to the record source on which the form or report is based.

V

validation rules   Rules that need to be met before the data can be entered.

variable name   A variable name is simply a symbolic name that you assign to a value. Creating variable names that make functions easy to understand can help make your database more user-friendly

virus   A virus is a computer program that is designed to reproduce itself by attaching to other programs in a computer.

W

wildcard character   A wildcard character is a character, such as an asterisk, that you can use to represent incomplete or unknown information when performing a search.

INDEX